Monochrome
Painting in Black and White

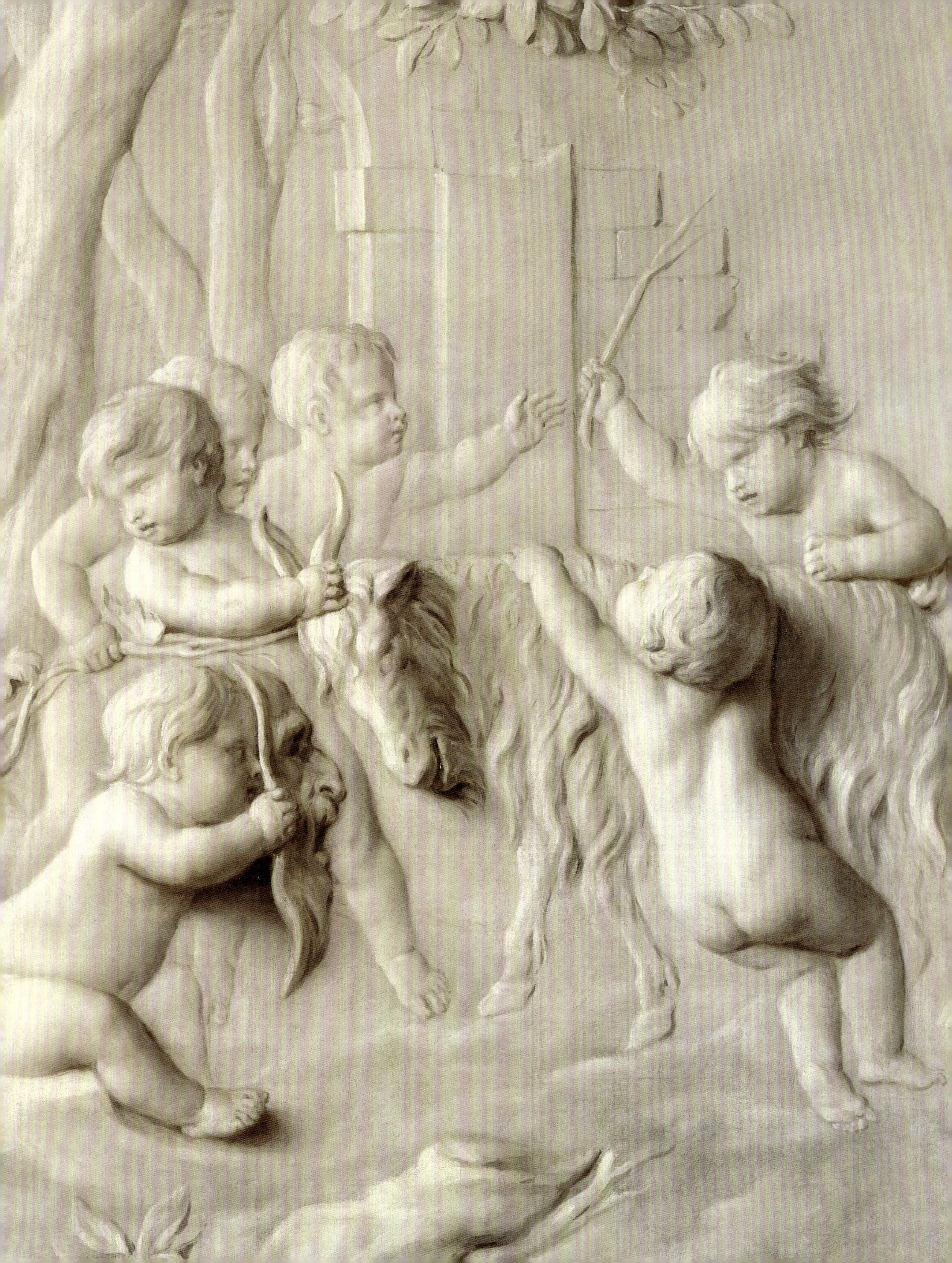

Monochrome
Painting in Black and White

Lelia Packer and Jennifer Sliwka

National Gallery Company, London
Distributed by Yale University Press

Exhibition generously supported by
Howard and Roberta Ahmanson

With additional support from
The Vaseppi Trust
David Zwirner, London and New York
and other donors

Published to accompany the exhibition

Monochrome: Painting in Black and White
The National Gallery, London
30 October 2017 – 18 February 2018

Black & White: Von Dürer bis Elíasson
Museum Kunstpalast, Düsseldorf
22 March – 15 July 2018

This exhibition has been made possible by the
provision of insurance through the Government
Indemnity Scheme. The National Gallery would like
to thank HM Government for providing Government
Indemnity and the Department for Culture, Media
and Sport and Arts Council England for arranging
the indemnity.

First published in 2017 by
National Gallery Company Limited
St Vincent House
30 Orange Street
London WC2H 7HH
www.nationalgallery.co.uk

ISBN 978 1 85709 614 9 HB
ISBN 978 1 85709 613 2 PB

1043422 HB
1043423 PB

British Library Cataloguing-in-Publication Data.
A catalogue record is available from the British
Library
Library of Congress Control Number 2017939575

Publisher: Jan Green
Project Editor: Sarah Derry
Editor: Rachel Giles
Picture Researcher: Félix Zorzo
Production: Jane Hyne and Amanda Mackie
Designed by Joe Ewart

Origination by DL Imaging, London
Printed in Italy by Conti TipoColor

All measurements give height before width

Front cover: Jean-Auguste-Dominique Ingres,
Odalisque in Grisaille, about 1824–34
(detail of cat. 28)

Frontispiece: Marten Jozef Geeraerts, *Children's
Game*, perhaps 1740–90 (detail of cat. 37)

Page 6: François Boucher, *Vulcan's Forge (Vulcan
presenting Venus with Arms for Aeneas)*, 1756
(detail of cat. 18)

Page 10: Jan Brueghel the Elder, *Visit to the
Peasants*, about 1597 (detail of cat. 26)

Pages 12–13: Willem van de Velde the Elder,
Departure of the Dutch Fleet the 9th of June 1645,
about 1650 (detail of cat. 47)

Pages. 212–13: Peder Balke, *The Tempest*, about
1862 (enlarged detail of cat. 53)

Pages 222–3: Anthony van Dyck, *Rinaldo and
Armida*, 1634–5 (detail of cat. 41)

Section introductions feature decorative details
from Andrea Mantegna's *Introduction to the Cult of
Cybele at Rome* (cat. 34). The full colour image is
reproduced on pp. 118–19.

Contents

Directors' Preface — 7
Acknowledgements — 11

Introduction — 15

1 Painting the Sacred — 27

2 Studies in Light and Shadow — 53

3 Independent Paintings in Grisaille — 79

4 Monochrome Painting and Sculpture — 107

5 Monochrome Painting and Printmaking — 137

6 Monochrome Painting in the Age of Photography and Film — 163

7 Abstraction in Black and White — 185

Beyond Painting: Monochrome and Installation Art — 205

Your monochromatic listening
Olafur Eliasson — 209

Notes — 213
Bibliography — 223
List of Lenders — 235
Photographic and Copyright Credits — 236
Index — 238

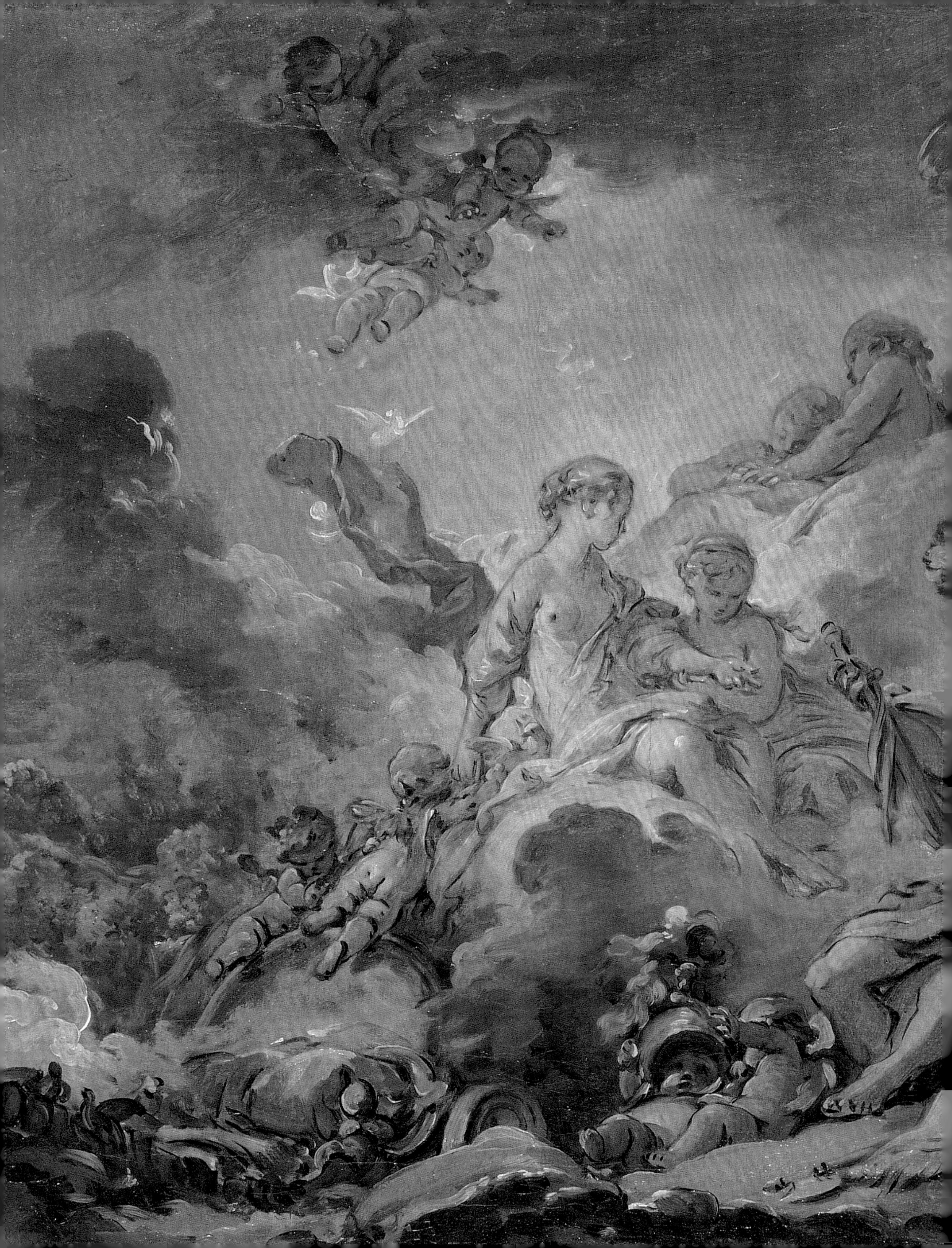

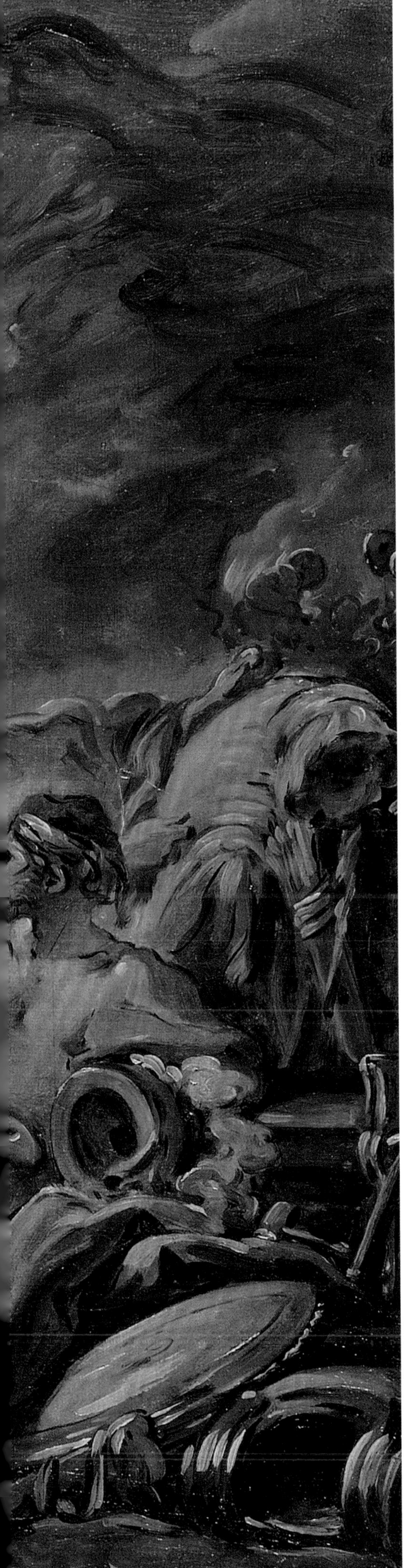

Directors' Preface

This is the first exhibition, we believe, devoted to the subject of painting in black and white from the Middle Ages to our own times. The theme is a truly fascinating one; it engages with the most important aspects of picture-making and has provoked the interest of numerous artists from van Eyck to Degas and from Ingres to Richter, as the selection of works reproduced in this catalogue demonstrates.

The decision to paint in black and white and consciously to exclude colour reflects many and varied motives, ranging from the strictly functional and aesthetic to the moral and philosophical. Artists in the Middle Ages limited their palette because liturgical austerity required it or because their works had to serve the contemplation of the divine mystery of God as pure light. Painters have relished the challenge of achieving verisimilitude without recourse to coloured pigments, honing their mimetic skills to demonstrate the superiority of painting over the other arts. Considerable rhetorical effort was expended on this question in the Renaissance in the theoretical debate referred to as the *paragone*, the comparison, or competition, between the different arts, a debate to which Leonardo and Michelangelo also contributed.

Painting in monochrome has enabled artists to focus on the essentials of light and dark, the primary elements of visual perception. The ancient Greeks invented 'skiagraphia', painting lights and shadows, while the Italians of a much later age painted in 'chiaroscuro'. From the French comes the artistic term 'grisaille', a painting in tones of grey, often a sketch or study made in preparation for a larger and more ambitious work; but a grisaille could also serve as the vehicle for a *jeu d'ésprit* or even a *trompe l'oeil*, something that deceives the eye on account of its visual persuasiveness. It could also be a finished work in its own right.

Many painters were also etchers or worked very closely with printmakers and were consequently familiar with seeing their coloured inventions reproduced in black and white. Van Dyck repeated his own polychrome *Rinaldo and Armida* as a reduced monochrome painting so that it could be made into a print and widely diffused, while the little known French painter Etienne Moulinneuf reproduced in oils an etching after Chardin's *La Pourvoyeuse* and intensified its *trompe l'oeil* qualities by showing a broken pane of glass over it. This kind of visual virtuosity reflects a common thread in the history of monochrome, from van Eyck and Mantegna's efforts to reproduce carved stone to Peder Balke's painted responses to early landscape photographs.

Photography, which means 'drawing with light', was effectively a monochrome technique until the twentieth century and was, from the moment of its invention, intimately bound up with painting. Painters consciously evoked the effects of the photographic image in their work and the relationship between photography and painting continues to be fertile and complex right up to today, as shown in the works of Chuck Close, for example. Black-and-white films and monochrome television have also had a profound impact on picture making, something which this exhibition can only allude to.

Because of its elemental visual qualities and the sense that it reduces everything to first principles, monochrome has played a very significant role in the twentieth century's avant-garde artistic movements, from Cubism's preference for a restricted and highly disciplined palette to Malevich's *Black Square*, a purported endpoint of art but in many ways an influential new beginning; from American Abstract Expressionism to British Op art. The German artist, Gerhard Richter has observed that his grey canvases aim for a very serious kind of beauty that invites thoughtful contemplation and like other contemporary artists he alludes to the emotional and participatory, even democratic, nature of monochromatic abstraction. In his eloquent text at the end of this catalogue, the contemporary Danish artist, Olafur Eliasson, states that, 'The "mono" in monochrome does not mean the elimination of complexity; rather, the monochromatic space holds plurality in it – it welcomes multidimensionality and offers it to us as viewers'. The exhibition of which this catalogue is the accompanying publication closes with Eliasson's *Room for one colour*, an immersive environment in which a set of monofrequency lamps turns everything into monochrome, making the viewer's retina much more sensitive in what ends up being a shared experience of heightened visual perception. Stripping away colour has always been for artists a way to explore the nature of seeing and the power of image making. In this sense, painting in monochrome is profoundly insightful.

In 2014 the National Gallery held an exhibition entitled *Making Colour* which explored the significance and mechanics of colour and in 2016 the Museum Kunstpalast in Düsseldorf devoted a large show to the motif of the curtain in art which explored questions of concealment and revelation, the metaphorical limits of the viewable and the artistic challenge of mimesis. Our two institutions are very pleased to work together on *Monochrome: Painting in Black and White*, an exhibition that explores another broad and important theme in the history of art, rich with memorable, striking and beautiful images.

We are particularly grateful to the exhibition curators, Lelia Packer and Jennifer Sliwka, who conceived the idea several years ago and have developed it with intelligence and enthusiasm. They are also the authors of this catalogue. Betsy Wieseman, formerly a curator at the National Gallery, provided very valuable advice in the early stages of this project. We would like to express our gratitude to all the lenders, both institutional and private, who have kindly agreed to deprive themselves of their works of art for a period so that they may be enjoyed by visitors in London and Düsseldorf. We want to thank all our staff at the National Gallery and at the Museum Kunstpalast, where Beat Wismer has prepared the exhibition as Director General.

In London we would like to express our gratitude to Howard and Roberta Ahmanson for their support of the exhibition and to The Vaseppi Trust and other donors who have made generous contributions to enable the exhibition to take place.

In Düsseldorf, we would like to thank the City of Düsseldorf, founder of the Stiftung Museum Kunstpalast, and E.ON SE, sponsors of the exhibition at the Kunstpalast.

Gabriele Finaldi
Director, The National Gallery, London

Felix Krämer
Director General, Museum Kunstpalast, Düsseldorf

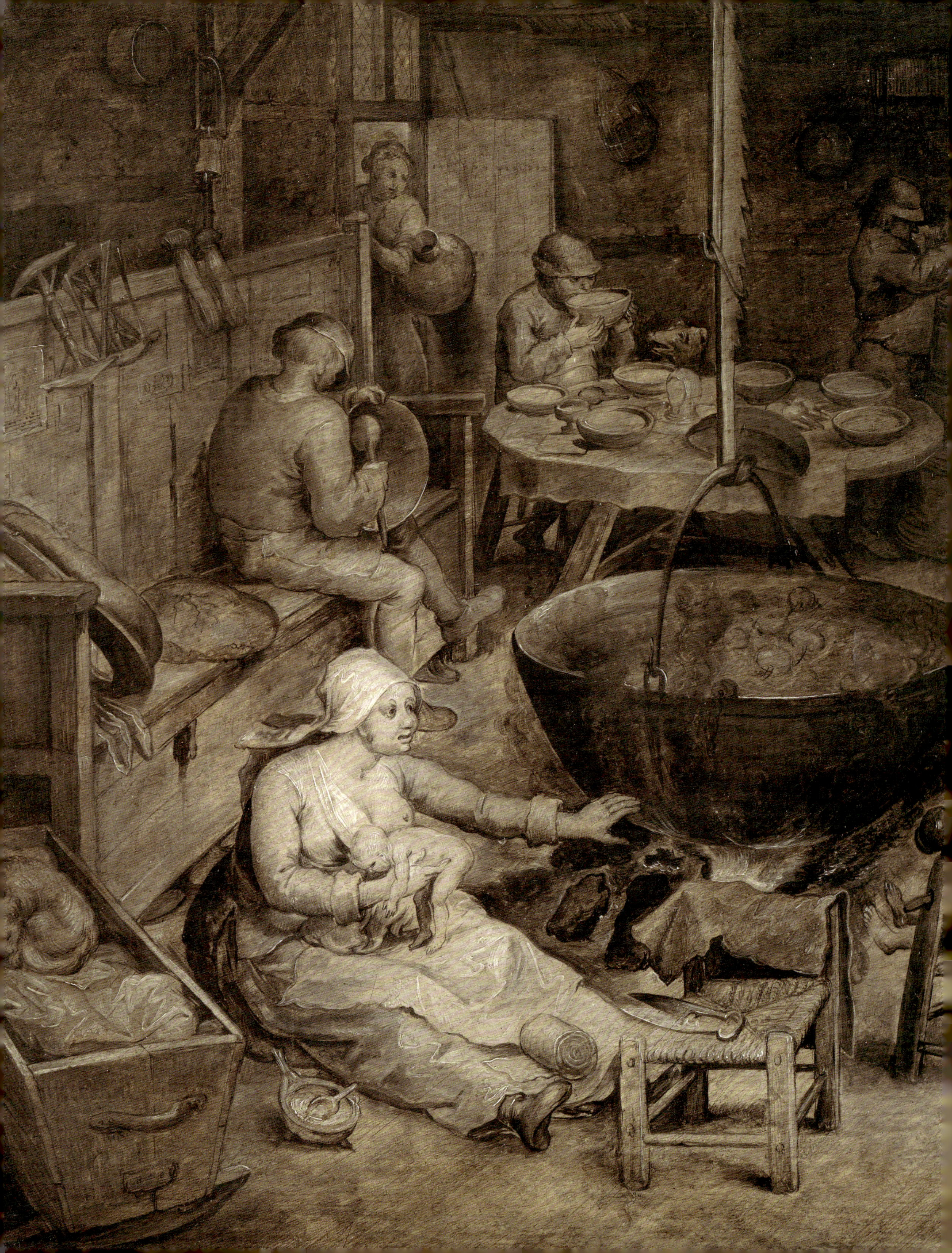

Acknowledgements

This study is greatly indebted to the research of many scholars working across a broad chronological and geographical scope whose interest in, and knowledge of, works painted 'without colour' have been a great resource for this wide-ranging catalogue and exhibition. The preparation of the catalogue has also benefited from the knowledgeable staff and invaluable resources at the Warburg and the Courtauld Institutes and the British Library in London, and the Kunsthistorisches Institut and the Berenson Library at Villa I Tatti in Florence. For their early enthusiasm for, and insight into, various aspects of this project we would especially like to thank Gabriele Finaldi, Nicholas Penny, Caroline Campbell, Betsy Wieseman, Jane Knowles and Letizia Treves, and our partners in Düsseldorf, Beat Wismer, Harry Schmitz and Sandra Badelt. We are particularly grateful to the institutions and individuals who have generously lent to this exhibition and to the directors, curators and conservators of those collections who facilitated our visits to study their works of art.

We would also like to express our gratitude to those individuals who assisted us with special access to objects, information and expertise: Paul Ackroyd, David Anfam, Karen Angne, Claire Baisier, Sophie Ballinger, Carmen Bambach, Giulia Bartrum, Bettina Baumgärtel, Andrea Bayer, Claire Bernardi, Rachel Billinge, Thomas Bohl, Duncan Bull, An van Camp, Barbara Castelli, Simonetta Castronovo, Hugo Chapman, Angela Choon, Keith Christiansen, Martin Clayton, Peter van der Coelen, Carly Collier, Tamara Corm, Samantha Cox, Alan Crookham, Nicholas Cullinan, Remmelt Daalder, Dexter Dalwood, Ana Debenedetti, Nicola Del Roscio, Charlotte Denoël, Christine Descatoire, Edith Devaney, Anthony D'Offay, Joel Draper, Blaise Ducos, Mimi Dusselier, Olafur Eliasson, Mark Evans, Susan Foister, Marie-Cécile Forest, Anne Forray-Carlier, Wells Fray-Smith, Michael Fried, Geoffrey Garrison, Audrey Gay-Mazuel, George Gordon, Gloria Groom, Hannah Gruy, Tatiana Gubanova, Emmanuel Guigon, Hannes Halder, John Hand, Jim Harris, Gill Hart, Kay Heymer, Zerlina Hughes, Oscar Humphries, Kyu Jin Hwang, Catherine Ingrams, Nancy Ireson, Jasper Johns, Elisabeth de Jonckheere, Pepe Karmel, Larry Keith, Dedo von Kerssenbrock-Krosigk, Leah Kharibian, Robin Kiang, Abigail Kikuchi, Minjung Kim, Hope Kingsley, Jack Kirkland, Kristina Köper, Dagmar Korbacher, Felix Krämer, Friso Lammertse, Aleksey Larionov, Kerstin Ludolph, Jona Lueddeckens, Ger Luijten, Emmanuelle Mace, Patrice Marandel, Philippa Martin, Paola Martini, Mark McDonald, Christof Metzger, Sophie Motsch, Jane Munro, Hans Op de Beeck, Pilar Ordovas, Marije Osnabrugge, Patrick O'Sullivan, Belinda Phillpot, Lauren Porter, Anne Pritchard, Leslie Prouty, Maureen Pskowski, Ben Quash, Bianca Raitz-Tinzmann, Xavier Rey, Chris Riopelle, Anne Robbins, Xavier Salomon, Xavier Salmon, Peter Schade, Arnika Schmidt, Svenja Schütte, Manfred Sellink, Annette Siegel, Kirsten Simister, Bernard Soens, Guillermo Solana, Matthew Stephenson, Luke Syson, Cécile Tainturier, Anna Testar, Alexandra Tommasini, Zelfira Tregulova, Anne Verdure-Mary, Christiaan Vogelaar, Dingenus van de Vrie, Sarah Vowles, Annie de Wambrechies, Henrietta Ward, Nicholas Fox Weber, Catherine Whistler, Colin Wiggins, Kimberley Williams, Humphrey Wine and Matthias Wivel.

We would like to thank Jan Green, Sarah Derry, Rachel Giles, Gillian Malpass, Félix Zorzo, Jane Hyne and Joe Ewart who transformed our text into this beautiful catalogue, and to the Development Department of the National Gallery for all of their energy and enthusiasm for this project. For their constant encouragement and support, we would like to thank our families Ryszard, Anne and Daniel Sliwka, Adam, Ana and Maia Packer, Mihaela Campion and Andre Kantar.

Lelia Packer and Jennifer Sliwka

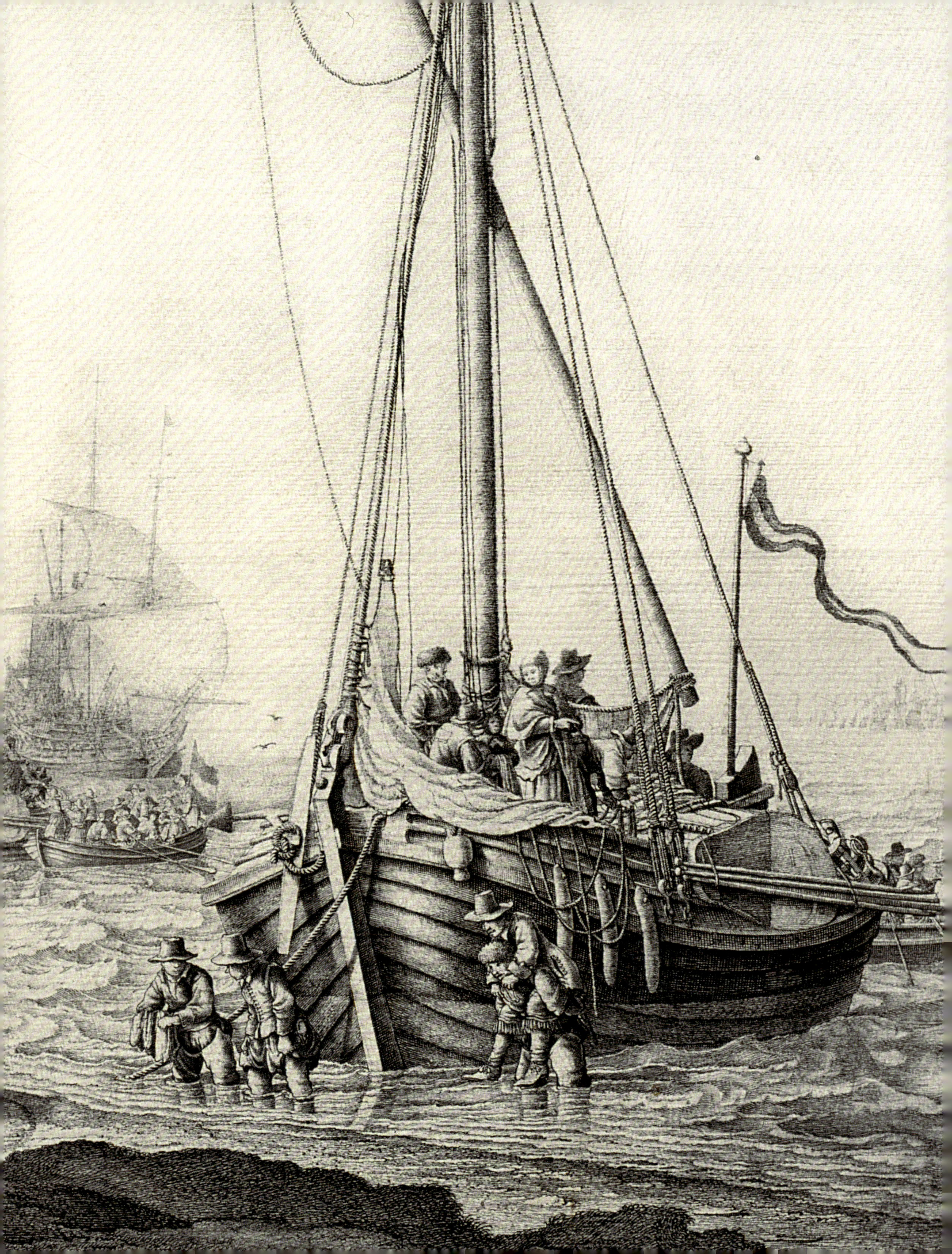

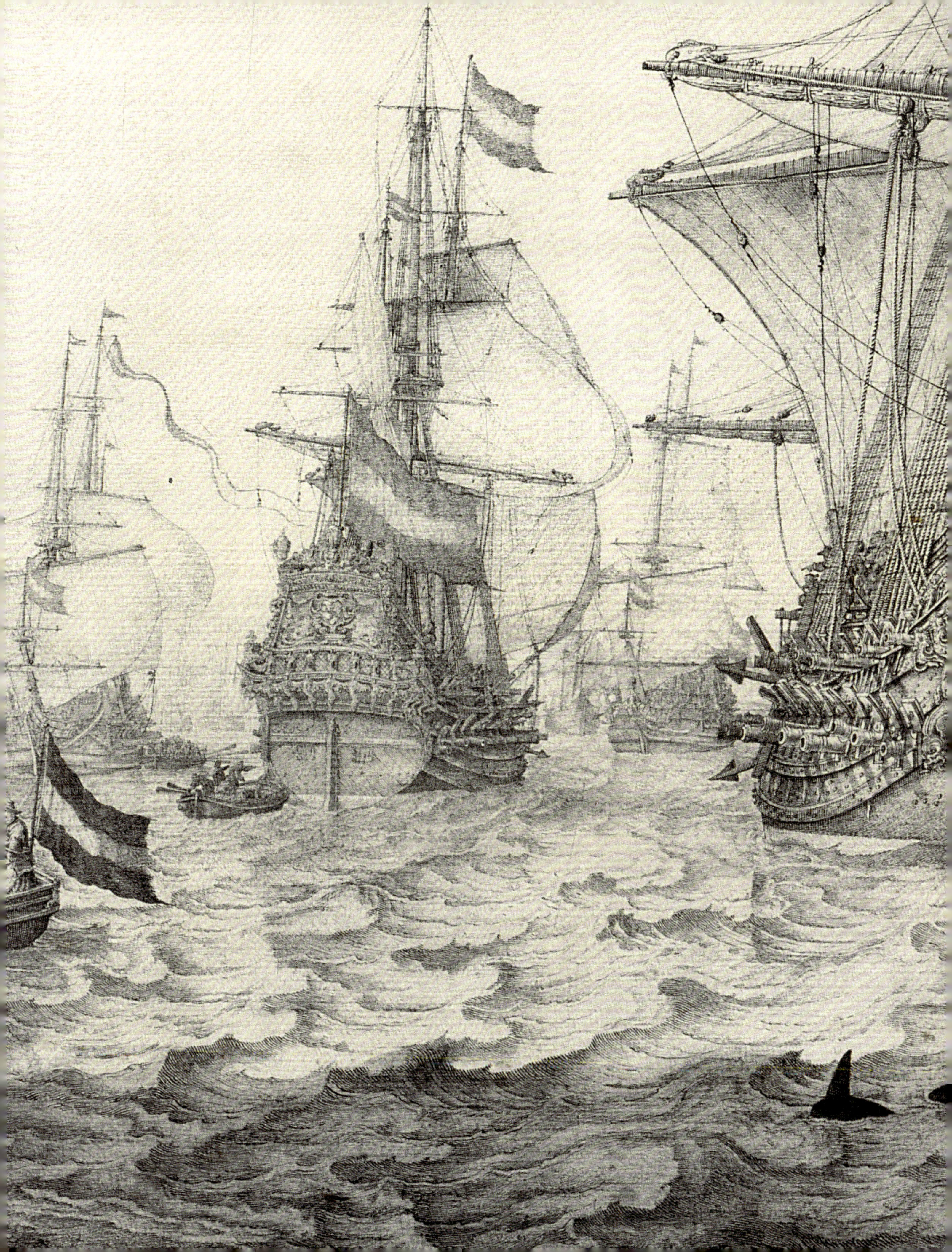

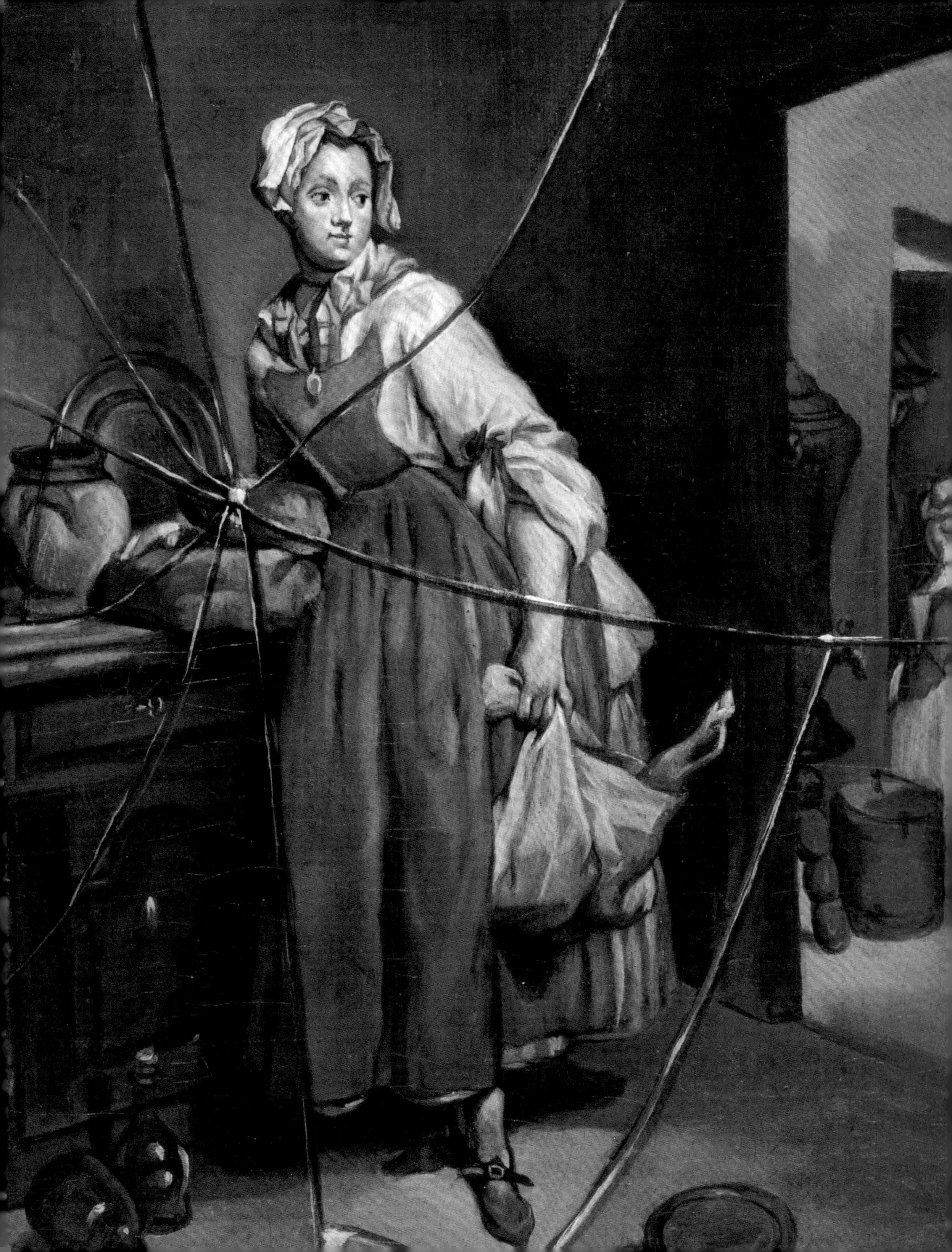

Introduction

Lelia Packer and Jennifer Sliwka

Painting in black and white is a thread that runs through the history and practice of art. In particular, it is a story of the connections between painting and other art forms – sculpture, printmaking, photography or film – and the impact those forms have made on painting. Painters have often, it seems, restricted their use of colour when they have wanted to demonstrate the superiority of painting over other art. To paint 'without colour', in other words, has been a means of demonstrating the intellectual power of painting. It takes us to the roots of why painting has mattered over time in the Western tradition and also the ways in which the practice and understanding of painting has changed.

A survey of black-and-white painting across nearly seven centuries reveals a number of shared aims and characteristics. Artists have long explored the psychological, emotional and spiritual effects engendered by viewing paintings in black-and-white and have been conscious that monochromatic pictures encourage the viewer to focus on a particular subject without the distraction of colour. In order to convey form and texture without colour, artists have developed innovative techniques. They have also been alert to the opportunity offered by a restricted – and economical – palette to demonstrate their artistic virtuosity. This palette, as our subtitle acknowledges, is made up predominantly of black and white, but some of the pictures illustrated here are painted not only in black, white and greyscale but also in tones from light tan to darkest brown.

In the modern period, painters working in black and white continue to push the boundaries of their medium in new directions. Some contemporary artists have provided first-hand accounts of their reasons for painting in monochrome, motivations that might offer insights into the practice of their artistic predecessors. The German artist Gerhard Richter (b. 1932), for example, has revealed that his entirely grey paintings 'come from a motivation ... that was very negative. It has a lot to do with hopelessness, depression and such things. But it has to be turned on its head in the end, and has to come to a form where these paintings possess beauty. And in this case, it's not a carefree beauty, but rather a serious one.'[1] Richter's approach, as well those of other modern and contemporary artists who similarly draw on monochrome's metaphorical associations and affective qualities, finds echoes in the work of some of the historic painters in this book.

Black and white: A brief history

The practice of painting using primarily black and white pigments has been discussed by authors and philosophers since antiquity, testifying, in the

Etienne Moulinneuf (1706–1789) after
Jean-Siméon Chardin (1699–1779)
Back from the Market (La Pourvoyeuse),
about 1770, detail of cat. 50

absence of surviving pictures, to its early origins and sustained appeal.[2] Painters in ancient Greece and Rome appreciated the value of black and white in representing light and shadow. The fifth-century BC Athenian painter Apollodorus, for example, is credited with developing a technique known as *skiagraphia* (literally, 'shadow painting'), using cross-hatching and light and dark tones to give the illusion of shadow and volume.[3] Centuries later, the Roman scholar Pliny the Elder (AD 23–79) traced the practice of creating monochrome pictures (*monocromatis picturis*) back to the very origins of painting and described the process of distinguishing between light and shade (*lumen et umbras*) in art as an intermediary step between an initial drawing and a final work.[4]

Italian Renaissance authors and artists revived these ideas, similarly drawing out the associations between white and black and light and shadow. Cennino Cennini, for example, in his *Libro dell'arte*, written in the early fifteenth century, describes how the use of 'chiaro e scuro' (light and dark) in painting might enhance the effects of volume and relief. While Cennino's discussion centred on coloured paintings, Giorgio Vasari, in the 1568 edition of his *Lives of the Artists*, appears to have been the first to apply the term 'chiaro scuro' not only to strong tonal contrasts between light and dark in coloured paintings but also to entirely monochromatic pictures, and specifically to paintings in imitation of sculpture or cameos executed in a single colour.[5]

While these descriptions concentrate on qualities of light and shadow, there is another early tradition that refers to the exclusive use of black and white in painting. The earliest surviving painted works in black and white are stained-glass windows produced for Cistercian monasteries in the twelfth century (fig. 2), but the earliest known written references identifying black-and-white painting as a specific genre appear two centuries later, in 1401–3, in the inventory of Duke Jean de Berry (1340–1416), which lists a panel painting executed in a technique described in French as 'de blanc et noir' (of white and black).[6] By this date, illuminators such as Jean Pucelle had been painting lively black-and-white illuminations, as seen, for example, in the Book of Hours he produced for the Queen of France in 1324–8 (fig. 3). Similar terms were coined to refer more specifically to works with an all-over grey tonality. The fourteenth-century inventories of King Charles V of France describe his painted altar hangings as 'cendré' (ashen) in reference to their ash-grey colour, while in the seventeenth century, the popular monochromes of the Dutch artist Adriaen van de Venne were endearingly dubbed 'grawtjes' (little grey ones) (cat. 23).

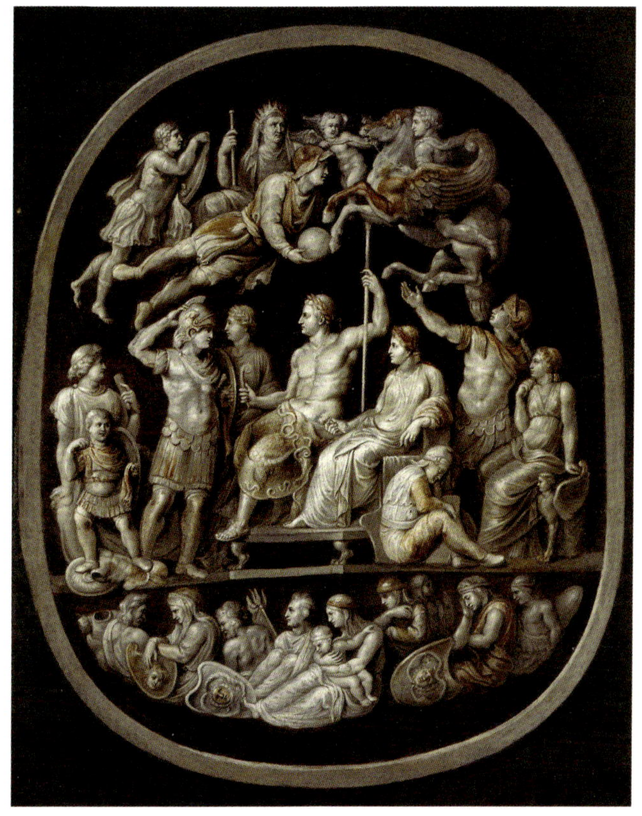

The term 'grisaille', derived from the French word 'gris' (grey), refers to works in greyscale. In 1625, the French antiquary Nicolas-Claude Fabri de Peiresc wrote to Peter Paul Rubens, commissioning him to paint an antique cameo 'en grisaille et non en couleurs' ('in grisaille and not in colour') (fig. 1).[7] The term began to be applied retrospectively to earlier, Cistercian stained glass, which became known as grisaille glass, but it is now most commonly used to mean grey paintings in imitation of sculpture or relief, or grey painting more broadly.

The more recent association of 'monochrome' with strictly black-and-white painting can be traced back to the work of the Russian Suprematists in the early twentieth century, led by Kazimir Malevich. Malevich's *Black Square* of 1915, a black square on a white background, sought to reduce painting to its simplest form, directing the viewer's focus to the purely physical and formal elements of the work (see cat. 60). Monochromatic painting became increasingly common in abstract art during the twentieth century, for example in the canvases of painters working in America such as Jackson Pollock (fig. 43) and Joseph Albers (cat. 61). The monochromatic momentum has persisted into the twenty-first century. Indeed, despite access to a variety of affordable and reliable coloured pigments, such artists as Christopher Wool (b. 1955) and Korean minimalist painters such as Park Seo-Bo (b. 1931) embrace an exclusively black-and-white palette, while Gerhard Richter continues to work in grey monochrome.

Fig. 1
Peter Paul Rubens (1577-1640)
The Apotheosis of Germanicus: copy after an antique Cameo (The 'Gemma Tiberiana')
Oil on canvas, 100.7 × 78 cm
Ashmolean Museum, University of Oxford

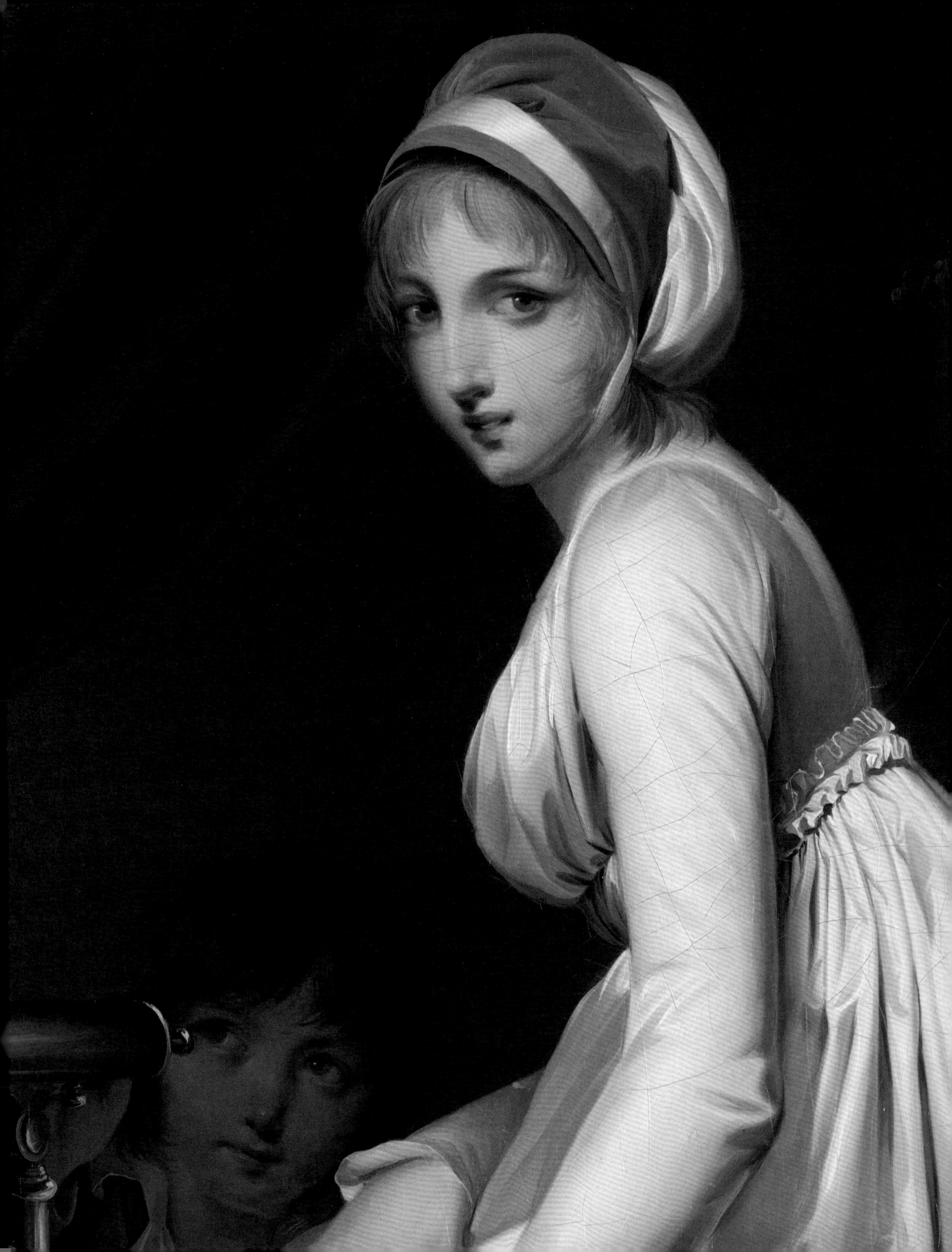

Why paint in black and white?

The earliest works discussed in this book are paintings commissioned by the medieval Church, and the restriction to black and white was intended to fulfil specific spiritual functions. Sparsely decorated monastic spaces were designed to focus the mind on meditation and prayer, and black-and-white paintings were displayed during Lent, a period in the liturgical calendar for fasting, reflection, abstinence and penitence, when images in colour were hidden from view. In medieval and Renaissance paintings that combined grisaille and polychromy, monochrome images were often restricted to the margins, functioning as a fictive frame or border, or were painted on the reverse of altarpiece shutters. The juxtaposition of colour and 'non-colour' usually signalled a hierarchy or a historical distinction in the subject matter. In Petrus Christus's *Nativity* (cat. 6), for example, Old Testament scenes in grisaille 'frame' an episode from the New Testament in colour.

From the fifteenth century onwards, artists began painting preparatory works in monochrome. Drapery studies such as that by Domenico Ghirlandaio (cat. 11), or figure and compositional studies in oil on paper such as those of Domenico Beccafumi (cat. 13) and later, Peter Paul Rubens (cat. 15), provided opportunities for innovation and experimentation. These sketches provided artists with a deeper understanding of the play of light and shadow over different surfaces and allowed them to map out a sequence of harmonious tones across a composition. Detailed studies of sections of a composition included careful, precise depictions of the fall of light on draperies, or the lineaments of a face. The finished works in colour that followed, be they panel paintings, frescoes or tapestries, benefited from these meticulous studies in black and white.

In the second half of the sixteenth century, artists began to produce monochromes as independent paintings that did not have a preparatory or religious purpose. Hendrik Goltzius's *Without Ceres and Bacchus, Venus would Freeze* (cat. 22) is one example. Such pictures provided artists with a means of demonstrating their skill and technical ingenuity, and the novelty of the works must have impressed prospective patrons and collectors.

Painters were most likely to turn to monochrome, however, to imitate or rival works of art in other media, beginning first with sculpture and later, following the development of new technologies, printmaking, photography and film. In these cases, the artist's skill in deceiving the eye is often as much the subject of the painting as the figurative image or narrative it represents. By convincingly imitating other media in paint, as in the case of Andrea Mantegna's representation of an ancient stone relief, *The Introduction of the*

Cult of Cybele at Rome (cat. 34), artists attempted to assert the supremacy of painting over other art forms and in doing so, demonstrated their own virtuosity.

From the late sixteenth century onwards, the widespread availability of prints presented new challenges and opportunities for artists, who responded with remarkable ingenuity. Goltzius, an artist best known for his prints, developed an innovative 'pen painting' technique to create convincing imitations of his own engravings, and on a large scale impossible to achieve in a single print on paper (cats 45 and 46). Similarly, the invention of photography in the nineteenth century, and that of film during the twentieth, prompted painters to respond to the distinct qualities and advantages of these media and to evoke the effects of a photographic image in their work. In Célestin Joseph Blanc's *Head of a Girl* of 1867 (cat. 54), for example, both the child's formal pose and the velvety effect of the paint make it easy to mistake the painting for an early photograph.

In the twentieth century, Picasso was one of several artists who took images from newspapers and from newsreel as source material for powerful black-and-white paintings. His *Charnel House* of 1944–5 (fig. 38) comments directly on contemporary social and political events. More recently, Marlene Dumas has used black-and-white photography and film as source images for her paintings. *The Image as Burden*, 1993 (cat. 55) is a painting derived from a film-still from George Cukor's classic black-and-white movie *Camille* (1936). Extracted from its original context and translated into paint, the subject becomes ambiguous, more reminiscent of the iconography of the Pietà rather than the lovers in a 1930s film. Conversely, filmmakers, perhaps taking a cue from historical painting, have contrasted black-and-white with colour film to signal shifts in place, meaning or time. In the classic film *The Wizard of Oz* (1939), scenes with Dorothy and her Kansas home are transmitted in monochromatic sepia tones, until she steps through the threshold of her farmhouse door and enters the Technicolor world of Oz, marking the dramatic transition from the dullness of her previous existence to her newfound adventure.[8]

The final chapter of this book is dedicated to abstract artists painting in monochrome in the twentieth and twenty-first centuries. In these works it is often the painting's support (panel, canvas or board) and the black and white paints themselves – their manipulation, placement and orientation – that are the central subject, as in the case of Ellsworth Kelly's *Black and White Bar I* (cat. 68).

Some of these artists have worked deliberately in an abstract mode to encourage a contemplative response and to evoke the spiritual rather than the material world. Malevich likened his *Black Square* to a Byzantine icon by

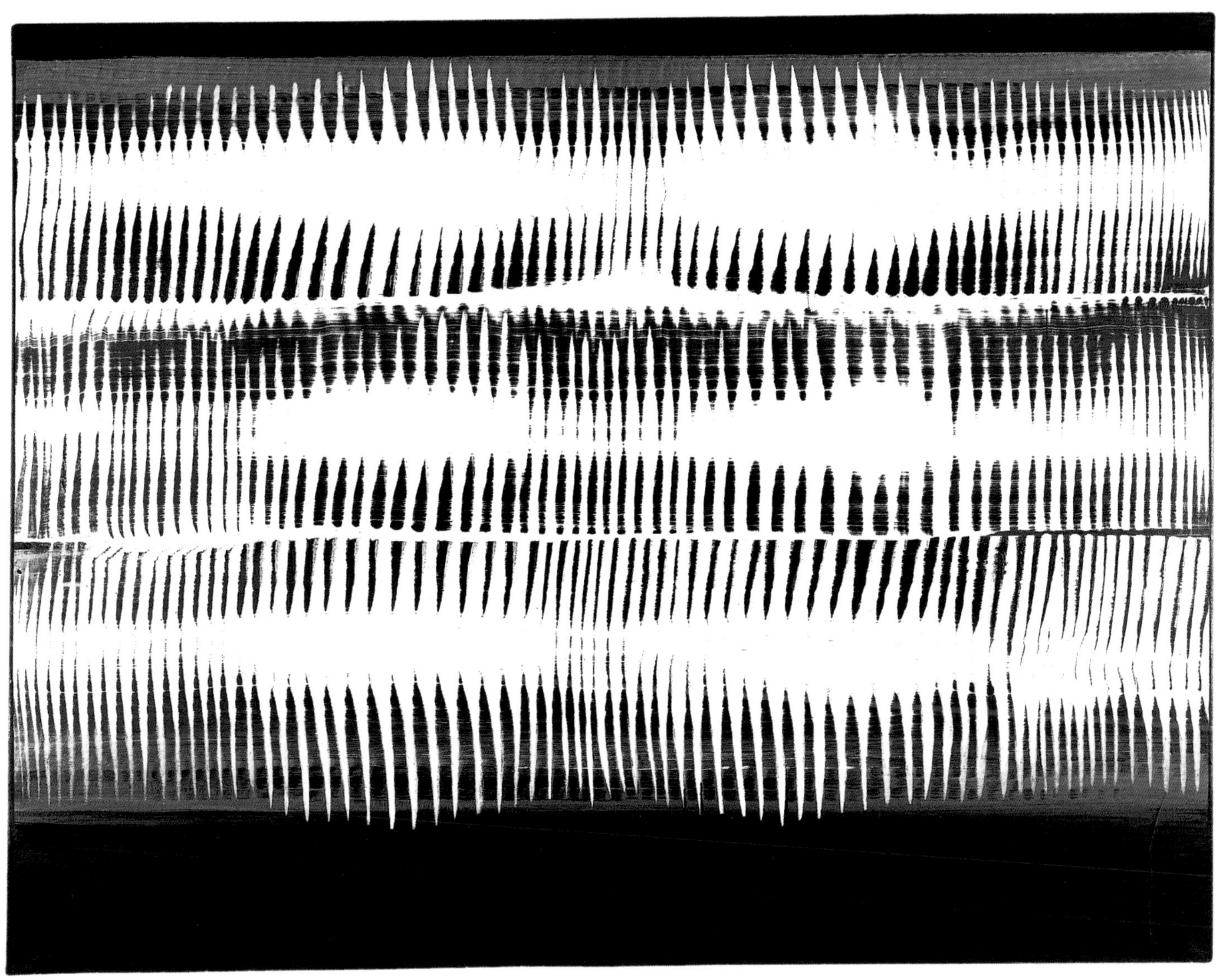

Cat. 1
Heinz Mack (b. 1931)
White Dynamic Structure on Black, 1962
Synthetic resin and pigments on canvas,
130 × 170 cm
Museum Kunstpalast, Düsseldorf – Stiftung
Sammlung Kemp
Exhibited Düsseldorf only

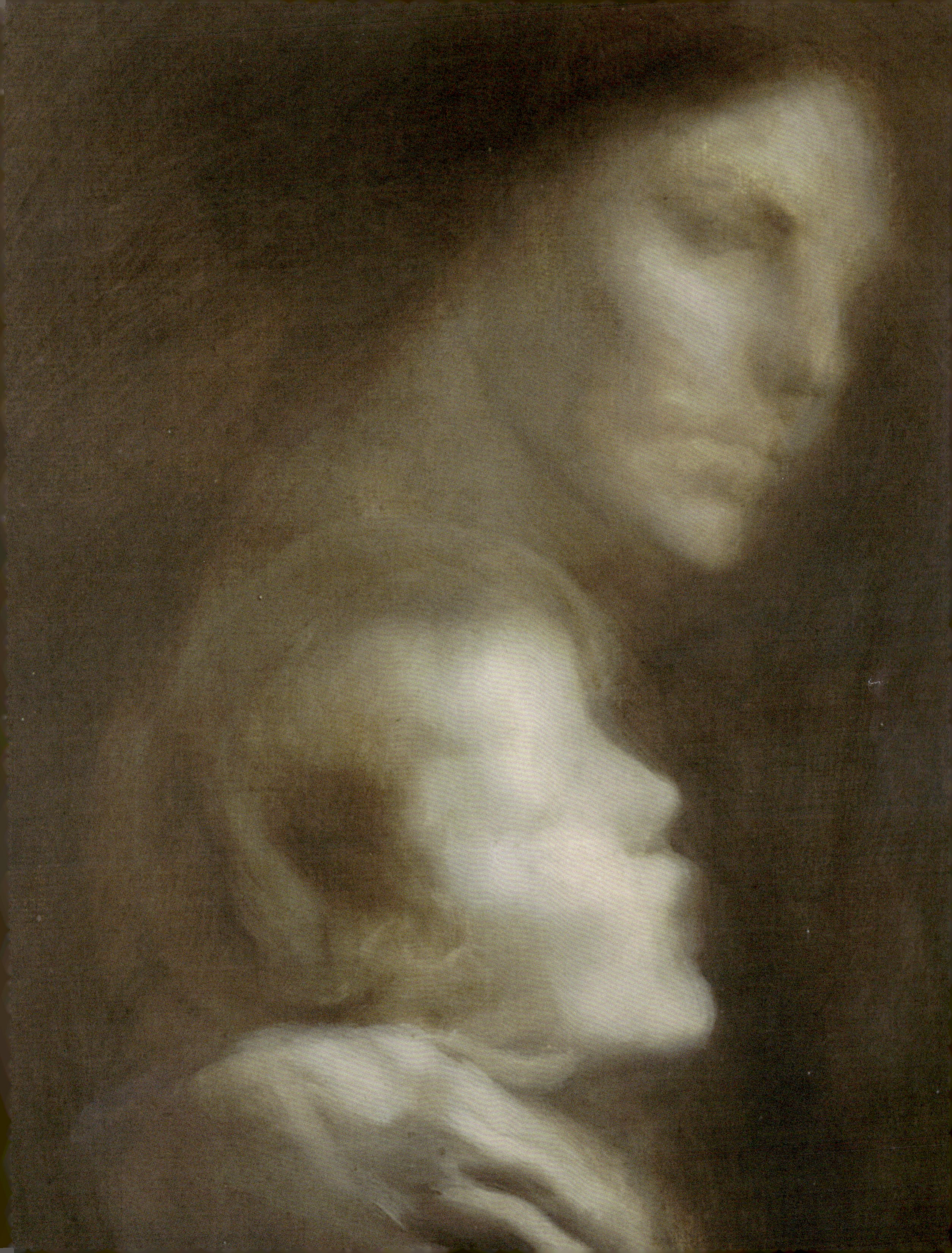

placing it high on the wall in the position usually reserved for sacred objects of that kind. In reducing an object or figure to its most simplified or abstracted form, many artists have refined their colour palette to the basics: black, white and grey. They draw the viewer's attention to the purely physical and formal elements of their works – their shape, texture, material and technique. The 'Zero' group of abstract artists working in the 1950s and 1960s, for example, used monochrome to highlight their artistic processes, often slashing or creating raised shapes on white or black canvases (cat. 1).

Like centuries of artists before them, abstract painters often associated black, white and grey with the virtues of order, purity, simplicity and spirituality. Gerhard Richter praises grey for its 'quietness' and often turns to monochrome when attempting a new technique or approach to painting so as to avoid what he identifies as the complications elicited by the use of colour.[9] In some ways, Richter's desire for chromatic quietness calls to mind the Cistercian prohibition of colour in their monasteries as a means of eliminating distraction from prayer, while his use of grey in the more experimental stages of a new project may recall Renaissance artists' use of monochrome preparatory oil sketches.

When asked why he has regularly returned to a reduced palette over the course of his career, Richter responded, 'I think grey is an important colour – the ideal colour … for states of being and situations that affect one, and for which one would like to find a visual expression.'[10] He has described grey as an inherently flexible colour, one able to convey both objectivity and ambiguity. Richter's comment on the objectivity of grey recalls the work of artists who use black-and-white photographs as source material for paintings, as he does himself in his *Helga Matura with her Fiancé* (cat. 56). His reference to the ambiguity of grey brings to mind enigmatic and uneasy symbolist or existentialist portraits, such as Eugène Carrière's *Maternité (Suffering)* (cat. 24) or Alberto Giacometti's *Annette Seated* (cat. 25). Richter also argues for grey's capacity to mediate between 'the visible and the invisible',[11] which reminds us of religious works such as the monochrome exteriors of shuttered altarpieces, the absence of colour preparing the viewer for the polychrome images hidden within.

Artists continue to be inspired by the possibilities afforded by painting in black and white. The meanings and purposes of monochrome painting are constantly shifting, yet the materials have altered little since the Middle Ages. Painting in monochrome has endured precisely because it allows painters to test the limits of their discipline. It enables them to conjure up spectacular effects of imagination with the simplest of materials and with remarkable virtuosity, and to challenge viewers to reconsider their perception of the world around them.

Eugène Carrière (1849–1906)
Maternity (Suffering), about 1896–7,
detail of cat. 24

RELIQVIAE
1

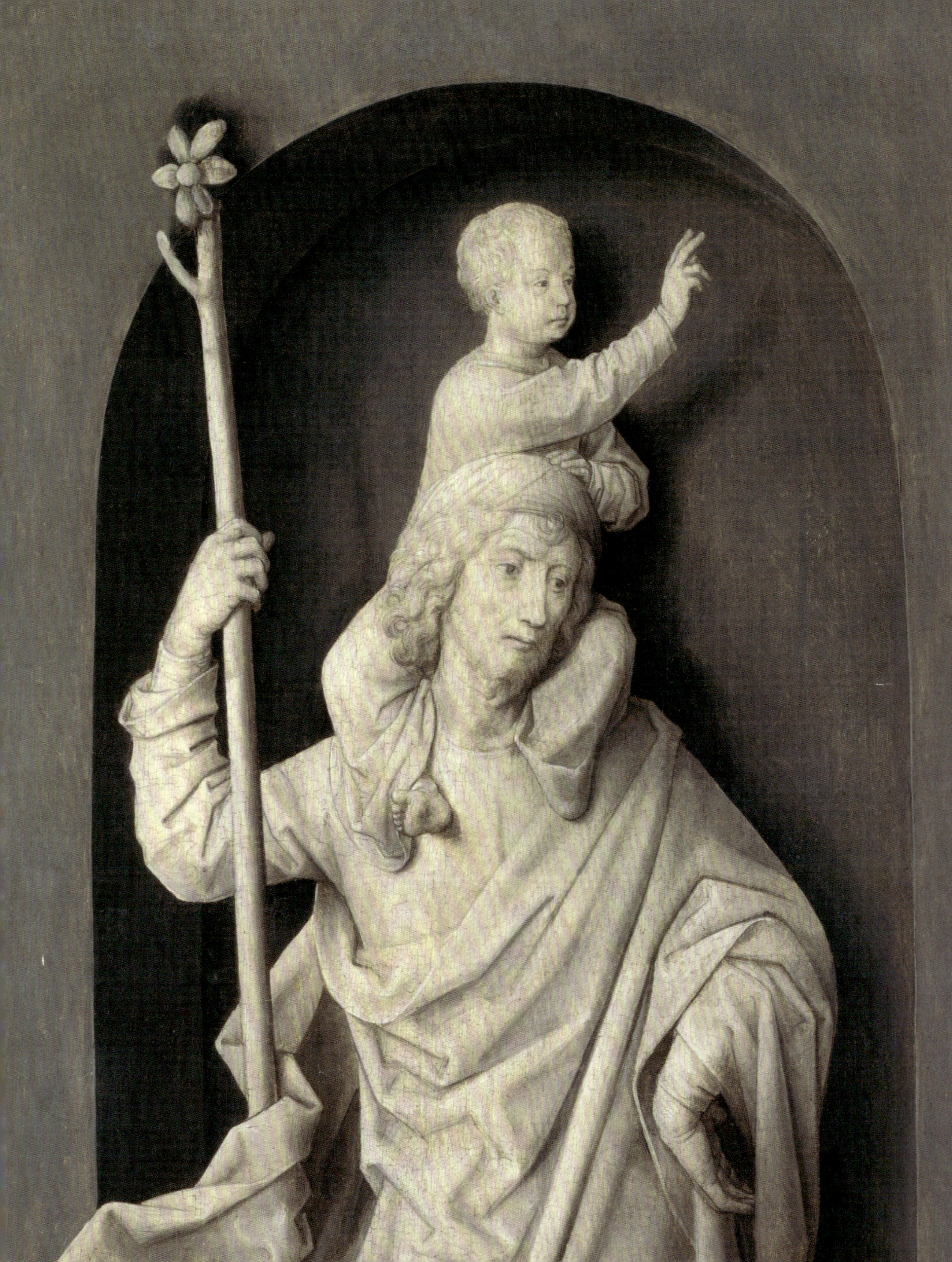

Painting the Sacred

Jennifer Sliwka

The earliest surviving works of art made exclusively in black and white were designed for specific devotional uses, or had particular religious functions. As colour is encountered everywhere and in almost everything, it can be associated with the familiar or the mundane, while objects made 'without colour' can suggest the otherworldly or the spiritual. Minimally decorated monastic spaces adorned exclusively with works in black and white marked a shift from the stimulation and concerns of the outside world of colour, to a simplified meditative space in which the mind and the eye could focus without distraction. A monochromatic palette was sometimes used alongside colour as a foil, to signal a hierarchy between different kinds of images. For example, black-and-white images are often found in the margins of medieval and Renaissance paintings, where they contrast with a central, or primary, coloured image. In many cases, the images painted in monochrome represent scenes from pagan antiquity or the Old Testament and are juxtaposed with New Testament images in vivid colour. Artists sometimes chose to paint personifications of religious ideals or concepts in grey monochrome to signify their symbolic or spiritual identity as opposed to an earthly or human one. Principally, black, white and often grey tones were used in works made specifically for use during Lent as a means of marking this period of penitence, fasting and mourning in the liturgical calendar. This restricted palette was taken up for the representation of Lenten themes more broadly, such as in illuminated manuscripts and on altarpieces painted with scenes from Christ's Passion. Although the examples of religious painting explored here range from the twelfth to the seventeenth century and use a variety of supports, including glass, textile and wood, they all employ a monochrome palette to create a distinction between the mundane and the spiritual, the past and the present or the everyday and a period of heightened religious solemnity.

Monastic austerity

In the early eleventh century, a group of Benedictine monks felt their fellow brothers had grown lax in the observance of the Rule as set down by Saint Benedict and formed their own more austere Order. They were known as the Cistercians, after the town of Cîteaux, where they established their first abbey. Among the strict reforms they enforced were dietary abstinence, manual labour and artistic asceticism – that is, an extremely minimal decor with an emphasis on function rather than ornamentation.[1] While other monastic orders made some or even all of these demands, the Cistercians were the only ones to stipulate artistic asceticism through written, mandatory laws. These statutes, dating to around 1119, are probably the earliest systematic restrictions on art in

Hans Memling (active 1465; died 1494)
*Saint Christopher carrying the Infant Christ
(The Donne Triptych)*, detail of cat. 9

the West.[2] In line with this, Cistercian buildings across Europe were sparsely ornamented with plain, white walls and altars simply furnished with crucifixes and white linen altar cloths.

A further statute was introduced around 1134 by the Abbot Bernard of Clairvaux (1090–1153). It prohibited in Cistercian churches and monasteries the use of colour, which was viewed as superfluous and unnecessarily exciting to the senses.[3] The aim of the Order's prohibition, of colour and of ornamentation more generally, was to create a sacred realm that subdued the senses and focused the mind as an aid to contemplation.[4] Although very little early Cistercian decoration survives, twelfth-century fragments suggest that it was common to decorate exclusively in shades of black and white as a more appropriate way to adorn religious buildings.[5] Walls, for example, were often painted with white limewash, and floors were laid with black-and-white tiles in simple geometric forms, or with tiles painted in black and white.[6] Instead of the coloured stained-glass windows commonly found in Romanesque and Gothic churches, early Cistercian windows were composed exclusively of pieces of greyish-white (grisaille) glass assembled in geometric or vegetal patterns, such as in the twelfth-century glass preserved in the Cistercian abbey of Aubazine (fig. 2).[7] This kind of stained glass, also known as Cistercian glass, is considered the oldest surviving form of grisaille in Western art.[8]

Around 1300, a new stained-glass technique, known as silver-stain painting, was developed, which gave artists greater creative and decorative freedom. Rather than forming patterns simply by joining pieces of glass together, this technique enabled artists to work with a black-brown or grey vitreous paint and a silver compound directly onto the glass panel. The silver compound, once fired in the kiln, produced a yellow-orange stain on the glass, and it was therefore known as 'silver-stain' glass. When applied to clear or grey-white glass, the technique produced a monochromatic effect that, like Cistercian glass, is also known as 'grisaille' stained glass. Following this development, and despite the Cistercian prohibition of representational and coloured decoration, small amounts of coloured glass and painted vegetal and scroll-work designs were soon introduced into grisaille glass panels. This more decorative style gained popularity outside the Order and, by the end of the thirteenth century, grisaille windows had become *de rigueur* in many non-Cistercian French churches.

A courtly style

At the Royal Abbey Church of Saint-Denis in Paris, the burial place of French kings, several chapels were added around 1320–4 on the north side of the nave, including one dedicated to Saint Louis (King Louis IX, who was canonised in

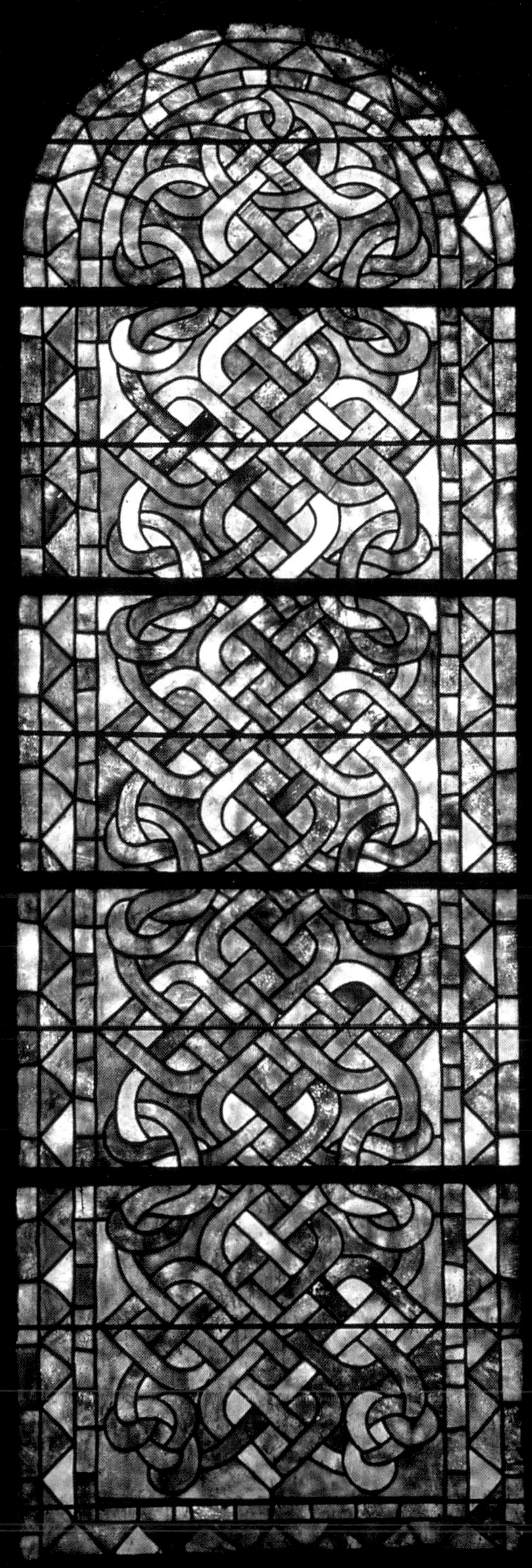

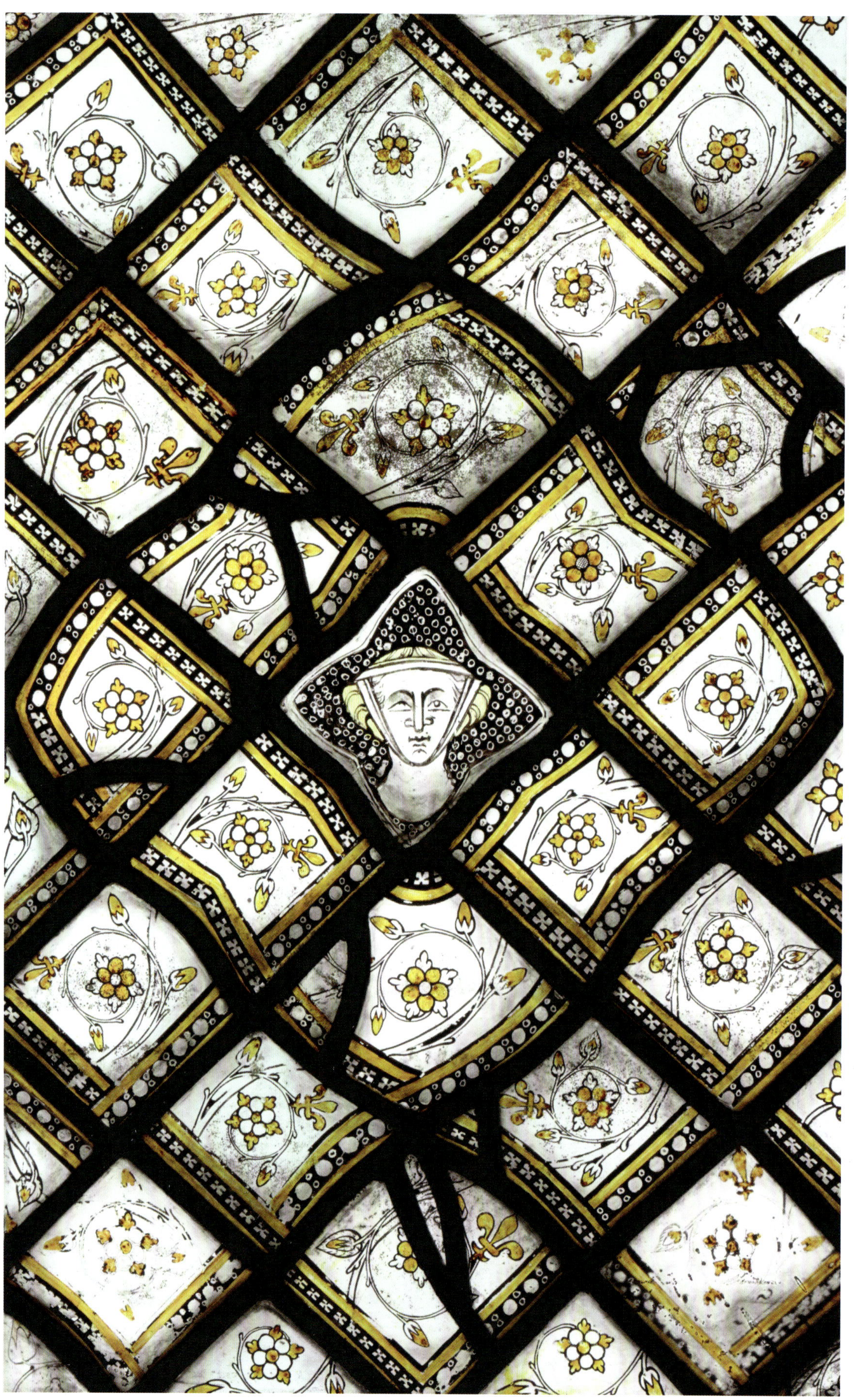

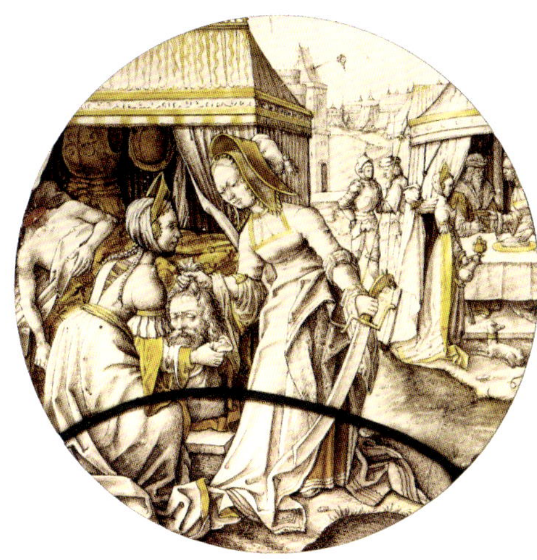

1297). It was adorned with beautiful grisaille glazing. Although the windows no longer survive intact, six fragments have been convincingly associated with this chapel (see cat. 2).[9] Each of the greyish-white glass panels making up the windows was painted in silver stain and black pigment, using several different techniques. At the centre of each is a fantastical figure painted in black and surrounded by a pattern of small circles, made using a *sgraffito* technique, in which a painted black ground is scratched through to reveal the glass beneath. The circle patterns are enclosed by a series of vegetal motifs, including a sprouting fleur-de-lis – a royal symbol that was originally visible throughout the decoration of Saint-Denis – outlined in black pigment and embellished with silver-stain.[10] The introduction of figures into these windows was exceptional, since it was not until the fifteenth and sixteenth centuries that naturalistic figures and landscapes appeared frequently in grisaille stained glass, as in the mid-sixteenth-century Netherlandish grisaille glass roundel depicting Judith with the head of Holofernes (cat. 2).[11]

The magnificent stained glass from the Royal Abbey Church is only one example of how popular grisaille became at the French court during the fourteenth century. It was also found on ivory carvings, on enamel work and, especially, in illuminated manuscripts. One of the earliest examples of the latter is *The Hours of Jeanne d'Evreux*, a small-format Book of Hours illuminated by Jean Pucelle (active 1319; died 1334), presented as a gift from the French King Charles IV to his wife some time between 1324 and 1328 (fig. 3). This tiny book, roughly the size of a hand, was created for the Queen's private devotions, to guide her prayers at specific times of the day and through different liturgical seasons. It is decorated with 25 full-page illuminations, which pair images from the infancy of Christ with scenes from the Passion. The text also contains illuminated scenes from the life of Saint Louis (the Queen's ancestor) and around seven hundred whimsical grisaille illustrations in the margins, including bishops, beggars and musicians, as well as animals and fantastical creatures, which provide a humorous and playful counterpoint to the accompanying religious text and larger illuminations.[12]

Pucelle made these grisaille illuminations using a fine pen and brush and black pigment (iron-gall ink and black carbon ink), thinned to varying degrees, with lead white paint. Using only these basic tools and pigments, the artist achieved astoundingly fine contours and delicate modelling. Openings such as that showing the Crucifixion and the Adoration of the Magi reveal the extraordinary sculptural appearance of the painted grisaille figures and architecture. In the Adoration, for example, the kneeling Magi's foot and the Virgin's elbow project beyond the architectural frame. Curiously, while the

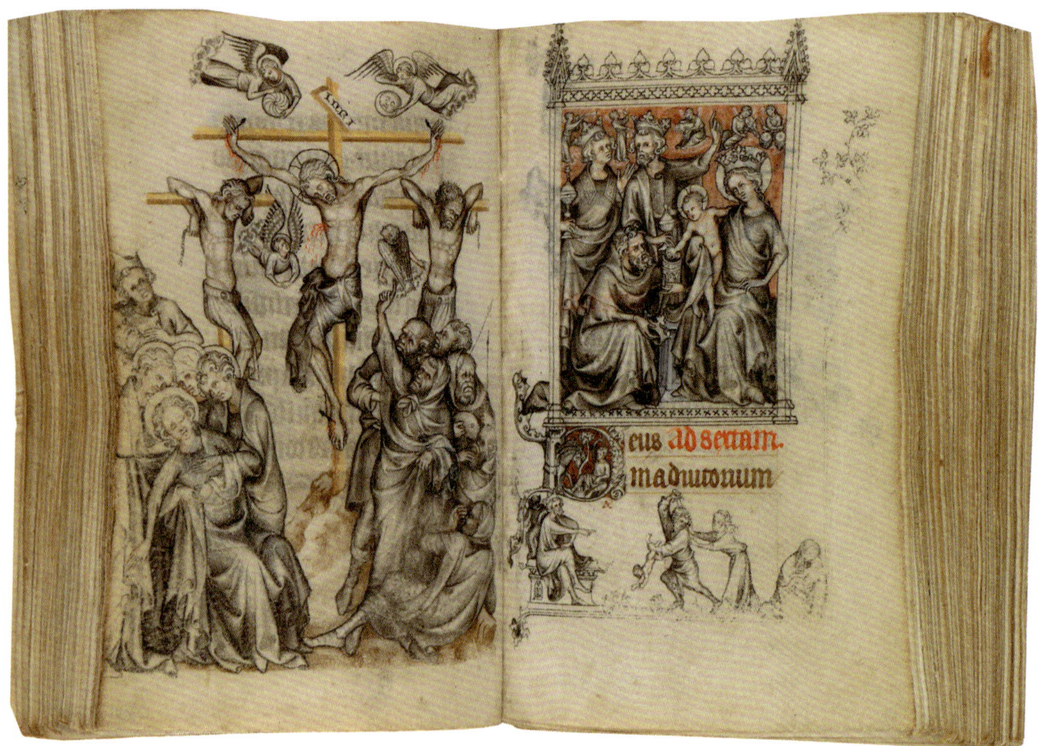

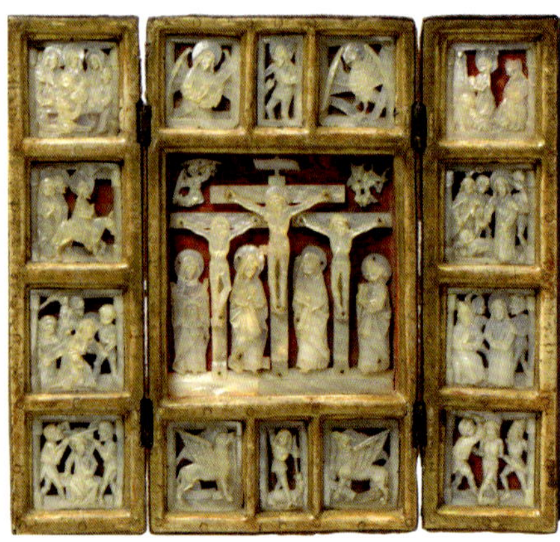

Fig. 3
Jean Pucelle (active 1319; died 1334)
The Hours of Jeanne d'Evreux, about 1324–8
Folio 68v, *The Crucifixion* and folio 69r,
The Adoration of the Magi
Illuminated manuscript, tempera and ink
on vellum, 9.2 × 6.2 cm
The Metropolitan Museum of Art, New York,
The Cloisters Collection, 1954 (54.1.2)

Fig. 4
Triptych with the Passion of Christ,
about 1475–85
Southern Germany
Mother of pearl, gilded wood frame, silk backing
and tooled leather covering, 21.2 × 24 cm
The Metropolitan Museum of Art, New York,
The Cloisters Collection (2006.249)

figures in Pucelle's highly detailed miniatures are depicted exclusively in grisaille, almost all of the non-figurative background details are rendered in colour.[13] In many of the illuminations there is a striking contrast between the three-dimensionality of the grisaille figures and the 'flatness' of the patterned coloured backdrops. In the Flagellation (fol. 53v), for example, the feet of all three figures protrude beyond the painted architectural frame, giving them a particularly lively and animated appearance; yet the red background denies any sense of recession into space. The unusual combination of grisaille illuminations with coloured backgrounds has led scholars to speculate as to whether Pucelle intended to emulate or draw associations with other artistic media such as stained glass, carved marble, ivory statuettes or relief figures in plaques.[14] Indeed, the juxtaposition of the grisaille figures and their coloured backgrounds recalls the practice of setting small-scale carvings in low relief against coloured backgrounds in the decoration of altarpieces, diptychs and reliquaries. Although carved over a century later, the *Triptych with the Passion of Christ* of about 1475–85 (fig. 4), a relief in mother of pearl set against red silk, is an example of an artistic practice established centuries earlier and provides a helpful comparison. Pucelle's wavy-patterned red backgrounds recall the watered silk lining relief carvings seen in the *Triptych*. Despite there being close parallels with these types of carved works, Pucelle does not seem to be evoking a specific material, such as marble or ivory, with his grisailles, but rather alludes more broadly to these kinds of finely worked precious objects in a way that draws attention to his artifice and artistic skill.

accoꝛde sa requeste. Elle ꝯ̃xpianne
seignꝰ en leuant ses reulx au ciel.

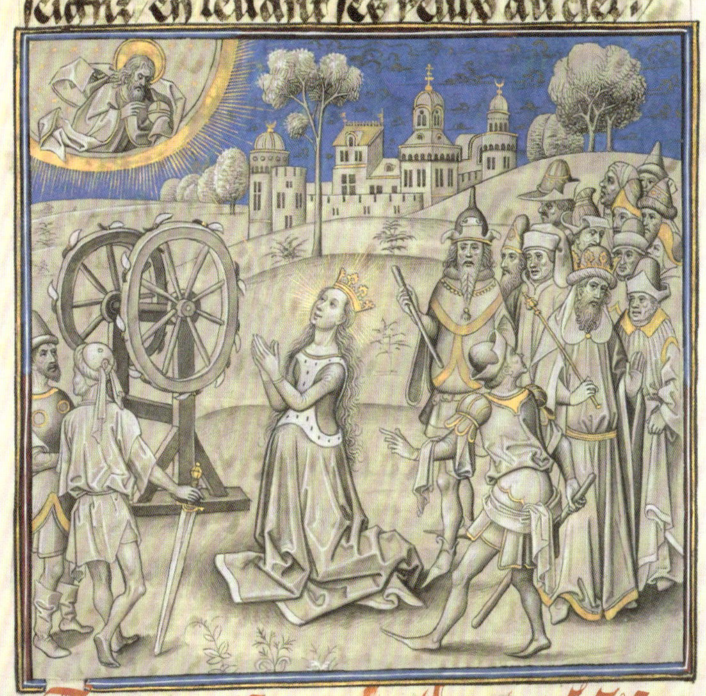

Don Ihesu qui es la beau
te et la salut de ceulx qui
croient en toy. Je te rens
graces et merciz, qui mas
daigne anombrer dedens le colliege

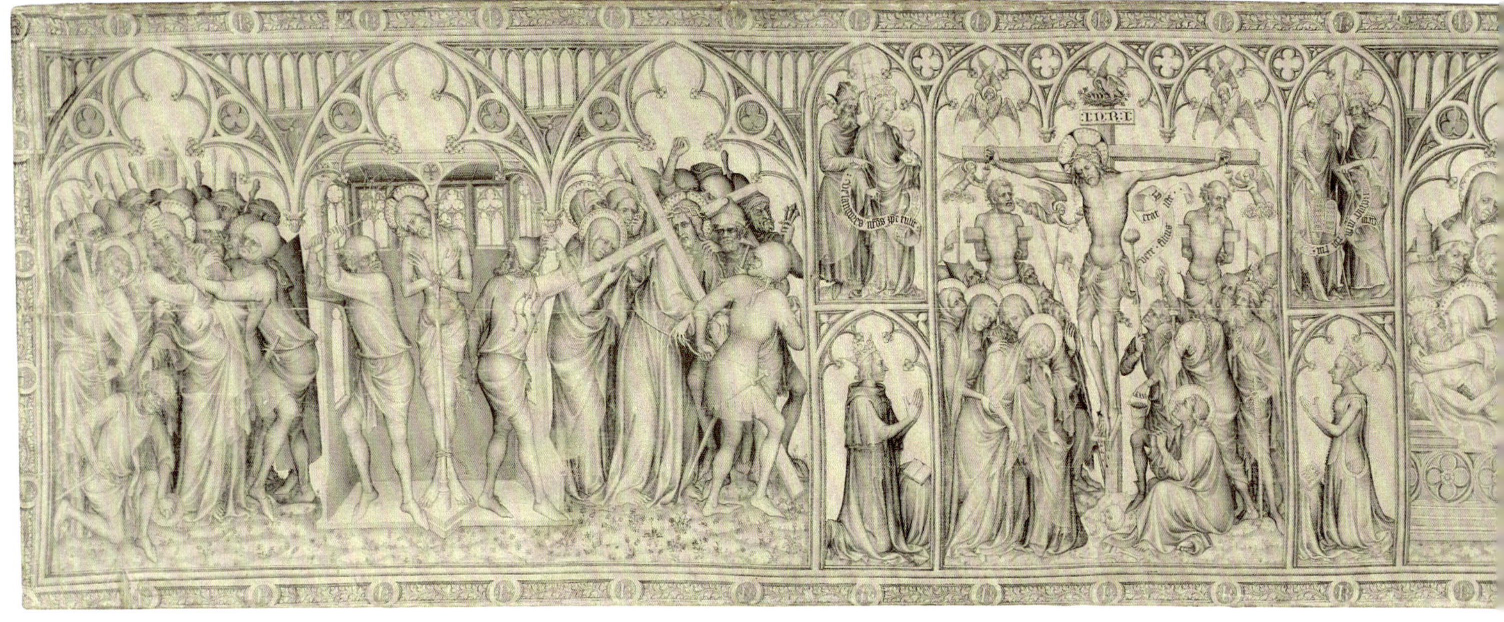

The great achievement of Pucelle's grisaille miniatures for the French Queen inspired a host of followers, in particular his pupil Jean Le Noir and his workshop. Indeed, from the middle of the fourteenth century onwards, manuscripts produced in Paris for members of the French court and their entourages were increasingly illustrated with grisailles. One beautifully illuminated example was made for Philippe le Bon, Duke of Burgundy, and includes 60 grisaille miniatures depicting scenes from the life of the fourth-century martyr Saint Catherine of Alexandria (cat. 4).[15] Executed in shades of grey against a vivid blue background, its engaging illuminations include rarely represented scenes as well as some of the most recognisable events from Catherine's life. One folio depicts the saint kneeling with her hands in a gesture of prayer before the wheel upon which she is to be martyred. The figures, outlined in black, are exquisitely modelled using white heightening for the brightest highlights and various greys for the shaded areas. The only other known illuminated manuscript of this text, made for Margaret of York, Duchess of Burgundy, was painted several decades later and contains coloured illuminations, making the grisaille edition entirely unique. The use of grisaille in the *Life of Saint Catherine* suggests an awareness of an older tradition of manuscript illumination seen in Pucelle's *The Hours of Jeanne d'Evreux*, which had initiated a taste for the grisaille aesthetic at the French court. Rooted in this earlier tradition, the *Life of Saint Catherine* demonstrates how the taste for grisaille illuminations continued into the following century and was taken up by those working in and for the Burgundian court.

The *Life of Saint Catherine* is just one example of the visual legacy of the Pucelle manuscript and other early grisaille illuminations. Indeed, following Jeanne d'Evreux's death in 1371, the Pucelle manuscript passed into the

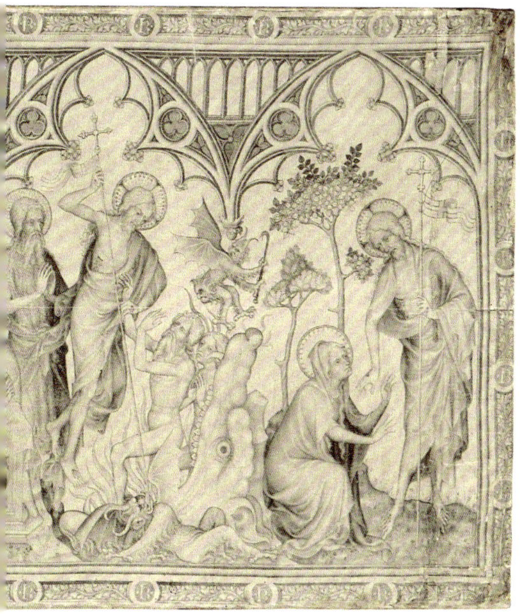

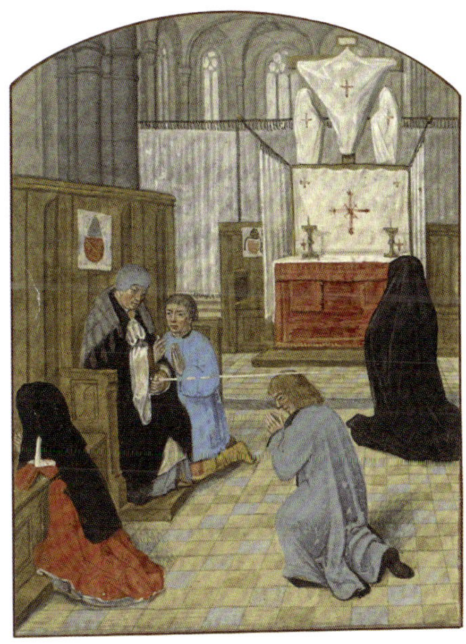

extensive library of Charles V of France, where it was clearly examined and admired by court artists, as we can see from their own works created *en grisaille*.

The most spectacular of these is the exquisite white silk altarcloth painted by Jean d'Orléans (about 1356–1408) by 1380 for Charles V using a brush and black ink (fig. 5). The technique of using subtle gradations between black and grey on a white background recalls Pucelle's *Hours of Jeanne d'Evreux*, and, like the grisaille manuscript, the cloth is also painted with scenes from the Passion of Christ, set within Gothic architectural arcades. The work, known as the Narbonne Altarcloth after the French city where the artist Louis-Léopold Boilly (1761–1845) purchased it in the nineteenth century, must have originally formed part of a *chapelle*, a collection of 15 to 20 elements of liturgical dress and altar adornments.[16] *Chapelles* provided a portable and flexible setting for the Mass and were variously coloured to correspond to a particular feast or period in the liturgical calendar. Charles V's inventories reveal, for example, that of his 57 richly decorated *chapelles*, two included simple white cloths painted with black, and one was 'cendré' (literally, 'ashen', here meaning ash-coloured or grey); they were probably designed for use during Lent. As well as describing the grey paint used on these cloths, the word *cendré* is also associated with the priest's custom of marking the foreheads of penitents with a cross of ashes on Ash Wednesday, the first day of Lent.[17] While making this sign, the priest would remind the penitents of their own mortality, saying, 'Remember that you are dust, and to dust you shall return' (Genesis 3: 19).

The 40-day Lenten period preceding Easter is devoted to fasting, abstinence and penitence, in commemoration of the 40 days Jesus spent fasting in the desert. The last week of Lent, known as Holy Week, commemorates Christ's Passion – that is, the events leading up to his death, from his entry into Jerusalem to his crucifixion on Mount Calvary – and is considered a period of mourning. Objects or images associated with the Passion or this liturgical period were therefore often decorously executed in subdued shades of grey. During the Lenten period, crosses, statues and pictures of Christ and of the saints throughout the church were traditionally shrouded with a veil (fig. 6).[18] This custom, practised possibly as early as the tenth century, is still observed in many churches today.[19] The absence of colour in the Narbonne Altarcloth suggests that it was used during Lent as one of these coverings. Its Passion iconography suggests that it served as a dossal – a cloth hung behind an altar – rather than as a frontal, which would have hung over the front, and which rarely depicted these subjects.[20] This hypothesis is bolstered by the choice of Lenten themes represented, although the scene of Christ's Resurrection is conspicuously absent.[21] It has been convincingly argued, however, that this

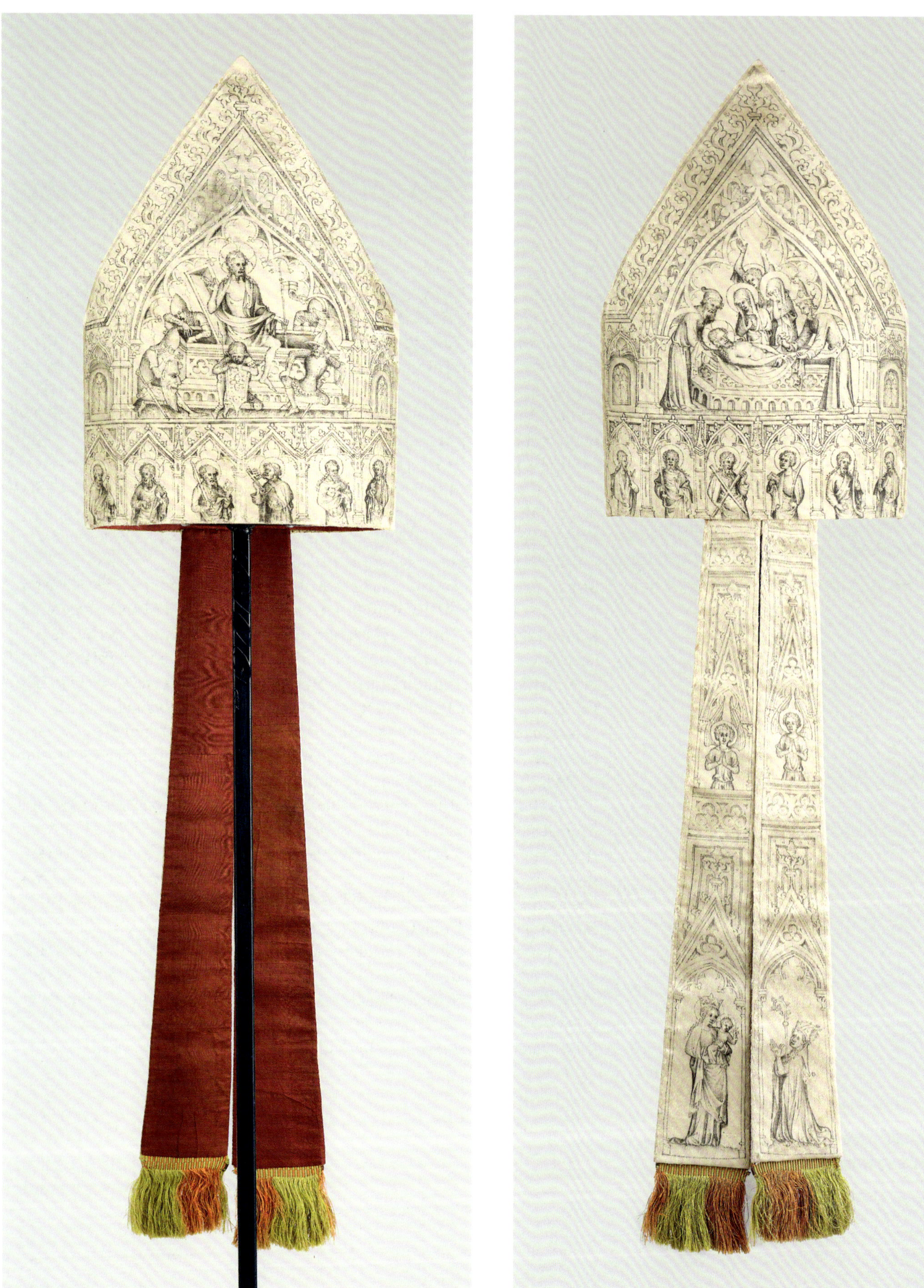

scene appeared on the painted panel or sculpted altarpiece that the Narbonne Altarcloth covered which would be revealed again only on the morning of Easter Sunday, when the cloth was removed.[22]

The Narbonne Altarcloth has long been associated with the so-called 'Mourning Mitre' (about 1360–70), because of their technical, stylistic and iconographic similarities (fig. 7).[23] Recently, it has been persuasively argued that the mitre and altarcloth were produced in the same workshop.[24] Ordinarily, the mitres and other liturgical vestments of medieval bishops were made from expensive brocades and ornamented with rich embroidery. By contrast, this white silk mitre is painted with figurative grisailles. The Resurrection and the Burial of Christ are represented on the front and back faces, or *tituli*, of the mitre. Below these scenes is a series of half-length apostles, and the two lappets – the cloth strips hanging down the back – are decorated with angels, a Madonna and Child and a bishop kneeling in prayer.

Inventories have revealed that the mitre originally belonged to the Sainte-Chapelle in Paris and, accordingly, the kneeling bishop may be identified with Bishop Etienne de Poissy, who presumably commissioned the mitre.[25] Like the Narbonne Altarcloth, the mitre formed part of a *chapelle* for use during the Lenten liturgy and was part of a larger decorative programme, which would have taken into account the surrounding architecture, the altar furnishings and, most importantly, the liturgical function it was meant to serve.[26] The principal painted scenes, the Burial and Resurrection, recall Christ's crucifixion as commemorated on Good Friday and his resurrection as celebrated on Easter morning, suggesting it was specifically intended for use during the celebration of High Mass at the Saint-Chapelle during Lent.

The mitre is also striking for the finely detailed and illusionistically painted architecture that frames each narrative scene or figure. This architecture evokes Gothic church facades, and unites the various elements of the mitre's design. To create a greater distinction between the architectural decorations and the figures, the artist painted the framing elements almost exclusively in black line (perhaps using a kind of pen and fine brush), while the figures, draperies and their shadows are all carefully modelled in varying tones of grey, using broader brushes. The use of black and white, clearly a reference to the Lenten observance, should also be understood as a display of courtly splendour, similar to that seen in the grisaille stained-glass windows at Saint-Denis, in Pucelle's Book of Hours and in Jean d'Orléans's altarcloth.

Fig. 7
Jean d'Orléans (about 1356 1408)
Bishop's mitre with the Resurrection of Christ and Saints *(The Mourning Mitre)*, about 1360–70
Chinese ink on silk, 93 × 24 × 15 cm
Musée de Cluny – Musée national du Moyen-Age, Paris, CL12924

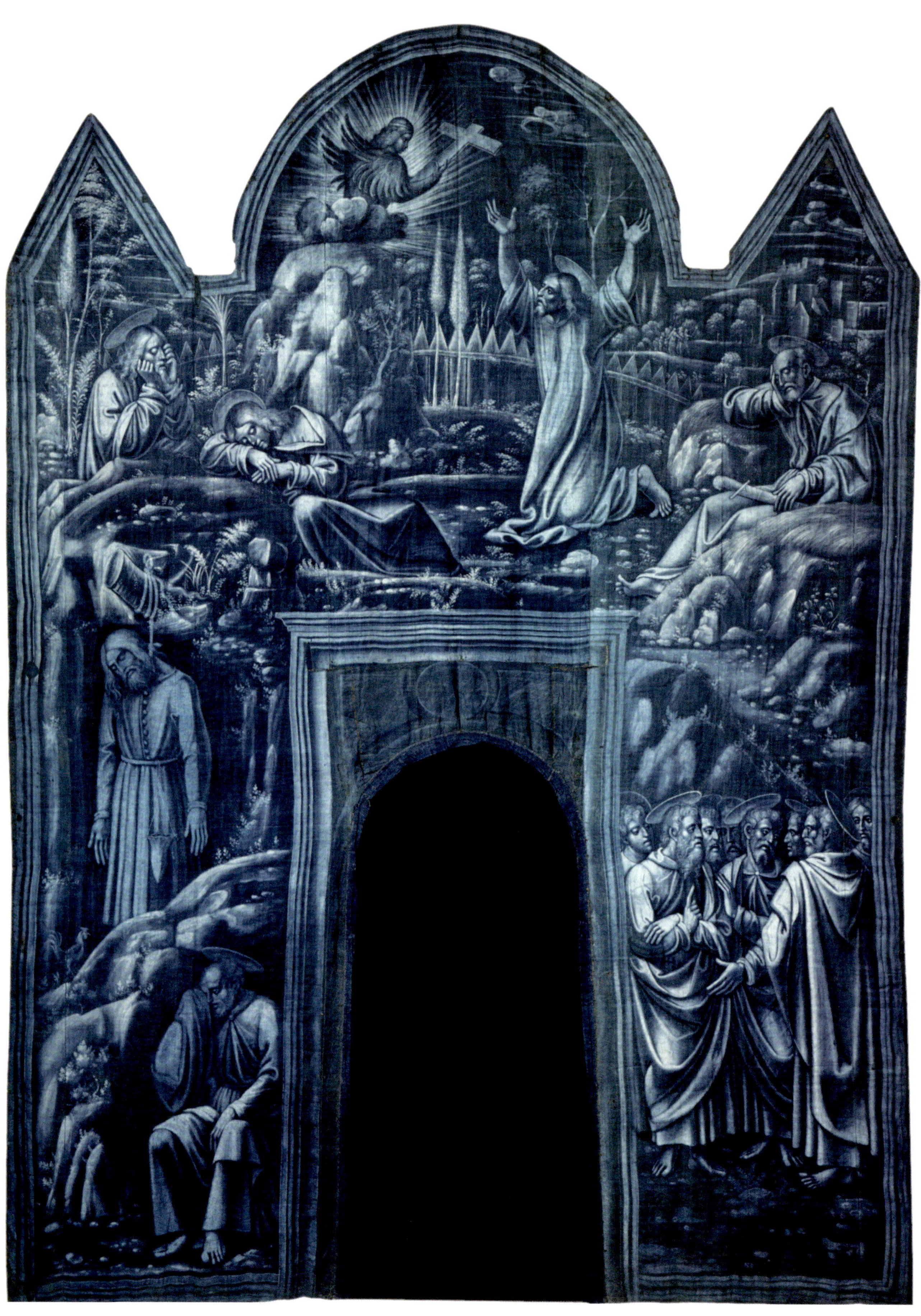

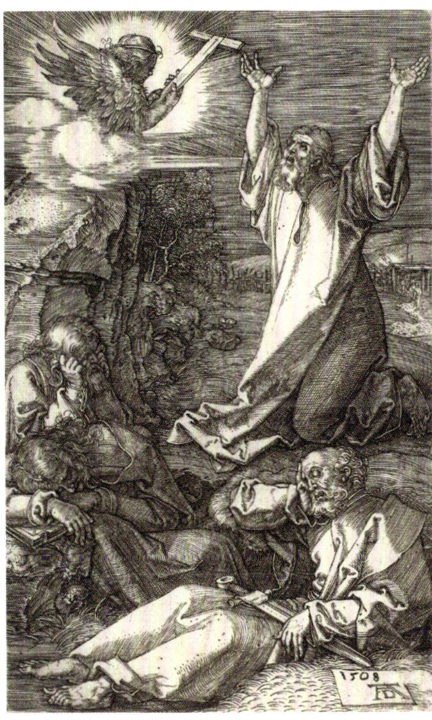

Cat. 5
Agony in the Garden, 1538
Oil on indigo canvas, 440 × 335 cm
State property on deposit in the Museo
Diocesano, Genoa

Fig. 8
Albrecht Dürer (1471–1528)
Christ on the Mount of Olives from
The Passion, 1508
Engraving, 11.4 × 7.2 cm
The Metropolitan Museum of Art, New York,
bequest of Alexandrine Sinsheimer, 1959
(59.534.41)

Ephemeral architecture

The great appeal of, and demand for, objects painted in grisaille was not limited to the French court, nor to the fourteenth century. Evidence indicates that textiles painted in grisaille were used in many parts of Western Europe well into the fifteenth and sixteenth centuries.[27] These were traditionally painted on white cloth, but a hardwearing blue linen canvas was invented in the sixteenth century in Genoa, where at least one set of 14 monochromes was painted on this blue textile.[28]

These painted cloths use the blue of the support as a middle tone and are executed entirely in lead white paint, much like a chiaroscuro drawing or woodcut print. Of the fourteen cloths, nine were commissioned around 1538 by Prince Andrea Doria, a famous admiral and statesman from the Republic of Genoa, with the remaining five added at an unknown later date. Doria commissioned the cloths to decorate either the presbytery or sacristy of the Benedictine Abbey Church of San Nicolò del Boschetto, Genoa (cat. 5).[29] Three of these cloths are exceptionally large, measuring up to 440 by 335 cm, and when assembled, create a kind of ephemeral 'chapel' within the church. One has an arch-topped pediment and a doorway cut through at the lower level. The lunette is painted with the Crucifixion and there is a scene of Christ carrying the cross with life-sized figures on either side of the doorway below, so that visitors passing through appear to join the solemn procession. The other two large cloths, also pierced by doorways at the lower level, are painted with the Agony in the Garden and the Crowning of Thorns respectively. A fourth, rectangular-shaped cloth is painted with the stars, sun and moon, while the remaining, smaller, painted cloths depict angels and other stories from the Passion. Although the original arrangement of the cloths is undocumented, a convincing recent reconstruction shows that the Crucifixion cloth formed the entranceway, the two other large cloths formed the side walls, and the rectangular cloth with celestial bodies formed the ceiling; the smaller remaining works, representing Christ's Deposition and Burial, adorned and surrounded the altar.

The cloths were installed only seasonally, probably during Holy Week. They would have formed a sacred enclosure within the church, possibly as one of the *sepolcri* (sepulchres) or 'altars of repose' popular in Genoa in this period which were intended to evoke Christ's tomb. The monochrome Passion scenes may have also provided a dramatic backdrop for the staging of sacred plays or re-enactments on the same themes that took place inside the church during the last week of Lent.

Although textiles such as these, which were regularly moved and handled, rarely survive intact, they are recorded in inventories and first-hand accounts.[30]

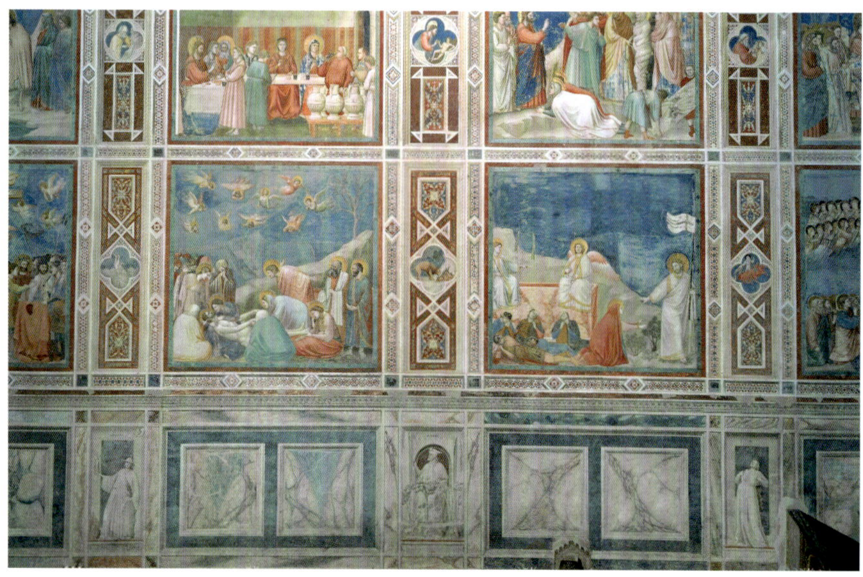

While these painted hangings were used as temporary decorations to mark the period of Lent, a branch of the Franciscan Order, known as the Minims, practiced perpetual Lent and therefore elected to have their monasteries painted with permanent decorations entirely in shades of grey.[31]

Grey in the margins

While early Cistercian and courtly traditions of using grisaille developed in France, its use on the Italian peninsula and north of the Alps was restricted largely to the margins of paintings. Between 1305 and 1308, for example, Giotto di Bondone (born about 1267 or 1276; died 1337) frescoed the Scrovegni Chapel in Padua with a History of Salvation in vivid colour, but decorated the dado below with a striking series of Virtues and Vices in grisaille (fig. 9).[32] Read against the coloured narratives above, the figures illustrate the programme's message of salvation and underscore the role of antithesis (also known as *oppositio*), a rhetorical device often used by artists, that appears throughout the chapel.[33] These early frescoed grisailles mark a watershed in the history of 'marginal' grisaille painting, a practice taken up across Italy and beyond for the purpose of representing abstract concepts, such as personifications of the Liberal Arts and Virtues. Raphael, for example, represented the Theological Virtues in grisaille on the predella (the box-like step supporting the main coloured panel) of his *Entombment* altarpiece of 1507 (Vatican Museums, Rome).[34]

In addition to the margins of fresco cycles or altarpieces, where they are intended to be read in association with the main, coloured image, grisaille paintings also appear as decorative sculptural reliefs in medieval and Renaissance devotional works. In these, the primary, coloured image is usually a subject from the New Testament, while the grisailles in the margins often depict figures or narratives from pagan antiquity or the Old Testament and serve as a typological gloss or counterpoint to the main subject.[35]

Fig. 9
Giotto di Bondone (born about 1267 or 1276; died 1337)
Fresco decorations in the Scrovegni Chapel, Padua, about 1305

Cat. 6
Petrus Christus (active 1444; died 1475/6)
The Nativity, about 1450
Oil on panel, 127.6 × 94.9 cm
National Gallery of Art, Washington, Andrew W. Mellon Collection, 1937.1.40

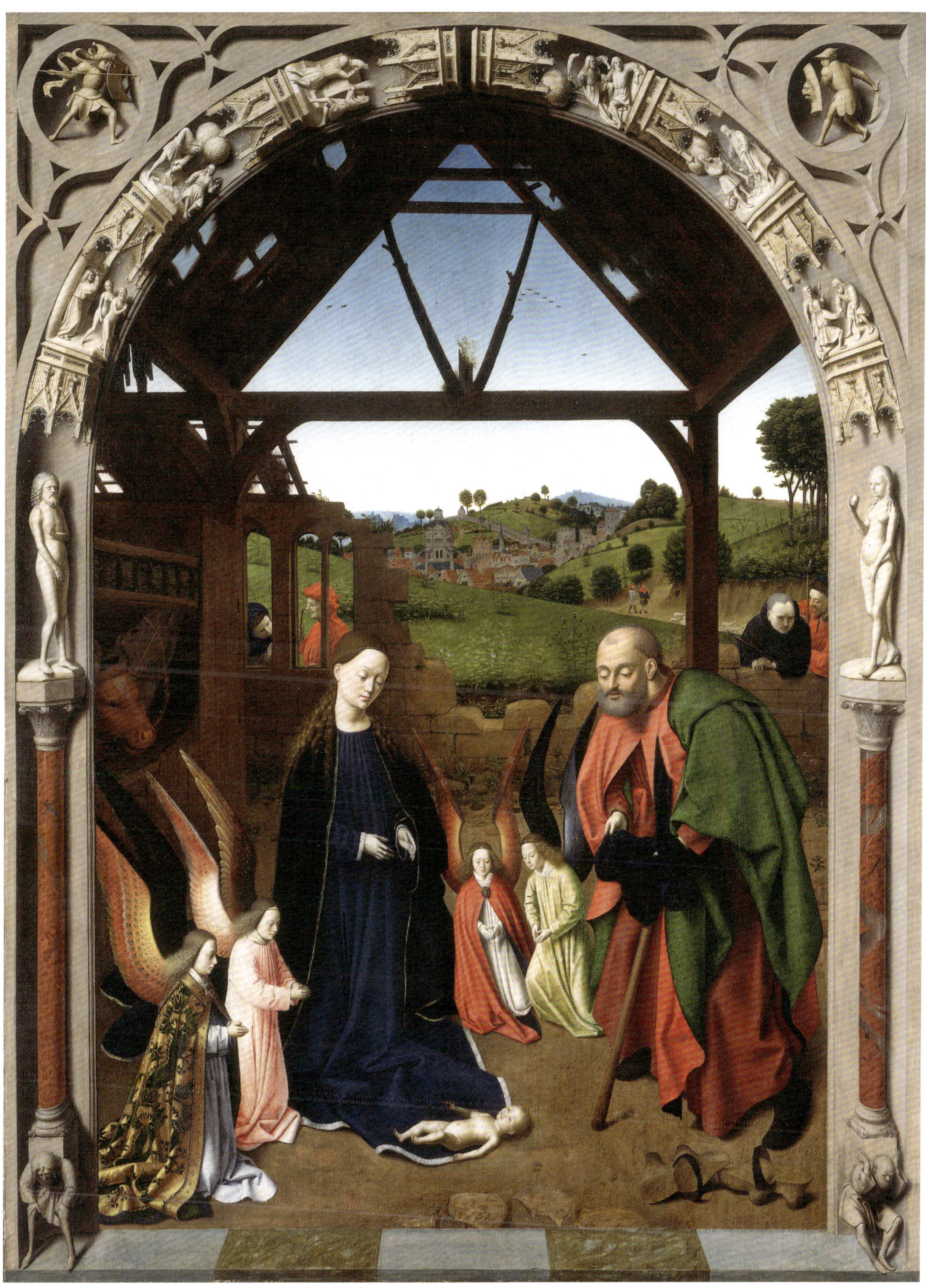

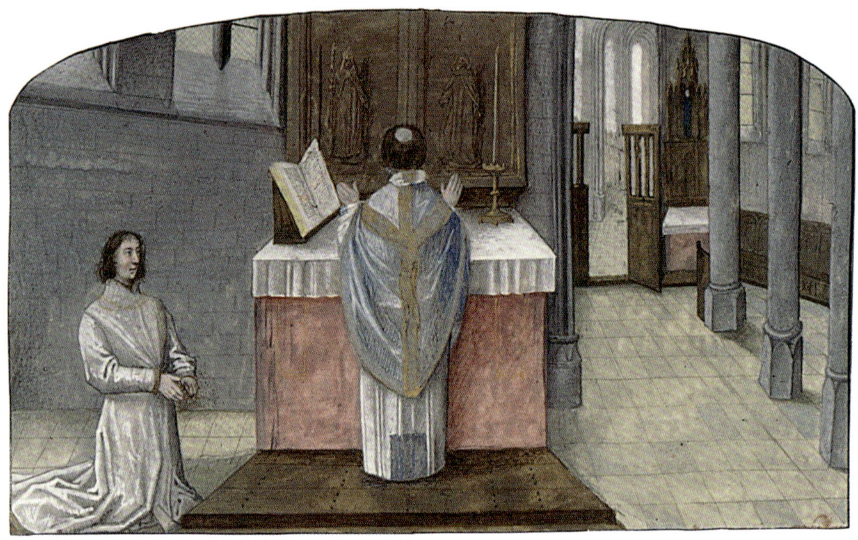

This treatment may have been prompted by an artistic metaphor repeated by several Church Fathers that the old dispensation was but a 'shadowy underdrawing' that was completed with colour only with the birth of Christ.[36] For example, John of Damascus's *On the Divine Images* states, 'As the [Old Testament] Law is a preliminary adumbration [shadow or foreshadow] of the coloured picture, so Grace and Truth are the coloured picture.'[37] From this, a visual tradition developed in which pagan or Old Testament scenes were represented in 'shadowy' grisailles, while scenes from the Life of Christ were shown in vivid colour.

The Early Netherlandish painter Petrus Christus (active 1444; died 1475/6), for example, used this juxtaposition in his *Nativity* (cat. 6), which he set within an architectural grisaille 'frame' recalling a medieval church portal, replete with carved statuary.[38] The illusionistic sculptural archway and its decoration function as a mediating space, or threshold, that divides the painted sacred space of the Nativity from the actual space of the worshipper contemplating the picture. On either side of the portal and facing inwards, towards the infant Christ, are the prominent grisaille figures of Adam and Eve, who are surrounded by sacrificial scenes from Genesis representing the Fall and Redemption of humankind. The scenes anticipate Christ's ultimate sacrifice and act as a kind of 'colourless' frame for the colourful representation of his Nativity.

The use of grisaille on the margins of paintings, either as a framing or veiling device, continued in the early fifteenth century in the Netherlands on 'winged' altarpieces.[39] These kinds of altarpieces had developed in Germany and the Netherlands early in the fourteenth century, and typically consisted of a main sculpted image flanked by two or more hinged panels that served as shutters. The shutters were decorated on both sides, with the either sculpted or painted interior shutters visible when the wings were open and with only the painted exterior wings visible when the shutters were closed (fig. 10).[40] The

Fig. 10
Master of the Moral Treatises and workshop
The Celebration of Mass
Illuminated manuscript
Bibliothèque royale de Belgique,
Ms 9272-76, folio 55

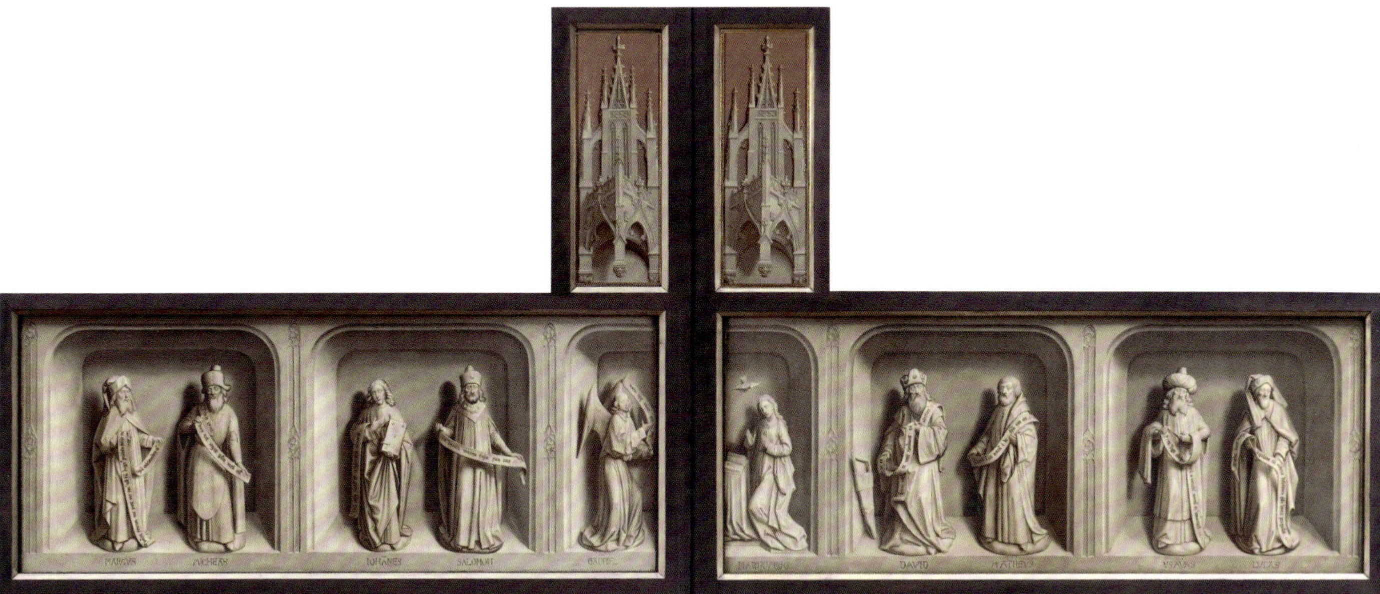

shutters were intended to cover and protect the central image and were usually opened only at key moments during the Mass or on specified feast days, such as the Annunciation, which celebrates the Archangel Gabriel's announcement to Mary that she will bear the Son of God (Luke 1: 26–38).

Accounts of the now fragmented Saint Bertin Altarpiece, made around 1455–9 for the high altar of a church in Saint-Omer (now northern France), describe a sculpted shrine illustrating scenes from the lives of Christ and the Virgin, executed in gold, gilded silver, copper, rock crystal, diamonds and other precious stones. Apparently, all of the figures were gilded save their hands and faces, which were painted in flesh tones. This richly decorated central section was enclosed by double-sided shutters painted by the Netherlandish artist Simon Marmion (active 1449; died 1489) with episodes from the Life of Saint Bertin in colour on the inside, and on the outside, remarkable illusionistic grisaille 'stone' niches containing 'sculpted' figures, perhaps in imitation of contemporary sculptured altarpieces. The shutters, later cut into fragments, are now in collections in Berlin and London (cat. 7 and fig. 11).[41] At the centre of the grisaille outer shutters is a depiction of the Annunciation, the moment of Christ's Incarnation, a term derived from the ecclesiastical Latin *incarnate*, meaning 'made flesh'. The word 'carnation' is also the traditional term used to describe flesh colouration in painting; appropriately, therefore, the external static figures are rendered in stony-grey, while the figures represented both on the inner shutters and in the main altarpiece – showing scenes from the lives of Christ, the Virgin and Saint Bertin – are rendered in vivid colour and painted with flesh tones.[42]

Representations of the Annunciation in grisaille were especially popular for the decoration of the exterior wings of an altarpiece, as in the monumental altarpiece painted by Marten de Vos (1532–1603) and his workshop after 1569

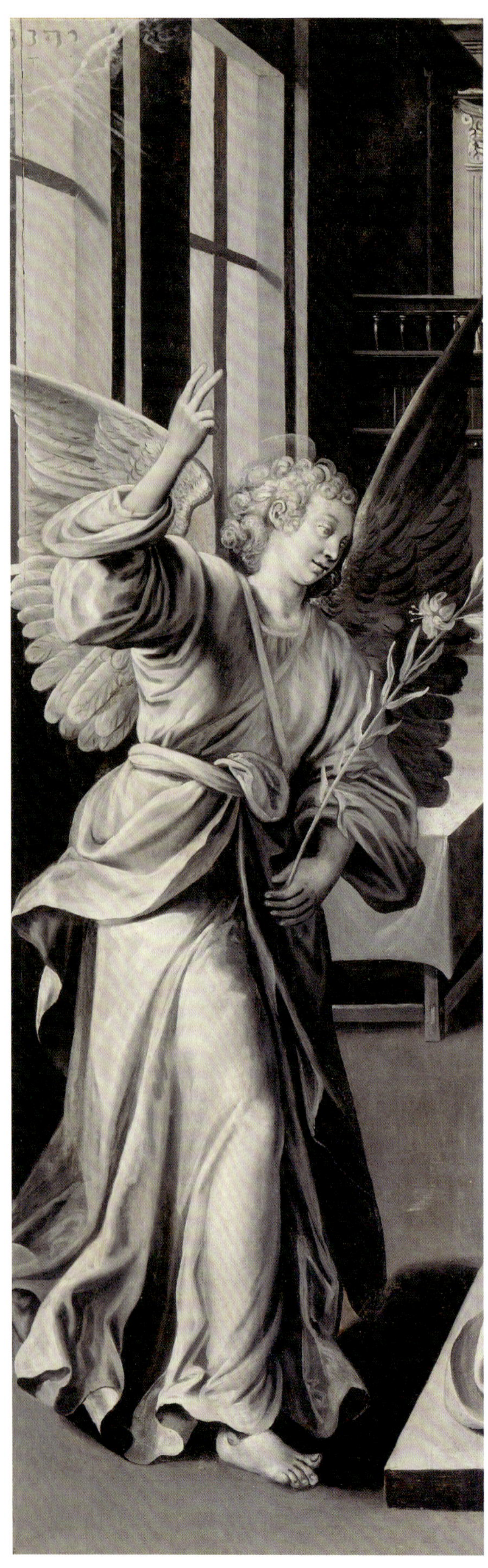
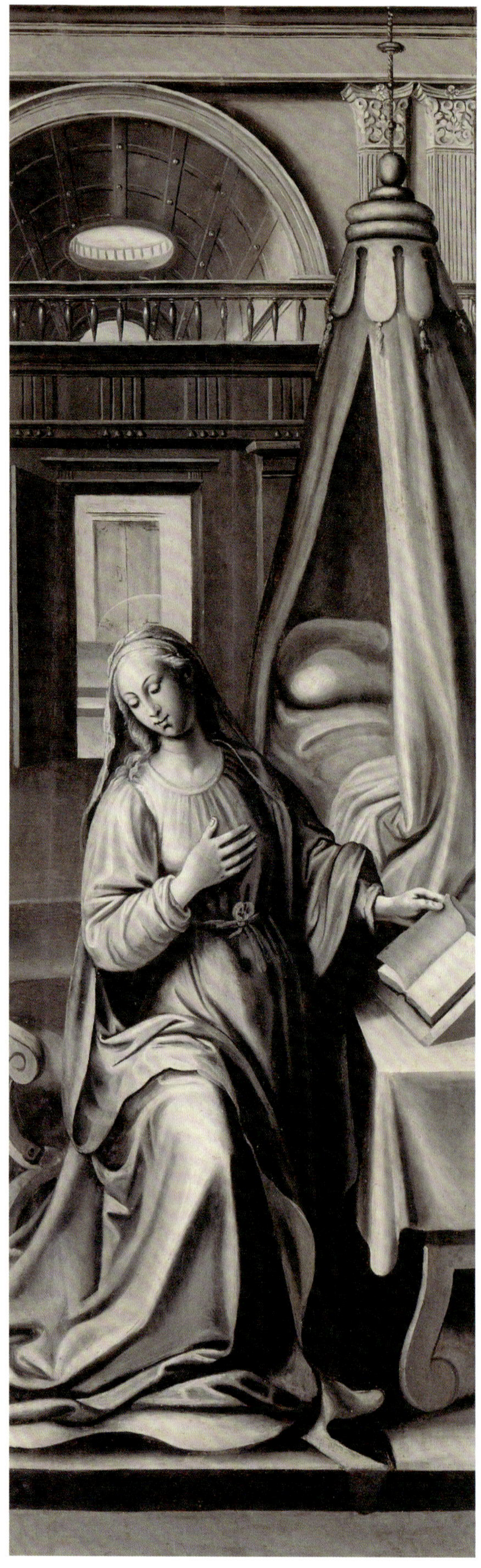

(cat. 8), and the appearance of the subject in this location had several purposes. Practically, it provided one figure for each shutter – the Virgin and the Angel Gabriel. Symbolically, it marked a key moment of the Incarnation, a turning point in the history of Salvation. Liturgically, it commemorated the feast of the Annunciation, which was celebrated during Lent, when altarpieces were usually covered.[43] Altarpieces adorned with depictions of the Annunciation could therefore remain closed throughout the observance of Lent without diminishing the importance of the feast.

The Netherlandish practice of painting shutters with figures in grisaille was soon taken up by foreign artists travelling and working in the Netherlands, such as the German-born painter Hans Memling (active 1465; died 1494), who lived and worked in Bruges. In about 1478, Memling painted a triptych for Sir John Donne of Kidwelly, a Welsh courtier, diplomat and soldier living in Calais (cat. 9). In the central panel, the Virgin and Child are flanked by saints and donors and, on the reverses of the shutters are Saint Christopher and Saint Anthony Abbot, painted in grisaille to resemble stone statues.[44] Known as the *Donne Triptych*, this relatively small work was probably made as a portable altarpiece that could be transported between the family's many houses to aid their private devotions.[45] Each of the outer grisaille saints stands within his own niche on a rock-like base, casting a dark shadow onto the grey stone wall behind him. Both saints were commonly represented in the period and would have been especially appropriate for a soldier and traveller such as Donne, given that Christopher was the patron saint of travellers and was invoked against sudden death, while Anthony was petitioned as a healer. Despite their sculptural appearance however, these grisailles retain a certain pictorial character through the apparent softness of their hair, their animated gestures (such as the extended, blessing hand of the Christ Child) and their fine draperies – with Christopher's fluttering beyond the limits of the niche. His flowering staff, too, protrudes beyond the confines of the recess.

Roughly two decades after Memling's *Donne Triptych*, the German artist Hans Holbein the Elder (1465–1524) painted the extraordinary 12-panel *Grey Passion* (about 1494–1500) (fig. 12).[46] Like Memling, Holbein probably had an intimate knowledge of Netherlandish painting and must have travelled to Brussels or Bruges early on in his training. Originally forming the shutters of an altarpiece of the Holy Cross, these panels illustrate the story of Christ's Passion, from his Arrest to his Resurrection, almost entirely in shades of grey. Unprecedented in scale and type, Holbein's *Grey Passion* demonstrates a new approach to the tradition of grisaille painting on winged altarpieces. Holbein painted the scenes in 'semi-grisaille', that is, in shades of grey, but with flesh

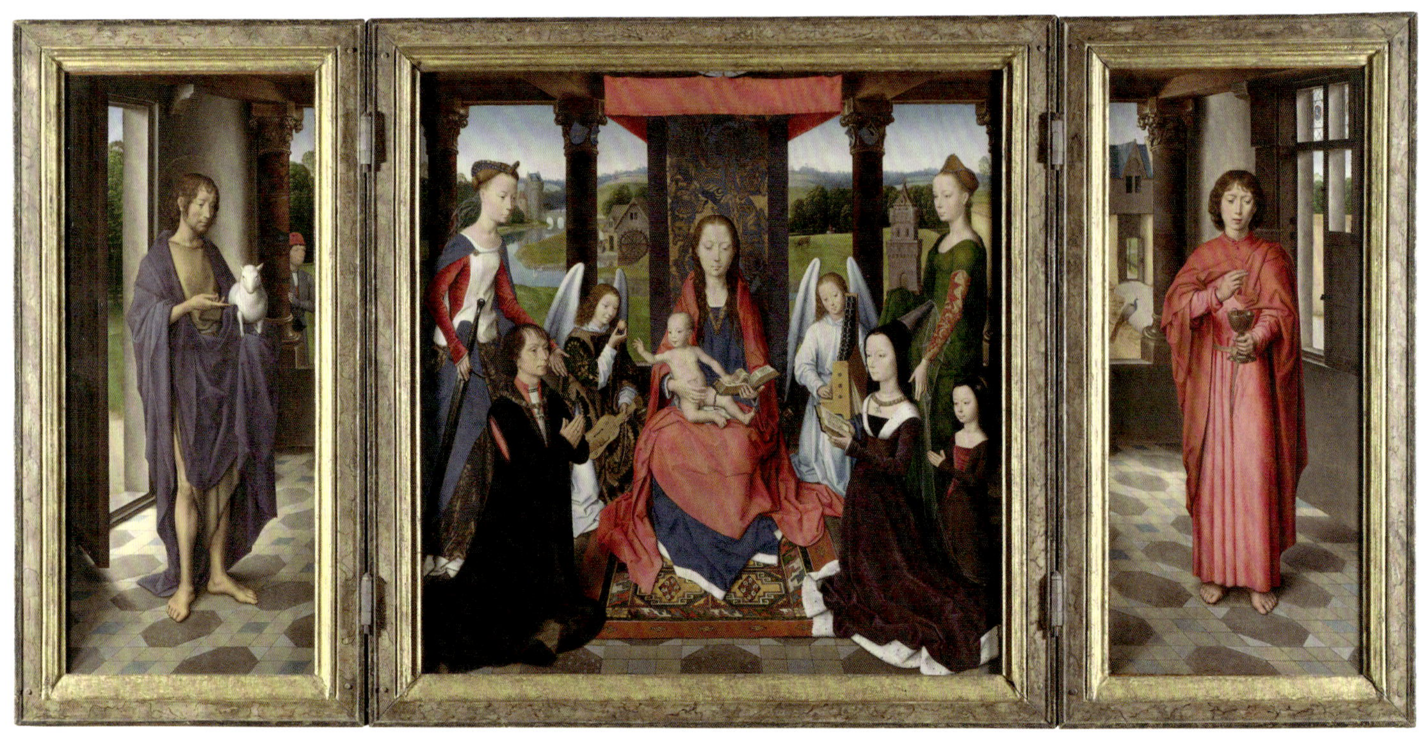

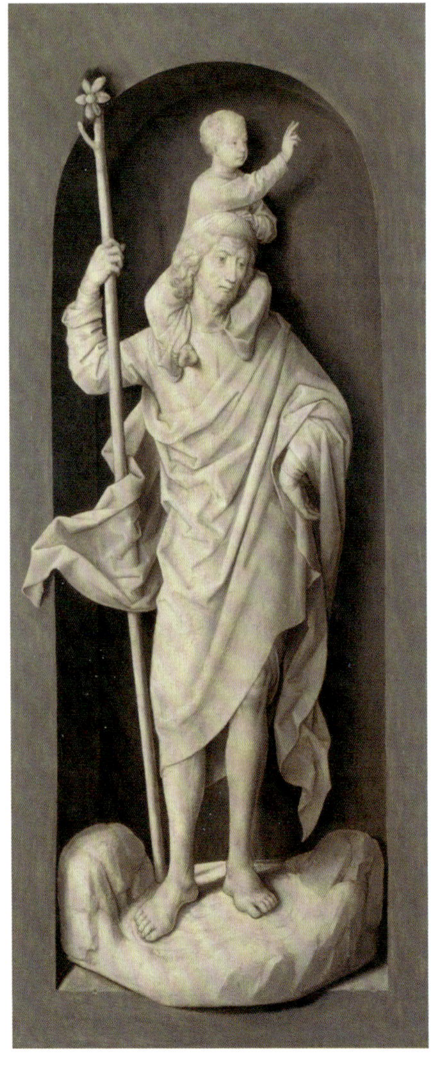

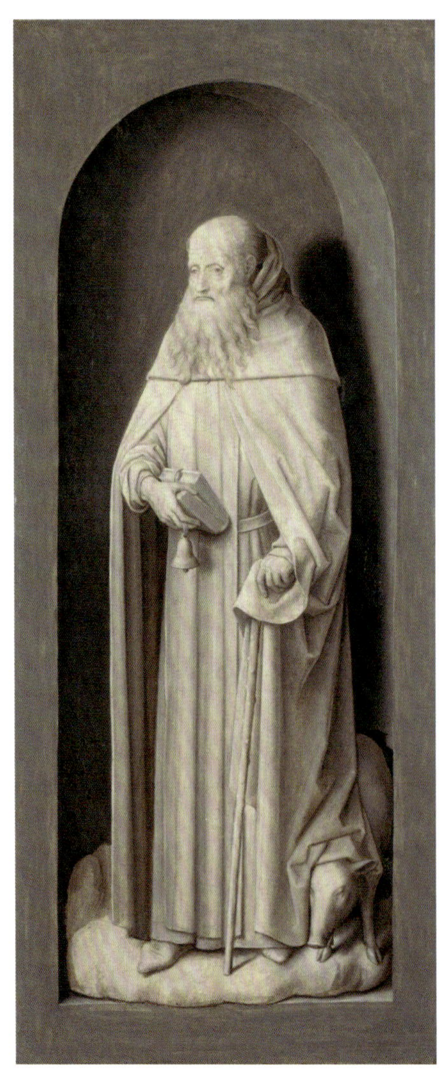

tones added to the figures, so that they appear to emerge, lifelike, from the stony colour of their garments.

Each wing was originally composed of three double-sided panels, with six narrative scenes represented on each shutter. The wings were dismantled and sawn into their individual scenes at a later date before making their way onto the art market. It is unusual that both sides of the shutters are painted in grisaille, but there are subtle differences between them. Reconstructions of the shutters reveal that the outer panels, which begin with Christ in the Garden of Gethsemane and end with the Ecce Homo, were executed in a cool grey tone, while the inner shutters, which pick up the narrative from Christ before Pilate and end with the Resurrection, were painted in a lighter, slightly warmer grey.

While earlier grisaille altarpiece shutters often provided a deliberate aesthetic and symbolic contrast with the coloured painted or sculpted interior, the central element of Holbein's altarpiece, now lost, was probably a sculpted Crucifixion group by Gregor Erhart (about 1470–1540), which appears to have been executed in an unpainted grey stone or in wood painted in grey, as a complement to the figures on the shutters.[47] This combination would have created a sophisticated interplay between painting that imitated sculpture and sculpture that imitated painting. The motivation for creating a painted grisaille Passion cycle resembling sculpture and an explanation for the curious absence of a Crucifixion within it are both clarified if we imagine the unpainted carved Crucifixion scene at the centre of Holbein's pictorial cycle.

While the 'marginal' function of grisailles continued into the seventeenth century, these later works often took a smaller format intended for the domestic interior. The Antwerp painter Frans Francken II (1581–1642), for example, began surrounding polychrome biblical scenes such as *The Parable of the Prodigal Son* (cat. 10), with smaller, related scenes in grisaille. These small scenes are arranged in such a way as to form a painted 'frame'; this frame recalls the stone reliefs decorating church portals, as well as their painted imitations in Renaissance paintings such as Christus's *Nativity* (cat. 6). Unlike the sculptural representations, however, each of Francken's grisaille scenes is represented in a lively, naturalistic and painterly manner and seem closer to a similar, earlier, Netherlandish practice of framing coloured images in illuminated manuscripts with narratives in monochrome.[48]

The parable in Luke's Gospel tells the story of the Prodigal Son, who, despite having wasted his inheritance, is welcomed back home by his father with compassion and is celebrated as one who had returned from the dead (Luke 15: 11–32). Francken's treatment of the narrative gives special attention

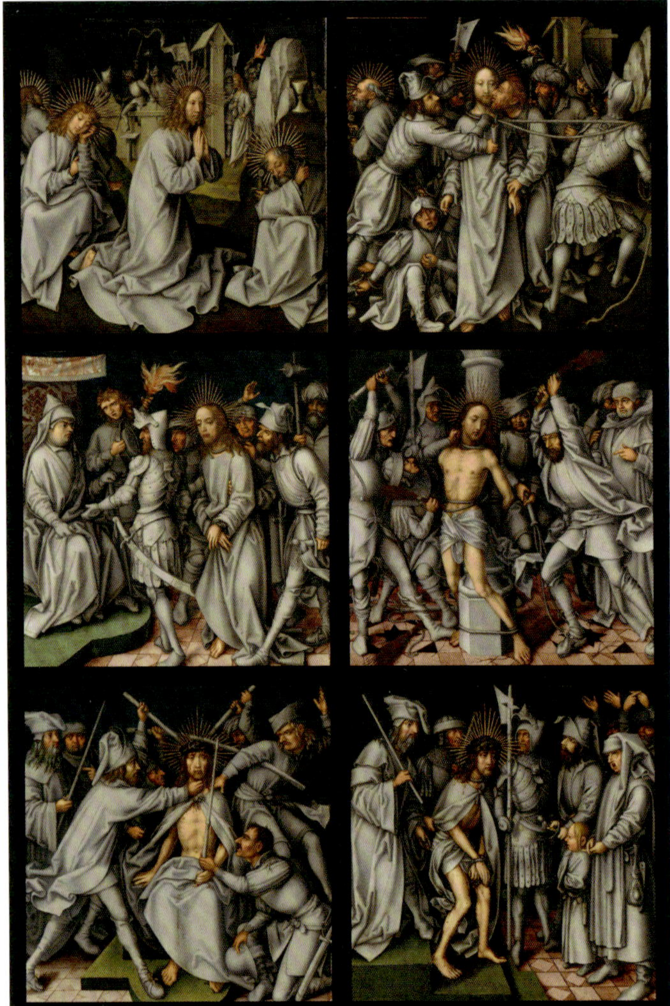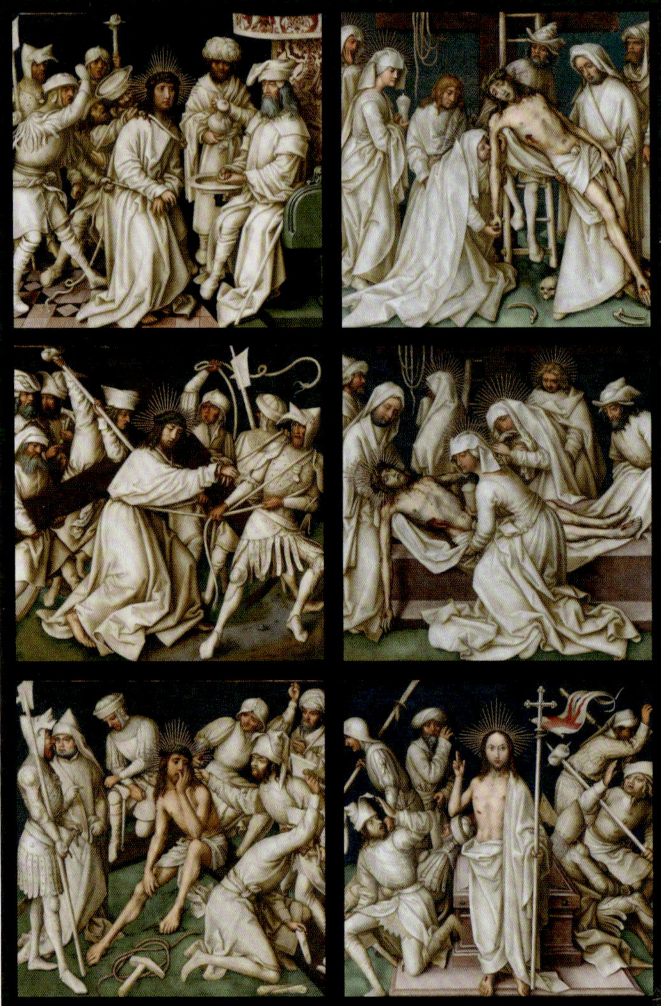

to the moment of the return, which is the largest scene and is rendered in colour at the centre of the composition, while eight other episodes of the parable are painted in a smaller format in grisaille, framing the coloured image. In this way, Francken represents the entire gospel account but juxtaposes colour and grisaille to underscore the parable's critical message of loss and forgiveness.

The earliest surviving artworks painted in monochrome were intended to mark solemn religious spaces and liturgical feasts in a decorously 'stripped-back' palette, but the novelty of this approach to painting, and the evident skill required to execute works without the use of colour, led to its adoption in royal and aristocratic circles for more sumptuous and increasingly secular settings. While independent black-and-white works often signalled a subject or object as special or distinct from the everyday, artists began combining grey monochrome with colour painting as a kind of rhetorical device in which the grey images alternately veil or reveal additional meanings in the polychromed

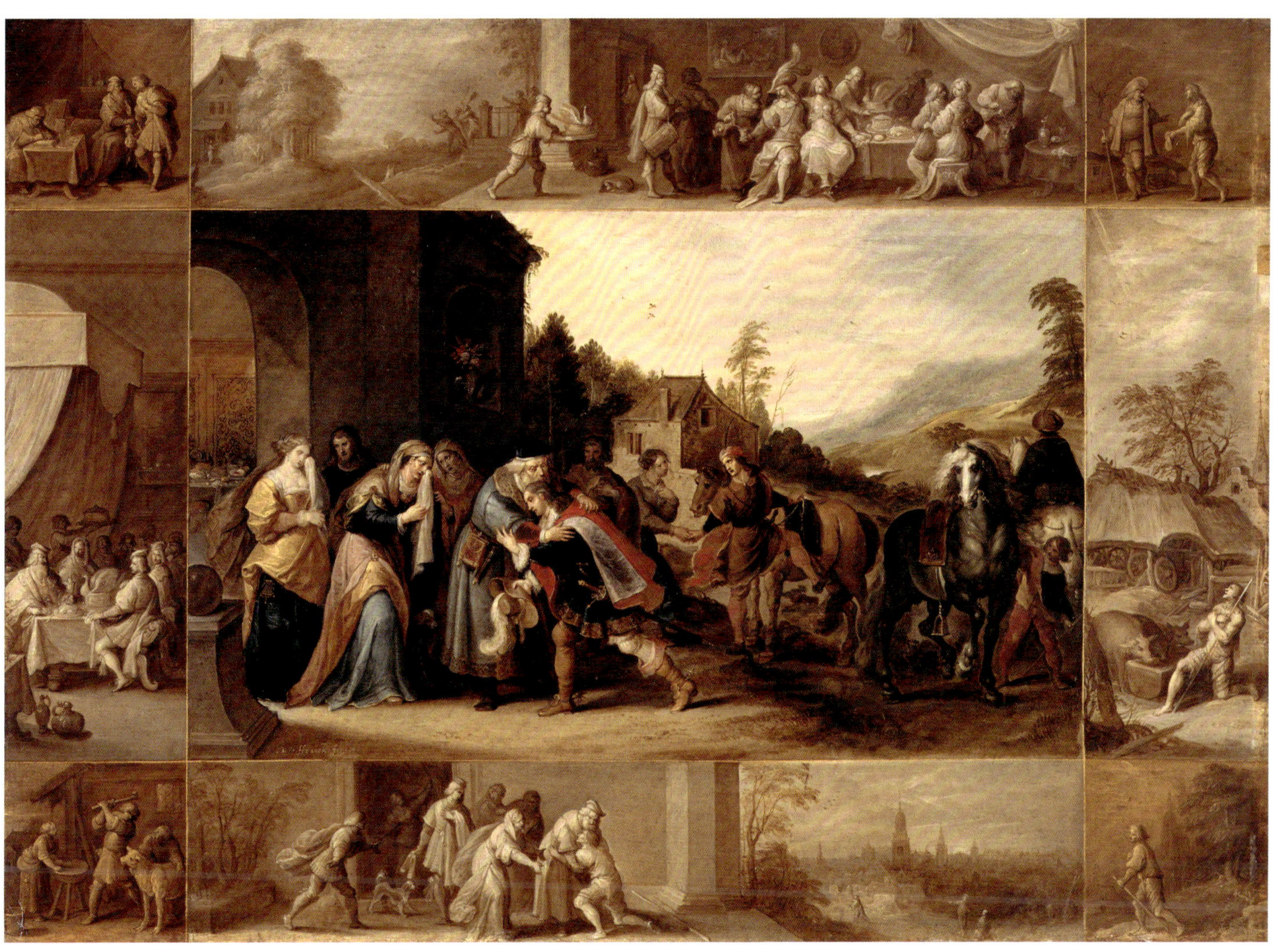

image. The practice of painting sacred subjects in grisaille continued beyond the seventeenth century, but black-and-white monochromes increasingly moved beyond the spiritually ascetic or subordinate functions discussed here to serve new artistic roles.

Cat. 10
Frans Francken II (1581–1642)
The Parable of the Prodigal Son, 1633
Oil on panel, 61 × 86 cm
Musée du Louvre, Département des Peintures,
Paris, inv. 1295

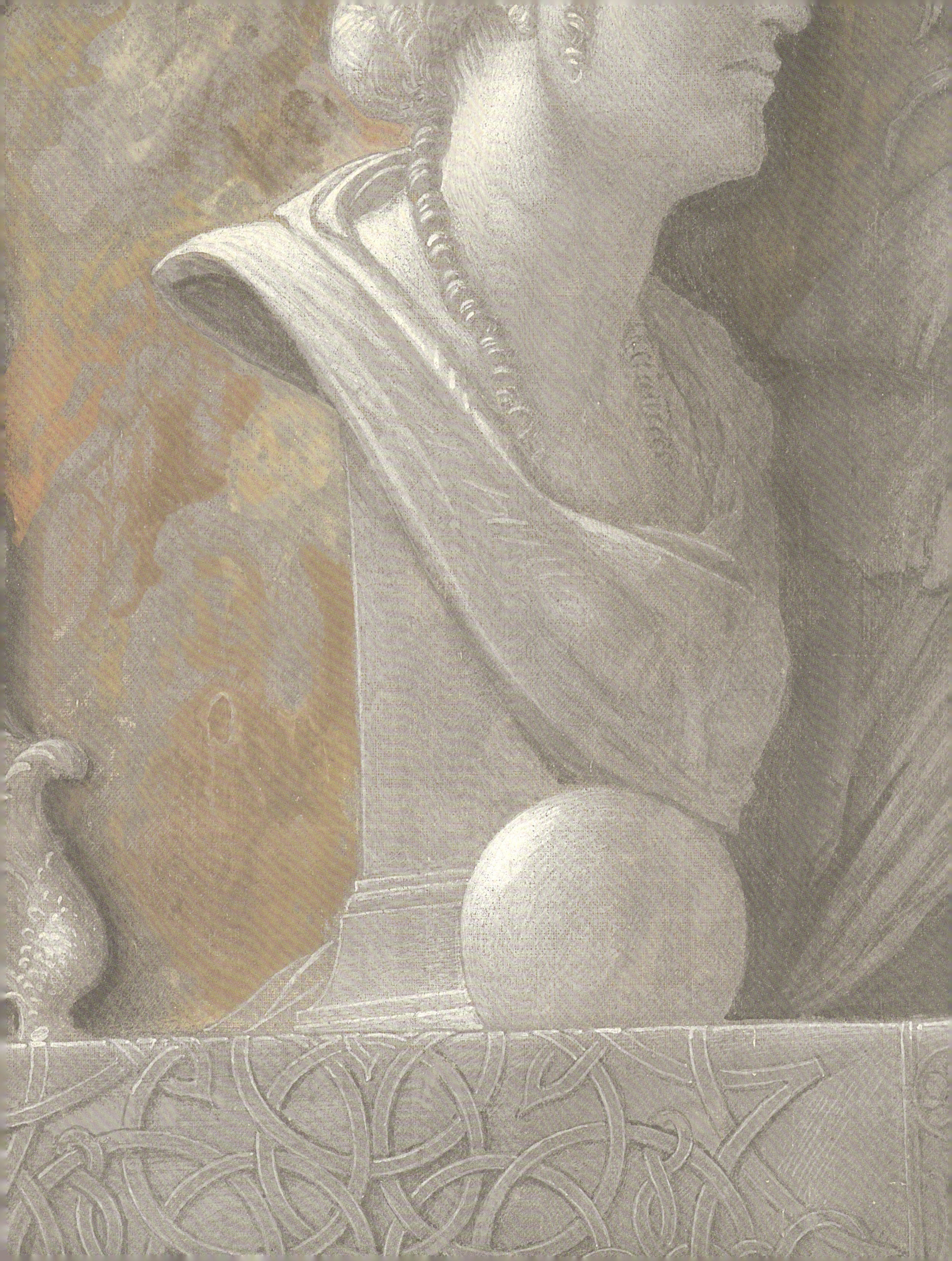

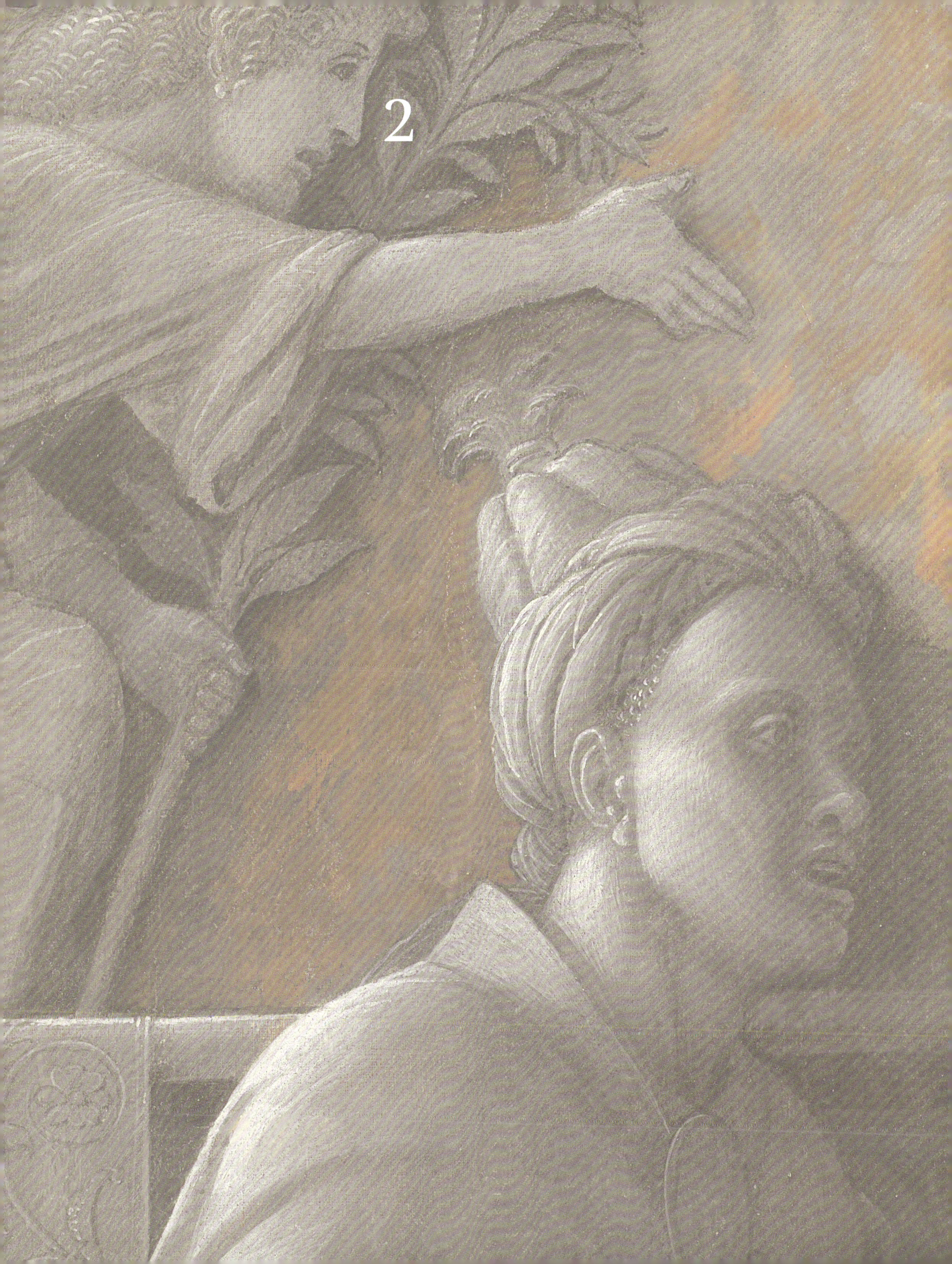

2

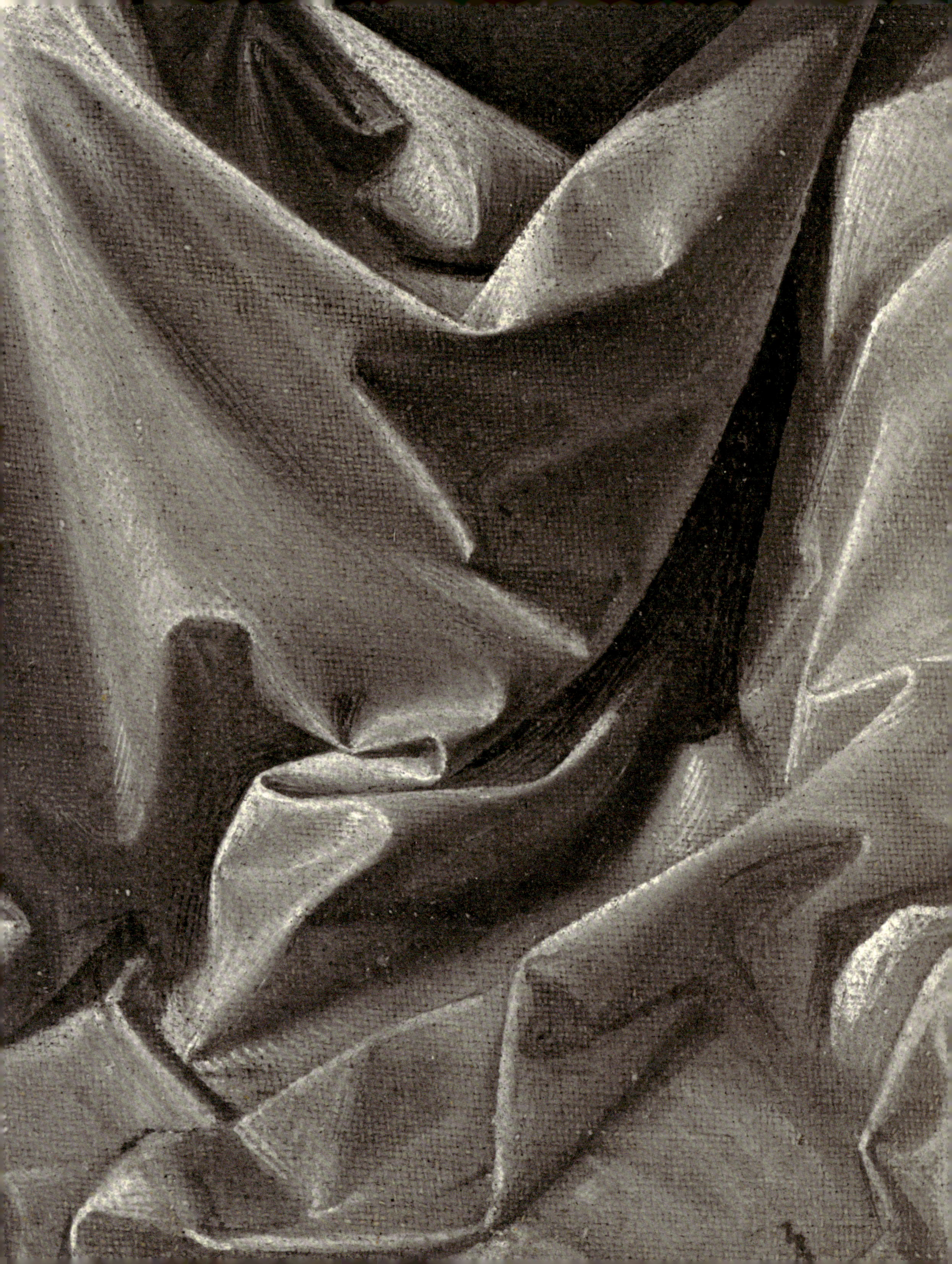

Studies in Light and Shadow

Jennifer Sliwka

This is one of a series of black-and-white painted drapery studies that have long been associated with Leonardo da Vinci but were more likely painted by several different pupils in the workshop of Leonardo's master, Andrea del Verrocchio. Verrocchio seems to have devised a new practice of studying the fall and hang of fabric. He draped clay models of figures with soft rags dipped in plaster and painted studies from them on fine linen. The meticulous painting illustrated here is probably the work of Domenico Ghirlandaio, another of Verrocchio's talented pupils. Ghirlandaio has carefully mapped out the fall of light and shade across the faceted surfaces on the lap of his draped figurine. He appears to have used and modified the study to suit different figures and compositions in colour, such as in the figure of Saint Matthew on his frescoed ceiling for the Santa Fina Chapel in San Gimignano.

Most people are familiar with the artistic practice of making preparatory drawings on paper – whether simple doodles or fully worked-up designs – before taking brush to paint. However, painted preparatory monochrome studies, in tempera or oil, on paper or small pieces of canvas, are less well known. The practice began towards the end of the fifteenth century and continued through the nineteenth, and is still used by some artists today. It was a swift, economical and effective way of planning a painting, and artists would paint sketches in black and white to work through challenges posed by their subjects or compositions and to determine the correct distribution of light and shadow. Having solved these problems in monochrome, artists would translate their studies into colour. Some artists omitted using paper altogether, making grisaille sketches straight onto the primary support and creating an initial monochrome version of their painting. This underpainted layer would serve as a guide and tonal foundation for the coloured paint laid over the top. Artists exploited the economical and adaptable qualities of painted monochrome studies to facilitate artistic experimentation and to prepare for works in colour. Some of these monochromes were highly finished and used as presentation models, known as 'modelli', for discerning patrons, and were later to be appreciated as independent works of art.

Studying drapery in tempera and ink

Among the earliest surviving painted studies in monochrome are a series of fifteenth-century drapery studies made using a brush and black-and-white tempera on linen (see cat. 11), long associated with Leonardo da Vinci (1452–1519).[1] In his *Lives of the Artists* (1550), Giorgio Vasari credits the invention of the technique to the young Leonardo when he was still an apprentice in the famous Florentine workshop of the painter and sculptor Andrea del Verrocchio (about 1435–1488). In his Life of Leonardo, Vasari describes how the artist

> would make clay models of figures, draping them with soft rags dipped in plaster, and would then draw them patiently on thin sheets of cambric or linen, in black and white, with the point of the brush. He did these admirably, as may be seen by specimens in my book of designs.[2]

Despite Vasari's early attribution of this technique to Leonardo, a group of about 16 surviving drapery studies, executed from the 1470s onwards, is now attributed to several artists working in Verrocchio's workshop, including Leonardo, Domenico Ghirlandaio (1449–1494), Lorenzo di Credi (1459–1537) and Fra Bartolommeo (1472–1517), which suggests that the practice may have

Domenico Ghirlandaio (1449–1494)
Drapery Study (possibly study for Saint Matthew and an Angel), about 1477, detail of cat. 11

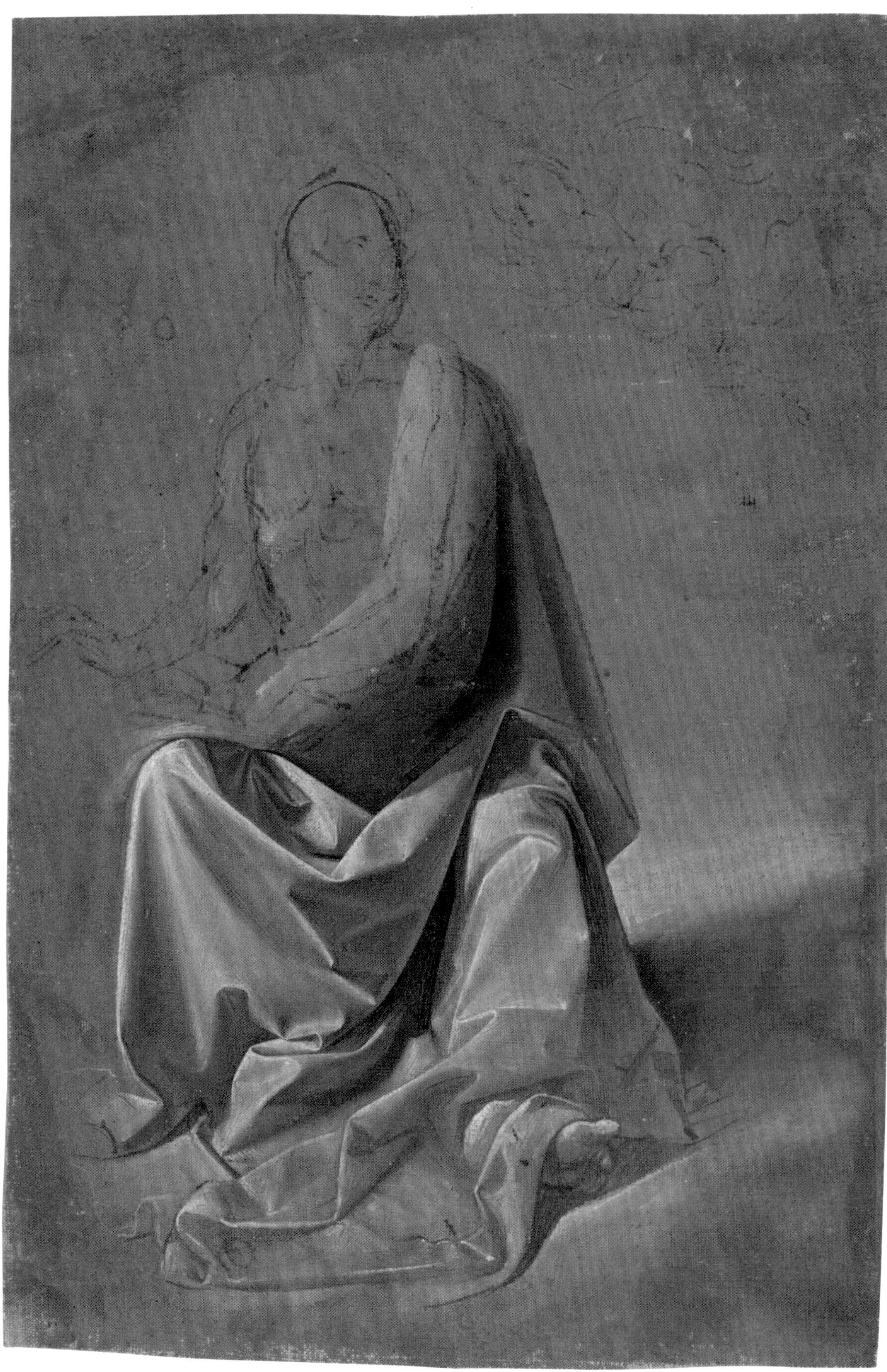

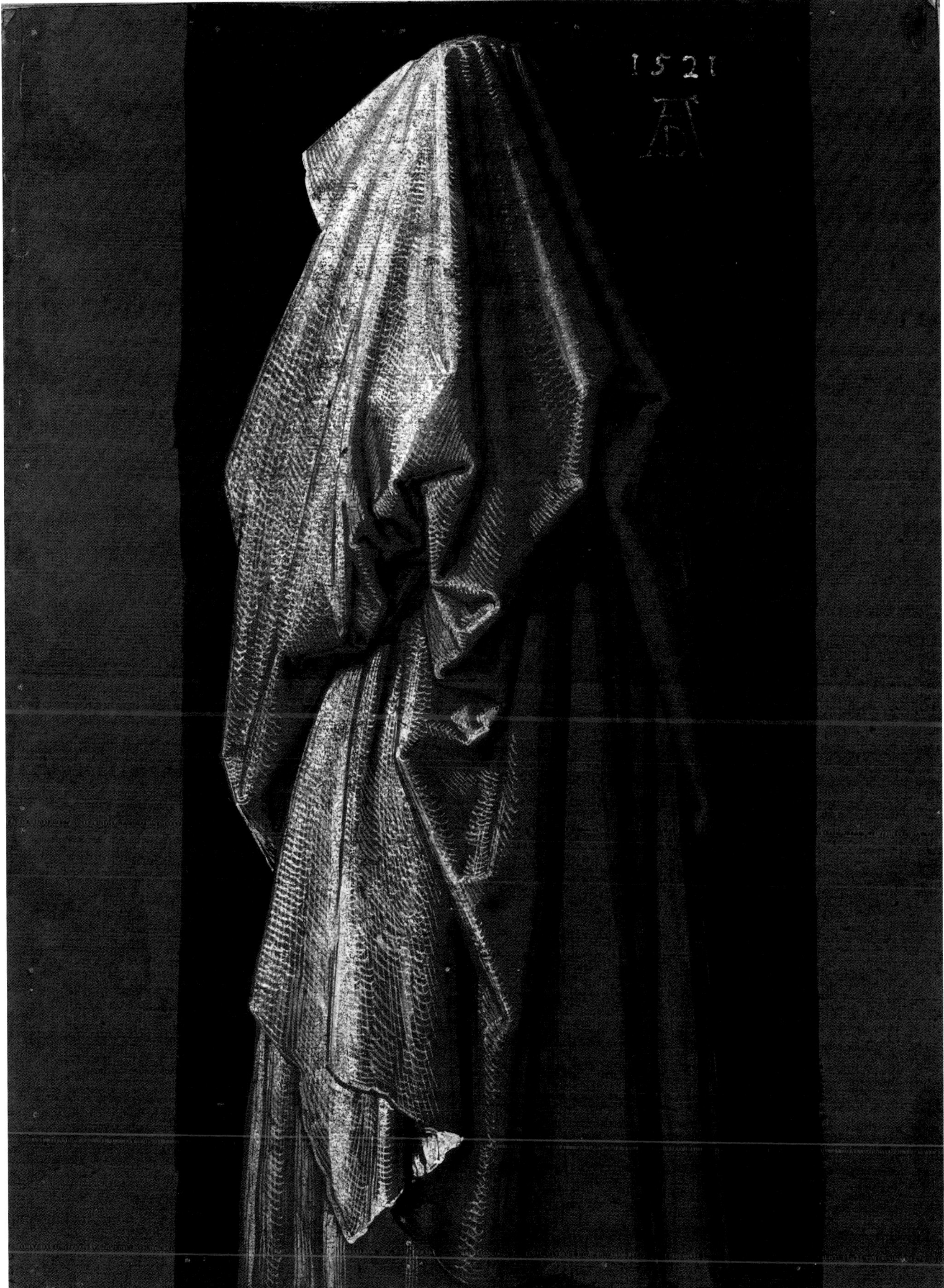

originated with the master of the workshop instead.[3] Making drawn studies from stiffened cloth carefully arranged over a figure or model under controlled lighting conditions actually predates Leonardo: it is a practice recorded by Filarete (about 1400–about 1469), a Florentine sculptor, artist and theorist, in his treatise of around 1465.[4] However, the great innovation by Verrocchio and his workshop was to execute these studies not as drawings on paper, but as monochromes brushed on linen, a support which, unlike paper, did not wrinkle when the wet paint was applied.[5] Most of the drapery studies produced in the Verrocchio workshop cannot be precisely matched with specific finished works and seem more likely to have provided a supply of drapery options that could be modified to suit different figures and compositions.[6]

These studies should be viewed in the context of the increased interest in representations of the body and its movements that developed during the fifteenth century, particularly in Italy. Artists grappled with the problem of how to represent the three-dimensional in two dimensions, as discussed by art theorists such as Leon Battista Alberti. In his treatise *Della Pittura (On Painting)* of 1435, Alberti states the importance of rendering drapery in such a way that it both articulates the body beneath and gives greater emphasis to the gesture or posture of each figure, aspects critical to conveying narrative.[7] Monochrome drapery studies on linen appear as an innovative response to this increased interest and, unlike in drawn studies, the looser handling of the brush facilitates a particularly fluid technique that more closely approximates the final, painted work. As much like paintings as they are like drawings, these studies on linen were clearly used to determine the precise location of the highlights and shadows and to establish the tonal range between the two as a way of creating a three-dimensional effect.

The frequent use and handling of such studies in the workshop is evident from their worn condition. One of the better preserved of these, however, is a drapery study which has been variously attributed to Leonardo or Ghirlandaio (cat. 11) – the latter attribution suggested by its resemblance to the drapery in the figure of Saint Matthew in the artist's fresco of about 1477 in the Santa Fina Chapel in the Collegiate Church of San Gimignano (see fig. 13, the figure in the lower left).[8] The study was made on finely woven linen prepared with a thin, grey-brown ground. The figure's silhouette was first roughly sketched out using a brush and black tempera and then heightened with white bodycolour. On the mantle, the artist carefully mapped the dramatic fall of light from the upper left, picking out the illuminated crests of the sharp folds rendered in white and modelling the variety of folds in the rest of the garment in subtle shades and gradations of grey. The study is very close to, but does

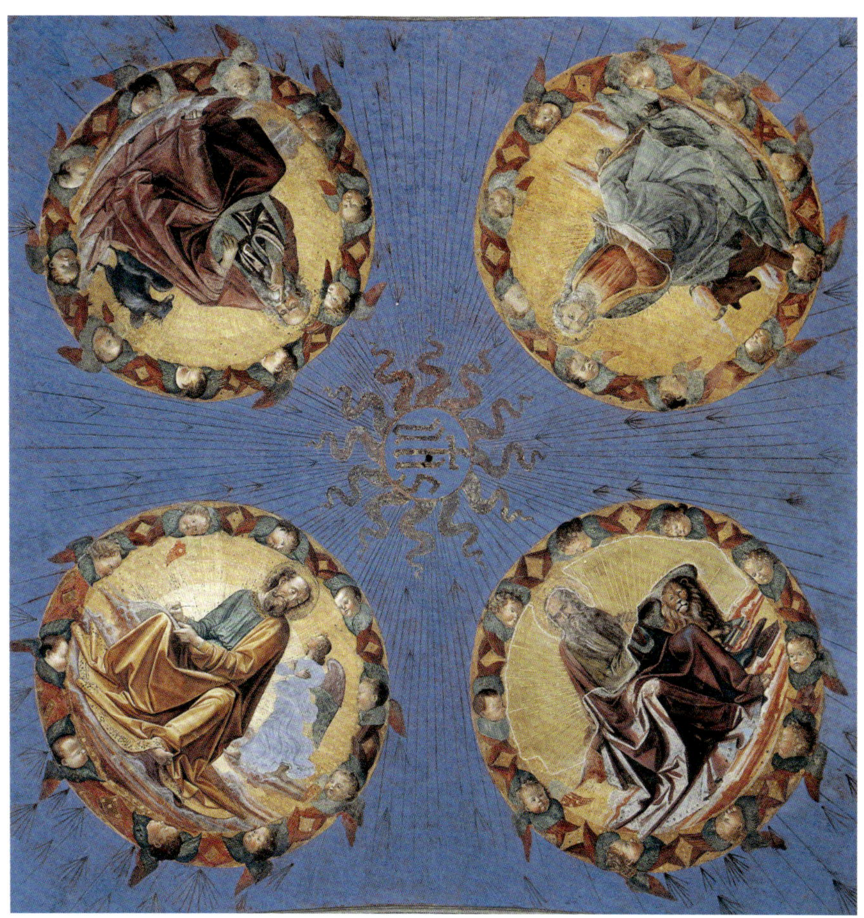

not correspond precisely with, the final fresco. Like the other drapery studies in this series, it may be understood as an investigation into the way light strikes different angles and surfaces, building an artistic vocabulary of light and shade to be used in subsequent paintings.

Drapery studies continued to be made in the following century, both south and north of the Alps, and they found a leading proponent in the German artist Albrecht Dürer (1471–1528). One of his finest examples is the *Woman in Netherlandish Dress seen from Behind (Drapery Study)* of 1521 (cat. 12), made using a brush and black ink, heightened with white, on grey-violet prepared paper. Dürer's writings reveal that he produced this work as a record of a type of dress he saw during his travels through the Netherlands in 1520–1.[9] The work is an impressive demonstration of Dürer's chiaroscuro technique: painting the drapery in shades from dark grey to white on the middle-ground of the prepared paper before adding a black background around the figure, he ensured that the figure would stand out against the coloured paper. The stiff, heavy folds in the woman's garment convey the thickness and weight of the fabric and Dürer's mastery of the technique, applying the white heightening with a brush in increasing degrees

Fig. 13
Domenico Ghirlandaio (1449–1494)
The Four Evangelists, about 1477
Fresco
Santa Fina Chapel, Collegiate Church of San Gimignano

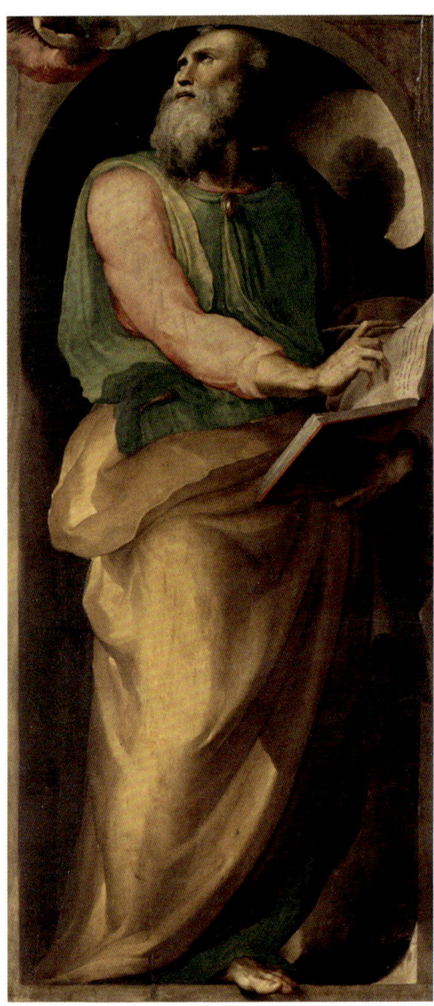

of intensity, amplifies the three-dimensional effect and renders areas such as the woman's head so bright that they appear to radiate light.

A comparison between the monochrome drapery studies made in the Verrocchio workshop and those by Dürer, made roughly 50 years later, demonstrates how these artists achieved similar effects through different means and that each had a very different aesthetic and aim. The dark preparation of the paper and black 'frame' surrrounding Dürer's drapery study make his figure stand out in stark relief. The sharp, almost calligraphic folds more commonly favoured by northern artists contrast with the textured appearance of Ghirlandaio's study on linen, in which the thick soft folds pool around the figure's feet in a manner reminiscent of contemporary Florentine painting and sculpture. However, not only do the medium and aesthetics make these works so distinct from one another, so do the different aims of each study: one is a kind of 'stock' image to be adapted and re-used in the workshop and the other is a more personal, visual account of the artist's travels.

The monochrome oil sketch

In the third decade of the sixteenth century, the Sienese artist Domenico Beccafumi (1484–1551) developed an innovative way to experiment with the effects of light and shadow. He used a different medium, oil on paper, to create monochrome sketches, a technique that would continue to be used and developed by artists in the following centuries.[10] Much more fluid and flexible than preparatory drawings, these oil sketches, painted mostly in shades of brown-black, grey and creamy white, enabled the artist swiftly to devise artistic solutions for complex problems of composition and illumination. Beccafumi would then translate these monochrome studies into vibrant colour in his frescoes and panel paintings.

One of the best-preserved monochrome sketches by Beccafumi is his *Saint Matthew* (cat. 13). Painted in brown, beige and cream-coloured oils and emulsion with a brush on paper, it is a study in light and shade for one of his panels of the Evangelists made for Pisa cathedral around 1538 (fig. 14). The *Saint Matthew* study is highly finished, suggesting it was used less for experimentation and more as a cartoon (*cartonetto*) – a fully worked-up model used as a guide for laying in highlights and shadows on the final panel.[11] Beccafumi modelled the forms through light with thick applications of white oil paint, as seen on Matthew's forehead, moustache, right knee and the left page of his book; the artist used a few swift, thin strokes in shades from grey to black that suggest the rest of Matthew's body and cloak and amplify the appearance of the shadows. In the final, large, coloured panel, Beccafumi translated his understanding of the

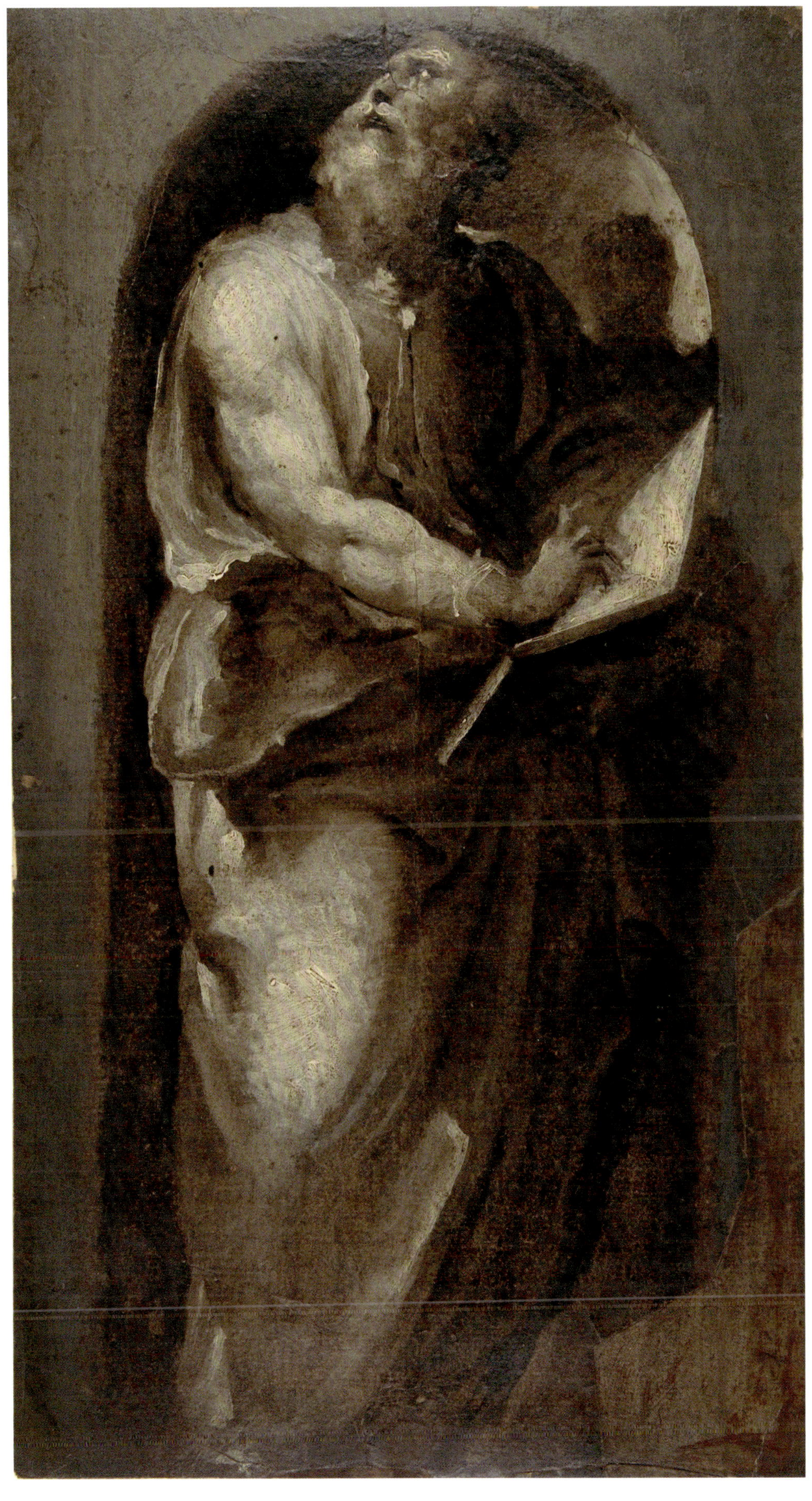

way light falls over different surfaces – the body, draperies and architecture – into his signature acidic greens, yellows and salmon pinks.

The monochrome oil sketch was often used to determine individual details or motifs, but it could also be used to work out the pattern of light and shadow across an entire composition. One of the artists who made the most extensive use of the technique after Beccafumi was Federico Barocci (about 1533–1612). An exceptionally talented and prolific draughtsman and painter from Urbino, Barocci took the practice to new heights during the second half of the sixteenth century. One example is the fine preparatory study *Aeneas and Anchises escaping from Troy* of about 1587–95 (cat. 14), executed in pen, ink and monochrome oil paints, mostly in shades of cool grey over a warm brown background with white heightening on paper. Although monochrome, the sketch implies a range of temperatures or tonalities that hint at the colour of the final work, and resolves the position of the main figures, their draperies and spatial relationships as well as the patterns of illumination across the composition.

This study is a prime example of Barocci's methodical practice of creating a small-scale monochrome cartoon (known at the time as a *cartoncino per il chiaroscuro*), before moving on to the prepared panel or canvas. In this case, the study was for a prestigious commission for the Holy Roman Emperor, Rudolf II, in Prague. Although the Prague painting is now lost, we have a sense of its original appearance from Barocci's second version of the work (fig. 15), painted over a decade later. Barocci presumably reused the same studies for this second version, given the inaccessibility of his first version in Prague. The monochrome *cartoncino* also appears to have served as a model for Agostino Carracci's 1595 engraved print of the composition, suggesting another function of monochrome studies as models for prints.[12]

Outside of Italy, one of the most famous painters of oil sketches was Peter Paul Rubens (1577–1640). Rubens used the technique extensively, leaving behind over 450 examples. Most of these, however, are in colour, and only relatively few could be termed strictly monochrome. It has been observed that oil sketches were an integral feature of the artist's working method and studio practice, to a degree that was unprecedented in the history of art.[13] Given the large scale of Rubens's workshop and the numerous commissions for works to be executed by specialists in a variety of media, including metalwork and tapestry, his autograph sketches are some of the few undiluted and most immediate representations of his personal invention.

Rubens's *The Birth of Venus* (cat. 15), a design in grisaille for an oval silver basin, depicts the sea-born Venus emerging from her shell onto a rocky shore, accompanied by nereids (sea nymphs) and a number of gods and goddesses.

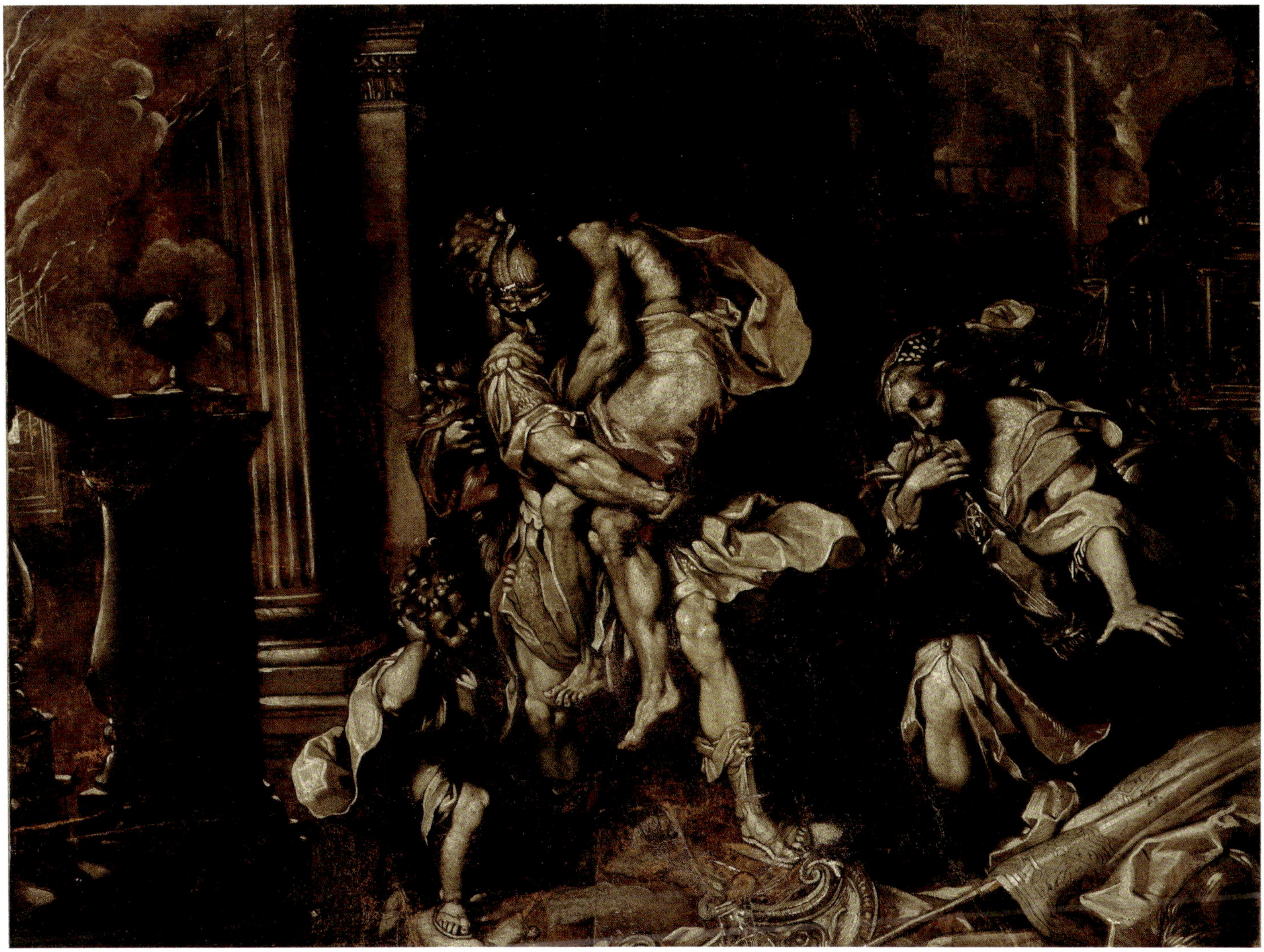

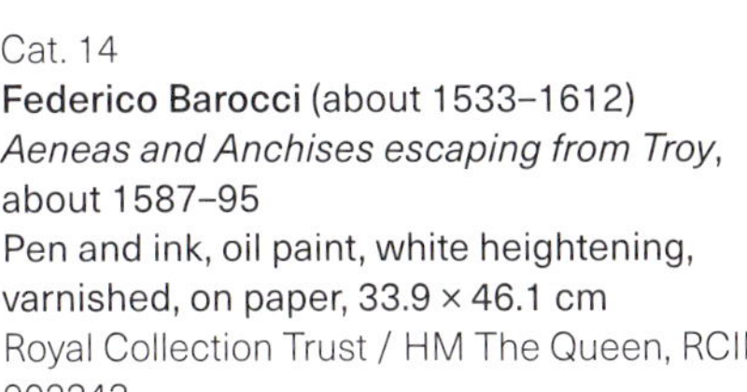

Cat. 14
Federico Barocci (about 1533–1612)
Aeneas and Anchises escaping from Troy,
about 1587–95
Pen and ink, oil paint, white heightening,
varnished, on paper, 33.9 × 46.1 cm
Royal Collection Trust / HM The Queen, RCIN
902343

Fig. 15
Federico Barocci (about 1533–1612)
Aeneas and Anchises escaping from Troy,
1598
Oil on canvas, 45.5 × 72.5 cm
Galleria Borghese, Rome

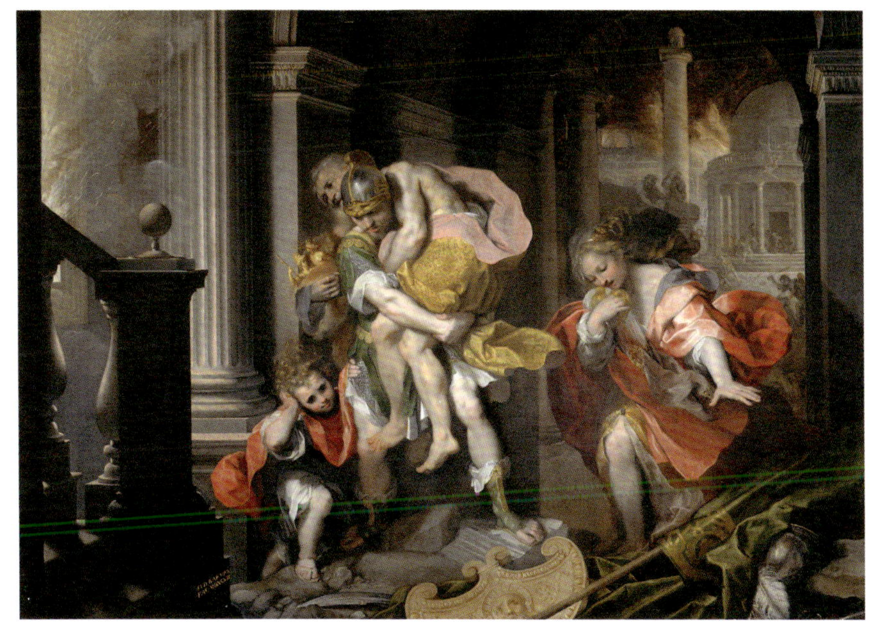

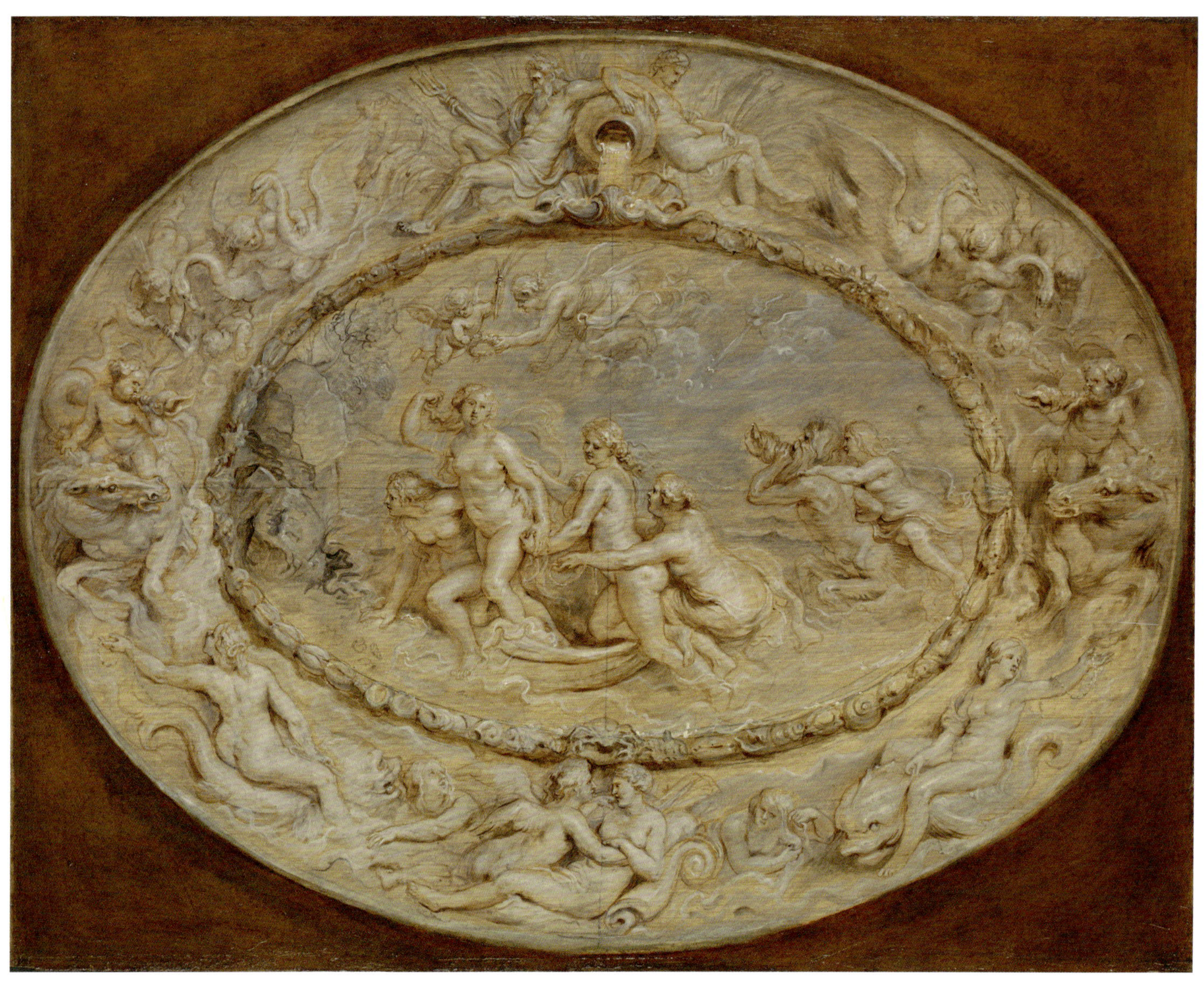

Rubens first drew the design in black chalk, which he then went over in brown oil, on a translucent brown priming. Over this, light grey was added to sketch the natural forms, such as the trees, rocks, waves and sky, and the white highlights further enhanced the sculptural quality of the composition. The artist clearly sought to approximate the three-dimensional appearance of the embossed and chased silver basin in relief. His design was keyed to the water theme: at the top of the basin Rubens included Neptune and Amphitrite holding a large urn, from which water flowed all around the inner rim. When actual water was poured into this luxurious object, it would have shimmered against the silver. Although the monochrome was evidently painted as a model for a silversmith, it remains uncertain if the basin was ever produced.[14]

Cat. 15
Peter Paul Rubens (1577–1640)
The Birth of Venus, about 1632–3
Black chalk and oil on oak, 61 × 78 cm
The National Gallery, London, NG 1195
Exhibited Düsseldorf only

The Lamentation over the Dead Christ (cat. 16) by Rembrandt van Rijn (1606–1669) is another monochrome sketch for an unrealised or unknown final work. One of about ten surviving monochrome oil sketches by the artist, it depicts the Virgin Mary and Mary Magdalene, among others, mourning the dead Christ after he has been taken down from the cross.[15] The fall of the light and shadows contributes to a reading of the narrative, with the brightest highlights illuminating the main figure group, which appears almost spotlit, and the brightest white reserved for Christ's winding sheet. The serene body of the 'Good Thief' on the cross on the far right is also bathed in light, and is so prominent that it might be mistaken at first glance for that of Christ. In contrast, the 'Bad Thief' suffers on his cross on the far left of the composition and is cast in shadow. This use of light is surely intended to contribute to the spiritual message of the subject. As recounted in Luke's Gospel, the Good Thief asks Jesus to remember him in his kingdom. Christ responds, 'Truly, I say to you, today you will be with me in Paradise' (Luke 23: 39–43). This passage is often interpreted as a confirmation that the thief became a saint in Paradise after his death. His peaceful, illuminated and Christ-like appearance here seems to reflect Jesus' promise.

Rembrandt's *Lamentation* underwent an extensive technical examination in 1998 which revealed that it was created in several stages: the artist took particular advantage of the flexible nature of the monochrome oil sketch to develop his final composition.[16] He first prepared the paper with a brown lay-in for the shadows and half-tones, on top of which he added grey and white oil for the highlights and dark brown and black for the darker shadows. Unsatisfied with these first results, Rembrandt rethought the lower part of the composition in a new drawing (*The Lamentation*, British Museum, London), then returned to his earlier grisaille, tearing out the portions he disliked and mounting the remaining, satisfactory parts to a canvas before reworking the entire composition. This elaborate process demonstrates how Rembrandt used the grisaille and drawing simultaneously, experimenting first in one medium, then transferring his iconographic and compositional solutions to the other.[17]

Curiously, this carefully composed grisaille does not correspond to any finished work known to have been made by Rembrandt. It has been compellingly argued that, like the artist's *Ecce Homo* of 1634 (see cat. 43), this sketch was intended as a modello for a print.[18] In this case, however, an etching of 1730 by Bernard Picart, was made almost a century after the design, making it unclear whether this was the oil sketch's original function. Another possibility is that the sketch was for part of Rembrandt's Passion series for the court in The Hague.[19] Support for the former theory over the latter is found in

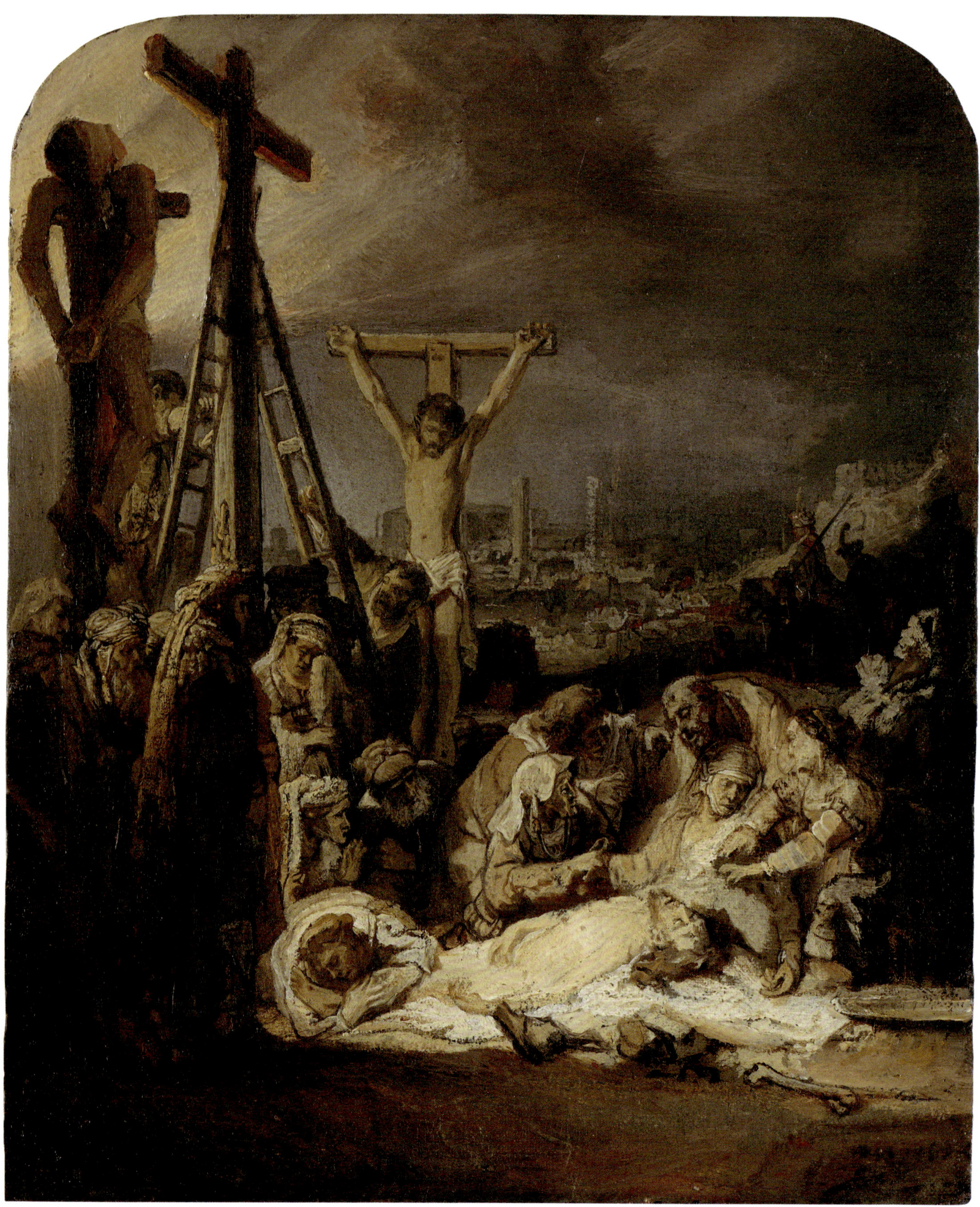

observing the position of the Bad Thief – on the cross to Christ's right. This is unusual, because this places him in the position traditionally reserved for the Good Thief in Christian art.[20] The anomaly may be explained by the fact that, when compositions were etched for transfer, artists often took into account that the printed image would appear in reverse. Regardless of the original function of Rembrandt's sketch, it reveals his deep understanding of the formal and symbolic effects of light and shade, and his ability to convey a subject entirely without colour but in a way that showed relative values of lightness or darkness. Indeed, a close examination of the different states of Rembrandt's etchings, such as *The Entombment* of around 1654, reveals that while the figures, contours or design details often remained the same, he continued to explore different distributions of light and shade across the entire composition.[21]

Grisaille studies for frescoes

The Renaissance practice of creating monochrome oil sketches continued into the late eighteenth century and was especially important in determining the correct fall of light and shade for works designed for specific locations. A case in point is the work of the Spanish artist Francisco Bayeu y Subías (1734–1795), the court painter of Charles III of Spain. Bayeu decorated a number of Spanish royal palaces; in 1794, for example, he was commissioned to decorate the ceiling of the Queen's boudoir at the royal palace in Madrid in fresco, for which he produced a fine grisaille study of *The Spanish Monarchy* on canvas (cat. 17).[22] For this prestigious commission, Bayeu designed a grand allegorical fresco in a dramatic *di sotto in su* (or 'seen from below') perspective, in which the Spanish monarchy is personified as an imposing matron wearing a helmet, surrounded by several allegorical figures including Religion to the left, holding a cross. Bayeu's swiftly executed study, painted in shades of brown-black and creamy white paint using a wet in-wet technique, maps out the parts of the composition to be picked out in bright light and those cast in shadow. His confident and economical brushstrokes convey the majesty of the final monumental work without colour, on a reduced scale.

Rather than an experimental sketch made early in the artistic process, this grisaille is a later product of Bayeu's dedicated study, as can be seen by the set of pencil lines visible in certain areas just below the thin paint layer. These lines form the grid that Bayeu presumably employed to transfer an earlier drawing of the composition to this canvas.[23] As the artist customarily made both monochrome and coloured oil sketches in preparation for his works, we may presume that he also made a colour sketch for this commission which has been lost or which remains unidentified.[24] In this case therefore, the artist

Cat. 16
Rembrandt (1606–1669)
The Lamentation over the Dead Christ, about 1635
Oil on paper and pieces of canvas, mounted onto oak, 31.9 × 26.7 cm
The National Gallery, London, NG 43
Exhibited Düsseldorf only

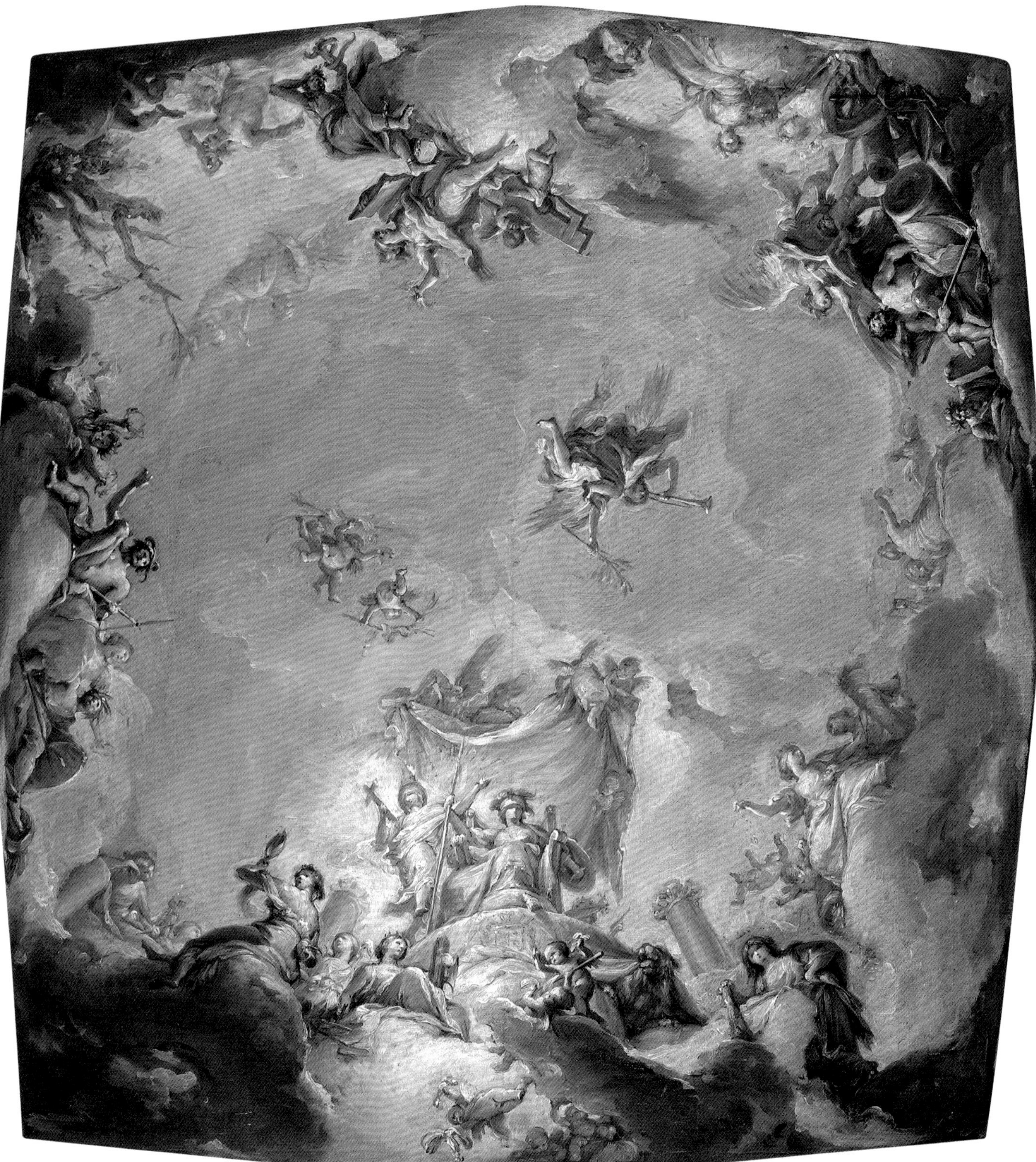

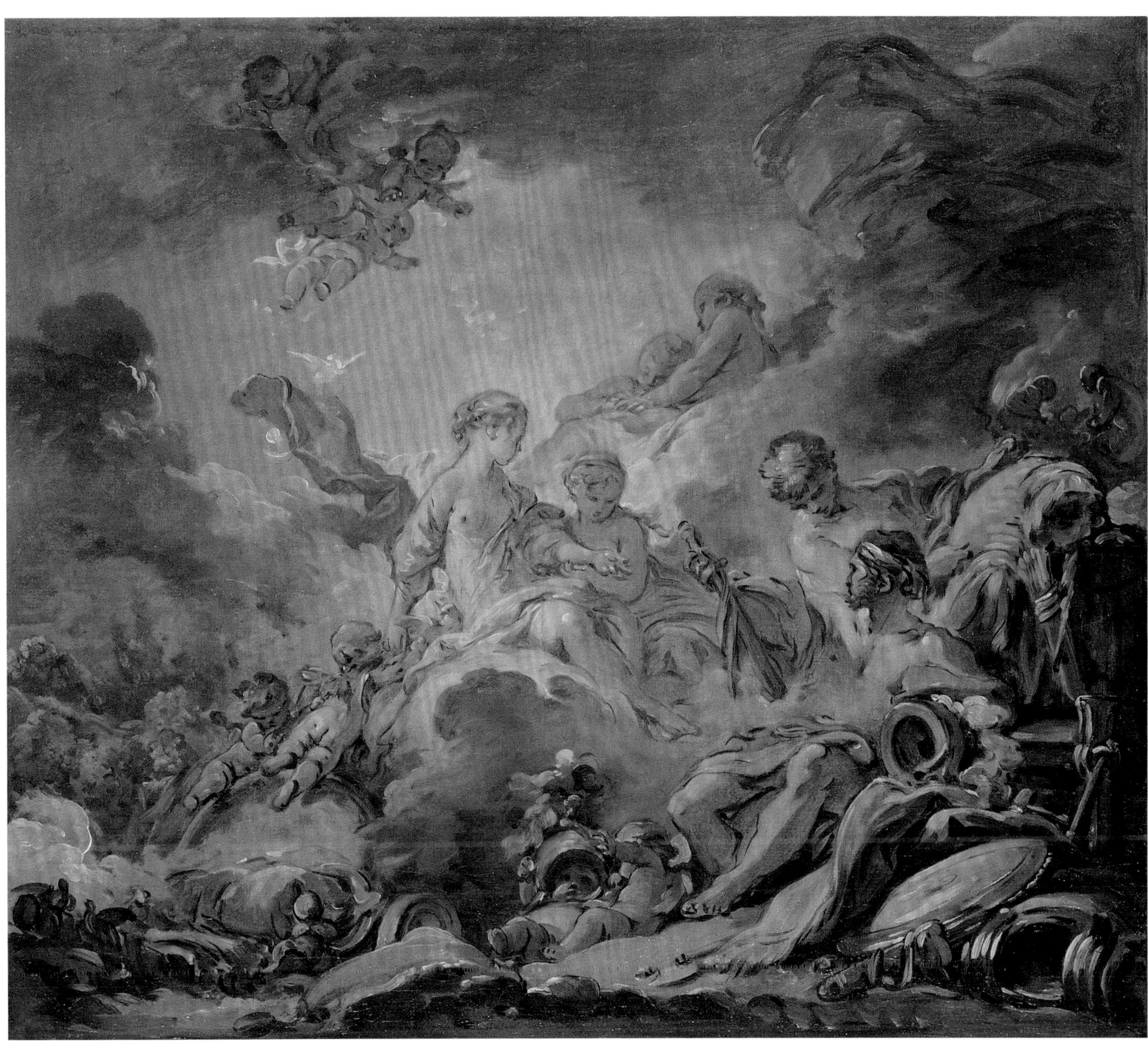

Cat. 17
Francisco Bayeu y Subías (1734–1795)
The Spanish Monarchy, 1794
Oil on canvas, 63 × 59 cm
Museo Nacional del Prado, Madrid, P02481

Cat. 18
François Boucher (1703–1770)
*Vulcan's Forge (Vulcan presenting Venus with
Arms for Aeneas)*, 1756
Oil on canvas, 38 × 43 cm
Musée des Arts décoratifs, Paris, 36231

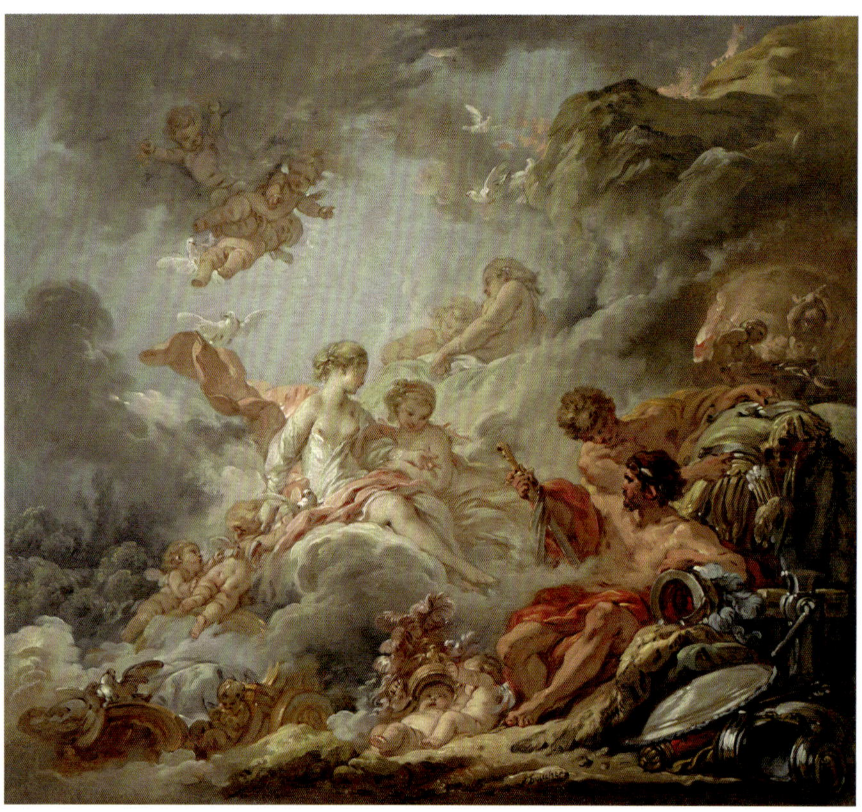

appears to have first established the composition in drawing and then used the grisaille as a means of determining the overall harmony of light and shadow across the surface, after which he most likely produced a colour sketch as a final preparatory stage to the final fresco.

The popularity of the fresco medium dwindled between the late sixteenth and eighteenth centuries, as did the associated practice of creating monochrome cartoons. In the nineteenth century, however, there was a renewed interest among painters in the art and techniques of medieval Germany and early Renaissance Italy. Artists such as Frederic Leighton (1830–1896) produced monochrome cartoons in preparation for his murals (1878–84) at the South Kensington Museum in London, now the Victoria and Albert Museum.[25]

Painting in monochrome, weaving in colour

The grisaille sketches discussed so far served as studies for works in painting, silverwork and fresco. In the eighteenth century, the French painter François Boucher (1703–1770), best known for his sweet and amorous subjects made in pastel hues, used grisailles as studies for two sets of tapestries representing the Loves of the Gods, the first woven before 1749 and the second between 1758–9.[26] These sensual subjects were in high demand as designs for tapestries woven in bright colours to decorate elegant domestic interiors. Although each set of the Loves of the Gods tapestries included different scenes, both included

Fig. 16
François Boucher (1703–1770)
Vulcan presenting Arms to Venus for Aeneas, 1756
Oil on canvas, 41.2 × 45.3 cm
Sterling and Francine Clark Art Institute, Williamstown, 1893.29

Cat.19
After **François Boucher** (1703–1770)
Loves of the Gods: Venus in the Forge of Vulcan, 1758–9
Tapestry, wool and silk, 355 × 333 cm
Collection du Mobilier national, Paris, GMtt 205/2
Exhibited Düsseldorf only

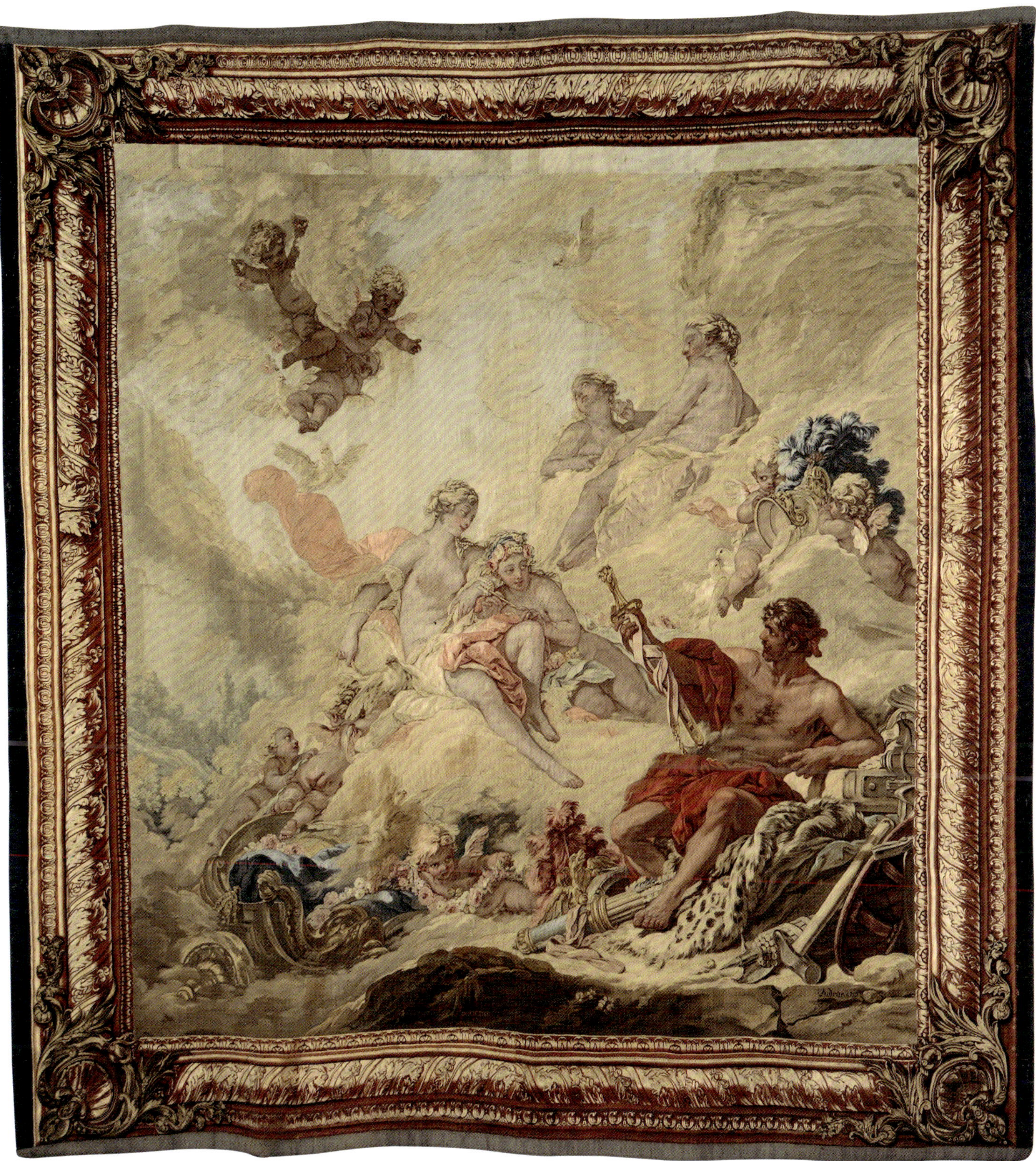

one of Boucher's favourite subjects: *Venus at Vulcan's Forge*. The story, from the eighth book of Virgil's *Aeneid*, describes how Venus visited her husband, Vulcan, to request that he forge weapons for Aeneas, her son by Anchises, and how she seduced Vulcan in order to convince him to do her bidding.

Two different grisaille sketches of the subject by Boucher survive. The first, made before 1749 (Musée du Louvre, Paris), formed the basis for a tapestry woven at the Beauvais manufactory, where Boucher served as director from 1734. The second, made around 1756 (cat. 18) was used for a tapestry woven at the rival manufactory of Gobelins, whose owners managed to entice Boucher to take up a directorship in 1755 and thus secured his designs for their company instead. Boucher also produced several coloured versions of the subject, including oil sketches and paintings.[27] Boucher's grisaille sketches for tapestries were generally painted swiftly and on a relatively small scale, as they are for the *Venus at Vulcan's Forge*. He then appears to have made the colour sketch, which almost exactly reproduces the composition of the grisaille (fig. 16). Interestingly, the final, highly finished painting sent to the tapestry manufactory as a guide for the weavers shows substantial changes to the composition when compared with the sketches (Musée du Louvre, Paris). It has been argued, therefore, that the coloured sketch does not represent a genuine stage in the creative process and was merely created as a favour to the commissioner, much like a presentation model (or 'modello').[28]

In the few cases where a full provenance for grisaille oils sketches have survived, the sketches seemed to have remained in the artist's studio until his or her death, probably because of their more personal nature as experiments or explorations in light and shadow.[29] Many grisaille sketches were subsequently owned by fellow artists, as is the case for Boucher's grisaille, which was acquired by the French sculptor Jean-Baptiste Lemoyne. This suggests that they held a special appeal for those who were familiar with and appreciative of these complex stages in the creative process.[30] Colour sketches were often acquired as independent works of art not only by artists but also by collectors and dealers.[31] The Marquis de Marigny, the Directeur Général des Bâtiments du Roi (Director General of the King's Buildings), for example, owned the full set of Boucher's colour sketches for the Loves of the Gods tapestries woven for Louis XV at the Gobelins manufactory.[32]

In addition to the preparatory studies, several versions of the tapestry of *Venus at Vulcan's Forge* based on cat. 18 survive, including the first, woven in 1758/9 in the atelier of Michel Audran at the Gobelins (cat. 19). The tapestry represents Boucher's signature style – from the glowing ephemeral clouds supporting the blonde goddess to the pink-and-cream silk draperies that set off her smooth, creamy skin and blushing red cheeks. Vulcan, seated on a leopard skin opposite Venus, provides a dramatic contrast to the luminous goddess, with his darker skin and muscular torso draped in deep red.[33] A comparison between the well-preserved but somewhat faded tapestry and the grisaille study reveals the subtlety with which Boucher worked out the play of light over the different surfaces in his oil sketch. Furthermore, given that the pale pastel colours of the tapestry have faded unevenly, the monochrome study is perhaps a more accurate record of the artist's intended balance between light and shadow.

Hidden and exposed: monochrome underpaintings

The practice of underdrawing, the preliminary outlining of a composition on a primed support, is relatively well understood thanks to artistic treatises such as Cennino Cennini's late fourteenth-century *Libro dell'arte (The Craftsman's Handbook)*, and through a study of unfinished paintings, x-radiographs and infrared photographs, which reveal artistic processes usually concealed under the paint surface.[34] Used by artists from the early Renaissance onwards to assist them in working out the details of a composition on a prepared support before applying coloured paints, underdrawings generally consisted of simple outlines, sometimes with hatching, made in a dry medium (charcoal or chalk) or a liquid one (ink) applied with a brush.[35] By contrast, underpaintings generally involved shading areas of a composition, such as drapery or faces, with washes, applied, according to Cennino's recommendation, with a blunt, soft brush.[36] In addition to these preparatory techniques is a related practice of monochrome underpainting known as 'dead-colouring', which is less well known but was similarly used for the outline and tonal organisation of a painting before the application of colour.[37] The term 'dead-colouring' (*dood-verf* in Dutch) can be traced back to the seventeenth-century Netherlands and must have originally referred to the colour of a corpse but, when used in connection with painting, implies the flat, predominantly dark grey-brown tones used.[38]

The use of dead-colouring before the application of colour is evident, for example, in the unfinished canvas *Lord Rockingham and Edmund Burke* (fig. 17) by Joshua Reynolds (1723–1792). Here Rockingham's suit has been laid with a dark, monochromatic ground, over which loose strokes of grey-white paint indicate the folds and where the highlights should fall. Similarly, Burke's face is underpainted in a blue-grey colour to create a cool foundation for the subsequent addition of the warmer pinky flesh tones.[39] The frequent reference to 'dead colour' in Reynolds's lists of 'portraits in progress' indicates that, for him, dead-colouring was synonymous with monochrome underpainting, on top of which the artist built up the colour in more or less transparent layers.[40]

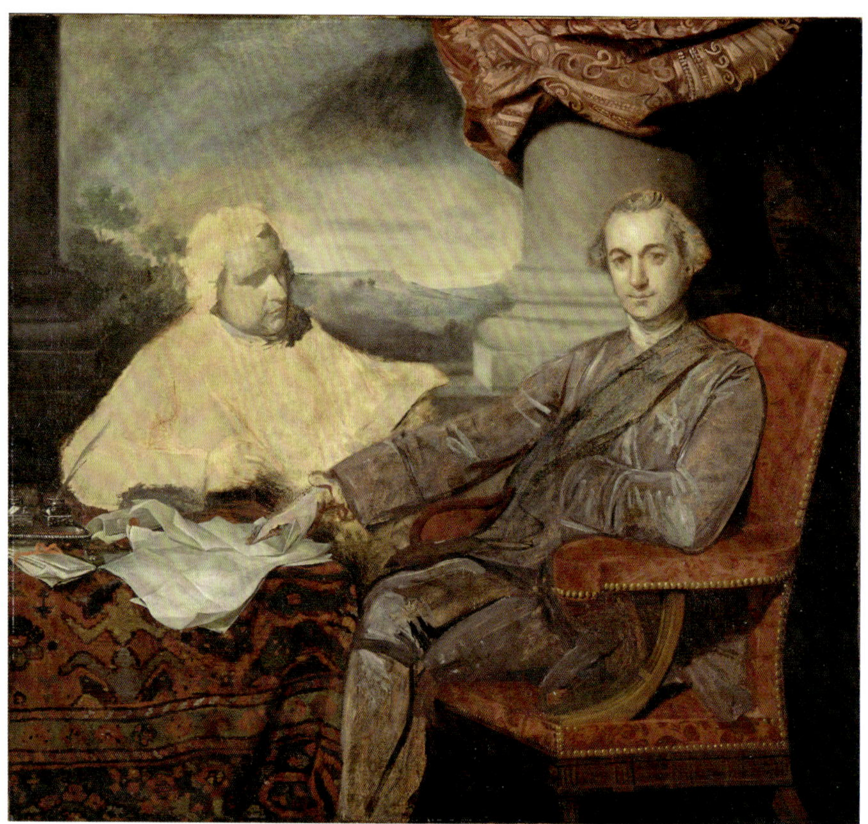

Fig. 17
Joshua Reynolds (1723–1792)
Lord Rockingham and Edmund Burke, 1766–8
Oil on canvas, 145.4 × 159.1 cm
Fitzwilliam Museum, Cambridge, 653

The process of dead-colouring was also taken up by the French painter Gustave Moreau (1826–1898). It can be seen in his many unfinished works, including his large horizontal canvas of *Diomedes devoured by his Horses* (cat. 20), which was abandoned at its monochrome, underpainted stage. Despite being unfinished, it was listed by the artist among a set of works to be retained for an exhibition, suggesting that he may have considered it fit for display even in its incomplete state.[41]

Moreau depicts the ancient Greek myth of Diomedes, King of Thrace (not to be confused with the Diomedes, son of Tydeus, described in the *Iliad*) and his wild, man-eating horses. As one of his Twelve Labours, the divine hero Hercules was challenged to steal Diomedes' uncontrollable mares. Unaware that the horses had an unnatural diet of human flesh, Hercules left his young companion Abderus in charge of them while he fought Diomedes, returning to find the boy had been eaten. In revenge, Hercules fed Diomedes to his own horses. The gruesome subject evidently fascinated Moreau, who painted it several times in a variety of formats, all of which feature powerful horses in dynamic poses indebted to works by the Italian Renaissance master Leonardo and the French Romantic painter Théodore Géricault.[42] In this unfinished version, Moreau has outlined his figures in black-brown paint and has begun building up the surrounding landscape through the use of shades of the same colour palette – from a light sandy-beige, to a darker red-brown, to the richest black – to indicate depth of space and the ground below the horses' stomping hooves and Diomedes' trampled body. The unpainted portions of the canvas are the brightest parts of the composition, suggesting areas Moreau intended to paint white (such as the horse at the far left), or where he might add highlights. The overall impression of the work is that of a large pen-and-wash drawing. The unfinished monochrome aesthetic clearly had a particular appeal for Moreau, who similarly abandoned one of his other paintings, *Hesiod and the Muses* (1860, Musée Gustave Moreau, Paris) at the red-brown underpainting stage and elected to frame and hang it in its unfinished state.

Moreau's dead-colour pictures show how monochromatic paintings were no longer used or considered only as preparatory to works in colour, but had come to be appreciated as independent and collectable works in their own right. Indeed, the practice of making preparatory studies in black, white and grey seems to have inspired artists to begin creating fully independent works without colour, a shift that began as early as the fifteenth century, but that did not really gain currency until the sixteenth. While artists continued to use monochrome sketches to experiment with or record areas of complicated light and shadow, they also began creating monochromatic works that advertised their status as something different, or apart from the everyday, through the absence of colour.

Moreau abandoned this monumental
painting at its monochrome,
underpainted stage, which accounts
for its resemblance to an unusually large
drawing. Indeed, the fury, power and
dynamism of the horses appear deeply
indebted to Leonardo da Vinci's drawn
studies for his lost painting of the *Battle
of Anghiari* (1505) and to Théodore
Géricault's numerous studies for the
Race of the Riderless Horses (1817),
which the artist may have known from
later (black-and-white) engravings.
Moreau was evidently pleased with
the effect of this work, even in its
unfinished state, as he included it
among a list of paintings to be retained
for an exhibition. Interestingly, Moreau's
contemporary, Auguste Rodin, was also
exploring an 'aesthetic of the unfinished'
in his sculpture around this time.

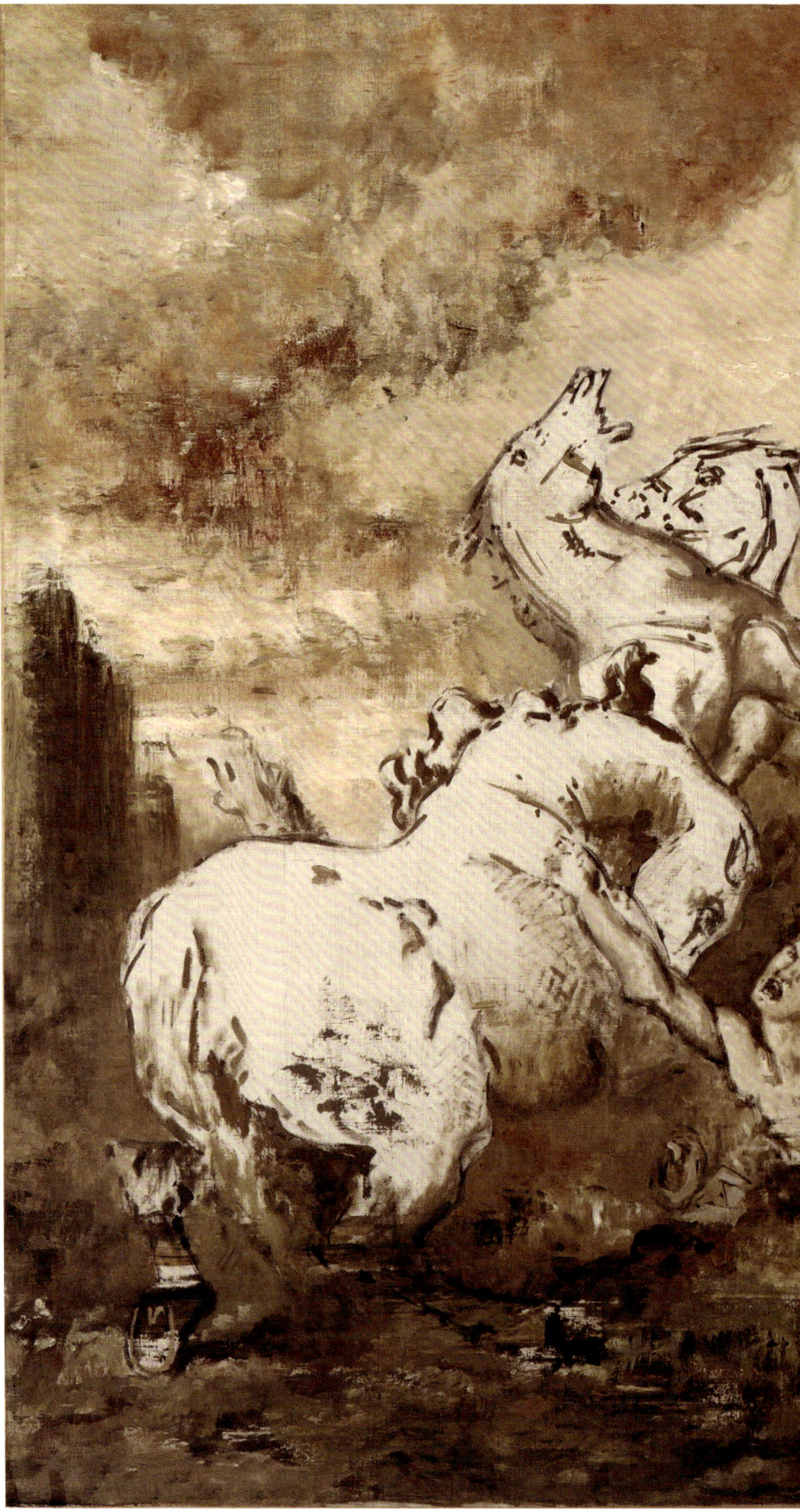

Cat. 20
Gustave Moreau (1826–1898)
Diomedes devoured by his Horses,
date unknown
Oil on canvas, 130 × 196 cm
Musée national Gustave Moreau, Paris
(Rouleau 38, no. 1)

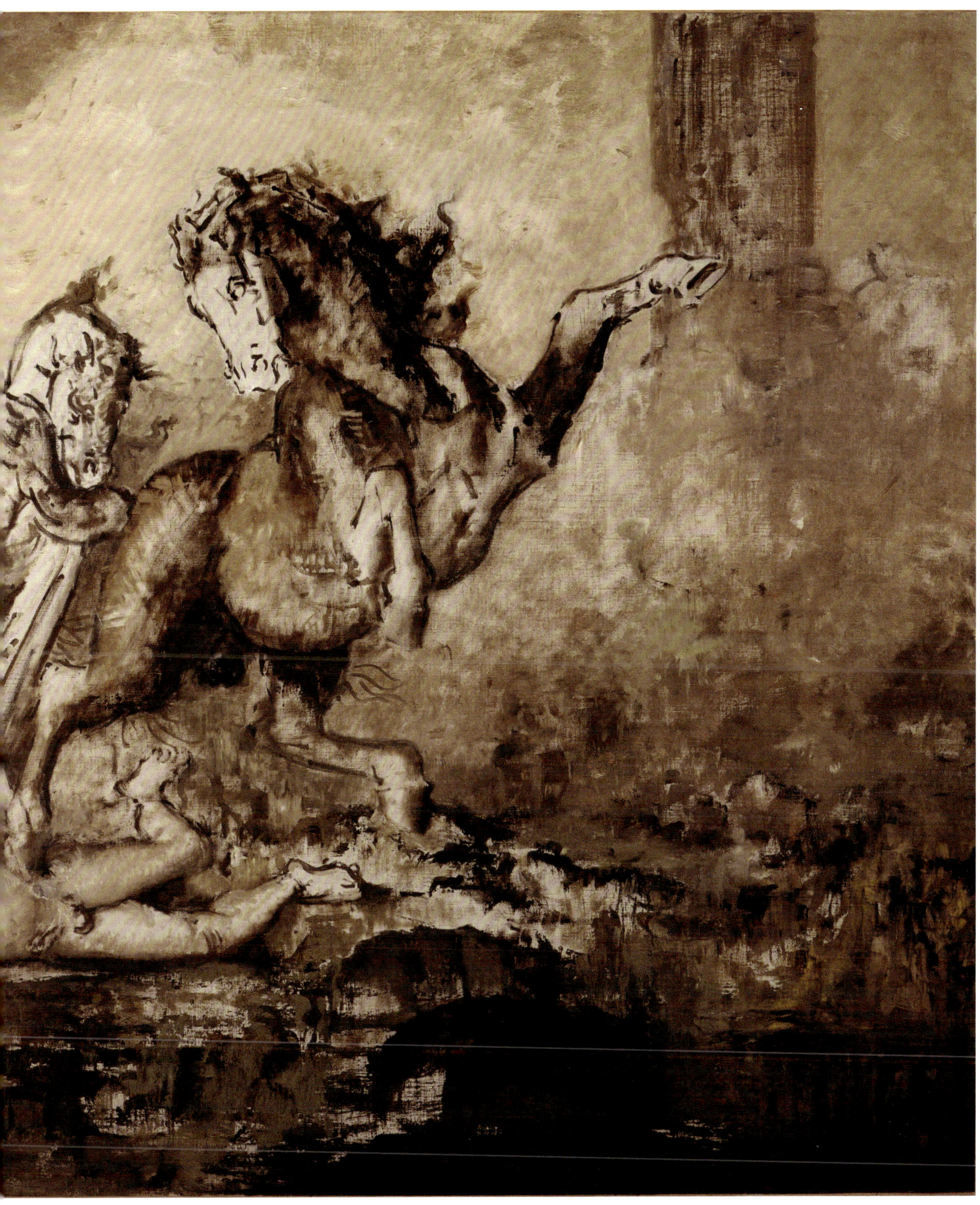

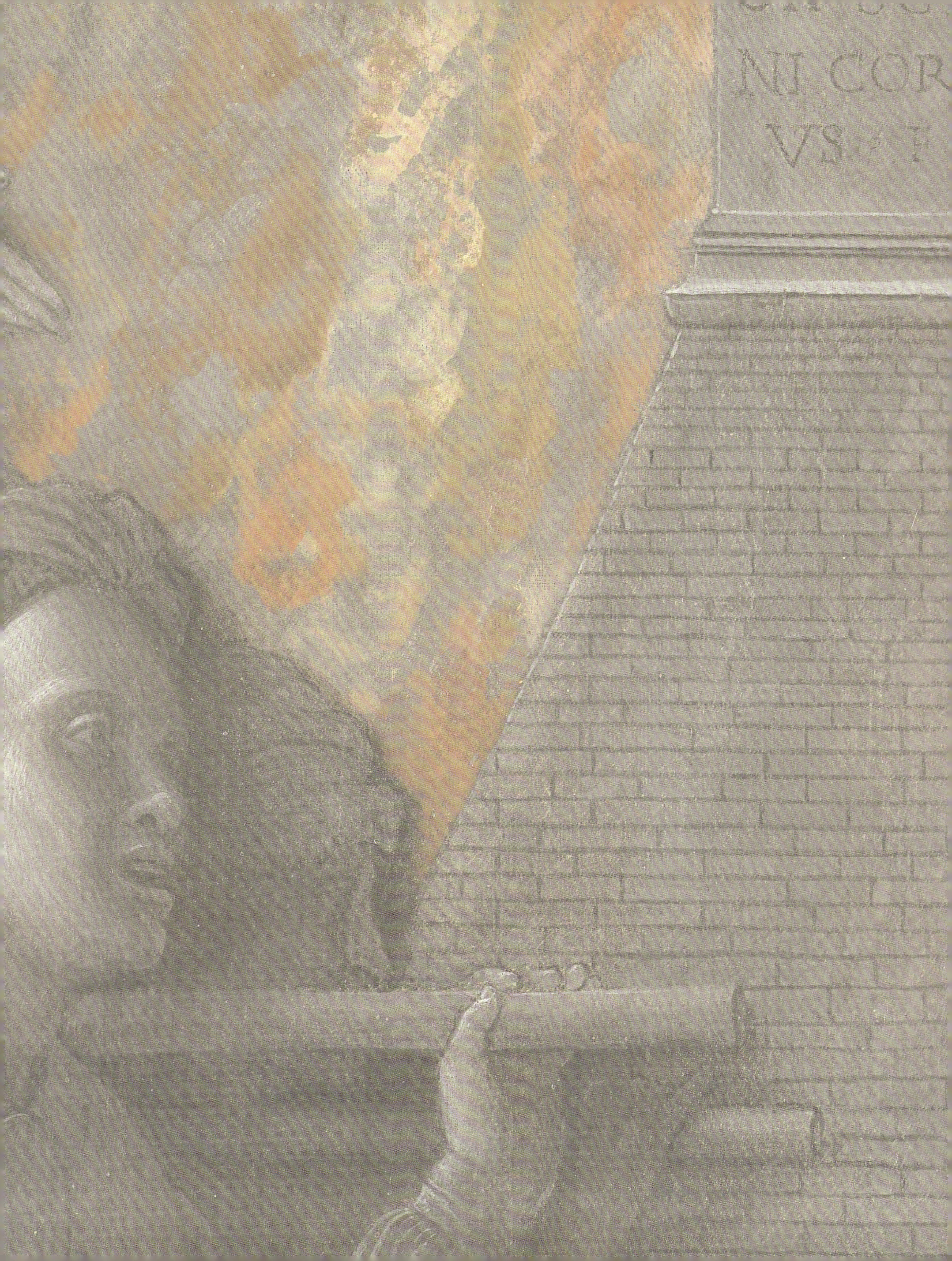
NI COR
VS F

3

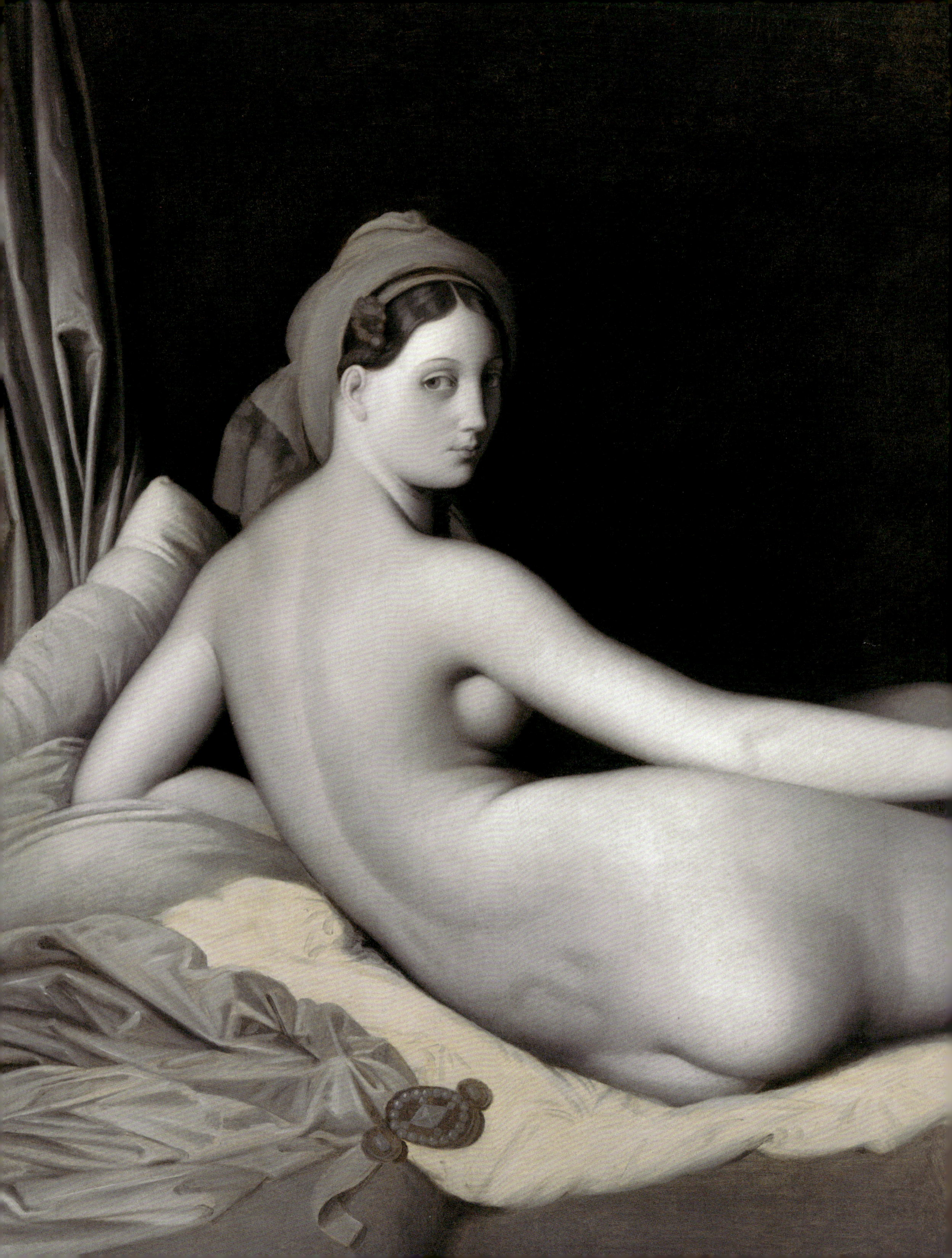

Independent Paintings in Grisaille

Lelia Packer

A new interest in independent monochrome paintings emerged during the sixteenth century, and was cultivated by painters and collectors alike. Before this period, grisaille paintings assumed a subsidiary role to the main coloured image in religious works, were employed as studies for works in colour, or were painted to imitate other materials such as stone. The grisaille paintings discussed in this chapter reflect a crucial shift in focus: they were produced as paintings in their own right, for contemplation or personal enjoyment. The interest in independent grisaille paintings was also evident in the production of monochrome versions after existing colour paintings. The black-and-white paintings discussed here were created and collected with several aims: to impress the viewer through artistic skill, without recourse to colour; to invite curiosity about how a painting was made; and to encourage deeper consideration of the subject portrayed. Moreover, working in monochrome liberated painters from the artistic conventions of colour images, challenging them to focus instead on the aesthetic or formal principles that interested them.

A century earlier, *Saint Barbara* (1437) by Jan van Eyck (active 1422; died 1441) anticipated the development of the independent grisaille (cat. 21). This extraordinary work is the earliest known example of a monochrome panel in its own right that was collected and appreciated as such. Van Eyck represented the Christian martyr seated in the foreground before a Gothic tower in the process of being built – a reference to both Saint Barbara's eventual imprisonment in a tower and to the building of Christendom. Drawing in metalpoint, India ink and oil on prepared ground, van Eyck used highly detailed hatchings to model forms and carefully applied paint to articulate areas such as the tower. The numerous *pentimenti* – the visible record of the artist's changes of mind – such as the saint's right hand and the upturned page of her prayer book – together with areas of heightened contrast in light and shadow, such as the folds of the saint's left sleeve, suggest that van Eyck was working out his composition directly on the panel, in monochrome. The detailed hatchings recall the common Netherlandish practice of underdrawing, where the preliminary outline of a composition was laid down on a primed support to guide the artist during the application of paint layers which would ultimately cover up the underdrawing.[1] However, the hatchings in the *Saint Barbara* are more worked up than was usual in contemporary underdrawings.[2]

The original semi-integral frame – with two mouldings carved from the same piece of oak as the support, and two carved separately and subsequently attached – is painted to resemble red marble, and enhances the impression of the *Saint Barbara* being an independent, finished work.[3] The painted

Jean-Auguste-Dominique Ingres (1780–1867)
and workshop
Odalisque in Grisaille, about 1824–34,
detail of cat. 28

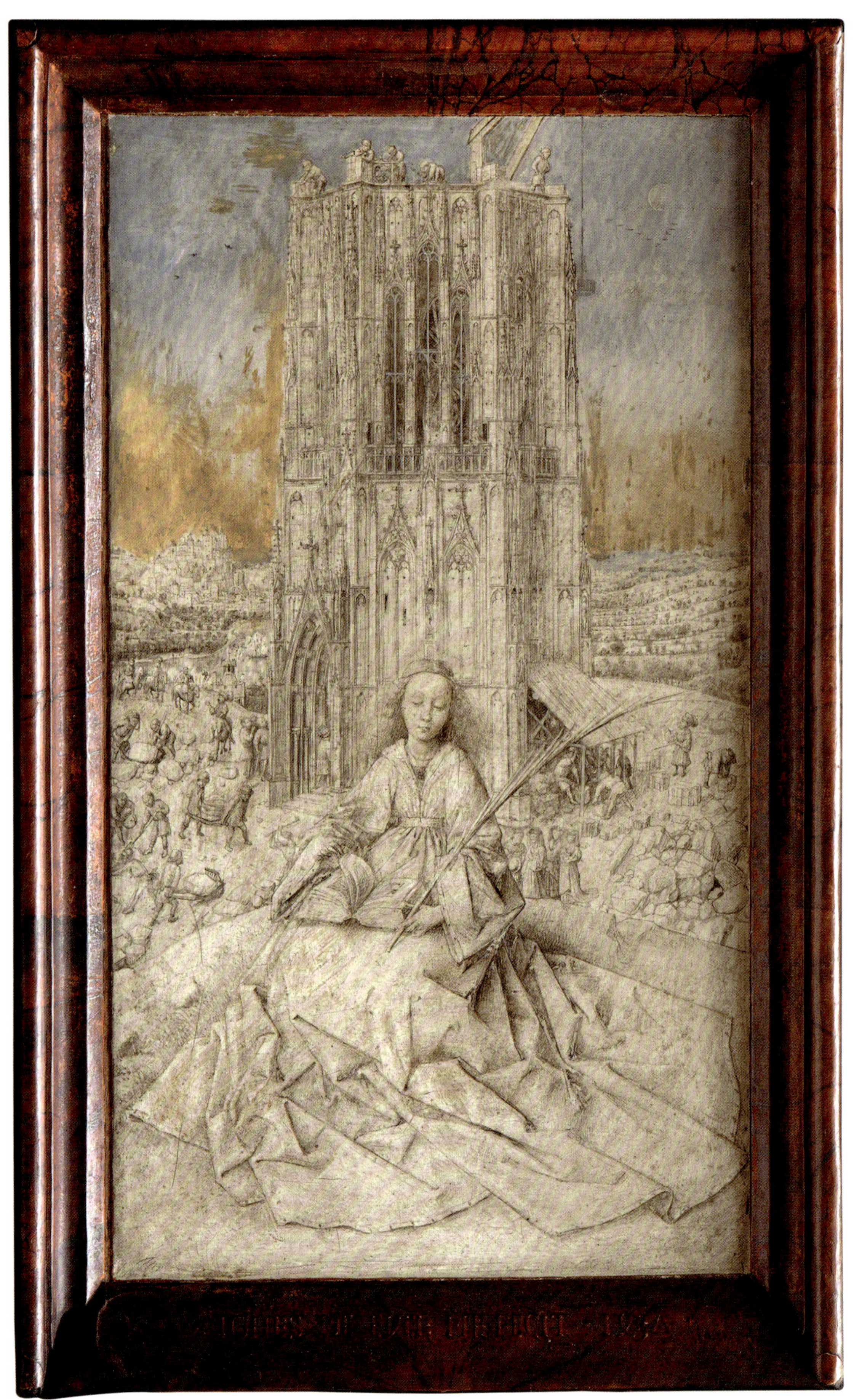
IOHES · DE · EYCK · ME · FECIT · 1437

Van Eyck's *Saint Barbara* constitutes the earliest known independent monochrome work on panel – that is, a work created neither as a preparatory study nor as part of a religious image – and it therefore holds a significant place in the development of grisaille painting. The unusual character of this work for the period – a fine drawing in metalpoint, India ink and oil with an original frame painted and signed by the artist – has been the subject of much debate about van Eyck's intention. Did he mean to produce a finished drawing, or is this an unfinished painting? Whatever the reason behind its appearance, the fact that the *Saint Barbara* was collected as a work of art in its own right, from as early as the sixteenth century or even before, is evidence of a nascent taste for independent monochrome works.

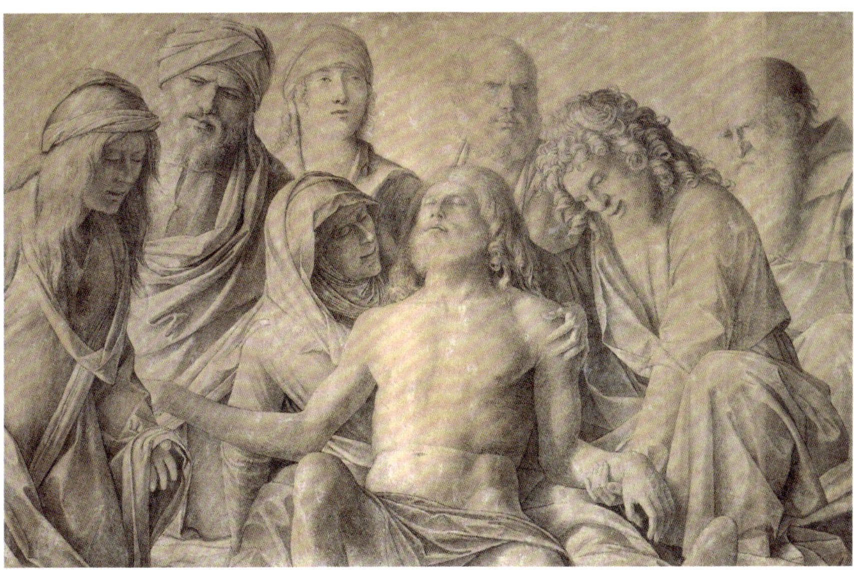

inscription, 'ioh[anne]es de eyck me fecit 1437' ('Jan van Eyck made me 1437'), in archaic lettering on the lower edge of the frame, looks as though it has been chiselled, creating an illusion of stone. It was customary at this time for a frame to be completed before the painting began; the presence of a frame here, therefore, does not necessarily reflect a finished work.[4] The *Saint Barbara* demonstrates how a master colourist like van Eyck thought visually in monochrome.

The panel's unusual appearance has sparked ongoing debate about what it is – a finished drawing, an unfinished painting or a work that began as one thing and became another.[5] However, the desire to classify the panel according to traditional categories obscures its very ingenuity. More telling is the fact that the *Saint Barbara* panel was collected and admired within erudite humanist circles early on. It was owned, for example, by the Ghent humanist painter Lucas de Heere during the sixteenth century, where it was seen and recorded by his pupil, Karel van Mander, the great Northern biographer of artists. In his 1604 *Schilderboek (Painter's Book)*, van Mander praised van Eyck's use of 'dead colour' in the panel, which is particularly interesting as an example of early notions of grisaille painting as a 'colourless' art.[6] This record reveals a fascination among Northern artists and collectors for monochrome painting at this date, a taste that developed in parallel with the appreciation of drawings as independent works of art.

A magnificent monochrome painting that has led scholars to pose similar questions is the *Lamentation over the Dead Christ* (about 1490) by Giovanni Bellini (active about 1459; died 1516), which has been alternatively described as a finished work or as a preparatory underdrawing for an unfinished painting (fig. 18).[7] In this large horizontal panel, the figures are arranged across the foreground in a manner similar to a frieze. The subtle differences in tonal values and in the modelling with light and shadow are far more sophisticated

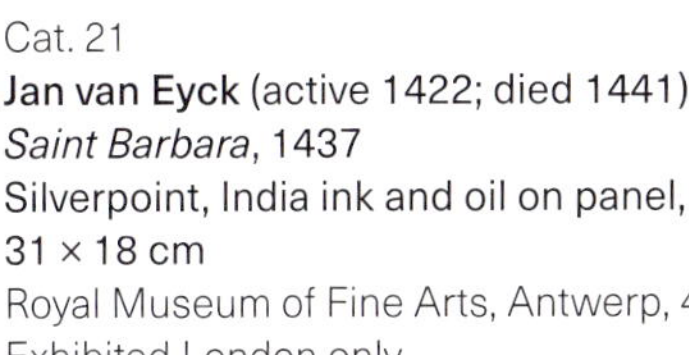

Cat. 21
Jan van Eyck (active 1422; died 1441)
Saint Barbara, 1437
Silverpoint, India ink and oil on panel,
31 × 18 cm
Royal Museum of Fine Arts, Antwerp, 410
Exhibited London only

Fig. 18
Giovanni Bellini (active about 1459; died 1516)
Lamentation over the Dead Christ, about 1490
Tempera on wood, 76 × 121 cm
Galleria degli Uffizi, Florence

and elaborate than in typical underdrawings, which, in Venice at this time, tended to be much more roughly outlined.

A new independent aesthetic

Aside from such early, isolated cases, independent grisaille paintings began to be produced on a wide scale during the latter half of the sixteenth century, particularly in Northern Europe. Pieter Bruegel the Elder (active 1550/1; died 1569), a pioneer of this technique, produced three independent grisaille panels during the 1560s.[8] *Christ and the Woman taken in Adultery*, for example, showcases Bruegel's mastery of chiaroscuro effects, an element he was better able to explore in a reduced black-and-white palette (fig. 19). The highly sophisticated and nuanced play of light and shadow in this picture enabled Bruegel to convey the dramatic narrative with great vividness. In the brightly lit foreground, Pharisees and Scribes accuse a woman of adultery, while Christ defends her with a silent, powerful reply that exposes all men as sinners. Christ's dispersal of the executioners is implied by the crowd's scattering into a gradually darkening background. The grey colour palette recalls stone and reinforces the subject: according to the Scriptures, the punishment for adultery was stoning. Interestingly, the picture remained in Bruegel's family long after his death in 1569.[9] This early provenance is noteworthy, since grisaille paintings were often particularly prized by artists, who made them either for themselves or for people close to them for personal enjoyment and contemplation.

The magnificent grisaille by Hendrik Goltzius (1558–1617), *Without Ceres and Bacchus, Venus would Freeze* (1599) is the only surviving work by the great Northern printmaker using this technique (cat. 22).[10] With astonishing facility, Goltzius employed the brush and oil paint, solely in shades of grey, to create virtuoso plays of light and shadow, convincingly modelling the forms of the three protagonists. Goltzius turned to a favourite maxim from the ancient poet Terence which elaborated that without food and wine, love grows cold. The artist seductively positioned Venus, Ceres and Bacchus on a four-poster bed with Cupid at their feet, surrounded by several flying putti and abundant food and drink.

The preparatory drawing for this work (about 1599, Royal Museum of Fine Arts of Belgium, Brussels) reveals that Goltzius initially conceived the composition with the use of some colour, particularly pinks for the flesh. The present work, in which Goltzius translated the design into complete monochrome, reveals a complex and sophisticated work process, involving two initial layers of underdrawing and an upper grisaille layer.[11] The existence of an engraving by Jan Saenredam after Goltzius's design, dated a year later, has led many to infer that Goltzius's grisaille was made as a model for that print.[12] But this would have been uncharacteristic for Goltzius, whose designs for prints were rather cursory. The high degree of finish and the presence of a signature and date suggest that the grisaille functioned as an independent work of art that was subsequently considered profitable to reproduce in print.[13] One year later, in 1600, the artist gave up printmaking for polychrome painting. It is interesting to note, then, that Goltzius, a printmaker accustomed to working in black and white, first experimented with the oil medium in monochrome before turning to colour painting.

The Dutch painter Adriaen van de Venne (1589–1662) was the first artist to specialise solely in grisaille painting for the majority of his career. Relocating in 1625 from Middleburg to The Hague, where he remained until his death in 1662, van de Venne abandoned his earlier polychrome panoramas depicting the Dutch political and cultural elite for small-scale, swiftly painted monochrome genre scenes, usually of marginal members of society.[14] van de Venne created a popular and entirely new pictorial genre known as the *grawtje* or 'little grey one', an endearing diminutive of the Dutch word for grisaille, *grauw* (grey), also synonymous with the dispossessed folk van de Venne represented. As the numerous surviving examples testify, the artist strategically diversified his artistic production to cater to a broad market, resulting in paintings of variable size and quality.[15]

Arme Weelde, A Procession of Revelling Cripples and Beggars (1635) is one of van de Venne's finest grisailles (cat. 23). Several paupers are shown dancing

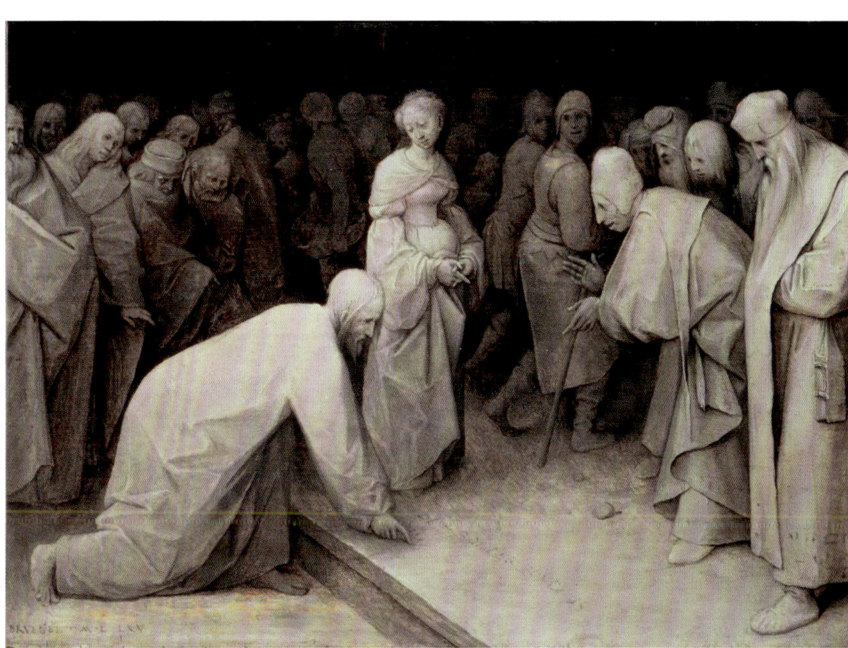

Fig. 19
Pieter Bruegel the Elder (active 1550/1; died 1569)
Christ and the Woman Taken in Adultery, 1565
Oil on panel, 34.4 × 24.1 cm
The Samuel Courtauld Trust, Courtauld Institute of Art Gallery, London, P.1978.PG.48

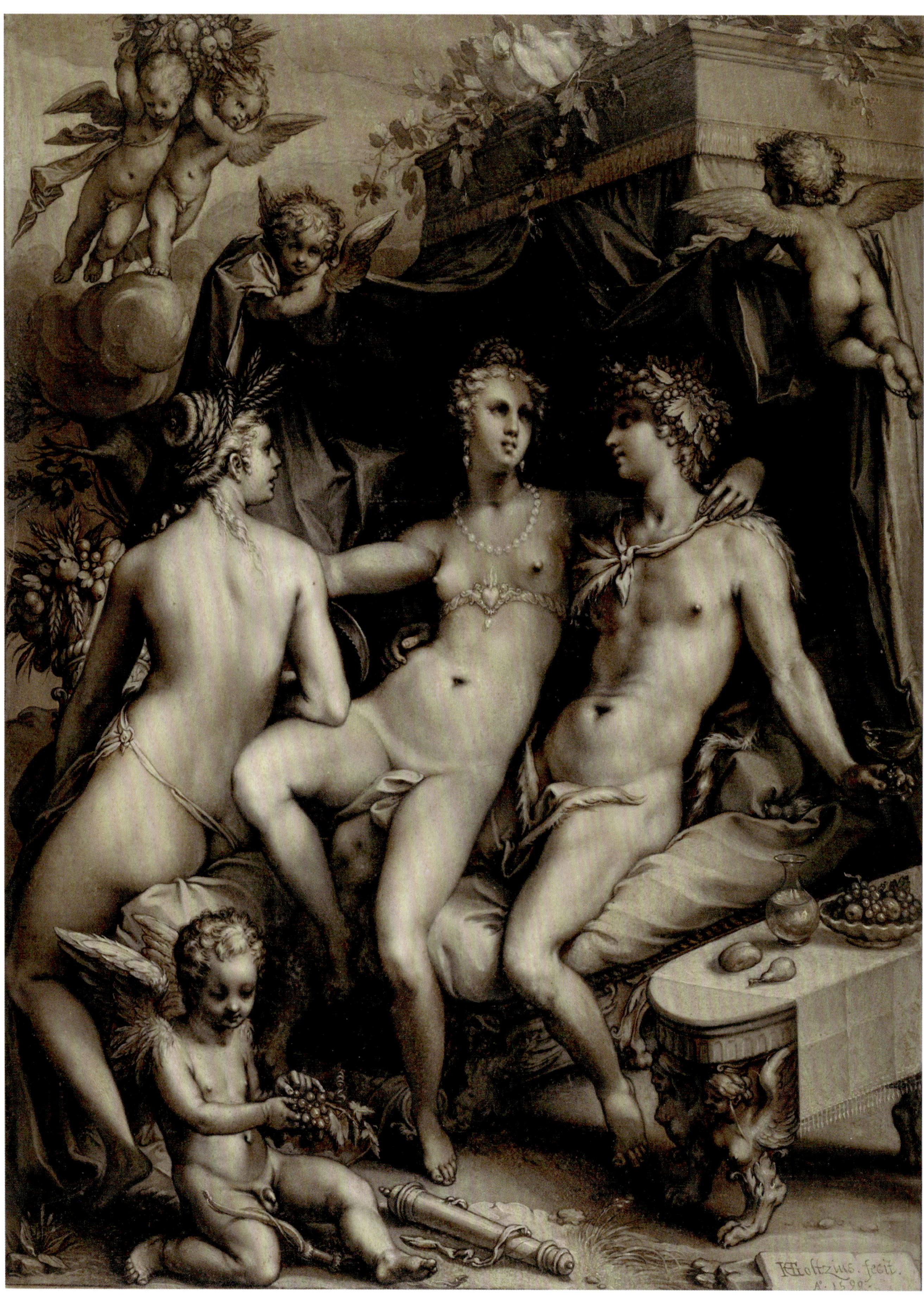

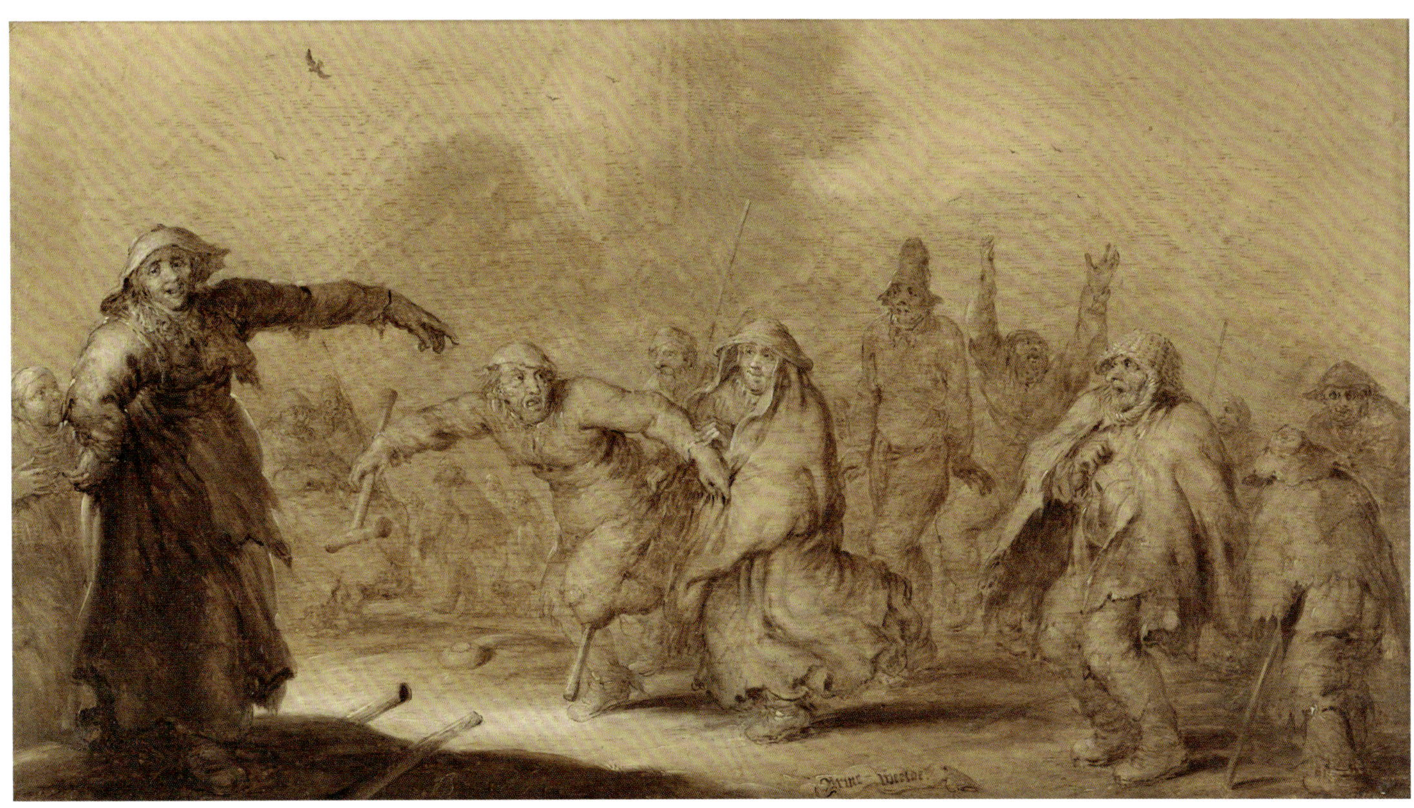

to the music of a hurdy-gurdy player on the right, who wears an inverted wicker basket on his head, alluding to a world turned upside down. The accomplished composition and the rare inclusion of a signature and date suggest that the work was aimed at a sophisticated client. The banderole with an inscription in the lower foreground has a double function, being both the title of the painting, 'Arme weelde' or 'poor luxury', and perhaps also alluding, via a contradictory and ambiguous figure of speech, to the pathetic spectacle of the peasants dancing – one of the few pleasures that they were able to enjoy, but that was most likely amusing to the beholder of such a work.[16]

The clever inclusion of an interlocutor, the raggedy-dressed woman standing with her arm outstretched in the left foreground, directs the viewer's attention to both the scene and the artist's fluid technique. Van de Venne's swift handling of the thin oil medium conveys a sense of dynamic movement, with the brushwork highly visible. This technique, along with the drab but richly nuanced palette, reinforces the low economic standing of the protagonists. Thus van de Venne's use of the grisaille medium was intimately linked to his low subject matter.

Cat. 22
Hendrik Goltzius (1558–1617)
Without Ceres and Bacchus, Venus would Freeze, 1599
Chalk, ink and oil on paper, 43.5 × 32.1 cm
The British Museum, London, 1861,0810.14
Exhibited London only

Cat. 23 and detail, overleaf
Adriaen van de Venne (1589–1662)
Arme Weelde (Poor Luxury), A Procession of Revelling Cripples and Beggars, 1635
Oil on panel, 33.3 × 56.3 cm
Museum Boijmans Van Beuningen, Rotterdam, inv. 1896(OK)

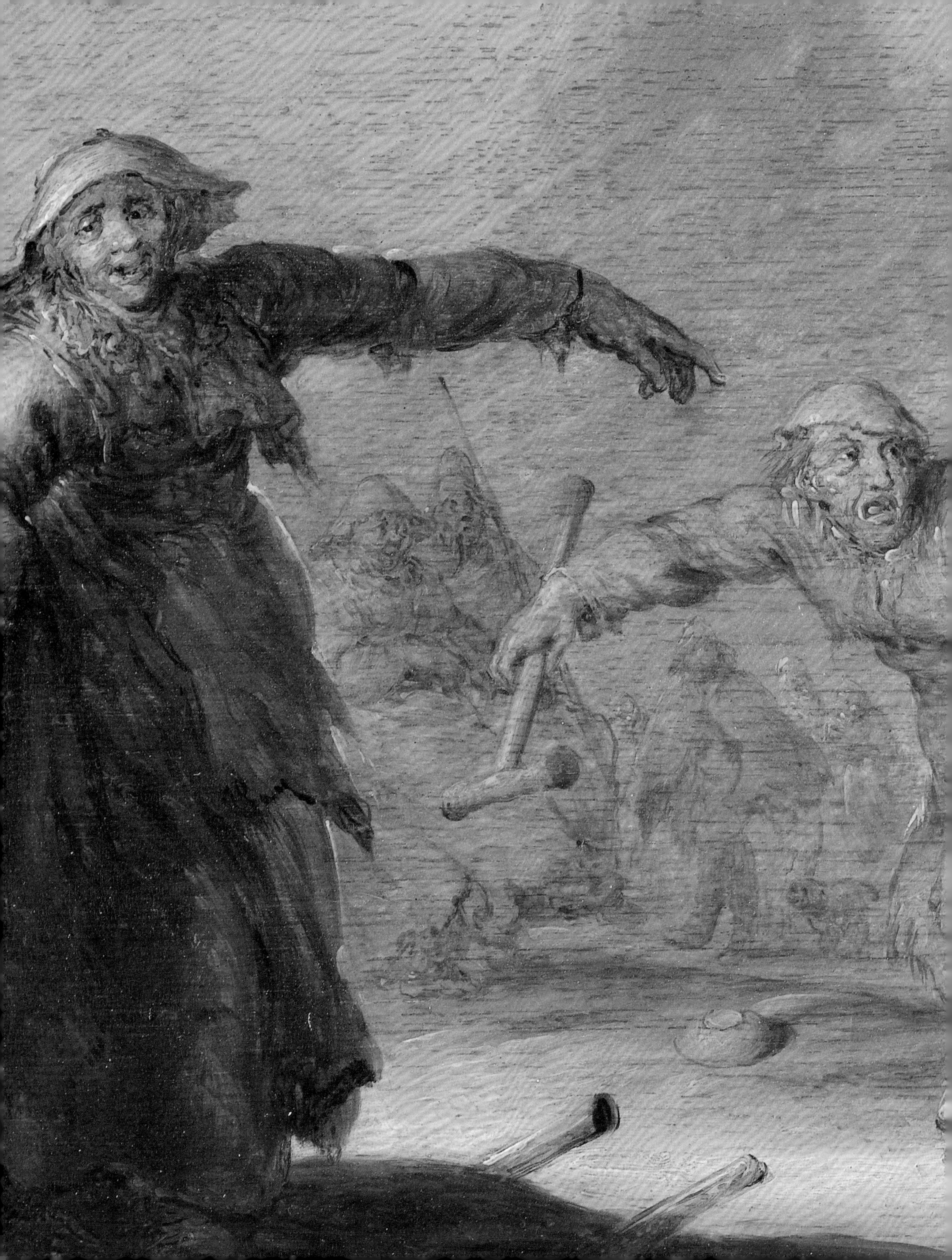

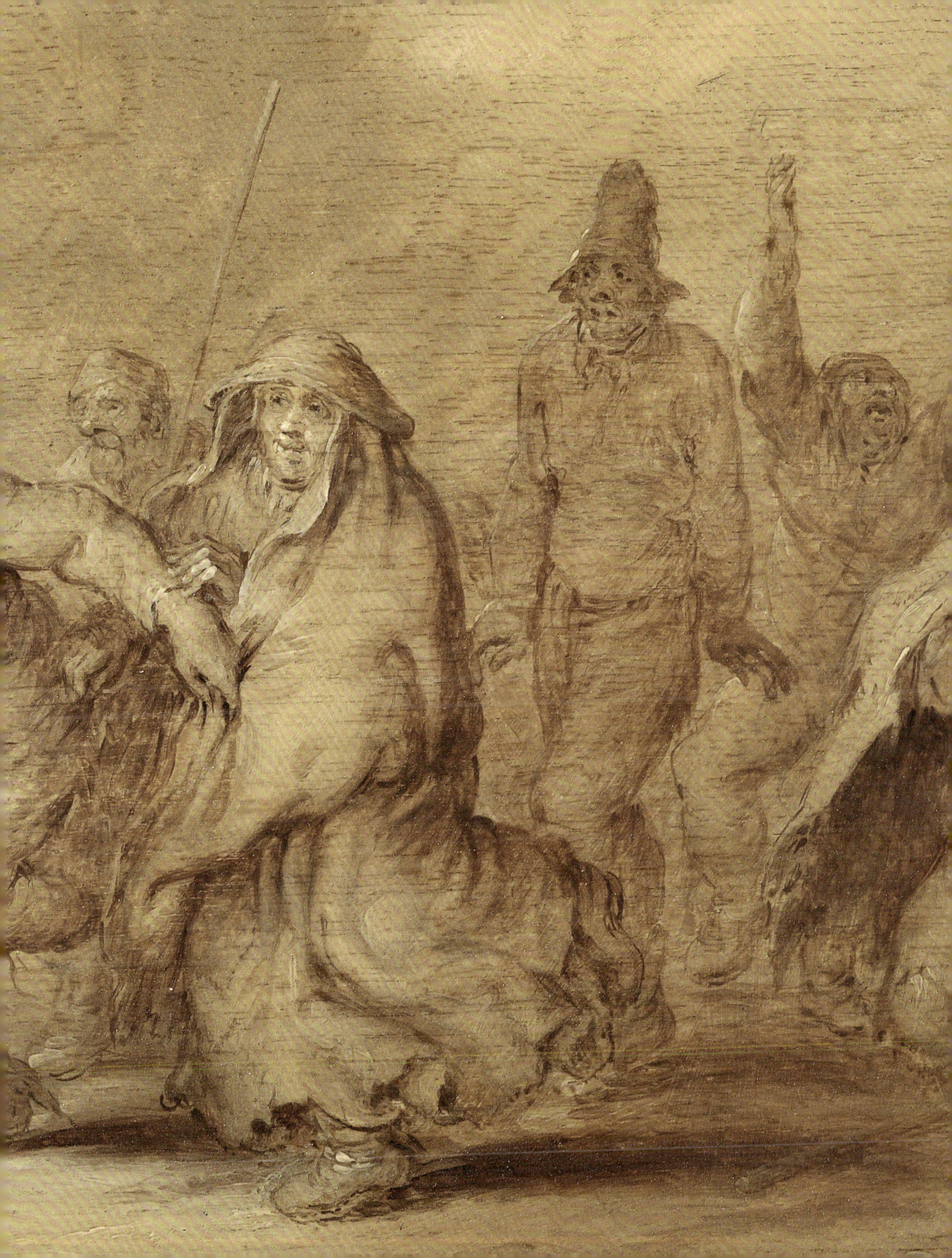

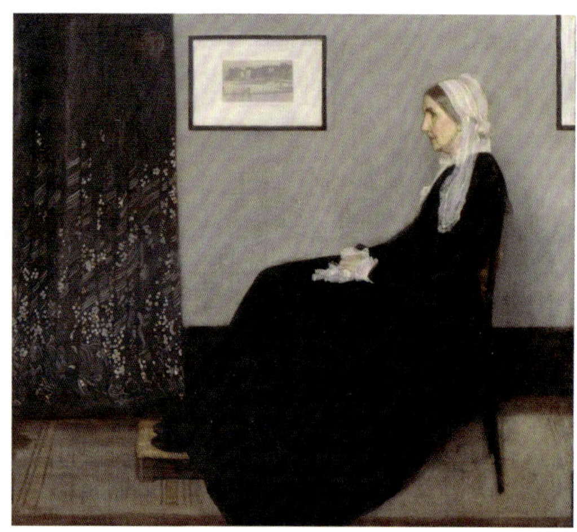

Unconventional monochrome portraits

A reduced black-and-white palette continued to captivate the imaginations of painters well into the nineteenth century. For example, James McNeill Whistler (1834–1903) became fascinated with exploring the delicate variations of certain colour hues, and in his *Arrangement in Grey and Black No. 1* (1871), Whistler created a harmony of vertical and horizontal black, white and grey accents (fig. 20). Seated in profile against a grey wall with black skirting and hung with Whistler's own black-and-white prints (enclosed by white mounts and black frames), Anna Matilda, Whistler's mother, inhabits a shallow yet charged pictorial space. Her black mourning clothes, stoic demeanour and intense gaze, combined with the cool tonality of Whistler's colour palette, imbue the work with a profound stillness. The painting was critically acclaimed, especially for its minimal colour.[17] This is the first time Whistler referred to a painting as an 'arrangement' of colours, choosing black, white and grey for his exploration.[18]

Paintings such as *Maternity (Suffering)* (about 1896–7) by Eugène Carrière (1849–1906) demonstrate how, by the end of the nineteenth century, independent black-and-white paintings were considered particularly appropriate for conveying subjective and symbolic meanings (cat. 24). Carrière, one of the most influential artistic figures in late nineteenth-century Paris, aligned himself with the Symbolist movement, first developed in French literature during the 1880s by writers such as Stéphane Mallarmé (1842–1898) and Paul Verlaine (1844–1896), who reacted against the rationalism and materialism they considered had come to dominate Western culture. Symbolist artists sought to evoke emotions and ideas rather than represent the world objectively – a deliberate reaction against Impressionism, which celebrated colour and its naturalistic representation, as well as Naturalism and Realism.

In reducing his palette to shades of grey and brown in *Maternity (Suffering)*, Carrière divorced himself from naturalistic representation, focusing instead on the suggestion of psychological states and on conveying symbolic

Fig. 20
James McNeill Whistler (1834–1903)
Arrangement in Grey and Black No. 1, 1871
Oil on canvas, 144.3 × 162.5 cm
Musée d'Orsay, Paris, RF699

Cat. 24
Eugène Carrière (1849–1906)
Maternity (Suffering), about 1896–7
Oil on canvas, 81.3 × 65.4 cm
Amgueddfa Cymru – National Museum
Wales, Gwendoline Davis Bequest, 1951,
NMW A 2434

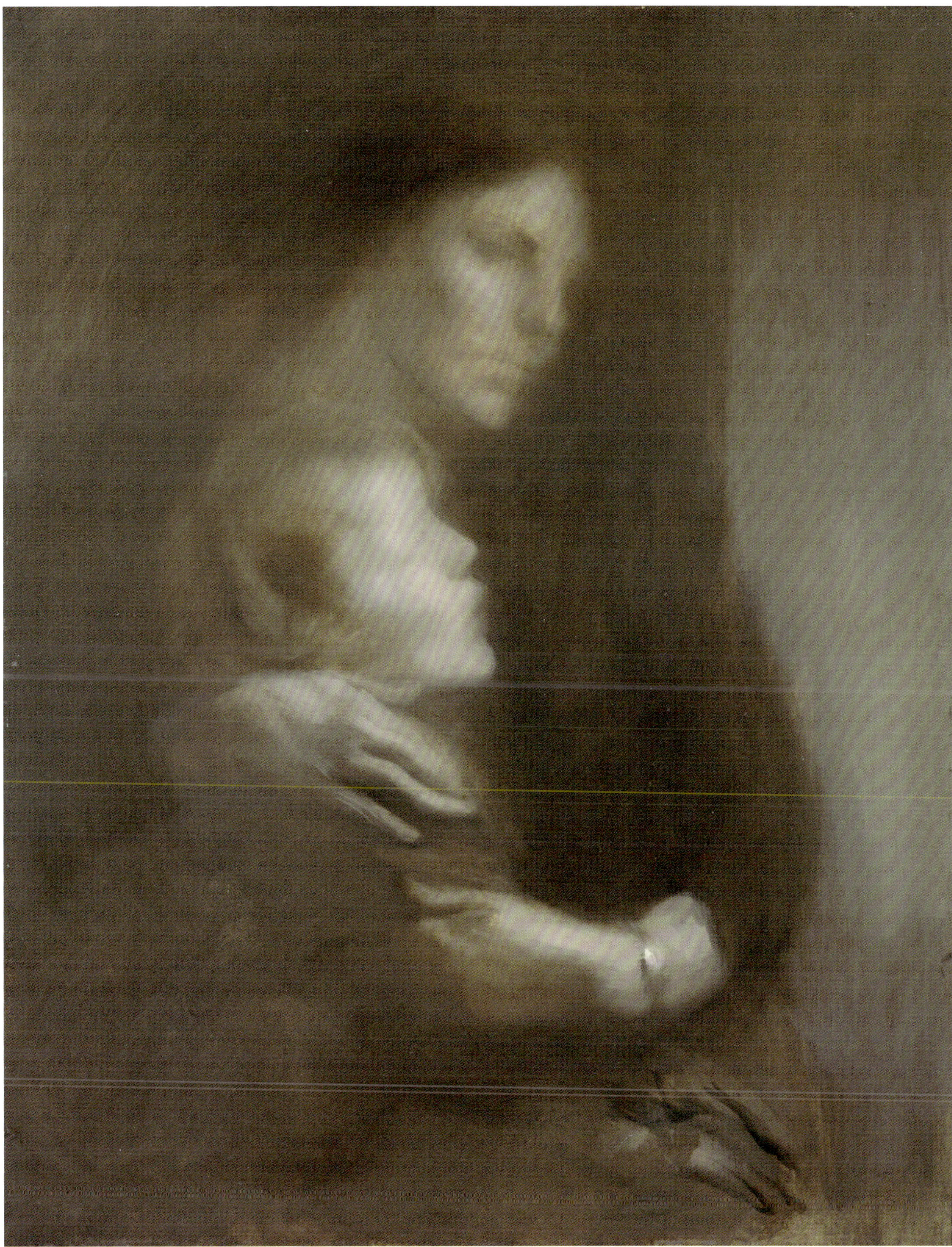

meaning. While Carrière's wife, Sophie, and his eldest daughter, Elise, were probably the models for this image, the dark palette and blurred effects create an unsettling family portrait. The mother and child, and the spiritual bond between them, were a frequent motif in Carrière's work, recalling one of the oldest image-types in Western art – the Virgin holding the Christ Child. The French art critic Gustave Geffroy commented on how Carrière transformed the traditionally calm and serene demeanour of the Madonna and Child into a pessimistic bourgeois vision of modern maternity: in a number of works the mother's worried and anxious appearance seems to be 'perpetually fending off illness and death'.[19] Carrière's gloomy reflections on contemporary motherhood are expressed through his dark and dreary palette. In addition, he omitted extraneous details, softened outlines and set the figures against a neutral background, encouraging the viewer's awareness of the figures' emotional states whilst creating a sense of timelessness. Carrière's aesthetic influenced early twentieth-century pictorialist photographers such as Edward J. Steichen (1879–1973).

More than half a century later, the prolific Swiss artist Alberto Giacometti (1901–1966) painted several powerful portraits in a reduced colour palette, such as that of his young wife and frequent model, Annette. *Annette Seated* (1957) is executed in grey, black and white (cat. 25). A relentless student of the human form, Giacometti is best known for his elongated figural sculptures, but he also produced a number of accomplished paintings, drawings and prints.[20] In *Annette Seated*, Giacometti used a series of dark grey linear brushstrokes to craft the silhouette of a nude woman sitting in a frontal position. Situated at some distance from the viewer and surrounded by a grey mandorla shape, the diminutive figure seems to be simultaneously appearing and disappearing. The rudimentary linear frame inscribed on the canvas, which Giacometti reinforced with a secondary outer border, accentuates and delineates the space inhabited by the sitter. Giacometti's insistence on using line to model his sitters has led to his paintings being regarded as drawings with a 'web of lines', in oil on canvas.[21]

Although Giacometti sculpted from memory, he painted from life. The distant, austere and mysterious character of paintings like *Annette Seated*, however, seems to contradict this, suggesting instead that the individual identity of the sitter was not a primary concern for Giacometti. Rather, the painting appears to represent something more profound and universal than an individual likeness: it reveals the artist's subjective experience of seeing whilst producing the image.[22] In portraits such as *Annette Seated*, Giacometti's reduced

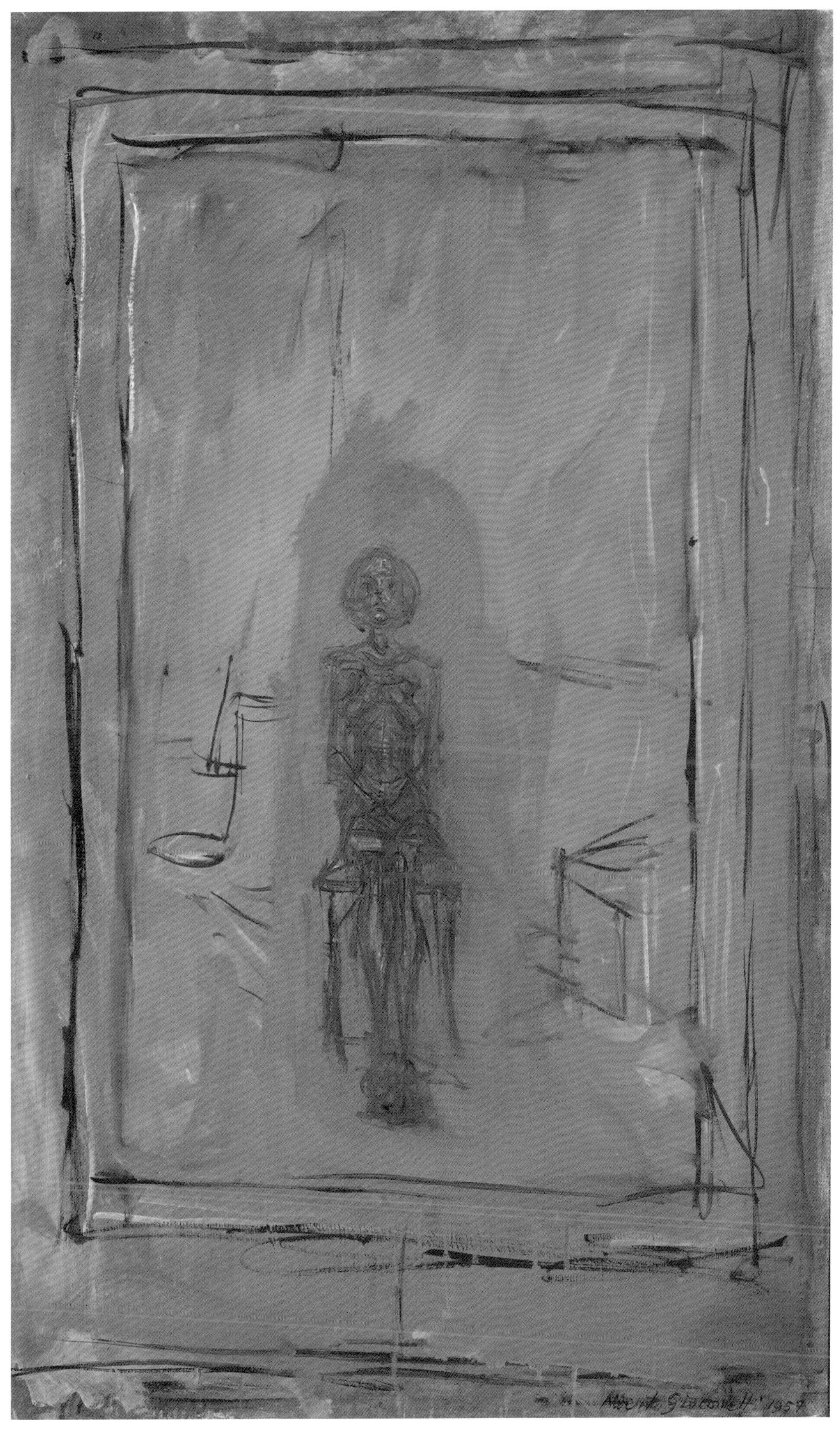

Alberto Giacometti 1958

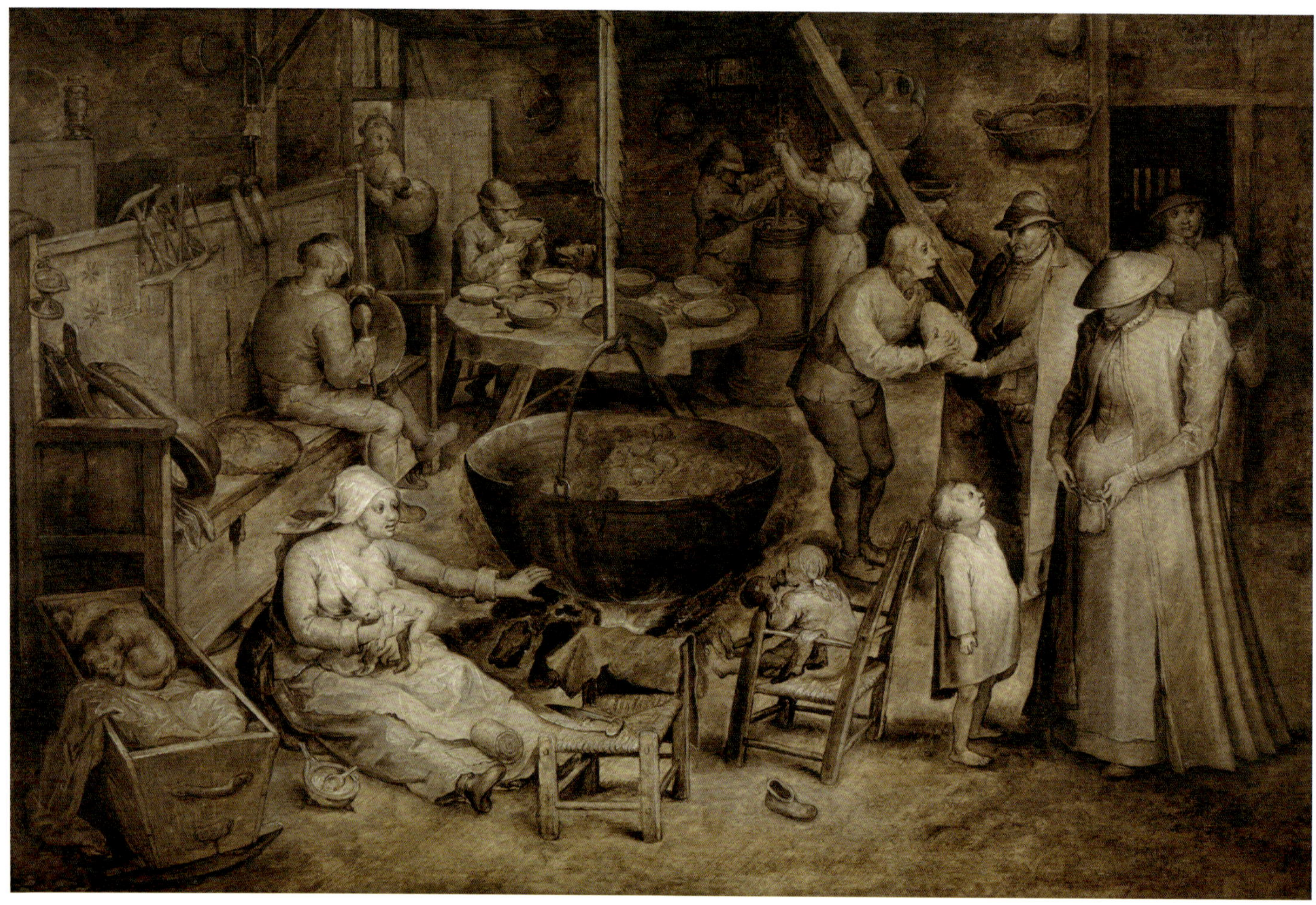

palette of grey hues is as much a protagonist as the sitter, emphasising – in painting as in sculpture – his personal, abstract approach to portraiture.

Colour translated to black and white

During the sixteenth century, around the same time that grisaille paintings began to be produced as independent works of art, the technique was also used to produce monochrome versions of existing colour paintings. These monochromes were more economical to produce and buy and were a new type of painting in a growing and varied art market. Handmade black-and-white painted versions also provided unique alternatives to reproductive prints that circulated in multiples. During the latter half of the century, artists working in Antwerp, then a vibrant artistic centre for the large-scale production of paintings, first produced such grisaille alternatives as collectable works of art.[23]

The posthumous fame of Pieter Bruegel the Elder was ensured by the numerous copies and variations after his compositions made by his two sons, Pieter Brueghel the Younger (1564–1637/8) and Jan Brueghel the Elder (1568–1625). The majority of these were painted in colour, but several were also

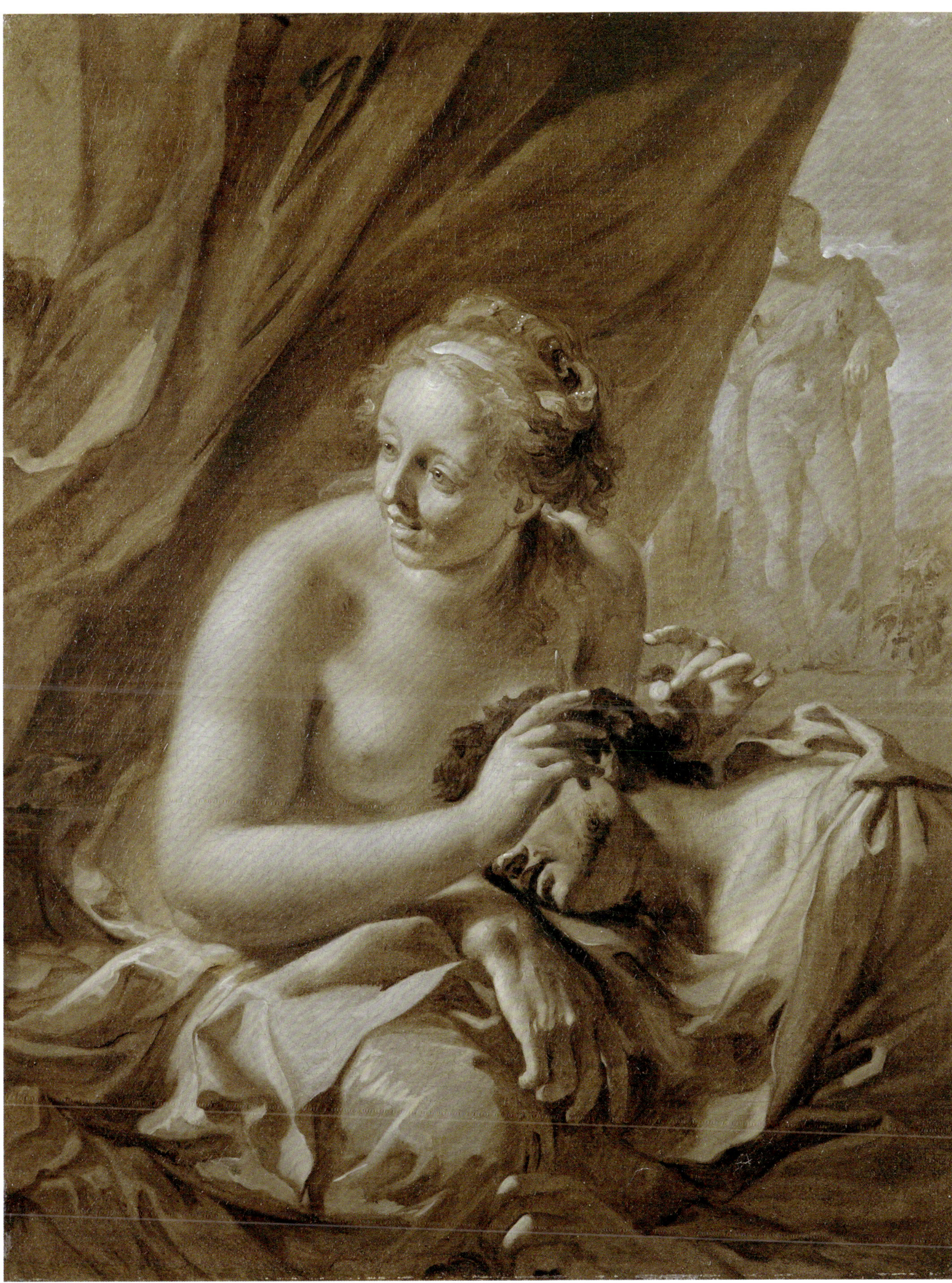

Ingres was a highly skilled and prolific draftsman who headed a large studio in which he trained numerous apprentices. In *Odalisque in Grisaille*, Ingres revisited his original 1814 polychrome composition, this time in greyscale. The painting remained in Ingres's studio until his death and may have been used as a tool for teaching. In the grisaille, Ingres has reduced and simplified the composition and removed the figure from its context by omitting the oriental details seen in the original oil painting. Moreover, he places her against a flat black background. The result is an unadorned, highly sensuous female nude. The painting was put on public display at the Metropolitan Museum of Art, New York, in 1938, and soon became a source of inspiration for many artists, including the Dutch-American abstract expressionist Willem de Kooning and the American painter Kerry James Marshall, who is known for his large-scale narrative history paintings featuring black figures.

realised in monochrome.[24] Both sons knew their father's grisaille technique, discussed above, as attested by their copies in colour and in monochrome after *Christ and the Woman taken in Adultery* (fig. 19).[25]

Jan Brueghel the Elder's *Visit to the Peasants* (cat. 26), a grisaille panel probably after a lost, polychrome painting by his father, represents a bustling peasant interior with figures of all ages engaged in a multitude of domestic activities. They are interrupted by the entry of an elegantly dressed couple, probably the landowners, who offer the father a gift of a cinnamon loaf, customary on the occasion of a birth. This popular composition engendered at least fifteen copies in colour and three in grisaille by both sons, of different sizes and on many different supports.[26] In the polychrome versions, the artists varied the colours in some of the figures' garments, suggesting a desire to distinguish the copies through subtle variations.[27] The complete reduction to grisaille ensured this distinction even more dramatically with all the elements translated to monochrome, including the coloured prints attached to the back of the wooden bench on the left.

The monochrome painting probably of *Samson and Delilah* by Adriaen van der Werff (1659–1722) attests to the continuation of this practice in Northern Europe throughout the seventeenth century (cat. 27). The work reveals a less familiar side of van der Werff, an artist particularly known for his refined use of colour. One of the most famous and successful Dutch painters at the turn of the eighteenth century, he fused the meticulously detailed *fijnschilder* (fine painter) technique, popularised by Gerrit Dou (1613–1675) and his followers during the middle of the seventeenth century, with a cool, classicising style. His elegant manner was admired by the wealthiest and most knowledgeable connoisseurs of the day, and earned him in 1697 the role of court painter to the Elector Palatine Johann Wilhelm II of Düsseldorf, where he was granted a knighthood for his services in 1703.

Samson and Delilah is a close variant of a now lost polychrome painting made by the artist in 1693 (formerly in the Gemäldegalerie, Schloss Sanssouci, Potsdam), of the same dimensions.[28] Van der Werff's monochrome copy varies slightly from the original: Delilah's left hand is above, rather than on Samson's shoulder, and her facial expression is more engaging; Samson's left hand is closer to Delilah's knee and the curtain in the background is drawn further out into the composition. These changes may reflect van der Werff's rethinking of details when working in grisaille. In the preparatory red-chalk drawing for the now lost polychrome painting, van der Werff included colour specifications, which suggests that he planned *Samson and Delilah* with colours in mind from the start and supports the idea that the grisaille was

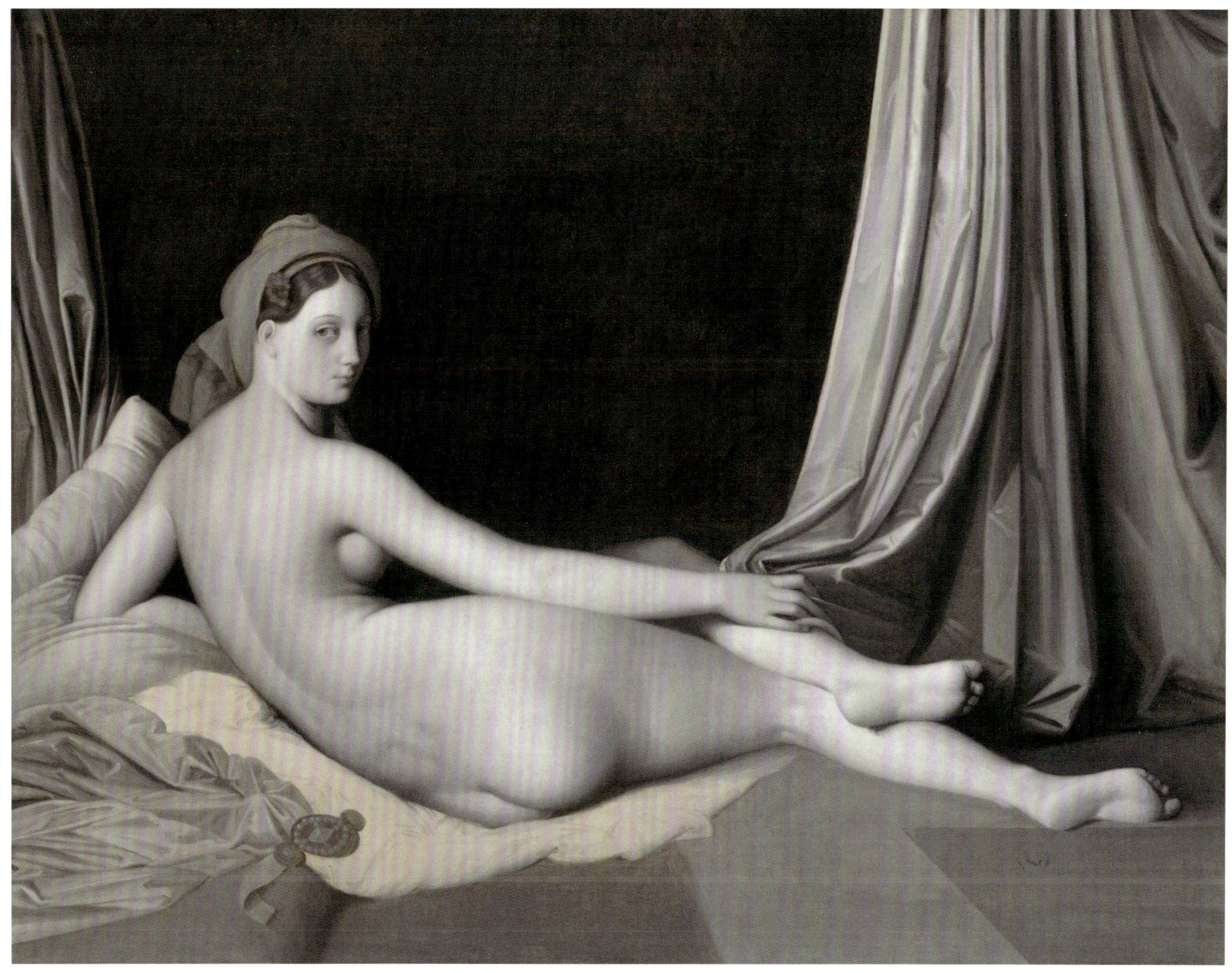

a subsequent exercise. Beyond the curtain, a colossal statue of the Farnese Hercules is visible, which when transformed into grisaille recalls one of the major functions of grey paintings – to imitate stone.[29] The term *ricordi*, that is, paintings that reproduce or record colour compositions in monochrome, has been used to describe such pictures.[30]

The most iconic grisaille made after a colour painting is the arresting *Odalisque in Grisaille* by Jean-Auguste-Dominique Ingres (1780–1867) and his workshop (cat. 28). It is a reduced version in black and white of Ingres's famous *Grande Odalisque* (fig. 21) and was painted for Napoleon's sister Caroline Murat, Queen of Naples. Of the at least five copies made by Ingres after his great masterpiece, this is the only version painted entirely in shades of grey. Ingres not only reduced the size of the canvas and the colour palette

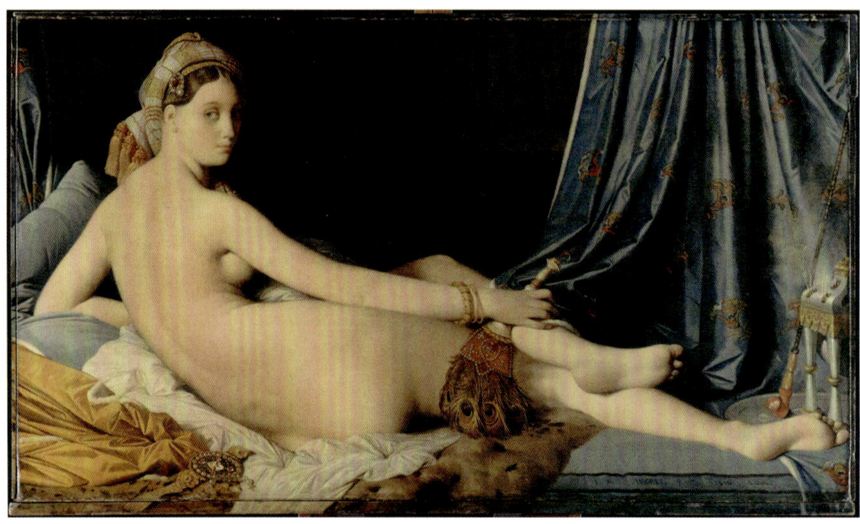

but also omitted a number of the oriental details and accessories, such as the figure's bracelets, peacock feathered fan, the decorative patterns on her headscarf and the brocade on the curtain on the right. Divorced from a recognisably oriental setting, the nude woman, no longer identifiable as a concubine in a harem, is abstracted and decontextualised, providing a pretext for Ingres to study the fall and nuance of light and shadow. The painting was recorded in the artist's studio at his death in 1867, suggesting that it held personal significance for the artist. It remained in the family until 1937, more than a century after its production.

Other artists famed for their mastery of colour also occasionally experimented with monochrome. *Ballet Rehearsal on Stage* (cat. 29), the only finished grisaille painting known by Edgar Degas (1834–1917), is a black-and-white version of a composition that the artist also realised in colour on two separate occasions, probably during the same year.[31] The grisaille is the largest of the three and the only one that is painted in oil on canvas. The presence of numerous *pentimenti* in the grisaille reveal Degas's reworkings directly on the canvas, making it likely that the grisaille was produced first, followed by a version in *essence* on paper (fig. 22) and then one in pastel, which is the most freely handled. This practice of first working out a composition in monochrome before considering colour is reminiscent of the long tradition of monochrome oil sketches first developed during the sixteenth century.[32] Degas's grisaille, however, is more worked up than an oil sketch and was independently exhibited at the first Impressionist exhibition of 1874, where it was both highly praised and, interestingly, described as a drawing. The painting was immediately acquired by the collector Gustave Mulbacher and, subsequently, by Count Isaac de Camondo, which indicates a regard for Degas's black-and-white painting as an independent work of art. The presence of the two colour versions suggests that Degas was experimenting with a variety of techniques and tonal ranges with this composition.

Fig. 21
Jean-Auguste-Dominique Ingres (1780–1867)
La Grande Odalisque, 1814
Oil on canvas, 91 × 162 cm
Musée du Louvre, Paris, RF 1158

Fig. 22
Hilaire-Germain-Edgar Degas (1834–1917)
Ballet Rehearsal, 1874
Oil, watercolour and pastel over pen-and-ink
on paper, 54.3 × 73 cm
The Metropolitan Museum of Art, New York,
H.O. Havemeyer Collection, Gift of Horace
Havemeyer, 1929 (29.160.26)

Cat. 29 and detail overleaf
Hilaire-Germain-Edgar Degas (1834–1917)
Ballet Rehearsal, 1874
Oil on canvas, 65 × 81 cm
Musée d'Orsay, Paris, RF 1978
Exhibited Düsseldorf only

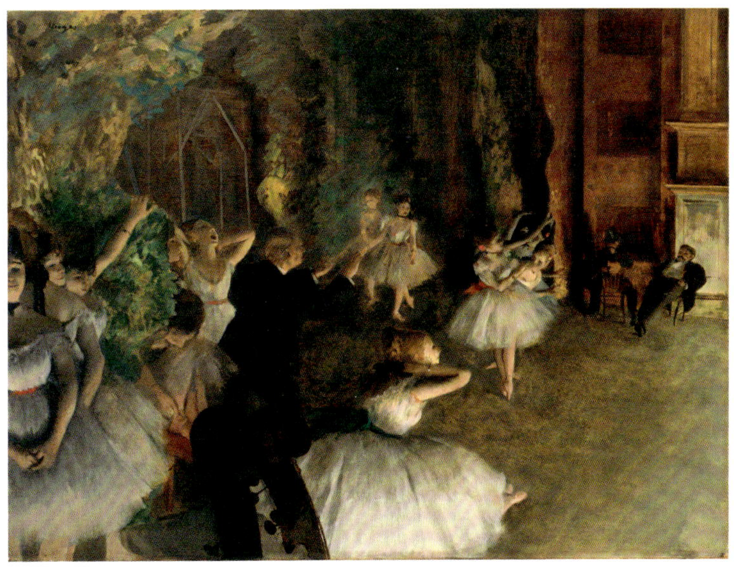

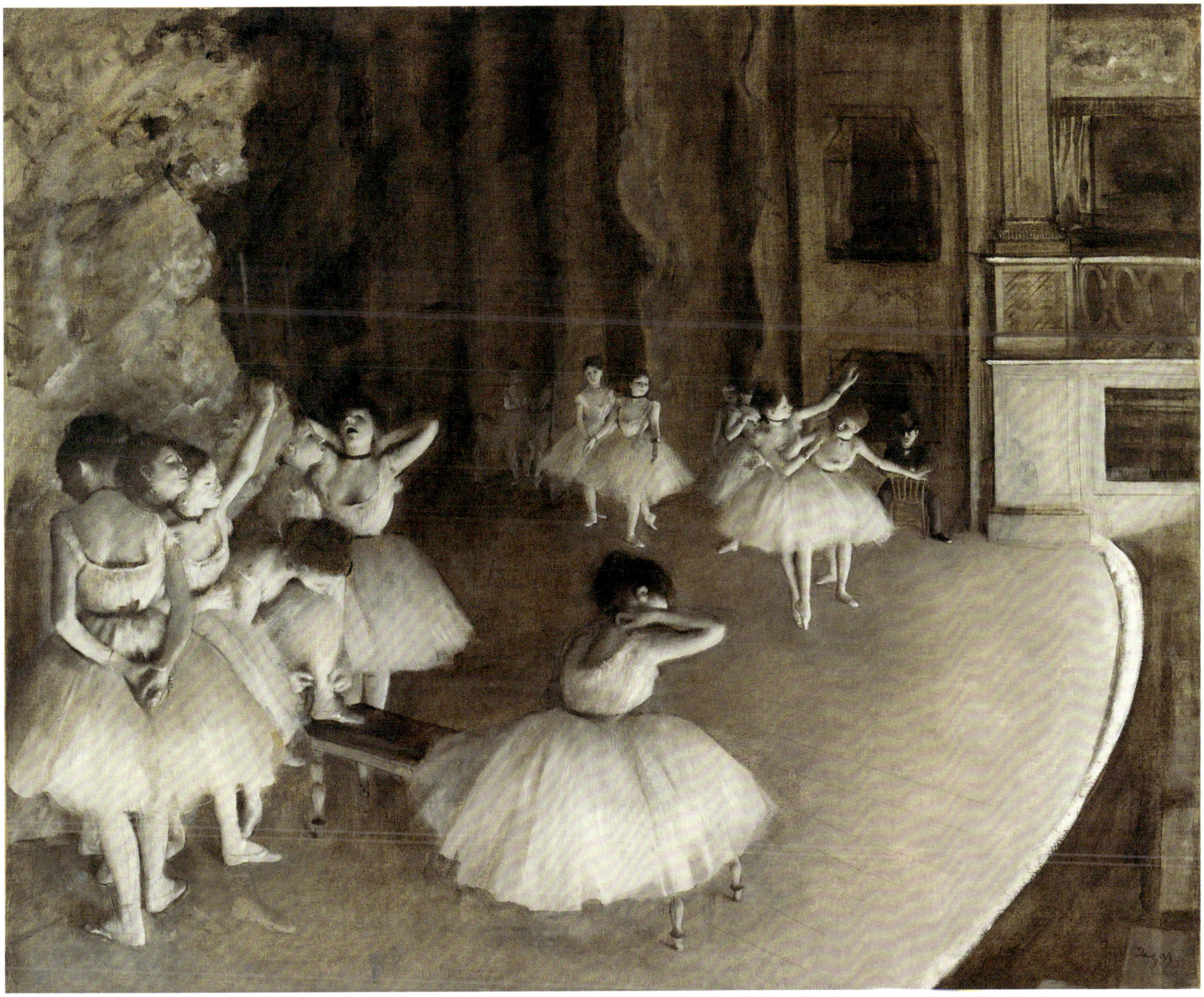

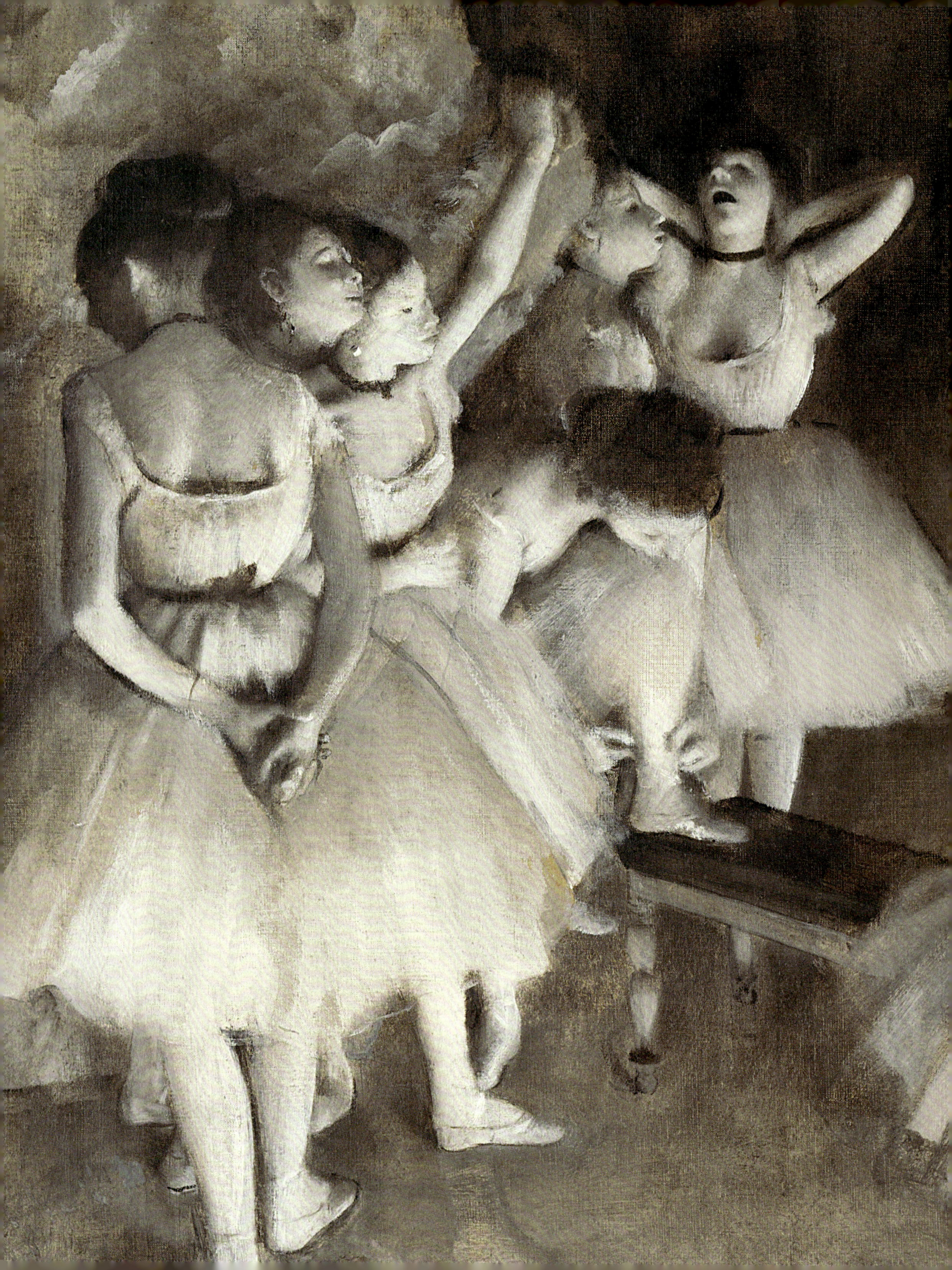

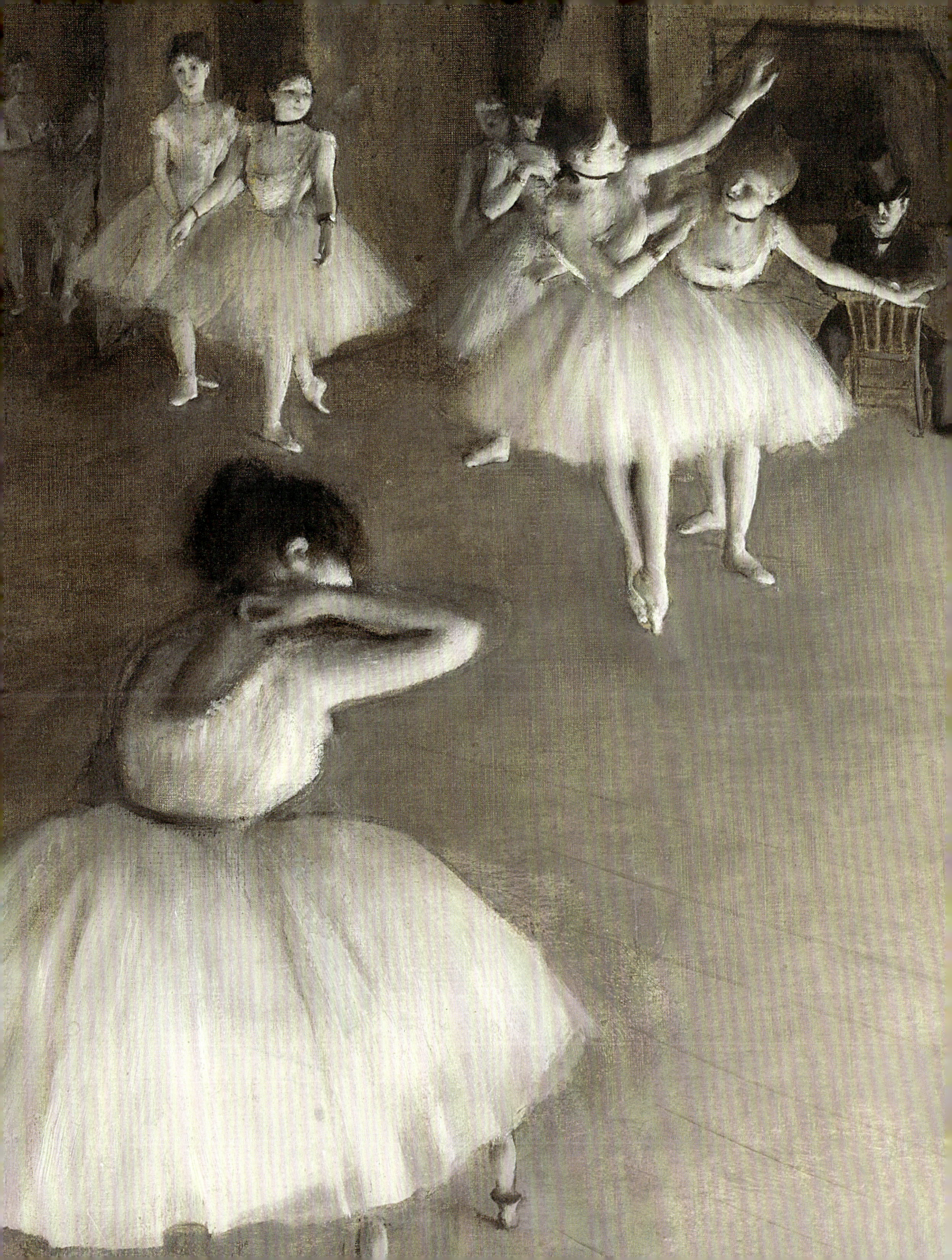

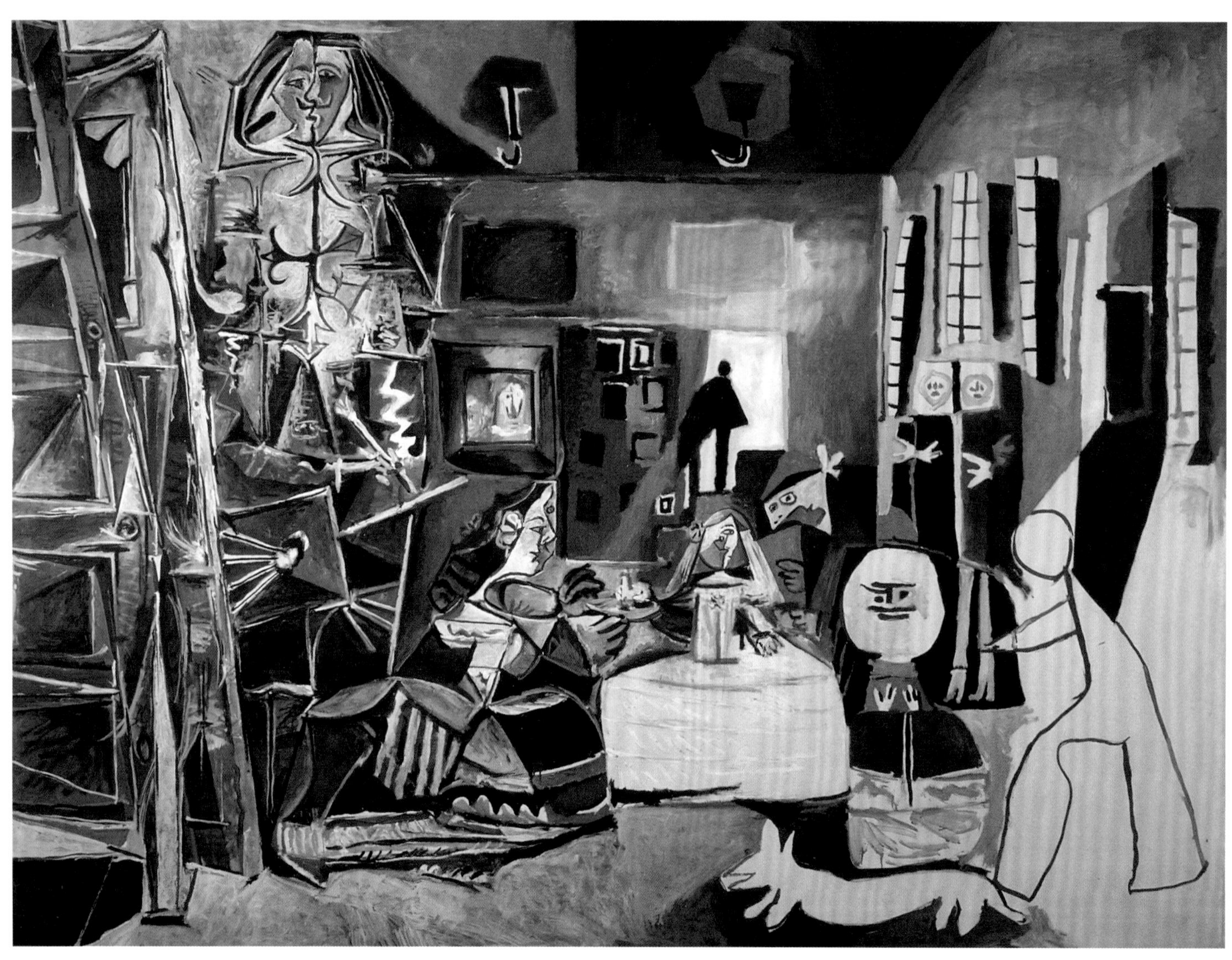

Fig. 23
Pablo Picasso (1881–1973)
Las Meninas (after Velázquez), 1957
Oil on canvas, 194 × 260 cm
Museu Picasso, Barcelona, MPB 70.433

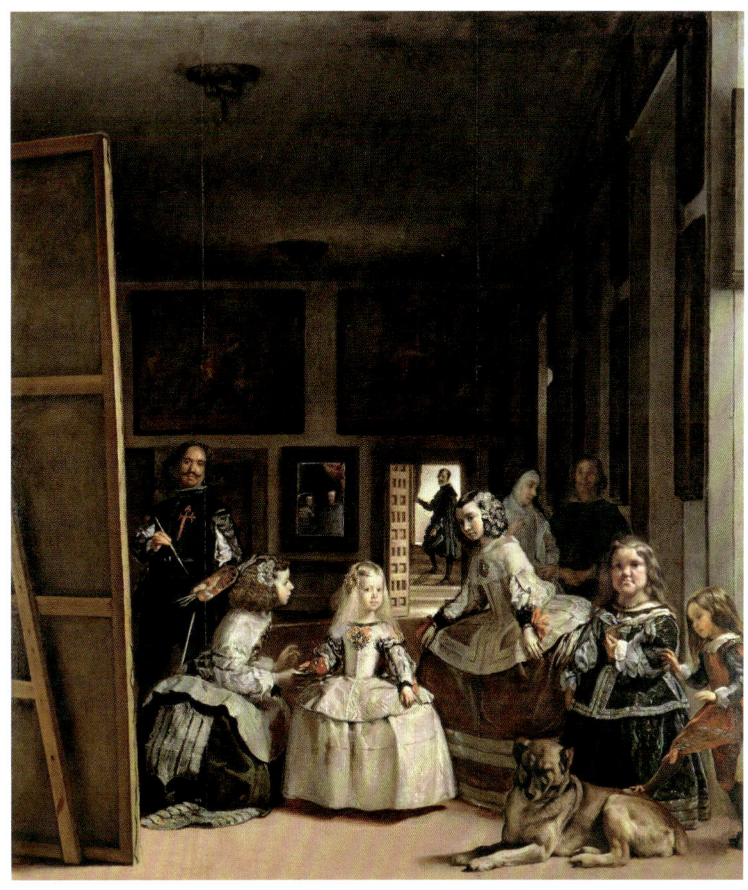

During the twentieth century, Pablo Picasso (1881–1973), a passionate
and knowledgeable student of Western European painting, produced works
intended to initiate a dialogue and competition with his artistic predecessors,
sometimes in black and white.[33] Picasso's *Las Meninas (after Velázquez)*
(fig. 23), a complex and nuanced appropriation of Diego Velázquez's *Las
Meninas* (fig. 24), is a prime example of Picasso's fascination with the old
masters, successfully translated into black and white. It is the first and largest in
a series of 44 paintings after Velázquez's work, either of the entire composition
or of certain figures. The series occupied Picasso from 17 August until 30
December 1957.[34] Although many of the paintings in the series are in colour,
this work, which reproduces Velázquez's entire composition, is the closest to
the original and most naturalistic despite its black-and-white palette. This first
attempt at dissecting Velázquez's painting in monochrome might be explained
by the fact that Picasso was working from a black-and-white photographic
reproduction. However, Picasso knew *Las Meninas* first-hand from his visits to
the Prado, where he had the occasion to study its rich colour palette in detail.
Subsequent works in the series were painted in colour, making it unlikely that
his reference to a black-and-white reproduction can fully explain his choice of
black and white.

After his initial exploration of Velázquez's entire composition, Picasso turned to individual figures or groups of figures. By far his favourite protagonist was the five-year-old Infanta Margarita María, first child of King Philip IV of Spain, who also occupies centre stage in Velázquez's masterpiece. Picasso studied her in full and bust length, in colour and in black and white, and in a variety of styles and levels of finish. He began by painting her in black and white in a Cubist idiom, as in the canvas painted on 21 August 1957 (cat. 30), in which he focuses on the placement of the lights and darks. His technique is quick and fluid; the lower portion of the Infanta's dress is swiftly painted with broad strokes. Despite the impression of spontaneity in Picasso's handling of the paint, the figure's upright, frontal pose exudes a sense of stability suitable for a princess.

At the age of 76, with a prolific career to boast of, Picasso's attempt to appropriate Velázquez in black and white recalls the ways in which apprentices were instructed to draw after the old masters in monochrome. But these exceptional paintings were no mere exercises: Picasso fundamentally transformed his model. In *Las Meninas (after Velázquez)* he altered the orientation from vertical to horizontal, shifted the position of the central figures, increased the prominence of the painter and multiplied and opened the windows on the right. More profoundly, working exclusively in black and white enabled Picasso to focus on contour and form and on spatial relationships, which he radically altered, rendering the figures and their surroundings flat against the picture plane. By opening the windows on the right, allowing bright light to enter the room, Picasso further enhanced the contrast between the darker interior and the lighter exterior.

Picasso played a pivotal role in the development of black-and-white painting during the twentieth century, producing countless works, in a variety of media, in monochrome.[35] His fascination with black and white also had a considerable influence on later modern artists working with a reduced palette. The monochrome versions by, in particular, Ingres, Degas and Picasso of colour compositions demonstrate how artists have used black and white as an innovative tool for exploring composition and perception.

Cat. 30
Pablo Picasso (1881–1973)
Las Meninas (Infanta Margarita María),
21 August 1957
Oil on canvas, 100 × 81 cm
Museu Picasso, Barcelona. Gift of
Pablo Picasso, MPB 70.436

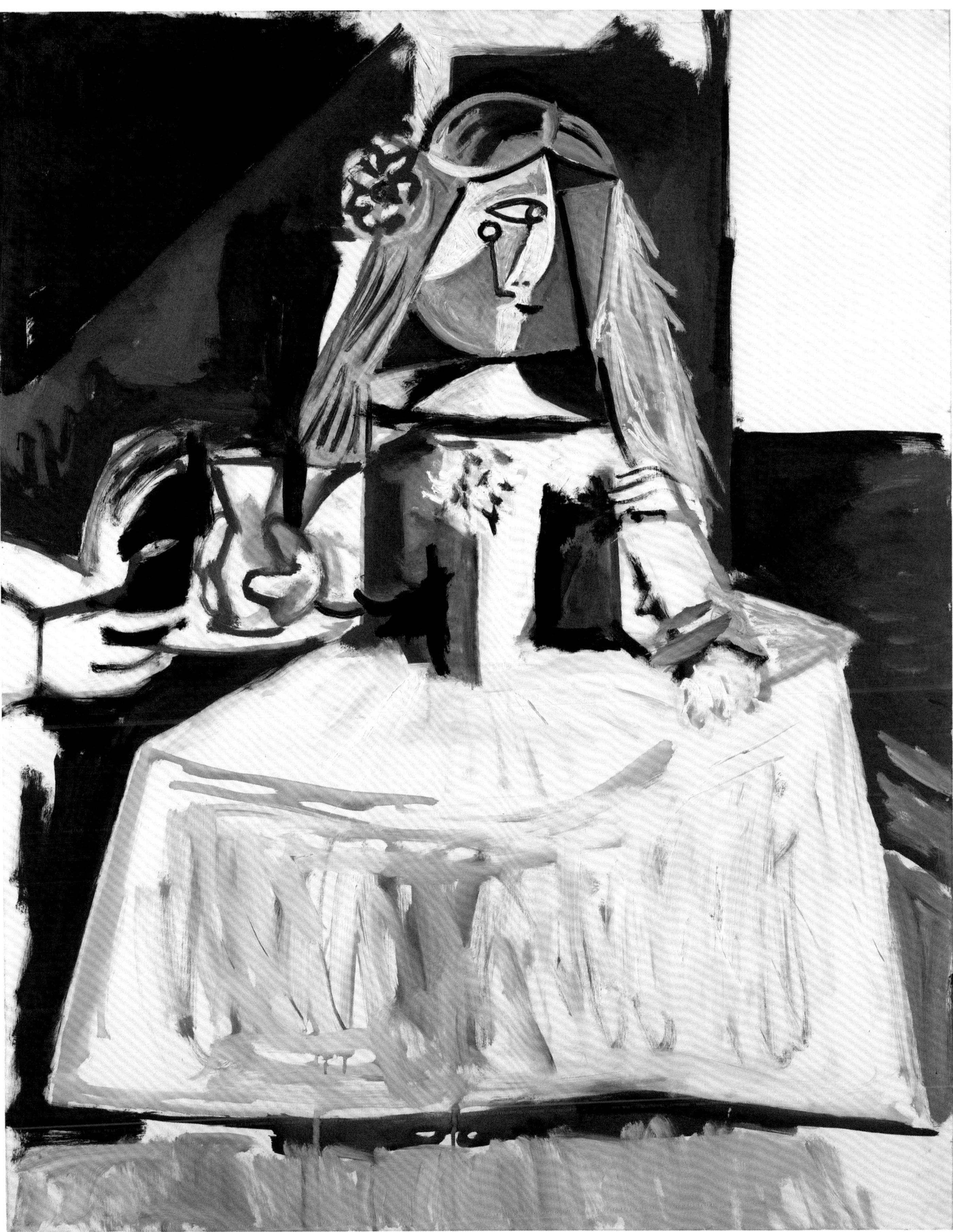

S P Q R

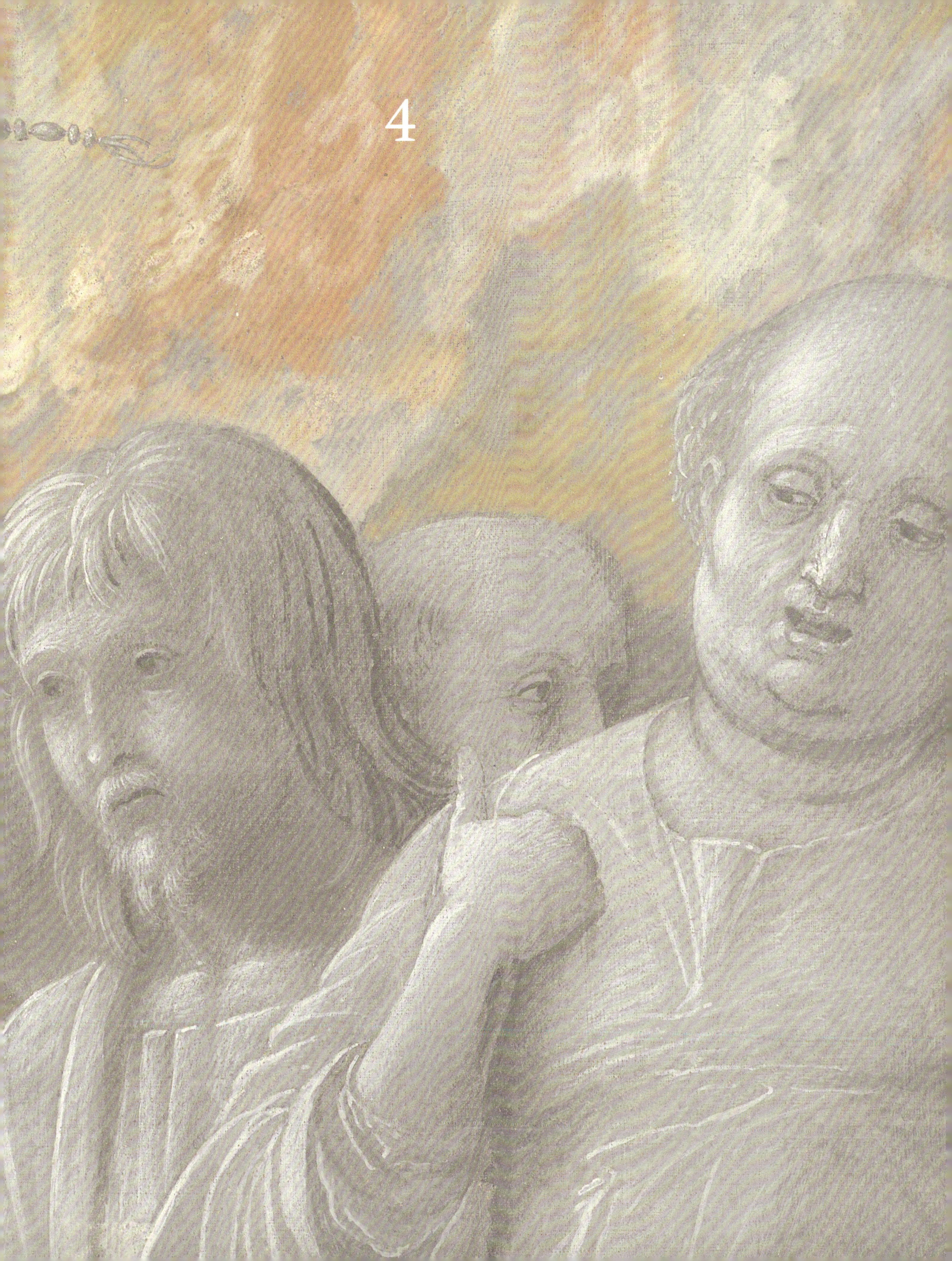
4

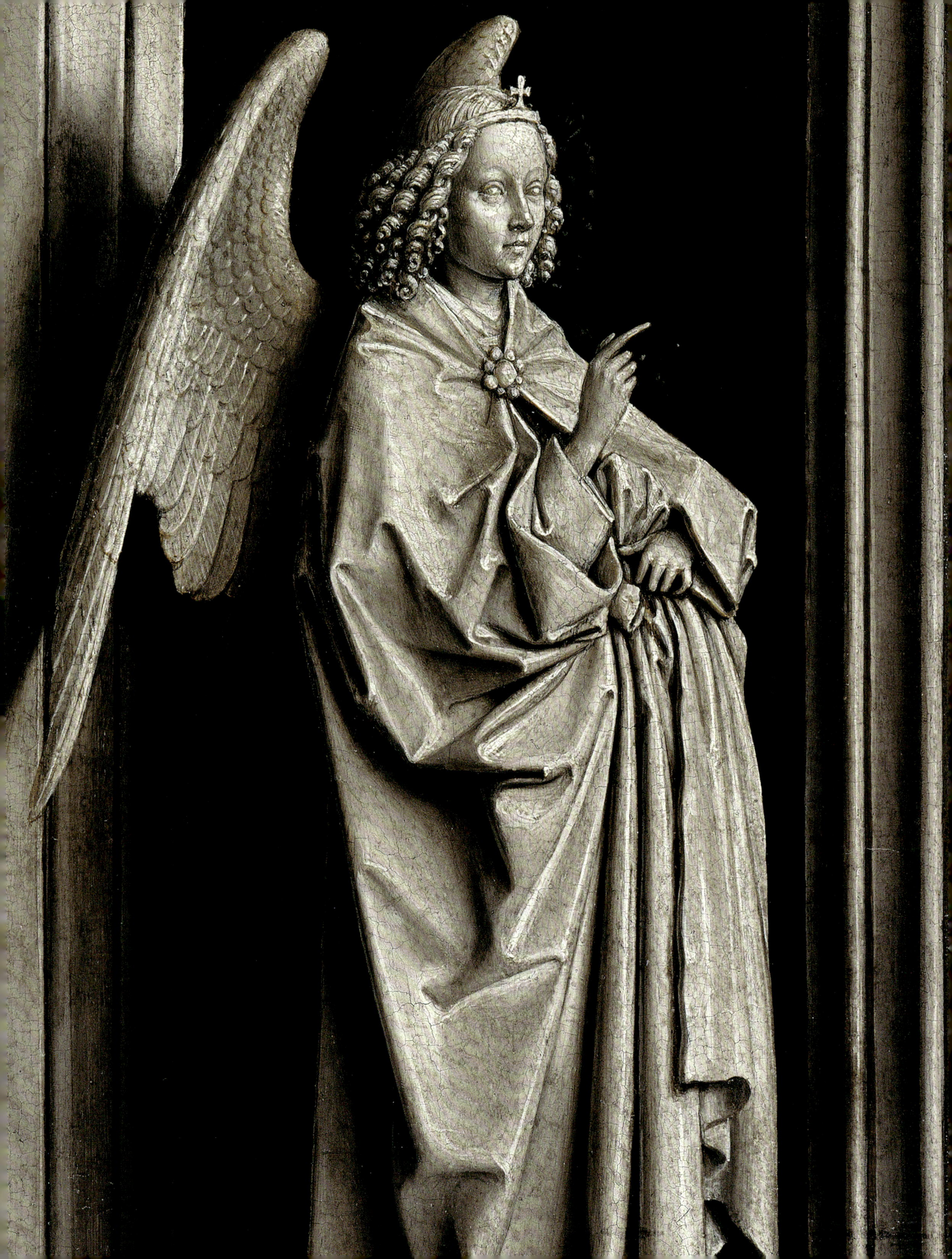

Monochrome Painting and Sculpture

Lelia Packer

For nearly five centuries artists have challenged themselves to represent sculpture and sculptural relief in paint. From medieval manuscript illuminators to eighteenth-century decorative painters, artists across Western Europe sought to create the illusion of stone sculpture in painting.

Italian Renaissance authors and artists who looked back at ancient literature would have been aware that painting in black and white had been closely linked to sculptural effects since antiquity. Pliny the Elder, for example, employed the term *color lapidum* (stone-coloured) to describe certain grisaille paintings, a term that was revived during the Renaissance and that alluded to the stone material monochrome painters sought to reproduce.[1] The architect and art theorist Leon Battista Alberti (1404–1472), in his treatise *De Pictura (On Painting)* of 1435, considered that the combination of white and black was important for a convincing three-dimensional effect.[2] Writing in 1550, the painter and biographer Giorgio Vasari (1511–1574) described monochromes as deriving from the copying of marble and bronze statues and figures in various sorts of stone.[3] Also during the sixteenth century, Italian artists and art theorists became engaged in the *paragone*, an intellectual and aesthetic debate about the relative merits of the different arts, such as painting and sculpture. By the eighteenth century, art critics such as Etienne La Font de Saint-Yenne, focused on the capacity of grisaille painting to imitate sculpture to the point of fooling the eye of the most astute connoisseurs.[4]

The earliest writings relating to the *paragone* date to the middle of the fourteenth century, when the Italian humanist and poet Petrarch (1304–1374) expressed his preference for sculpture over painting because of its durability, as testified by the numerous surviving ancient statues and the dearth of ancient paintings.[5] More than half a century later, Alberti considered sculptors mere craftsmen, requiring the guidance and rules of painters, whose task was more difficult.[6] Similarly, Leonardo (1452–1514) regarded painting as a science based on rules of perspective that demanded great *ingenio* (mental effort) in contrast to the mechanical art of sculpture, which in his view required greater mental than physical exertion.[7] A painting such as Titian's *Portrait of a Lady ('La Schiavona')* (cat. 31), in which the sitter is simultaneously portrayed as both colour painting and monochrome sculptural relief, reveals how artists engaged visually with these concepts. By showing the woman both from the front and in profile, Titian responded directly to advocates of sculpture who criticised painters for being able to depict only a single view of a figure, in contrast to sculptors who were able to work in three dimensions. The supremacy of painting over sculpture is further alluded to in the placement of Titian's initials (T. V.) on the raised parapet, the 'sculptural' element in the composition.

Jan van Eyck (active 1422; died 1441)
The Annunciation Diptych (The Archangel Gabriel), about 1433–5, detail of cat. 32

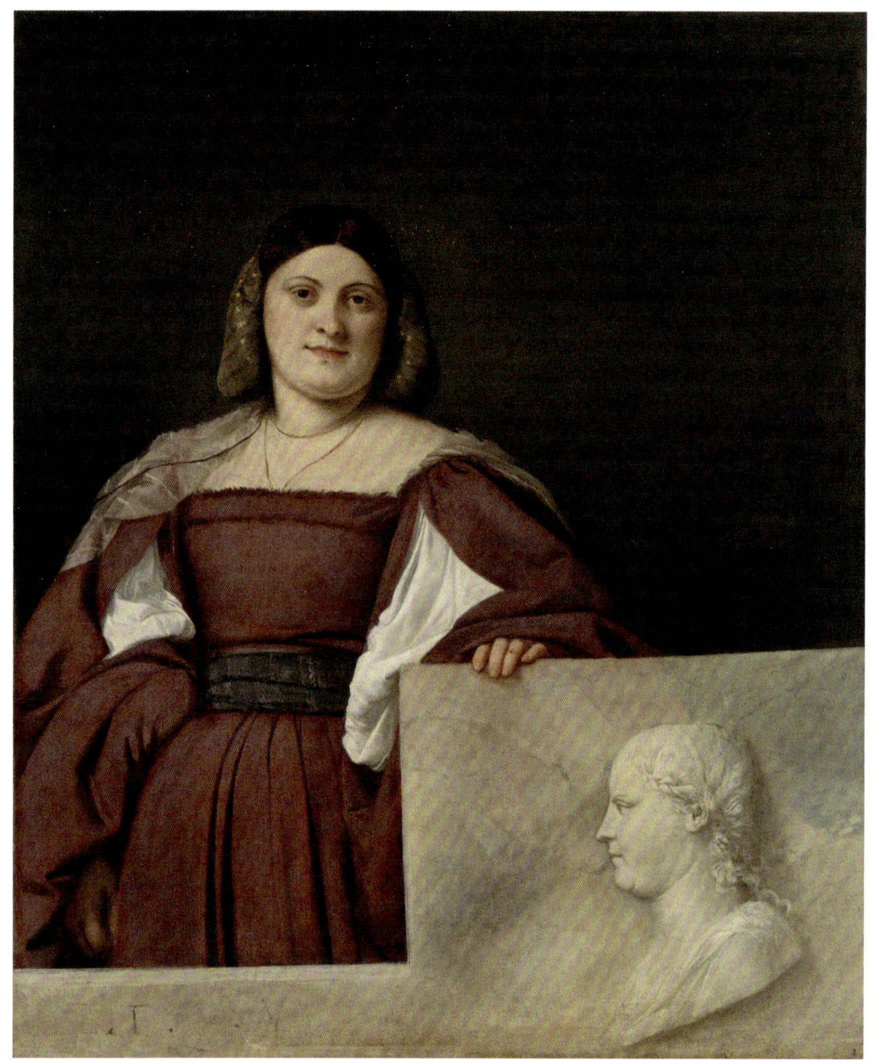

The debate about the relative merits of sculpture and painting reached its peak in 1546 in Florence, when the humanist Benedetto Varchi gave two lectures in which he argued for the superiority of sculpture above all the arts. Later, Varchi published eight letters (dating from 1546 to 1549) by painters and sculptors he had asked to comment on the subject.[8] Perhaps unsurprisingly, Michelangelo (1475–1564), a master painter and sculptor, affirmed that 'painting and sculpture are equal' and that every painter should practise both arts.[9]

It might seem evident to assume that monochrome painting in imitation of sculpture emerged as a result of these *paragone* debates, but examples of this type of painting appeared much earlier. For instance, Giotto's frescoed personifications of Virtues and Vices on the dado of the Scrovegni Chapel in Padua (fig. 25) were produced in the early fourteenth century, before the earliest documented commentary on the *paragone* by Petrarch. Each of Giotto's fourteen figures painted in grisaille is positioned within a rectangular

Cat. 31
Titian (active about 1506; died 1576)
Portrait of a Lady ('La Schiavona'),
about 1510–12
Oil on canvas, 119.4 × 96.5 cm
The National Gallery, London, NG 5385

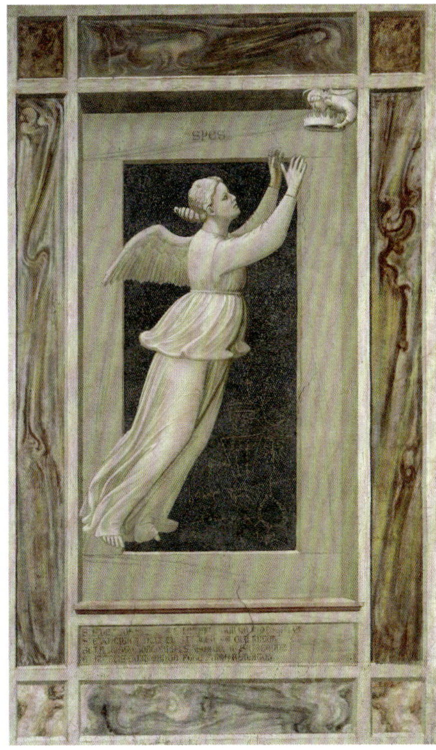

Fig. 25
Giotto di Bondone (born about 1267 or 1276; died 1337)
Hope, 1305
Fresco
Scrovegni Chapel, Padua

Following pages
Cat. 32
Jan van Eyck (active 1422; died 1441)
The Annunciation Diptych (The Archangel Gabriel; The Virgin Mary), about 1433–5
Oil on panel, left wing 38.8 × 23.2 cm, right wing 39 × 24 cm
Museo Thyssen-Bornemisza, Madrid, 1933.11.1–2
Exhibited London only

niche against a fictive, dark-stone background, echoing in its stylistic treatment and drapery such statues as Giovanni Pisano's marble *Madonna and Child* (1305–6) situated nearby on the chapel's high altar.[10] The allusion to stone is further enhanced by a secondary, outer illusionistic frame around each figure, impressively composed of eight different panels, each of feigned coloured marble.

Yet Giotto's grisaille personifications also display features that could never be realised in sculpture. For instance, the figure of Hope hovers implausibly in mid-air with her arms raised, leading some scholars to note the non-sculptural nature of these figures (fig. 25).[11] Given the absence of immediate precedents to Giotto's grisailles, it seems plausible that the Virtues and Vices are a sophisticated early attempt at once to represent sculpture in painting and to engage visually with ideas about painting's supremacy over sculpture. Moreover, the distinctive grisaille technique employed for the Virtues and Vices distinguishes their allegorical nature from that of the historical figures in the narratives painted above them in colour. Around the same time, a parallel tradition emerged in manuscript illumination, in which artists worked in grisaille to evoke sculpture. In Jean Pucelle's exquisite *Hours of Jeanne d'Evreux* (fig. 3), for example, the delicate figures recall contemporary statuettes in alabaster and ivory that were produced in Paris and northern France.[12]

Imitating stone in Netherlandish painting

In the Netherlands, the convincing representation of sculpture in painting was first achieved in the early fifteenth century by Jan van Eyck and Robert Campin.[13] In the absence of any literature on the *paragone*, Northern artists reflected upon painting's supreme merits visually, in painting itself. These artists perfected the use of the oil medium, in which transparent glazes are applied in successive layers. This resulted in a more detailed application of paint for a wide range of optical effects, including the ability to reproduce the appearance of stone with unprecedented precision. The earliest surviving grisaille paintings of sculptures that constitute the principal subject of a panel are the figures of Saint John the Evangelist and Saint John the Baptist, situated on the lowest register of the exterior shutters of the Ghent Altarpiece (fig. 26). The altarpiece was created in the van Eyck brothers' workshop, where Jan collaborated with his brother Hubert and where the successful imitation of sculpture in panel painting was developed.[14]

Van Eyck's highly sophisticated *Annunciation Diptych* (about 1433–5), painted in oil on panel, is a watershed in the history of monochrome painting

The representation of stone sculptures in grisaille became increasingly prevalent on the exterior of winged altarpieces in the Netherlands from the early fifteenth century onwards. Van Eyck's *Annunciation* is unusual because it locates these grisaille scenes on the interior of a diptych. Diptychs, composed of two hinged wooden panels that could be opened and closed like a book, were painted, sculpted or both, and were often relatively small in order to be used as portable devotional works. Numerous medieval portable diptychs were carved out of elephant ivory tusks, a costly material that, by the time van Eyck painted the *Annunciation*, had become difficult to procure. The intimate size of van Eyck's *Annunciation* suggests that the artist was trying to evoke such portable, carved, monochromatic objects. Van Eyck painted the *Annunciation* during the 1430s when the content and purpose of the diptych format was still being established, which might further explain the unusual placement of the grisaille on the interior.

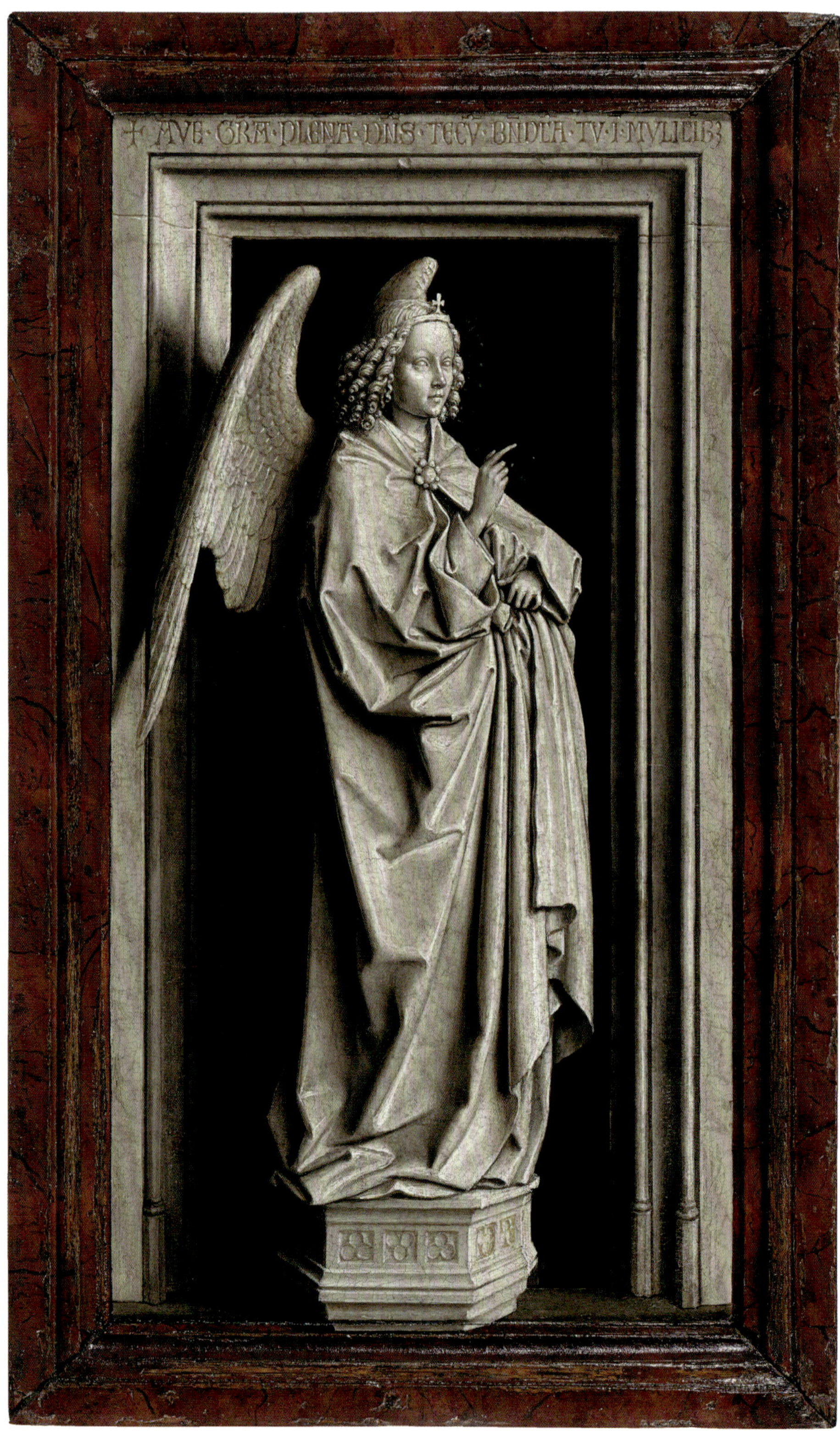

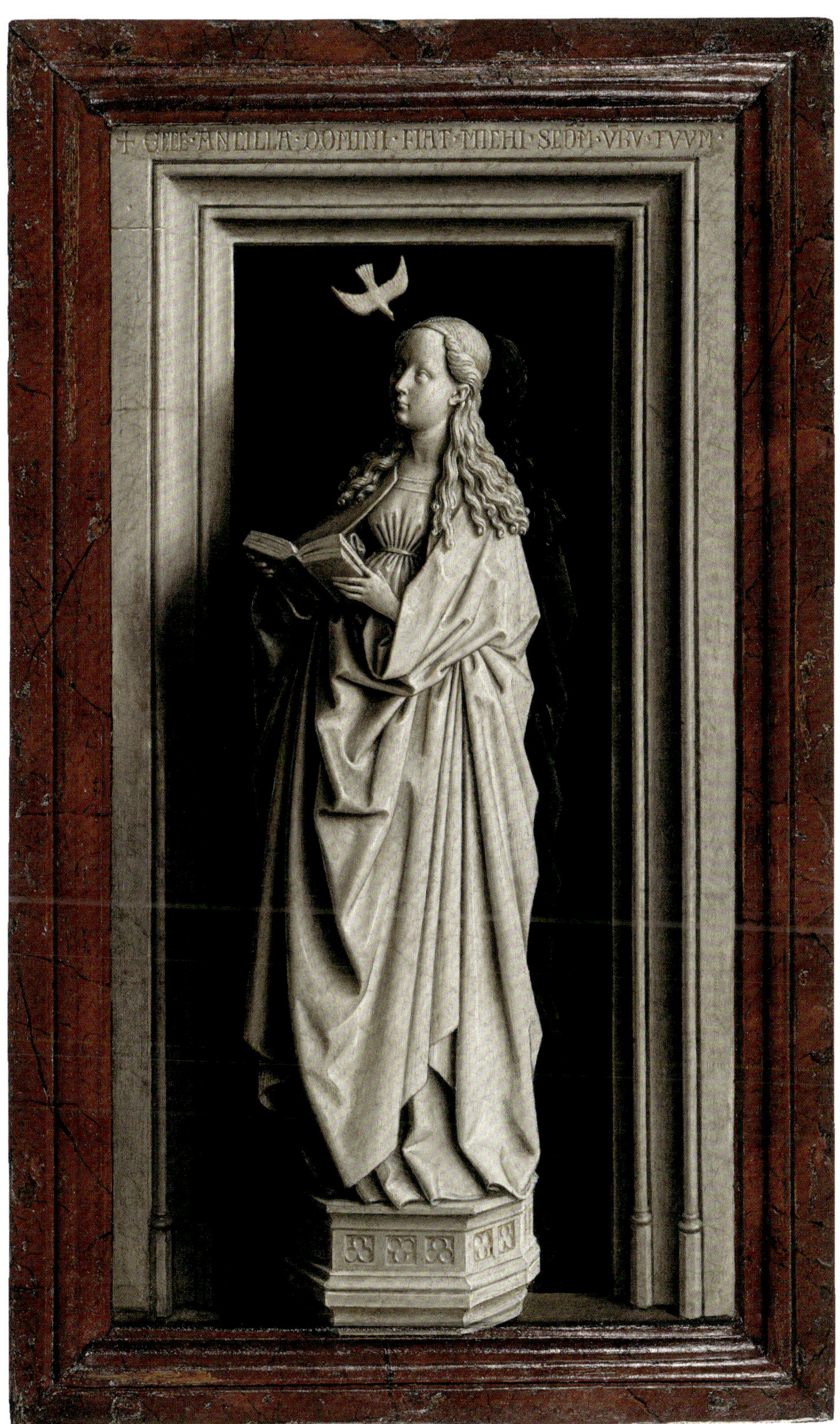
+ ECCE ANCILLA DOMINI · FIAT · MICHI · SCDM · VBV · TVVM ·

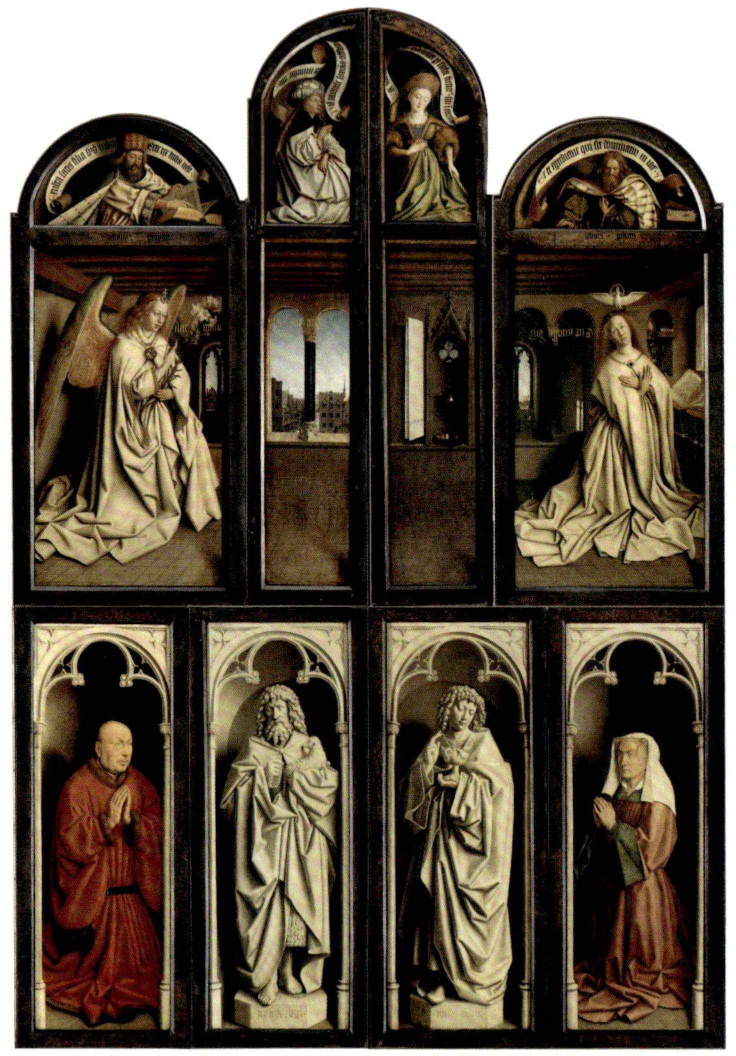

(cat. 32). The Virgin and the Archangel Gabriel are painted to represent palpable stone statues on octagonal plinths set within stone niches with a polished, reflective black background. The curls of their hair are rendered as though they were drilled rather than carved, a technique used in ancient Roman sculpture. Gabriel turns, gesturing towards Mary, as he delivers the news of her miraculous conception. His words, the genesis of the Ave Maria prayer, are inscribed as if chiselled in the upper edges of the fictive stone frames, further enhancing the sculptural illusion. But the stone-coloured dove of the Holy Ghost hovering implausibly in mid-air above the Virgin's head reminds the beholder that what he or she is viewing is a highly effective pictorial fabrication.

Van Eyck's skilful modelling, particularly of the folds of the Virgin's and Gabriel's robes, enhances the impression that the figures are three-dimensional. His dramatic use of light, which enters from the right, casts convincing shadows, such as that of Gabriel's wing on the left inner stone frame, adding

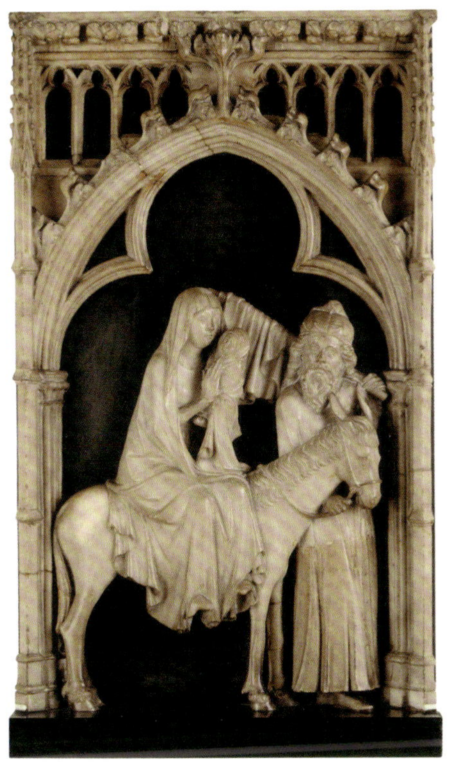

to the illusion that the figure projects forward into the viewer's space. It seems plausible that van Eyck had in mind carved retables produced in Paris during first half of the fourteenth century, such as the white marble *Flight into Egypt*, in which the holy figures are placed within a carved architectural frame against a similar black stone background that reflects their backs (fig. 27).[15] The comparable reflection of Mary's back on the black 'stone' behind her in van Eyck's diptych enabled the artist to represent her from all sides, demonstrating that painting can be the equal of and even exceed the qualities of sculpture.

While the exact identity of the types of stones van Eyck painted is uncertain, there may be as many as five different kinds represented: Italian marble or marble-like white alabaster from Liège for the statues of the Virgin and Gabriel; black marble from Tournai or Dinant for the background; white limestone for the secondary, inner frame; red-flecked marble for the outermost frame; and porphyry for the reverse of the panels.[16] Van Eyck's comprehensive knowledge of various stones and his evident understanding of their distinctive properties are made all the more impressive by his ability to reproduce them convincingly in paint.

Given that sculptures were often painted in colour during the medieval and Renaissance period, it might seem curious that painters left the stone material visible when depicting sculpture in grisaille panels. The art historian Erwin Panofsky was first to point out that the 'colour of stone' was rarely revealed since the majority of stone sculptures, until the end of the fifteenth century, were painted or gilded.[17] For Panofsky, Netherlandish grisaille paintings represent unfinished sculptures, which only painters, including van Eyck and Robert Campin, who painted statuary themselves, could have seen in sculptors' workshops. Panofsky further asserted that the grisailles cultivated a new-found appreciation for monochrome:

> Seeing the statues in the nude, as it were, the painters could observe the operation of light on form as under laboratory conditions, and the grisailles, in which they recorded this experience in 'black and white', may well have been instrumental in gradually educating the public – and the sculptors – to appreciate the beauty of the monochrome.[18]

Although Panofsky was correct in underscoring the prevalence of polychromed statuary of stone or wood, there were several sculptural materials that were considered to have intrinsic or symbolic value, or were appreciated for the technical difficulty they presented to sculptors,[19] and such materials – costly African ivory, precious metal, alabaster or marble – were rarely completely covered by paint. Marble became increasingly prestigious during the Renaissance, and so Italian sculptors frequently left it unpainted, influencing the practice of sculptors all over Europe. The grisailles, therefore, represented an existing, if once less common, practice of creating sculpture in monochrome, with painters somehow anticipating the increasing preference amongst sculptors for leaving their materials visible.

Grisaille sculpture in Germany

By the late fifteenth century, the practice of painting sculptures on the exterior of altarpiece shutters had become widespread in the Netherlands but was less common elsewhere. In Italy, there were shutters that were sometimes painted in grisaille on the outside, and canvas organ shutters, the backs of panel paintings, the covers of canvas paintings and the lids for panel paintings were also sometimes painted in grisaille. In Germany, outer shutters were often painted swiftly and in a reduced colour palette but not necessarily imitative of sculpture.[20] A rare exception to this general practice are the remarkable *Saint Lawrence* and *Saint Cyriacus* by Matthias Grünewald (1470–1528), two of four grisaille panels originally on the exterior of the Heller Altarpiece, a work named after its benefactor, the Frankfurt cloth merchant and councilman Jakob Heller, who commissioned it in 1508 for a side altar in Frankfurt's Dominican church (figs 28 and 29).[21] Grünewald collaborated with Albrecht Dürer on the altarpiece, with Grünewald responsible for the grisaille exterior. In a letter of 1508 updating his patron on the altarpiece's progress, Dürer wrote that the altarpiece shutters '... have been painted in stone colours [*Steinfarben*] on the outside', a passage that underscores both the monochromatic and sculptural qualities of Grünewald's paintings.[22]

Yet Grünewald simultaneously adhered to and departed from the work of his Netherlandish counterparts – most notably in the vividly realistic depiction of the saints. Although painted predominantly in shades of grey to represent stone, and positioned on feigned stone slabs inscribed, as though chiselled, with the saints' names, the figures of Saint Lawrence and Saint Cyriacus exhibit lifelike qualities, sensed through the agitated folds of their garments, the fluttering pages of their books and their setting in a landscape rather than a stone niche.

Albrecht Dürer, a gifted printmaker working in black and white, also explored monochrome in painting in a group of brush drawings produced between 1519 and 1522. The monumental *Head of a Woman* (1520) is the most sculptural sheet in the group and probably reflects Dürer's engagement with representing figures reminiscent of sculptures as a means of investigating and

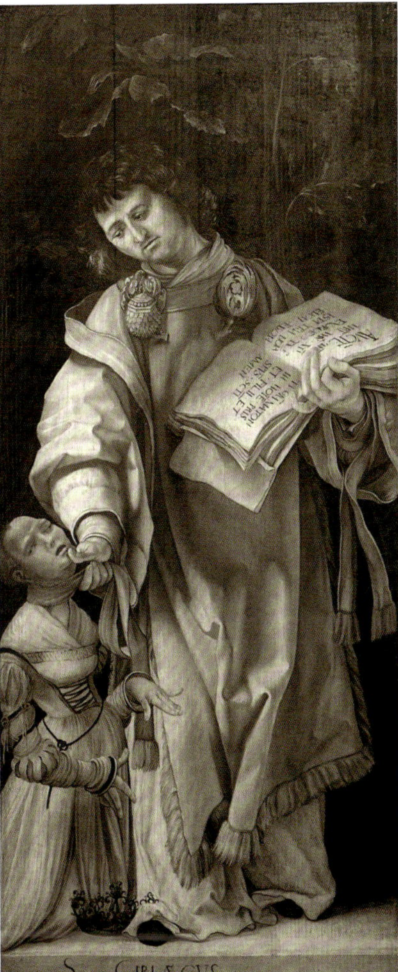

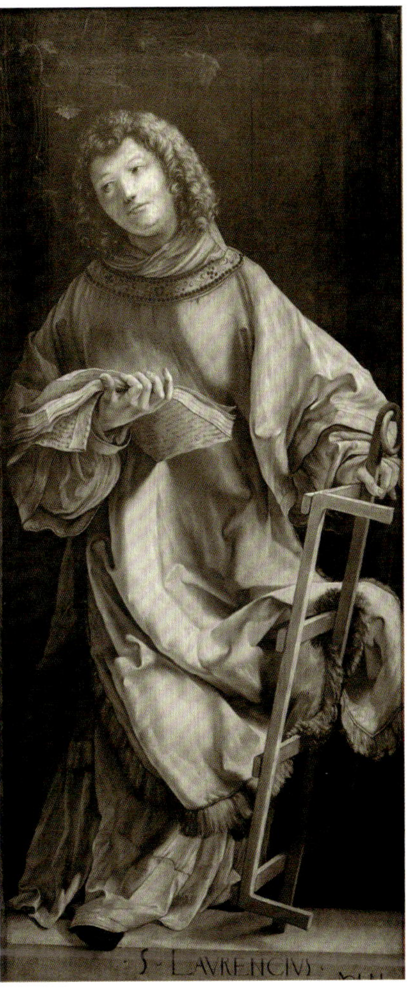

Fig. 28
Matthias Grünewald (1470–1528)
Saint Cyriacus, from the *Heller Altarpiece*,
about 1509–10
Oil on oak panel, 99.1 × 43 cm
Historisches Museum, Frankfurt, on long-term
loan to the Städel Museum, HM 37

Fig. 29
Matthias Grünewald (1470–1528)
Saint Lawrence, from the *Heller Altarpiece*,
about 1509–10
Oil on oak panel, 98 × 43 cm
Historisches Museum, Frankfurt, on long-term
loan to the Städel Museum, HM 36

expressing ideal human proportions, which he was carefully studying at the time (cat. 33). Dürer's masterly modelling with the brush in black-and-white bodycolour on unprimed paper, made more impressive by the absence of any preparatory lines, creates strong contrasts of light and dark that project the head forward, giving the illusion of a three-dimensional, sculptural bust.

The idealised and stylised head is symmetrically conceived as a forward-facing oval, disturbed only by a slight tilt to her right. The figure's hair is parted in the middle in line with the nose and is loosely pulled back, softly framing her face and covering her ears. Together these details enhance the symmetrical division of the face. The woman's lack of expression and closed eyes and mouth create an effect quite unlike that of a believable likeness often found in portraiture. Moreover, Dürer's careful modelling of the surface texture is more reminiscent of polished metal than skin.

Dürer painted in monochrome in the last decade of his life, either to prepare other compositions in colour or to produce independent works of art. His *Head of a Woman*, inscribed with his monogram and the date in the

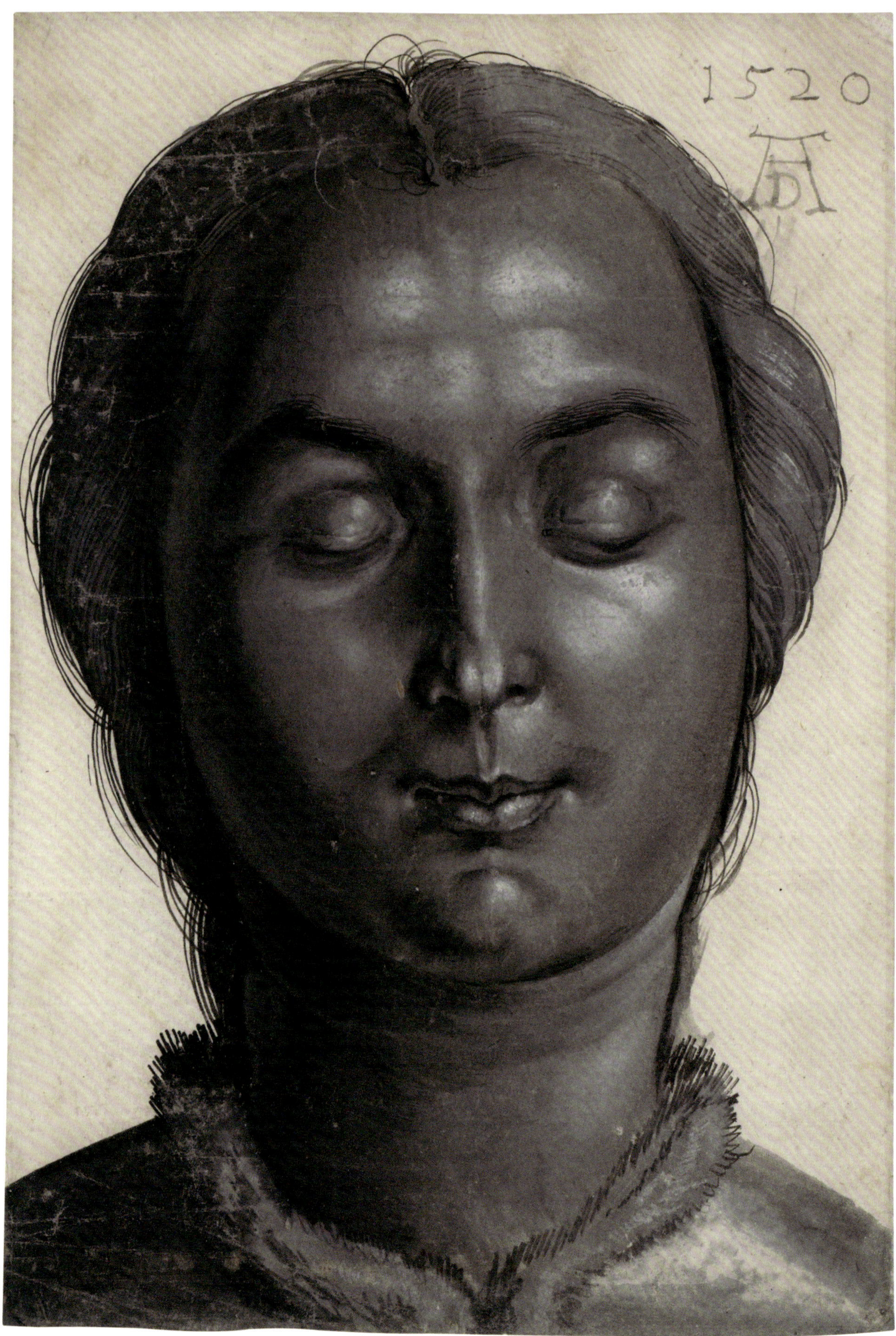

upper right, is unrelated to any known polychrome painting and was probably produced as an independent, collectable work of art.

Grisaille and the rediscovery of the Antique

In Italy, the earliest independent monochrome paintings of sculpture were rooted in the Antique. Beginning in the 1490s, Andrea Mantegna (about 1430/1–1506) produced a number of paintings that simulated ancient marble or bronze reliefs representing secular themes.[23] Mantegna possessed an interest in classical sculpture that was nurtured early on by his teacher Francesco Squarcione in Padua and fuelled by the great archaeological excavations of antique statuary taking place in Italy during the late fifteenth century. Mantegna often included ancient fragments of stone, and figures carrying stones, in his paintings.[24] His interest in classical statuary was also reflected in his figural style, or *maniera dura* as it became known, described by Vasari as 'somewhat hard and sometimes suggesting stone rather than living flesh'.[25]

Moreover, the avid collecting of classical sculpture at the Gonzaga court in Mantua, where Mantegna served as court painter, may well have stimulated his turn to grisaille during the 1490s. It was then that Isabella d'Este, the young wife of Francesco Gonzaga, Duke of Mantua, began eagerly to collect ancient and modern sculptures to decorate her *studiolo* in the Castello di San Giorgio. Around the same time, contemporary artists, such as Antonio del Pollaiuolo and Francesco di Giorgio Martini, were creating sculptures after the Antique. Mantegna's interest in grisaille also coincided with the escalation of the *paragone* debate. His grisailles evoke ancient statuary without depicting any actual antique sculptures. Mantegna's original compositions encourage the viewer to reflect on the painter's ability to produce something novel and unique that at once recalls classical antiquity without reproducing it, thereby asserting painting's ability to surpass sculpture as an art form.

The most imposing and monumental of Mantegna's grisailles is *The Introduction of the Cult of Cybele at Rome* (cat. 34). The frieze depicts the arrival in Rome of the cult of Cybele from Pessinus in Asia Minor in 204 BC. Cybele was an Eastern goddess associated with Victory, and she is represented in the painting by a bust and a round sacred stone. The painting, commissioned by the Venetian nobleman Francesco Cornaro to laud his family's Roman ancestry, was conceived as part of a series of four works but was the only one completed by Mantegna before his death. Mantegna's technique in this work complements his subject, the illusion of ancient relief statuary providing a fitting way to visualise the ancient Roman story recounted by Livy, Valerius Maximus and Ovid.

The figures are arranged across the foreground of the picture plane and

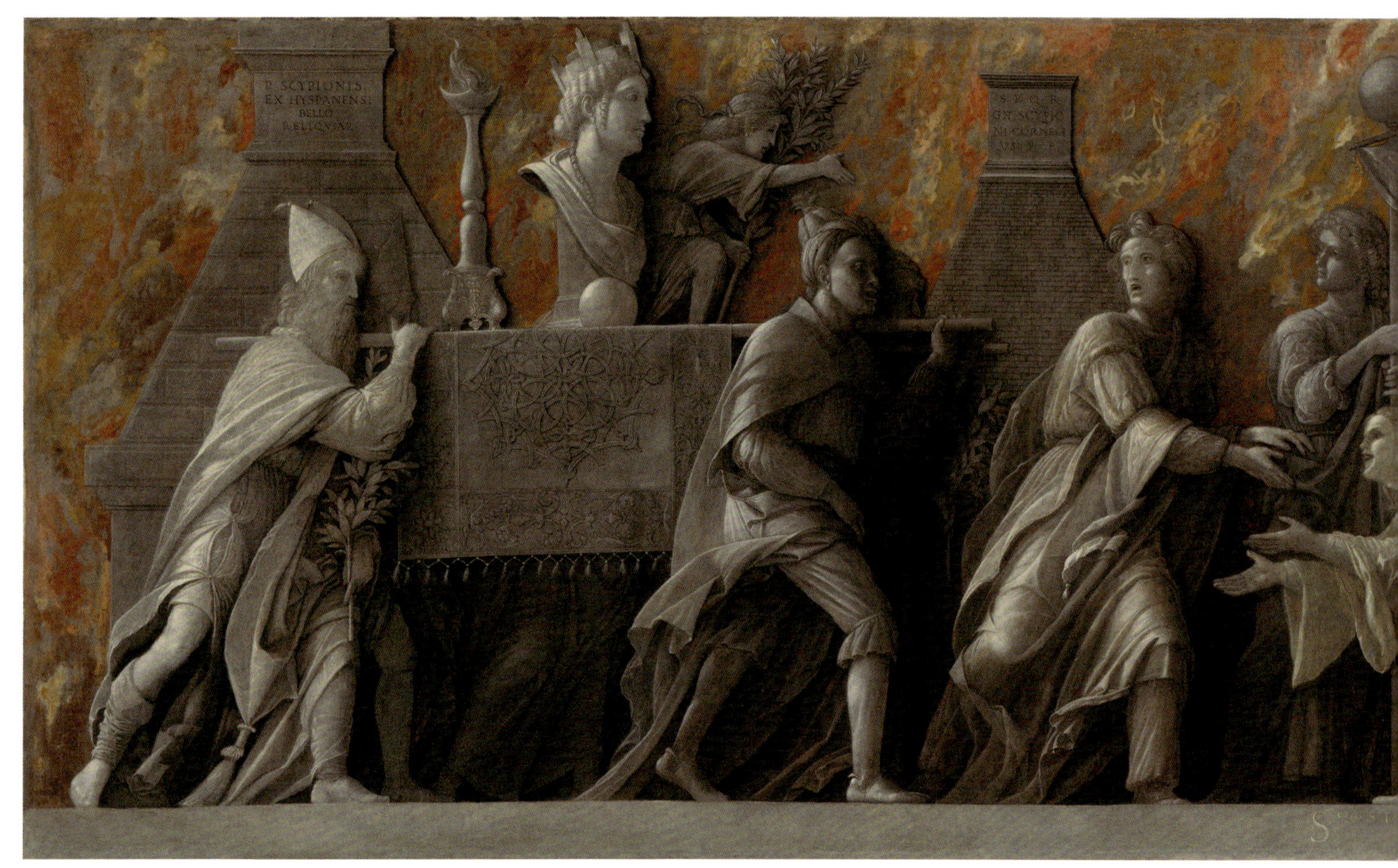

are represented at a low vantage point. This is probably accounted for by the
intended setting of the painting, high on a wall in a position similar to that of
a sculptural frieze in antique architecture that would be viewed from below.
Light enters the painting from the left, together with the priests, who carry
the goddess's attributes (the bust and round sacred stone). The success of
Cybele's cult in driving the Carthaginians from Italy (the motivation behind the
cult's relocation to Rome) depended on its being received by the most worthy
Roman citizen. The young Cornelius Scipio was selected for the task and is
probably the standing figure just right of centre, with his head turned, engaging
in conversation. Roman senators and soldiers intermingle with men in Eastern
attire. In the centre, the dynamic figure of Claudia Quinta, a Roman matron with
a questionable reputation, kneels in a gesture of public thanks to the goddess.

Mantegna's allusion to stone in the grey-painted figures is enhanced by
his inclusion of elements that would in reality have been made of stone, such
the platform and steps leading to the entrance of Scipio's house and the tombs
inscribed with the names of Scipio's father and uncle in the left background.
Most notable is the fictive coloured marble background similar to the type
employed for palace or church walls which provides a distinctive contrast to

Cat. 34 and detail overleaf
Andrea Mantegna (about 1430/1–1506)
*The Introduction of the Cult of Cybele at
Rome*, 1505–6
Glue on linen, 76.5 × 273 cm
The National Gallery, London, NG 902

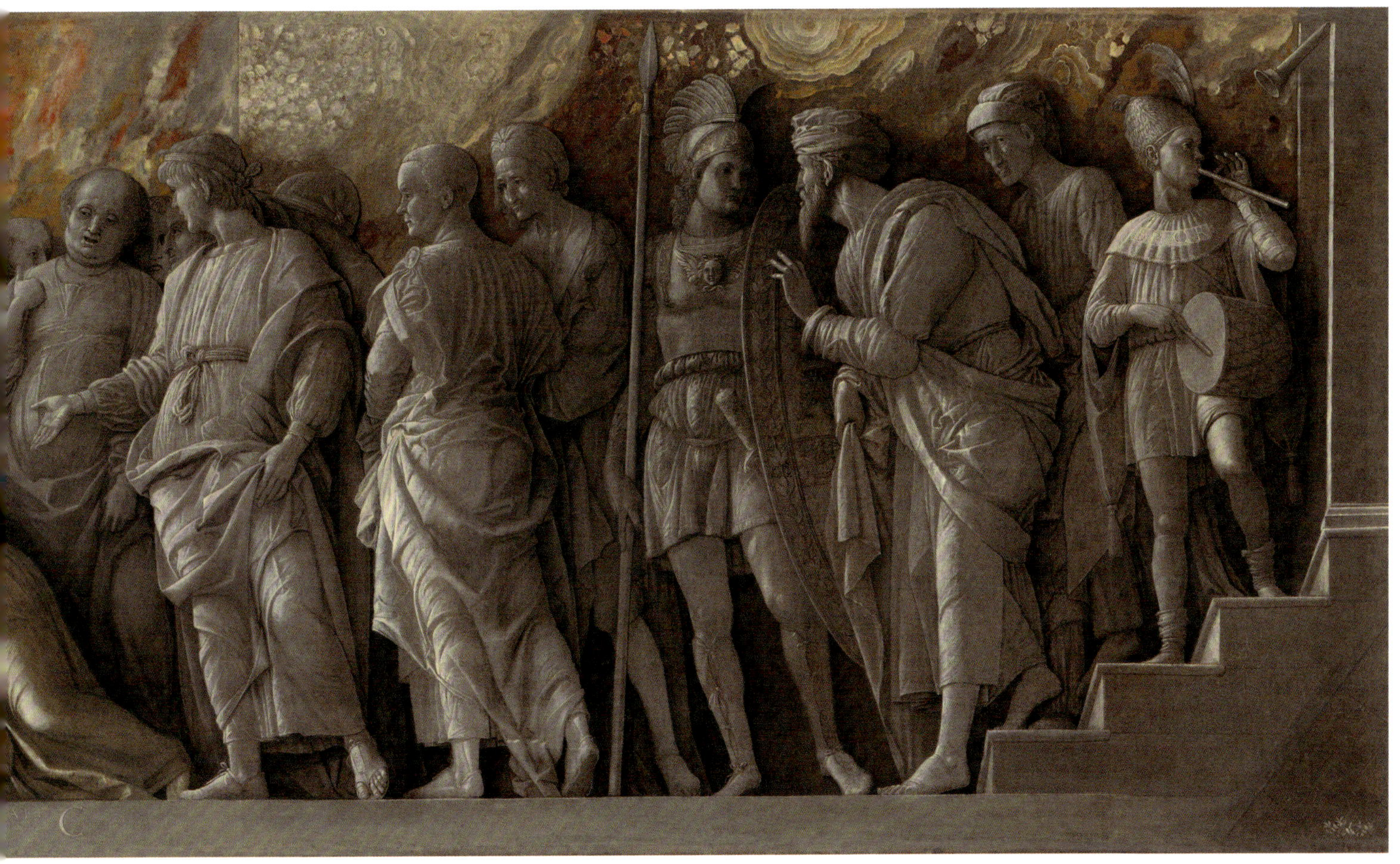

An avid student of the Antique, Mantegna painted a number of grisailles in imitation of ancient relief statuary, beginning in the 1490s. This painting represents the return to Rome of the cult of Cybele, a goddess symbolising Victory. The classical subject matter is complimented by Mantegna's choice of technique. Arranged as in a frieze, the grey stone figures are set against a painted representation of coloured marble, thereby combining stone materials that sculptors themselves could not. Mantegna's convincing imitation of two types of stone invites contemplation on the sister arts of painting and sculpture, and on the *paragone* debates prevalent in Italy around the time this work was produced. Originally planned as part of a series of four for interior decoration, the painting was one of Mantegna's last, and the only one of the series he completed before his death in 1506.

the grey figures and enhances their sculptural effect. In this way, Mantegna demonstrated his superiority over sculptors by combining sculptural materials that they, in turn, could not. Indeed, no relief sculptures that combine stones in this way are known from antiquity.

Grisaille and architectural decoration

The use of grisaille for mural decoration has a long history after Giotto, in both Southern and Northern Europe, with a number of murals conceived to represent sculptural relief. A rare and important surviving example in England is preserved at Eton College.[26] Along the north and south walls of the college chapel's nave are scenes executed in grisaille that date from 1477 to 1487 and represent the miracles of the Virgin (fig. 30). Each scene is bordered on either side by an elaborately canopied niche in which stands a saint on a plinth, clearly intended to represent sculpture. The single, sculptural figures contrast with the figures re-enacting the miracles inside the rectangular frames, who lack any suggestion of sculpture (such as a plinth) and instead are reminiscent of early Netherlandish polychrome paintings. Indeed, the artists of the cycle may have been from the Netherlands, or from England but working in a

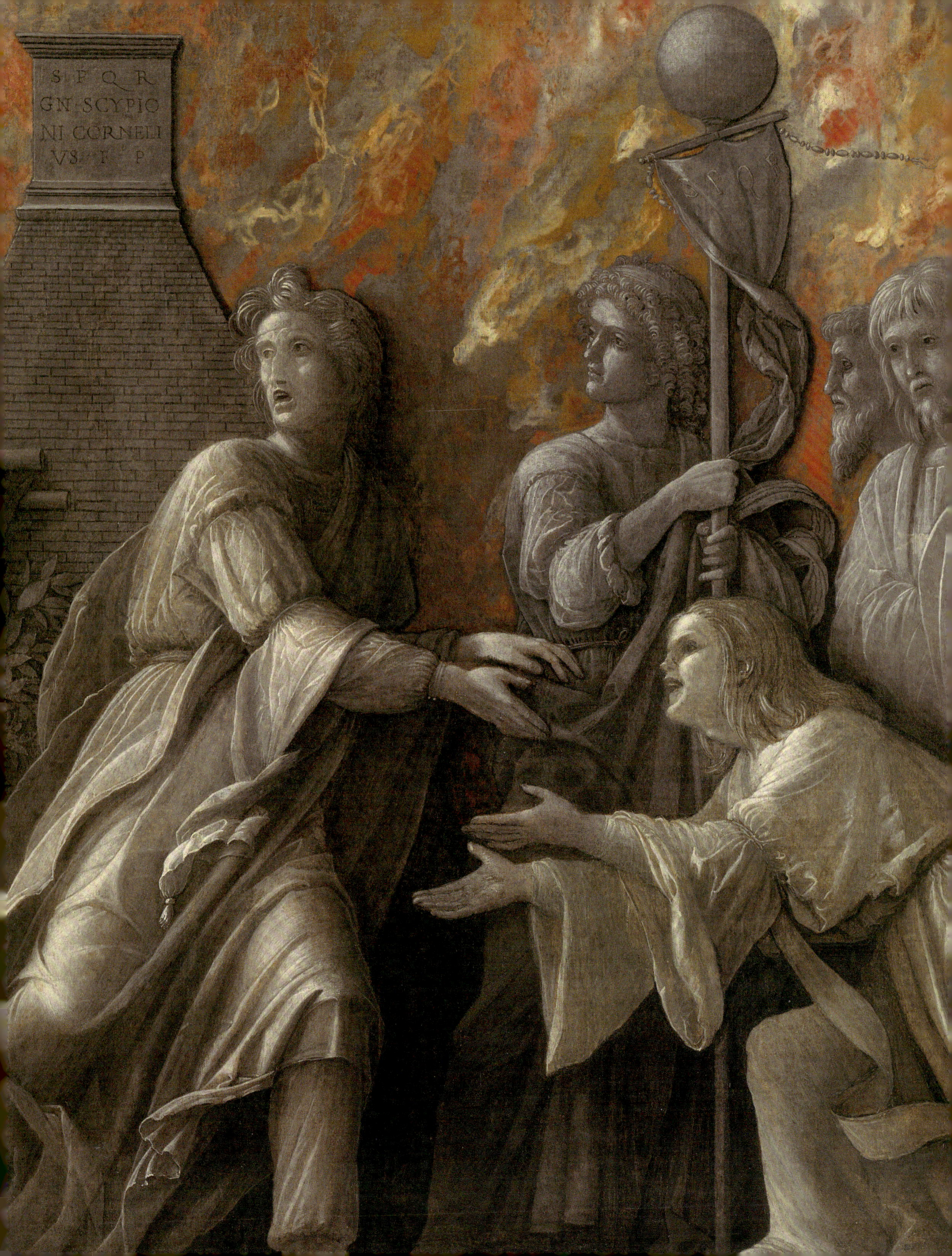
S . P . Q . R
GN . SCYPIO
NI CORNELI
VS T P

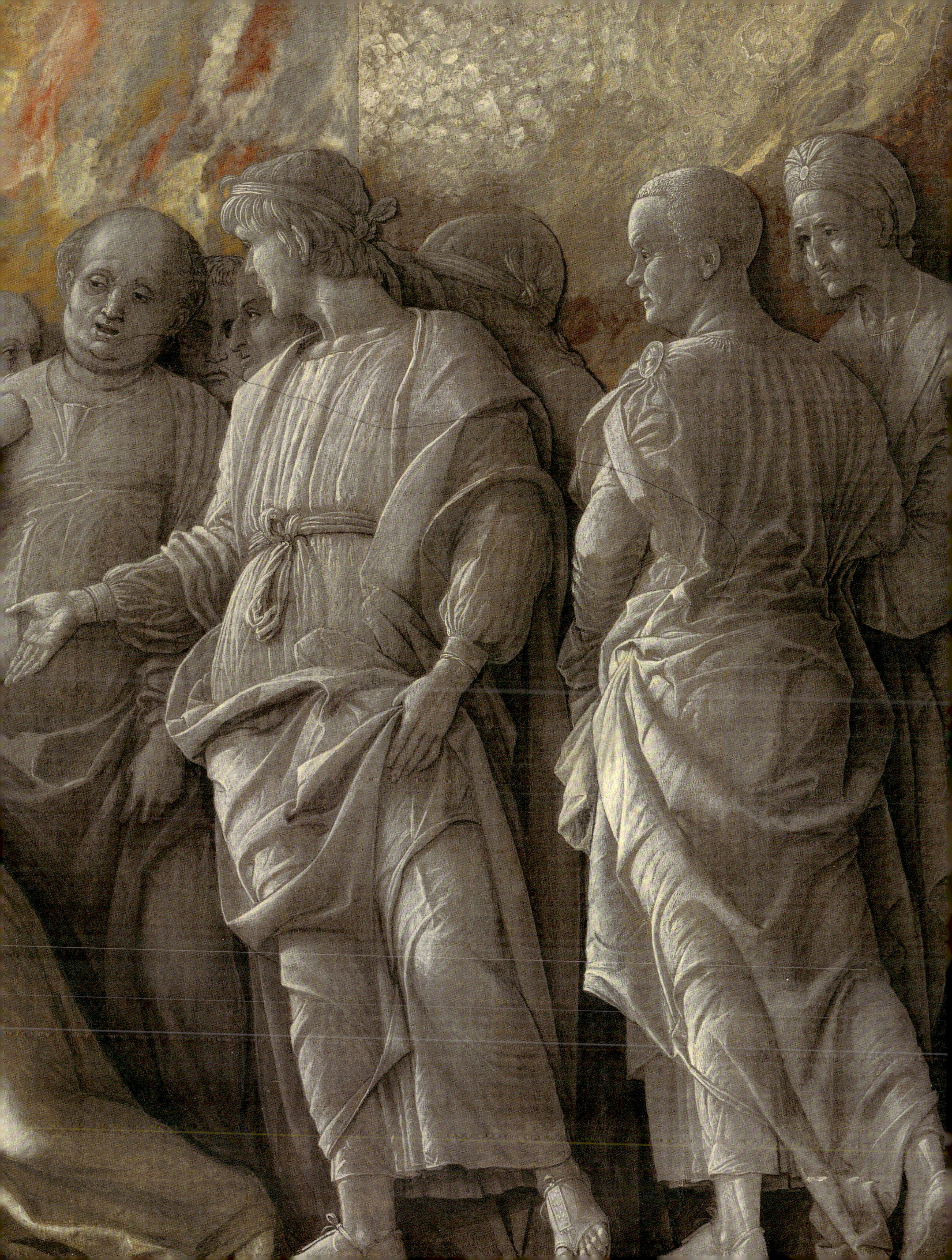

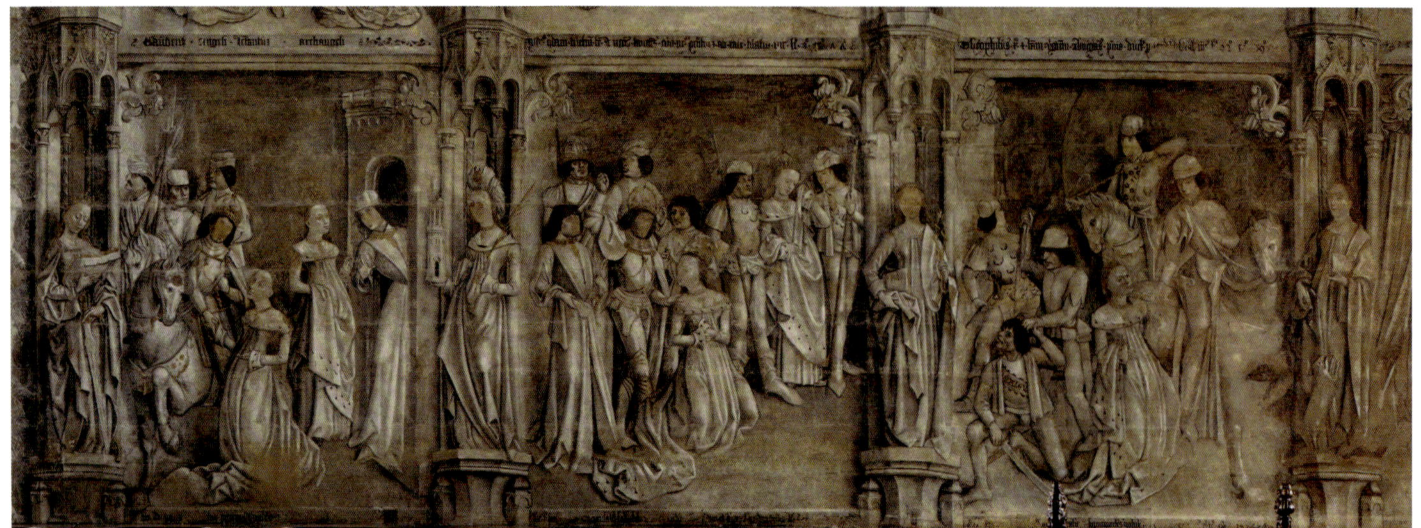

Netherlandish style.[27] The grisaille sculptures in this case provide a framing device for and a point of transition between each miracle, which is also painted in grisaille.

In Italy in the late fifteenth century, palace facades, especially in Rome, were painted to imitate antique reliefs using fresco, a technique that was faster and cheaper to execute than any form of sculptural decoration. The narratives depicted on these 'chiaroscuro facades' were highly rhetorical and were often taken from Roman history to represent the ideals and allegiances of the building's inhabitants.[28] Writing in 1586, the Italian art theorist Giovanni Battista Armenini claimed that the practice of painting feigned sculpture onto building facades dated back to antiquity.[29] Renaissance artists revived this practice. Vasari described these facades, emphasising their links to sculpture:

> artists have been accustomed to decorate in monochrome the facades of palaces and houses ... making them appear to be built of marble or stone, with the decorative groups actually carved in relief; or indeed they may imitate particular sorts of marble, and porphyry ... or other stones.[30]

The greatest Italian proponents of monochrome facade decoration that imitated sculpture were Polidoro da Caravaggio (about 1499–1543) and his collaborator Maturino da Firenze (1490–1528).[31] This prolific pair painted at least forty facades between the years 1520 and 1527.[32] Their decorations imitated ancient Roman facade sculptures and classical reliefs so convincingly that Vasari described them as 'counterfeiting' the ancient works of marble.[33] Polidoro and Maturino conceived their compositions as long narrative friezes which covered entire portions of a facade.[34] They worked not only in fresco but also in *sgraffito*, which in grisaille decorations involved laying down two layers of colours, first white then black, and scratching away the topmost black layer of paint to reveal the white underneath.[35]

Fig. 30
Grisaille paintings at Eton College chapel,
south wall, 1477–87
Eton College

Although few intact examples of monochrome facades survive, a drawing by Federico Zuccaro illustrates this practice (fig. 31).[36] The sheet depicts Federico's brother, Taddeo, sitting precariously high on scaffolding and painting with a long brush the facade of the Palazzo Mattei in Rome. From the evidence in the drawing, the painting consisted of scenes from ancient history rendered in monochrome to represent carved sarcophagi set into the wall. In the foreground, great artists (identifiable by inscriptions) such as Michelangelo, on horseback on the left, and Vasari and Francesco Salviati engaged in conversation on the right, marvel at Taddeo's progress from below. This important commission, carried out in 1548, established Taddeo's reputation at 18 years of age.

Large-scale, site-specific, secular fresco decorations painted in monochrome to imitate sculpture continued to be produced in Italy into the eighteenth century, especially to decorate the palaces and villas of the wealthy. Giovanni Battista (Giambattista) Tiepolo (1696–1770) and his son Giovanni Domenico (Giandomenico) (1727–1804) contributed significantly to this ongoing tradition of decorating villas and palaces in the Veneto, practised most notably by Veronese during the sixteenth century. Their work in this genre stands out, however, with the prevalence of grisaille imitating sculpture, a taste they catered to and cultivated during the eighteenth century.

The cycle of six life-size commemorative frescoes, celebrating the triumphs and military prowess of the wealthy and patrician Porto family from the eleventh to the seventeenth centuries, is a fascinating example of this monumental practice. The series, painted around 1760, was part of a larger decorative programme for the Palazzo da Porto Festa in Vicenza. Orazio Porto

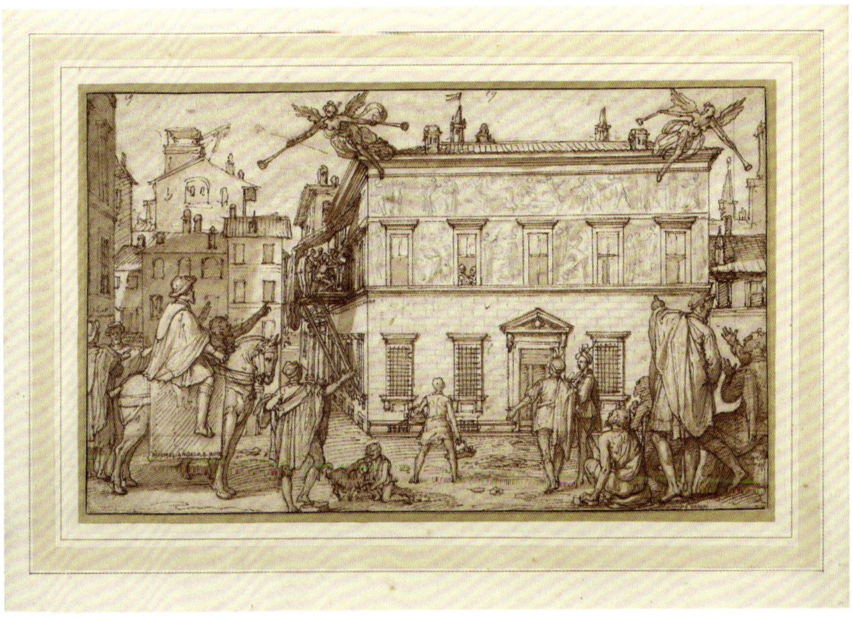

commissioned both Giandomenico and his more famous father to decorate
his palace, which has led to confusion about the authorship of the cycle. On
stylistic grounds, the cycle is now accepted as by Giandomenico, but there is
no doubt that the work was influenced by Giambattista, who was skilled at
representing sculpture in such decorative programmes. Around the same time,
Giorgio Marchesini commissioned Giambattista to decorate his Palazzo Valle-
Marchesini-Sala, also in Vicenza, which resulted in a series of grisaille frescoes
imitating sculpture, to which Giandomenico is likely to have contributed.[37]

The fresco *Jacopo Porto appointed Governor of Vicenza by Holy Roman
Emperor Henry II in 1022* represents Jacopo Porto wearing armour and kneeling
before Emperor Henry II, who embraces him with his left arm (cat. 35). Behind
them are soldiers carrying the imperial standard. With his right arm, the
Emperor points down to two river gods, who look up from a reclined position.
The left background opens into a vista of the city of Vicenza. Giandomenico
effectively modelled the standing figures and reclining river gods in shades
of grey to suggest a stone relief. The shadowy contours, prominent especially
around the right side of the river gods, work to project the figures forward.
As was common in such pictures, Giandomenico took account of the natural
light and the position of the fresco within the great room on the ground floor,
as suggested by the consistent contours across the scenes in the cycle.[38] The
ceiling of the great ground-floor room was painted with a fresco by Domenico
Bruzazorzi, *The Fall of the Giants*. Tiepolo's choice of monochrome may have
been intended to complement the bright colours of the ceiling.[39]

The gold background adds a sumptuous element to Giandomenico's
frescoes and provides a contrast to the grisailles, enhancing their sculptural
appearance. The inclusion of the gold calls to mind the Renaissance practice
of placing relief sculptures against gold mosaic. It also recalls Mantegna's and
other artists' fictive depictions of other materials, such as coloured marble, as
the background of grisailles (cat. 34). Giandomenico labelled each scene in the
cycle with a Latin-inscribed cartellino on the lower edge, which identifies the
subject. The writing suggests chiselled lettering and amplifies the impression of
stone. Giandomenico also painted a fictive grey frame around each scene, giving
each episode its own individual status. The border resembles dark marble,
further intensifying the illusion of stone.

Cat. 35
Giovanni Domenico Tiepolo (1727–1804)
*Jacopo Porto appointed Governor of Vicenza
by the Holy Roman Emperor Henry II in 1022*,
about 1760
Detached fresco transferred to canvas, gold
ground, 270 × 169 cm
Private collection

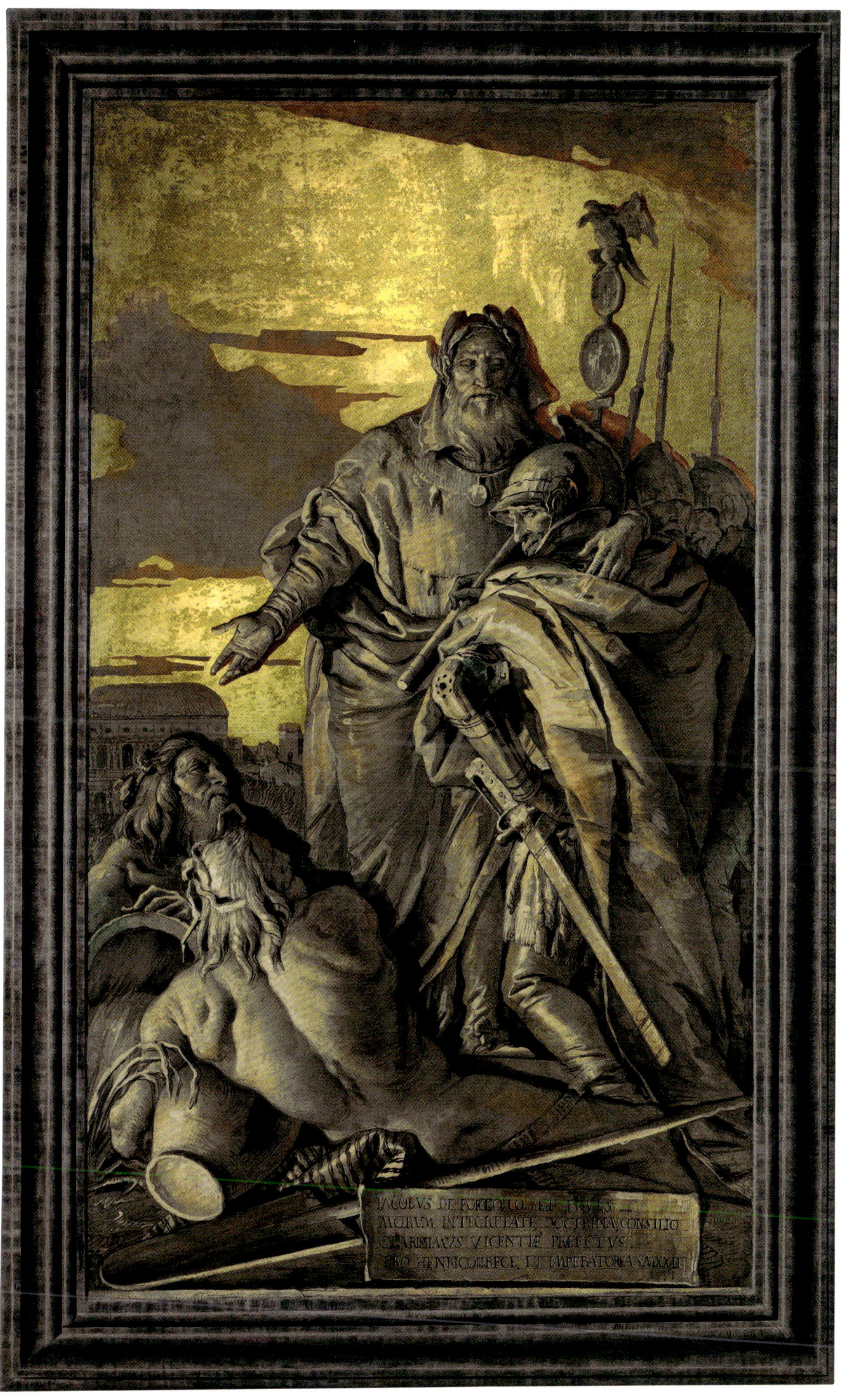

IACOBVS DE PORTEO CO. ET EQVES
MORVM INTEGRITATE DOCTRINA CONSILIO
CLARISSIMVS VICENTIÆ PRÆFECTVS
PRO HENRICO III REGE ET IMPERATORIA S.M.XXII

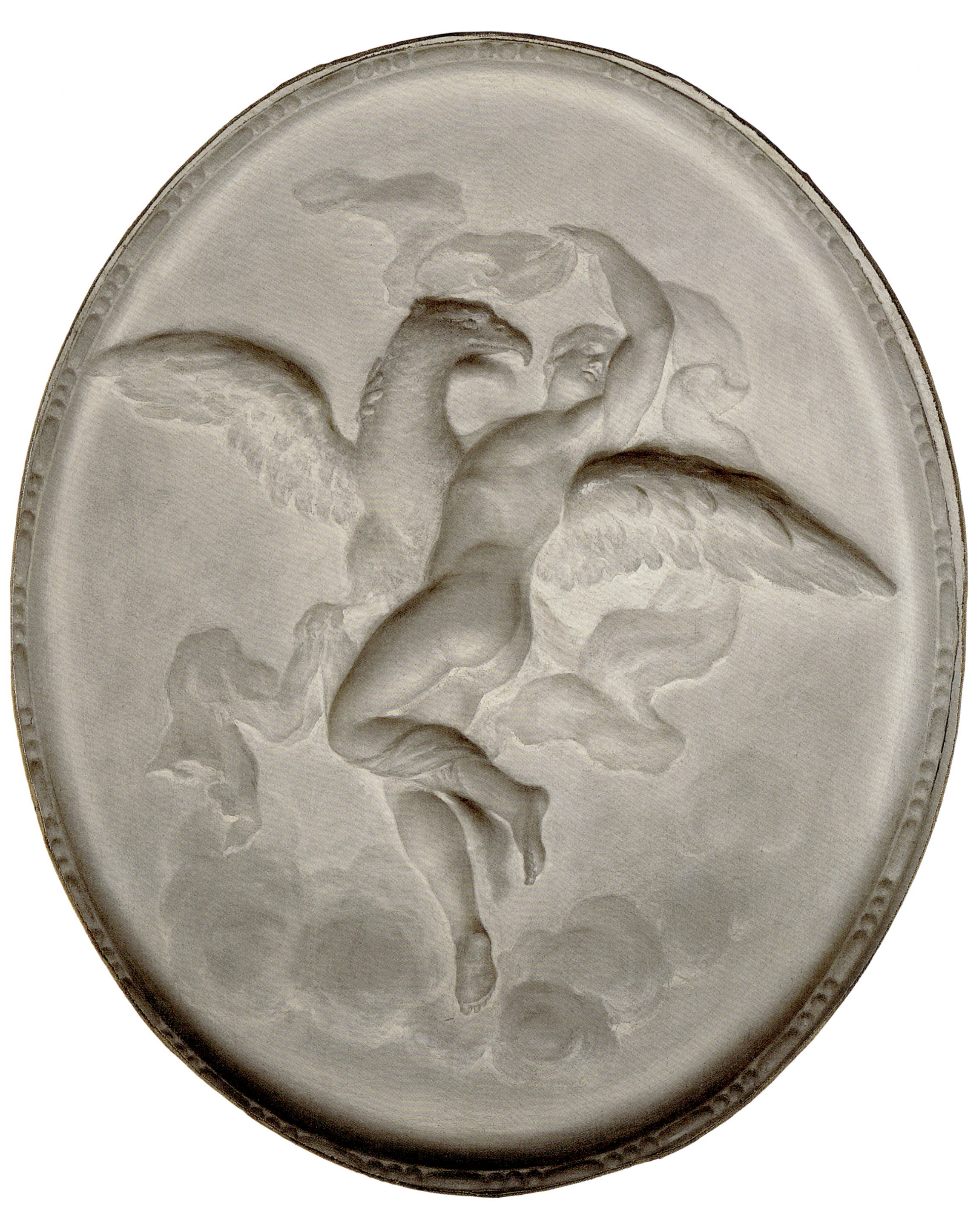

Grisaille and sculptural *trompe l'oeil*

Such large-scale fresco decorations were uncommon in Northern Europe, probably owing to the unfavourable cold and wet climate. Instead, the eighteenth-century imitation of sculpture in grisaille developed into highly illusionistic works of *trompe l'oeil* painted on panel or canvas. Like fresco, such paintings were a far more cost-effective way of achieving the effects of carving. In Amsterdam, Jacob de Wit (1695–1754) excelled at this practice with grey-and-white paintings such as *Jupiter and Ganymede* (cat. 36), made in imitation of stucco wall reliefs that usually formed part of larger decorative ensembles designed for domestic or public interiors, most of which were subsequently dismantled and lost.[40] Originally surrounded by plasterwork painted in cream or white that would have enhanced the sculptural illusion, De Wit's grisailles enjoyed great popularity in the period and became known as *witjes*, a witty double allusion to the Dutch word for 'white' and the artist's name. The relatively modest size and oval shape of *Jupiter and Ganymede*, along with the angle of the composition, suggest it was meant to be seen from below as part of a ceiling decoration in a domestic interior.

The subject was taken from Ovid's *Metamorphoses* and Virgil's *Aeneid*. After falling in love with the beautiful young shepherd Ganymede, Jupiter turned himself into an eagle and swooped down to Mount Ida to capture and carry off Ganymede to Mount Olympus, where he made him his cup-bearer. De Wit represented the two figures in mid-flight, amid clouds, a fitting subject for a ceiling painting. Unlike grey paintings by earlier artists such as Albrecht Dürer and Andrea Mantegna (cats 33 and 34) which deliberately draw attention to the artist's skill in creating a sculptural appearance, here the artist's presence is concealed by the success of his illusion, a feature of decorative grisaille painting at which De Wit was particularly skilful. The extent to which beholders were really fooled or merely enjoyed the visual play in De Wit's paintings remains to be determined. It is possible, however, that before the invention of electric light, De Wit's fictive low reliefs were mistaken for real carvings.

The Northern tradition of feigned sculptural reliefs in *trompe l'oeil* continued during the latter half of the eighteenth century, a period characterised by a renewed interest in classical antiquity and by an abundant taste for interior decorations in grisaille.[41] An important proponent of this practice was the Antwerp-born Marten Jozef Geeraerts (1707–1791), who further popularised the genre long after De Wit's death in 1754.[42] Following De Wit's example, Geeraerts became a renowned specialist in grisaille bas-reliefs imitating stone, bronze or wood for the decoration of grand domestic and church interiors, most often representing putti at play, which he adapted from

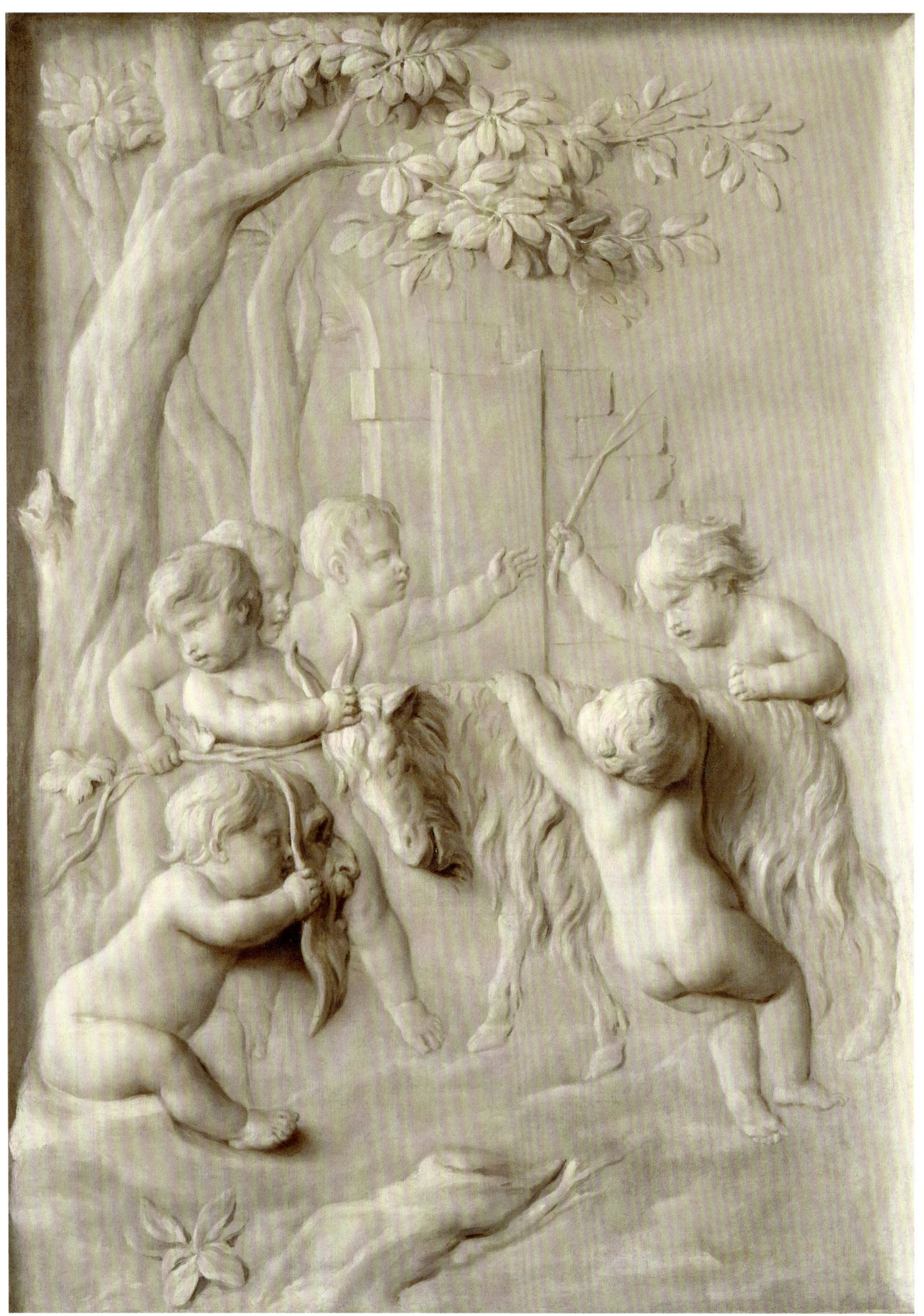

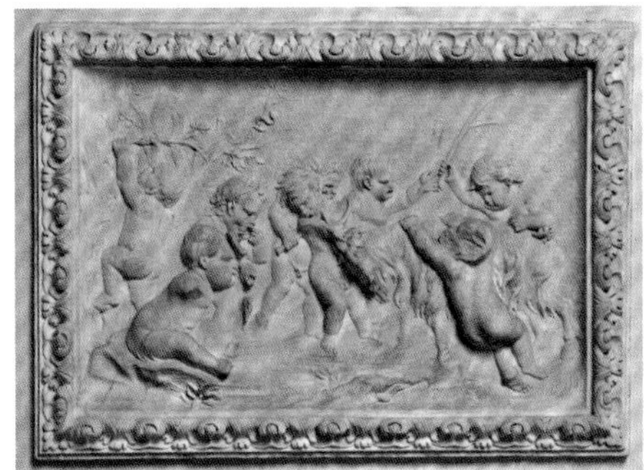

the sculpted putto bacchanals of François Duquesnoy (1597–1643). Geeraerts's deceptively convincing grisailles attained such renown that they were commissioned by the greatest courts of Europe.

Geeraerts's *Children's Game* constitutes a highly persuasive imitation of a marble sculptural relief depicting six naked putti teasing a goat in a landscape with ancient ruins (cat. 37). The artist's skilful modelling in shades of white to dark grey gives the impression of an actual relief, with the figures seemingly projecting and receding beyond the flatness of the two-dimensional canvas. *The Children's Game* is an adaptation of a famous relief by Duquesnoy made in Rome in the seventeenth century which captivated contemporaries with the charm and naturalism of the putti (fig. 32). Duquesnoy's relief recalled ancient sculptures found on Roman sarcophagi. It was known in many versions, including plaster, ivory and marble. The composition of Geeraert's *Children's Game*, which includes a mask, a symbol of imitation, is a commentary on the fabricated illusion in the painting. The subject of children's play underscores the visual game that Geeraerts successfully achieves in this work.

Such secular paintings usually formed part of larger decorative ensembles in domestic interiors. The existence of a pendant to *Children's Game* (also entitled *Children's Game*, Palais des Beaux-Arts, Lille) indicates that it, too, was part of a larger decorative programme. Such *trompe l'oeil* paintings were less costly than the sculptures they imitated and therefore affordable by a larger clientele. Contemporary critics also celebrated their illusory character. In 1774, for example, Geeraert's best pupil, Piat Joseph Sauvage (1744–1818), who became a great grisaille decorator in his own right, sent a dozen such paintings to that year's Paris Salon and was praised for being a playful genius with a great ability to fool the eye.[43]

Grisaille as an aid to the sculptor

While the production of grisaille paintings for interior decoration was widespread, a less common but important and often overlooked function of monochrome painting was to create paintings of sculptures as a means of assisting sculptors in their artistic process. The Venetian artist Antonio Canova (1757–1822), for example, employed such painters as Bernardino Nocchi, Stefano Tofanelli and even Pierre-Paul Prud'hon to make paintings of his plaster preparatory casts.[44] The paintings assisted the sculptor in testing the composition in different lighting conditions, such as candlelight, and were more effective than using a maquette. They also enabled him to present a modello or example of his composition to his patrons for approval before producing the final work in expensive marble. Such paintings could also serve as models

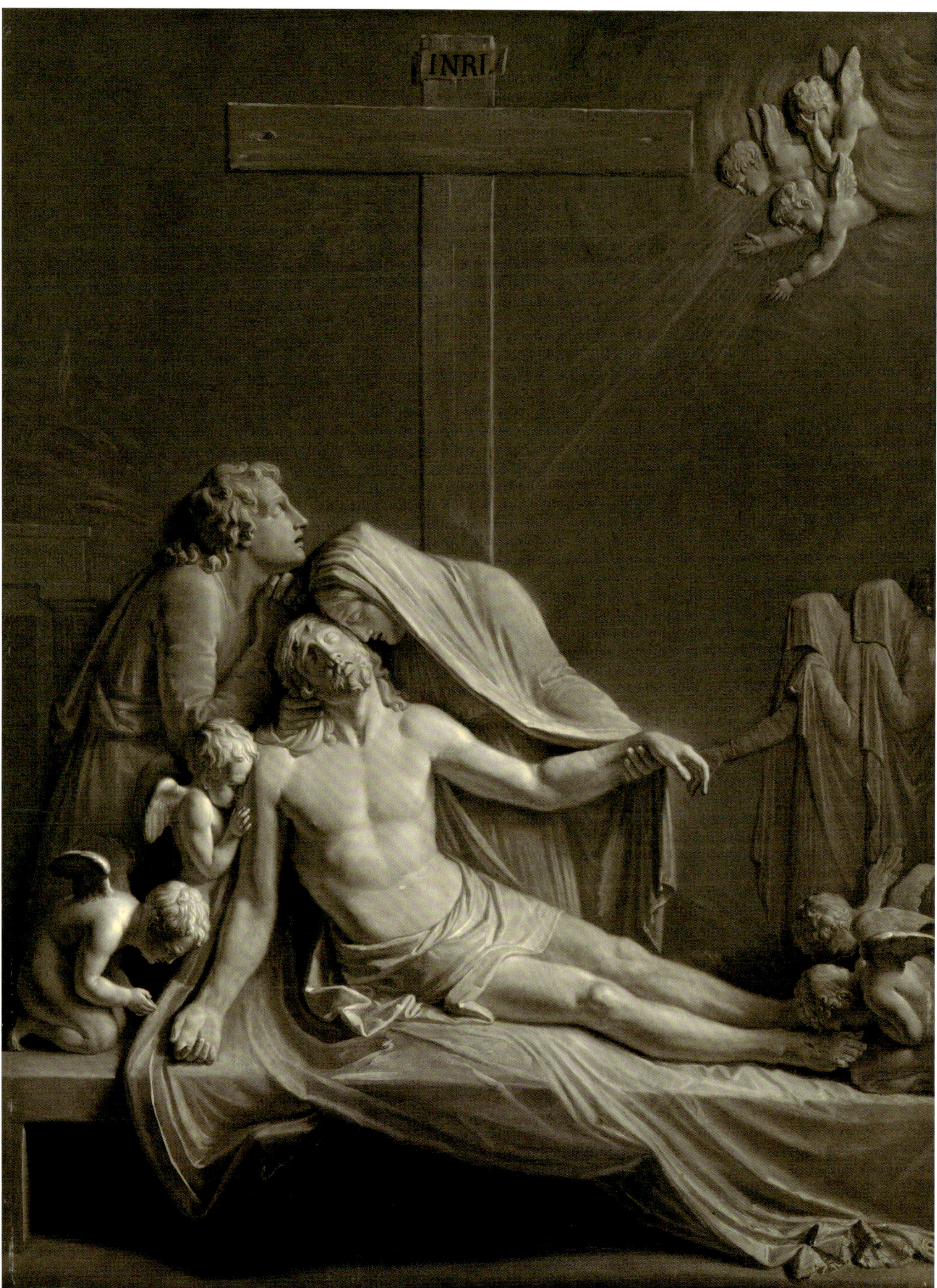
INRI

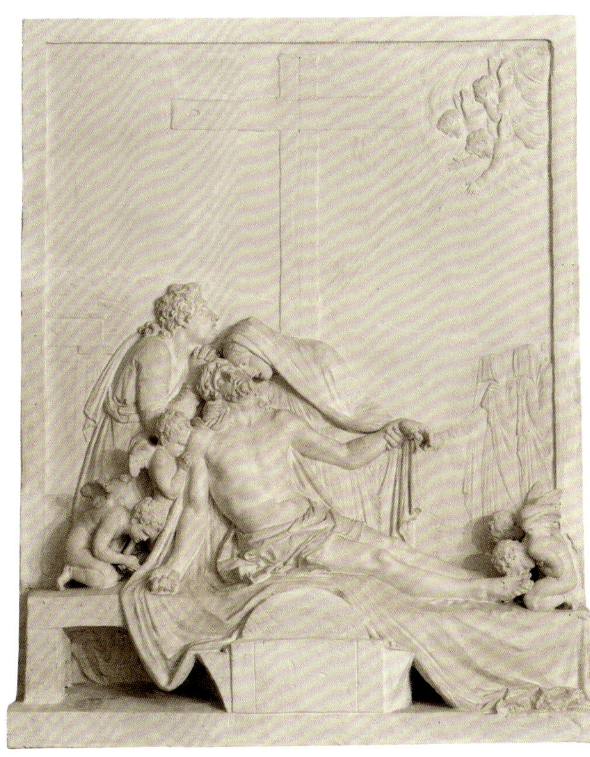

for prints, which allowed sculptors to disseminate their works to a wide and
varied public.[45]

Nocchi's painting of the *Deposition* after Antonio Canova's plaster
model of the same subject from 1800, is a case in point (cat. 38 and fig. 33).
Nocchi, the official painter of the Apostolic Palace, was an ideal candidate
for this kind of work, having studied antique bas-reliefs, which informed his
paintings after sculptures such as the *Deposition*. Nocchi's skilful modelling
with light and shadow effectively imitates Canova's transitions between deep
and shallow relief. In this case, Nocchi's convincing imitation is likely to have
served as a 'stand-in' for Canova's original with the patron, the Venetian Count
Antonio Widmann. Canova probably conceived the work for a tomb, given
the presence of the coffin underneath Christ and of the two mourners in the
right background of the plaster modello. X-radiographs of Nocchi's painting
reveal that the coffin was originally included but subsequently covered up by
an extension of the drapery, the only place where the painter departed from
Canova's plaster model.[46] Interestingly, it was not Canova but a pupil and close
collaborator, Antonio d'Este (1754–1837), who carved a marble *Deposition*
after Canova's plaster modello much smaller than was originally intended
(cat. 39), possibly using Nocchi's grisaille as an aid in the process. D'Este
directed Canova's studio in Rome and often made replicas after his works. In
d'Este's marble, the coffin is missing, as in Nocchi's grisaille, but the drapery
forms a rounded arch to imply its presence. Nocchi and d'Este's versions of
the *Deposition*, in monochrome and marble, demonstrate how monochrome

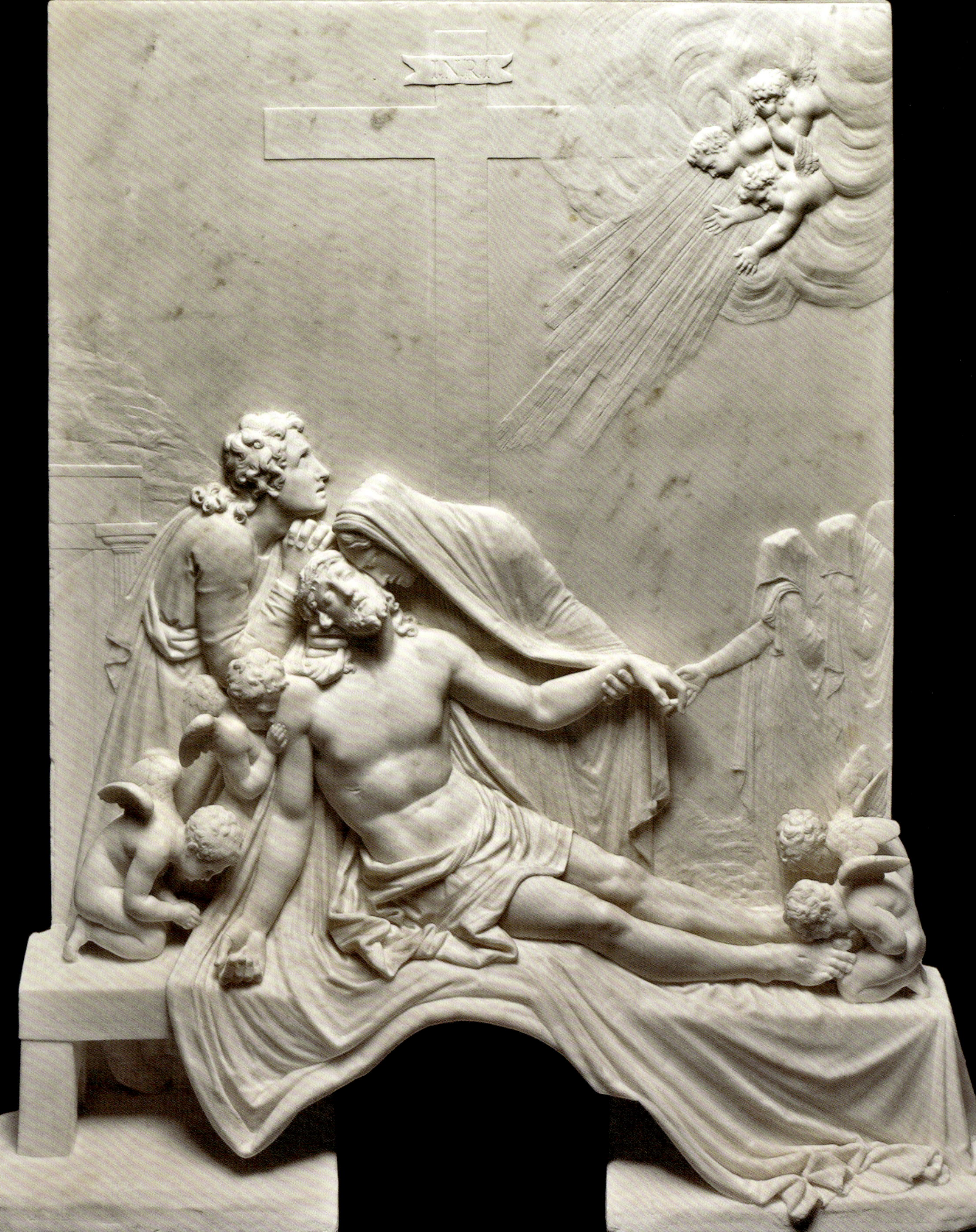
INRI

painting of sculpture served as an intermediary between the initial model and the finished work, in this case not executed by Canova himself.

While the tradition of monochrome painting continued to thrive into the nineteenth century and beyond, the practice of painting feigned sculptures in grisaille gradually diminished, as tastes changed. The consistent production of sculptural grisailles from the fourteenth to the nineteenth centuries, however, attests to their enduring appeal for a multitude of purposes, such as personal or public devotion, a revival of interest in the Antique, an overt engagement with the *paragone*, or for sumptuous secular decoration.

Cat. 39
Antonio d'Este (1754–1837) after a model by
Antonio Canova (1757–1822)
Deposition, after 1800
Marble, 86 × 80 cm
The Art Institute of Chicago. Bequest of
Mrs Bertha C. Loomis, 1966.130

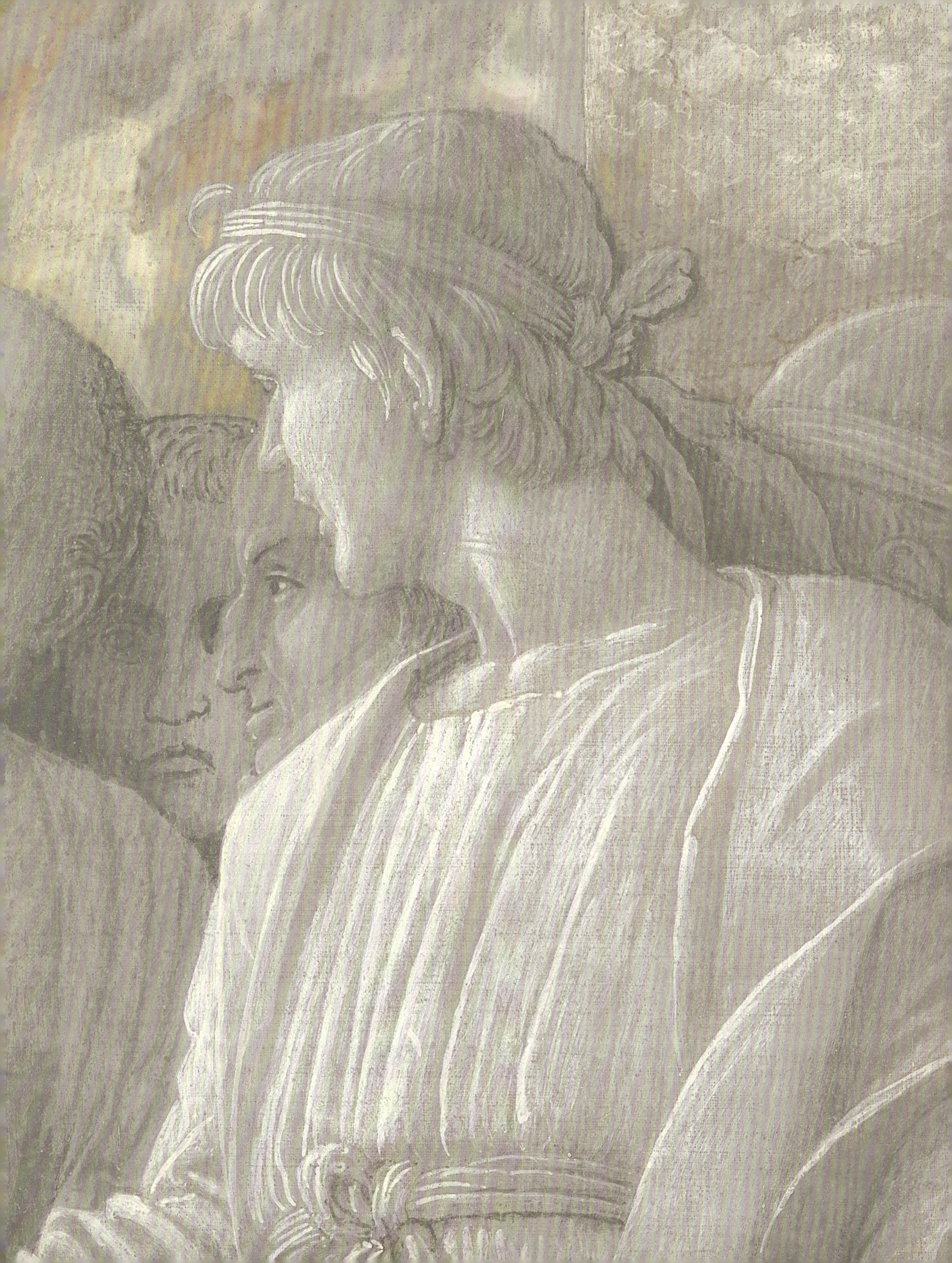

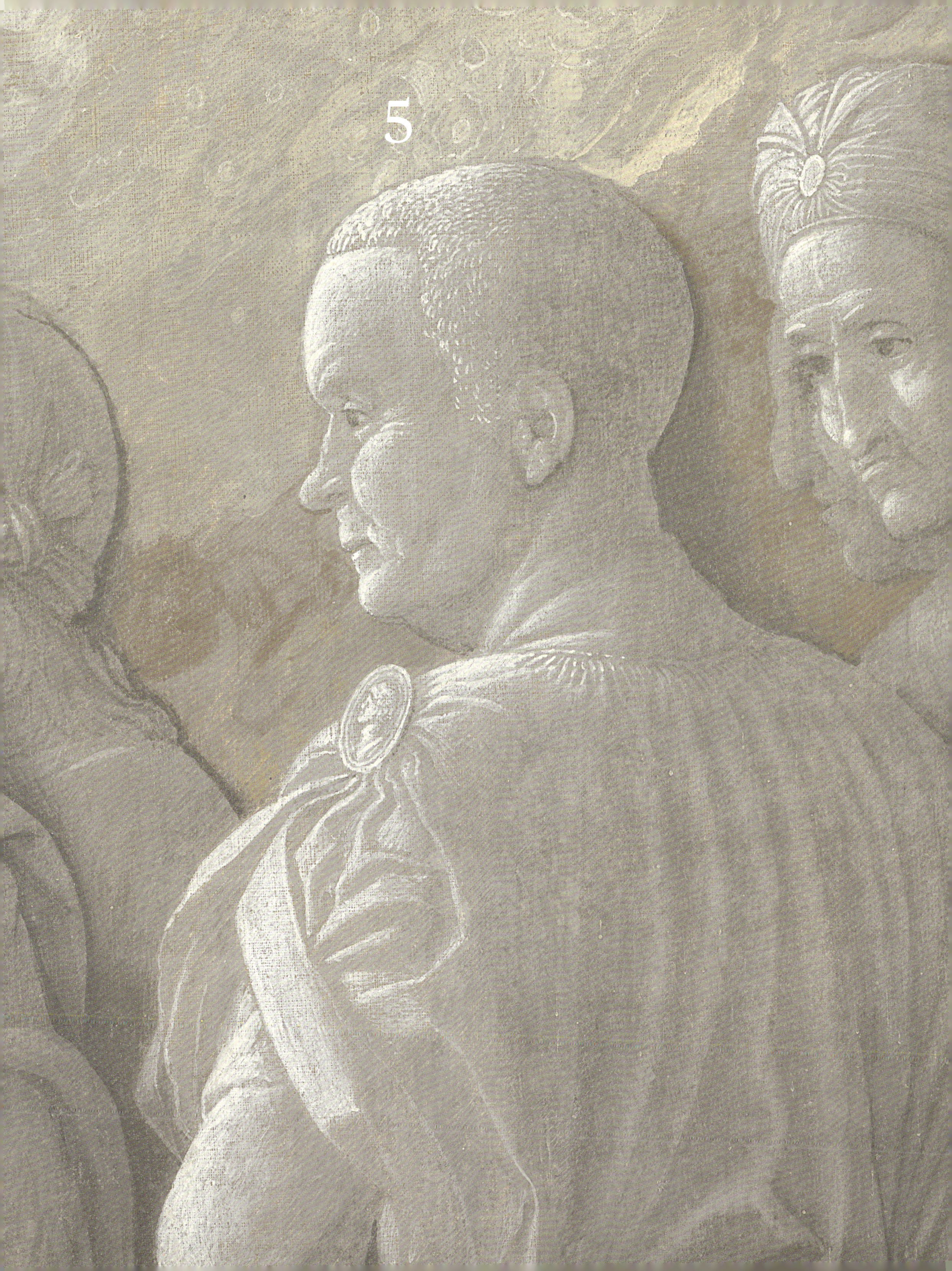
5

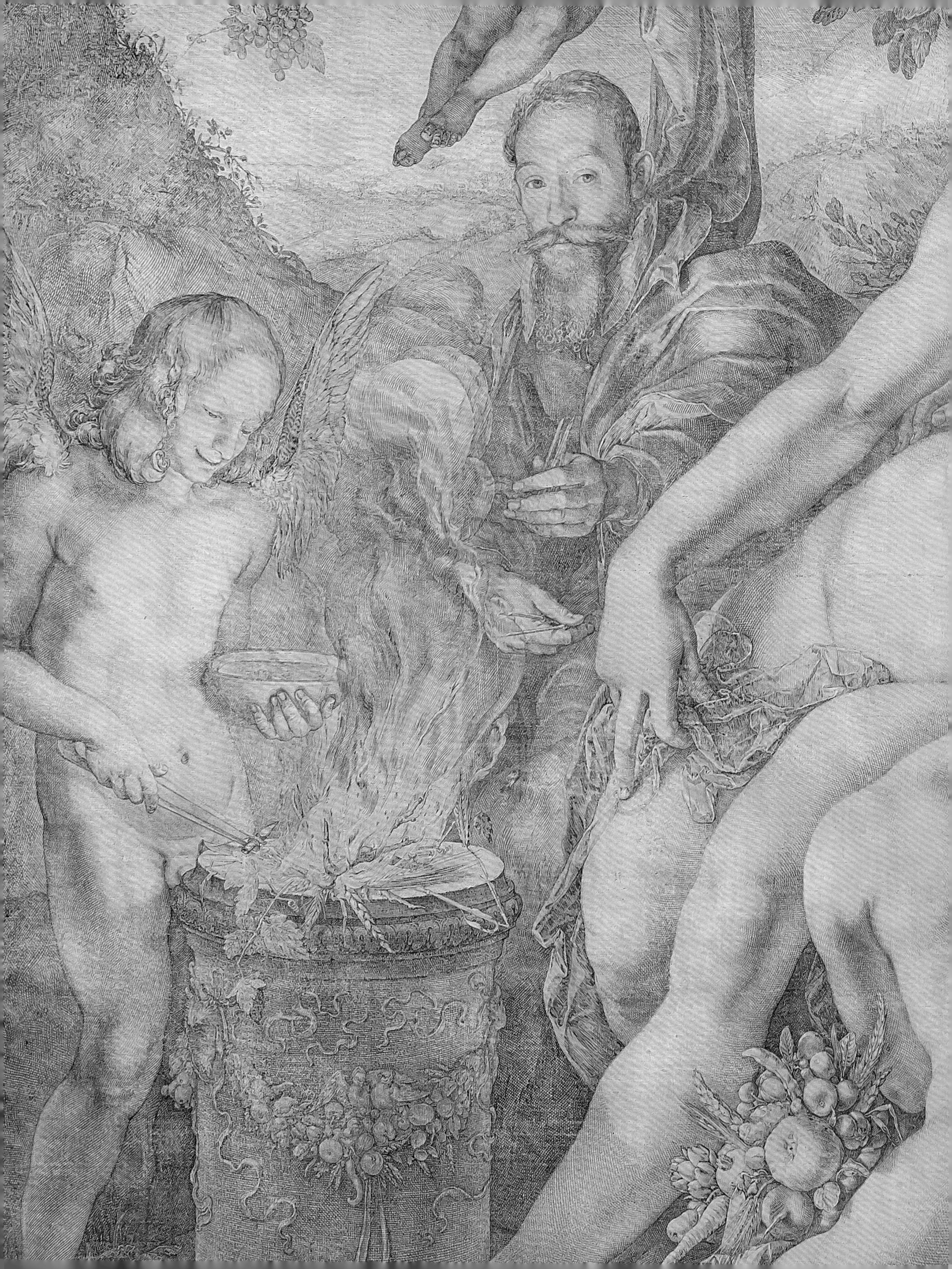

Monochrome Painting and Printmaking

Lelia Packer

From the sixteenth century onwards, painters were highly conscious of the visual language of printmaking. Many young artists first learned to draw by copying prints, which ensured that, at an impressionable stage in their artistic development, they understood the medium's graphic idiom before that of any other art form. Prints were easily accessible and affordable, so they could be used repeatedly and replaced easily as models in painters' studios. Polychrome paintings were often reproduced as prints, enabling painters to disseminate their works widely. Given the widespread availability and use of prints, it is no surprise that artists responded to the medium in monochrome painting. Grisaille paintings were used in varied and often unprecedented ways, not only in preparation for making prints but also to compete with them.

Preparing prints

From the second half of the sixteenth century, monochrome oil sketches played a critical role in the process of making engraved prints. Their limited palette was useful for planning designs, which were most often (but not exclusively) printed with black ink on white paper. The monochrome oil sketch allowed artists to concentrate on tone, texture and volume, expressing nuances of light and shadow, which the printmaker could then translate into a linear design in print.[1]

Engraving, a highly specialised and laborious print process, involves incising grooves with a sharp tool called a burin onto a metal (usually copper) plate. Making an engraving often involved a number of people – the designer, the engraver and the publisher – although one individual could sometimes play more than one role. Compositions were carefully planned in preliminary designs to avoid having to make changes once the lines were engraved. Print designs started out as drawings on paper; in time, oil sketches were also adopted for this purpose. For example, in the middle years of the sixteenth century, such artists as Pieter Bruegel the Elder and Maarten van Heemskerck (1498–1574) produced detailed preparatory drawings for prints that outlined each burin stroke, line by line. By contrast, late sixteenth-century printmakers such as Hendrik Goltzius were less prescriptive, creating sketchy wash drawings to plan and emphasise the interplay between light and dark, or chiaroscuro. Other Northern artists such as Dirck Barendsz. (1534–1592) and Otto van Veen (1556–1629) were among the first to turn to black-and-white oil sketches on paper for similar effects in their preparatory designs for prints.[2] In parallel, chiaroscuro woodcuts circulated at the time and influenced the development of oil sketches for print designs. This relief print process used multiple blocks printed in different colours, the final print recalling wash drawings which sat somewhere between monochrome and colour images. Gradually, by the

Hendrik Goltzius (1558–1617)
Without Ceres and Bacchus, Venus would Freeze, 1606, detail of cat. 46

seventeenth century, artists introduced panel and canvas as supports for oil sketches, which gave them greater longevity in the studio and, in time, led to their becoming collectable works of art in their own right.

The process of designing prints using monochrome oil sketches was fully explored during the first half of the seventeenth century by the Flemish master Peter Paul Rubens.[3] Rubens, a great self-promoter, understood the potential of printed images for popularising his style and reputation, and for financial gain. He instructed his assistants to produce oil sketches after his paintings which he, in turn, corrected to his liking.[4] He also made oil sketches himself, both of independent compositions and after his own paintings, which he used for print designs. Keeping close supervision over production, Rubens employed the greatest reproductive engravers of the day to translate these designs into prints.[5]

Rubens's most gifted collaborator, Anthony van Dyck (1599–1641), began producing oil sketches for prints while in the master's studio in the 1610s.[6] In 1629, Van Dyck began commissioning prints after his own paintings, some of which he prepared using oil sketches.[7] Van Dyck's sketches were largely monochromatic and thus bear close resemblance to the work of a draughtsman. Van Dyck produced numerous oil sketches for his *Iconography*, an ambitious portrait print series of illustrious contemporaries, first published as a bound edition in 1645 or 1646, after his death.[8]

One of Van Dyck's most highly finished grisaille sketches is *Rinaldo and Armida* (cat. 41), a monochrome version of an earlier, larger polychrome painting produced for Stadholder Frederik Hendrik, Prince of Orange, and his wife, Amalia van Solms (cat. 40). The painting represents an episode from the Italian poet Torquato Tasso's *Gerusalemme Liberata* (1581), an extremely popular epic poem set during First Crusade. Van Dyck depicted the moment when the crusaders Carlo and Ubaldo, hidden behind shrubbery on the left, discover their companion Rinaldo lying enamoured in the lap of Armida, a Saracen sorceress and one of Satan's instruments against the Christian knights.

Van Dyck began the grisaille version of the painting in 1634, two years after his original, with the aim of translating it into a print. However, the composition was not engraved until after Van Dyck's death, by Pieter de Jode the Younger (1606–about 1674) in 1644 (cat. 42). The grisaille reproduces the original painting faithfully, in the same direction, aside from the inclusion of more foliage in the upper section, which has been read as an indication that the original has been cut down.[9] It is more likely that this upper extension in the grisaille was meant to parallel the space left underneath the image for an inscription in the print. Van Dyck's careful modelling with light and shadow in the grisaille provided a clear guide for De Jode, who faithfully

Cat. 40
Anthony van Dyck (1599–1641)
Rinaldo and Armida, about 1632
Oil on canvas, 133 × 109 cm
Musée du Louvre, Département des Peintures, Paris, inv. 1235

Following pages
Cat. 41
Anthony van Dyck (1599–1641)
Rinaldo and Armida, 1634–5
Oil on wood, 57 × 41.5 cm
The National Gallery, London, NG 877.2

Cat. 42
Pieter de Jode the Younger
(1606–about 1674) **after Anthony van Dyck**
(1599–1641)
Rinaldo and Armida, 1644
Engraving, 61.8 × 42.3 cm
Museum Boijmans Van Beuningen, Rotterdam, FA 76/16154 (PK)

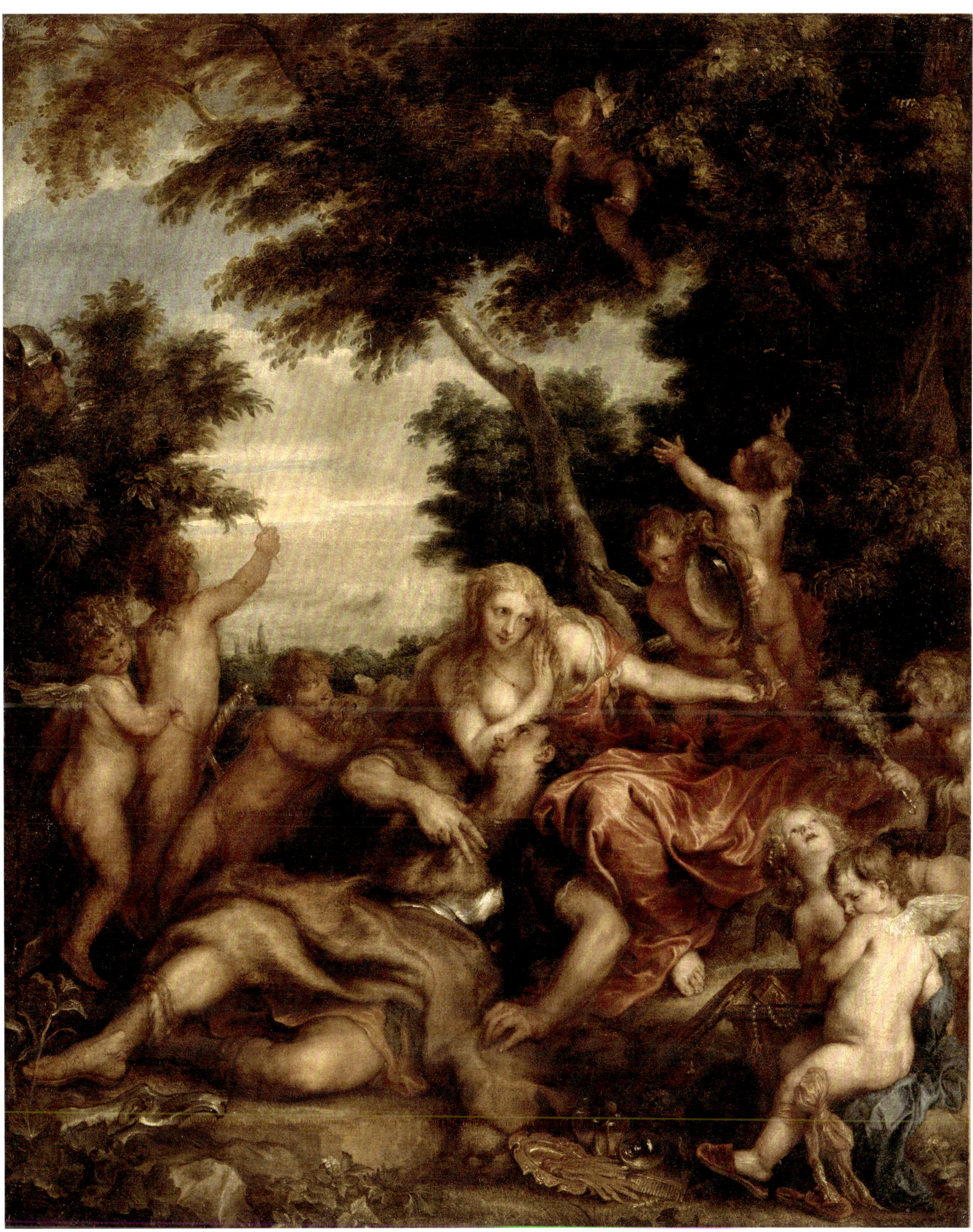

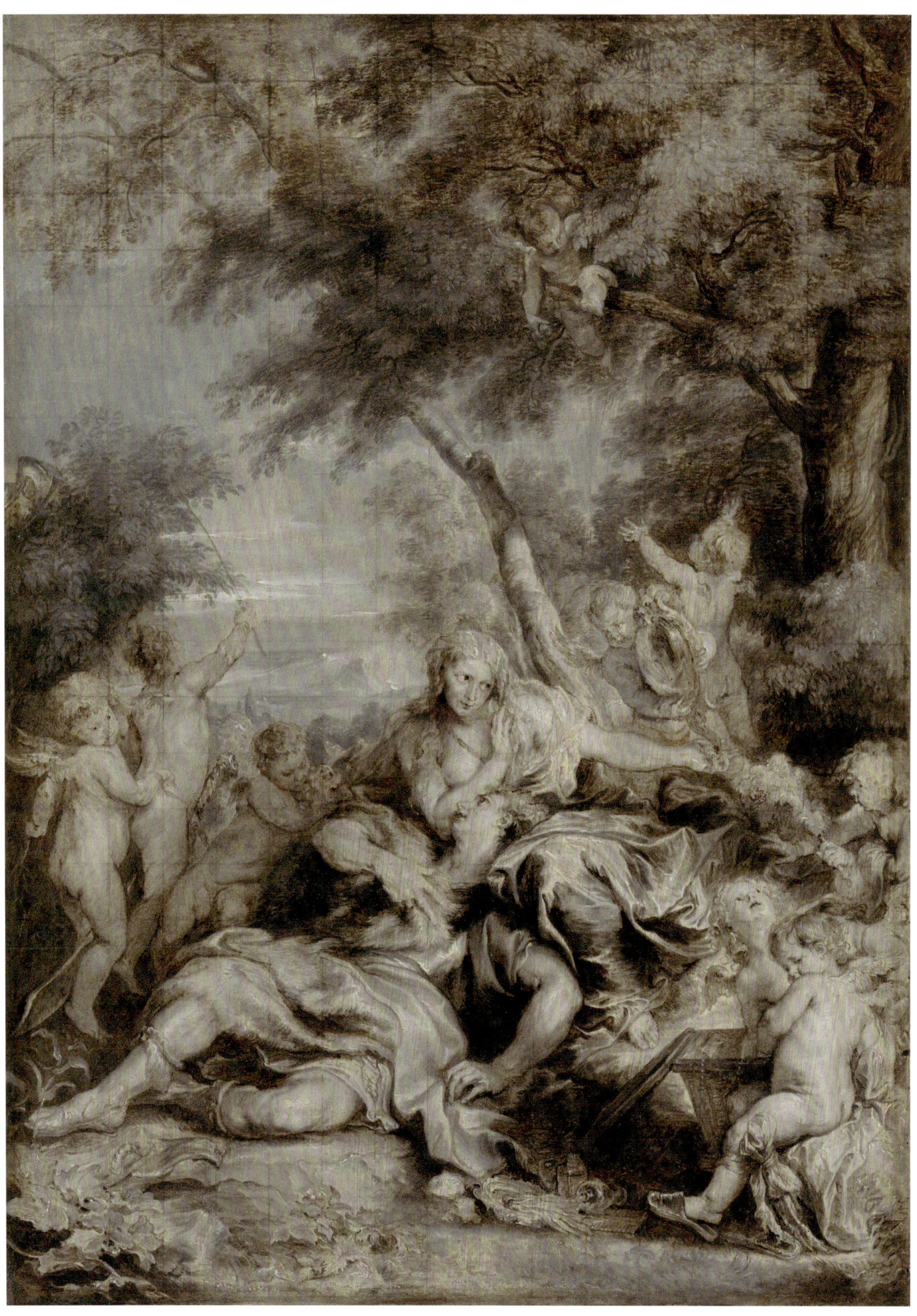

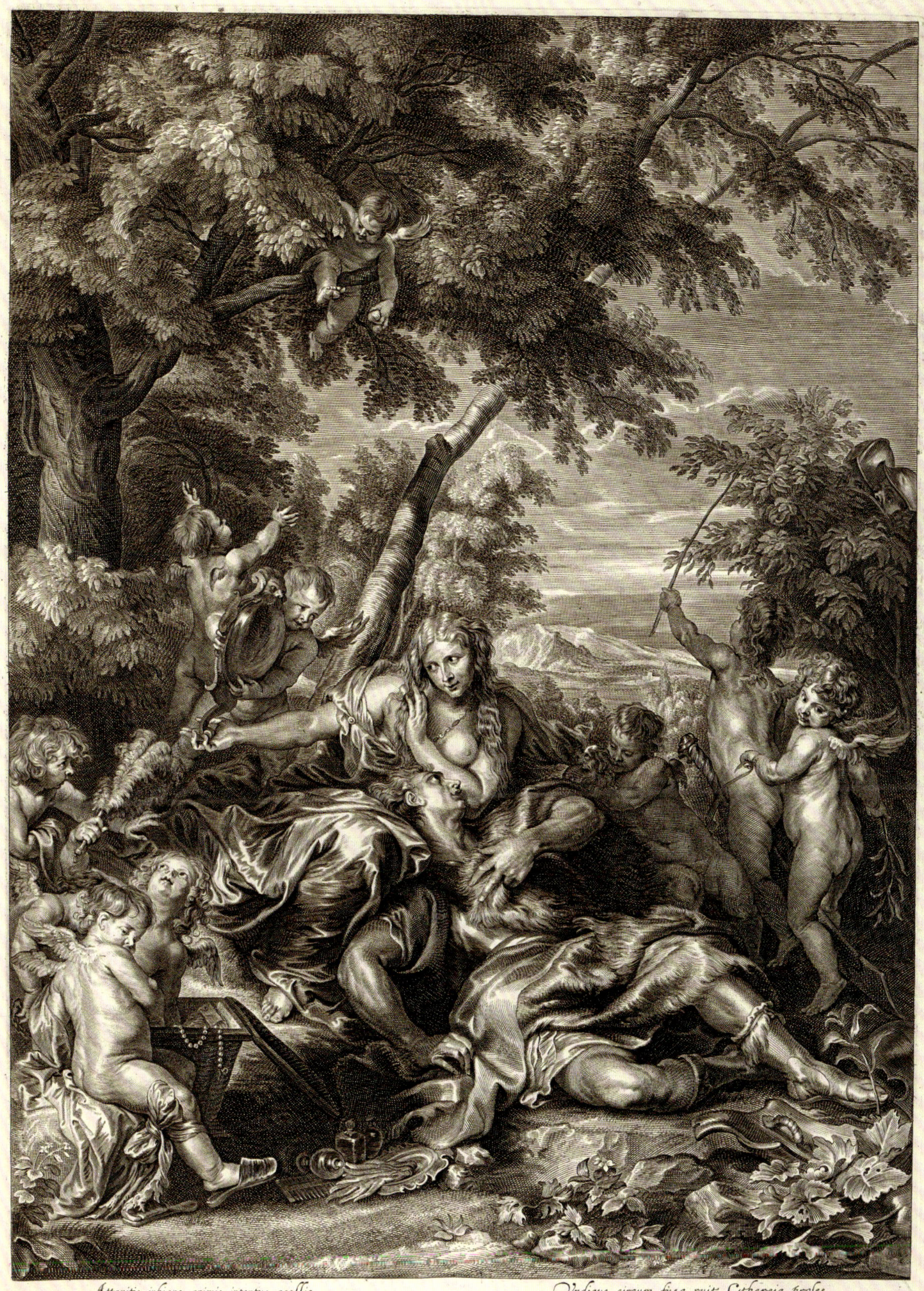

Attonitis inhians animis, intentus ocellis,
Armidæ in fusus gremio meditatur amorem,
Heros Rinaldus, speculoque in fixa moratur
Illa; fouens tenero flagrantes pectore flammas.

Vndique circum fusa ruit Cithereia proles
Et referens equitem latum consurgit in ensem
At parte ex aliâ contrectant Virginis arma
Hæc ridet stupet hæc opibus confusa superbis.
L. Lancelottus Lud.

Antonis van Dyck Eques pinxit.   Ioan. Lespeel excudit Antuerpiæ.   Petrus de Iode sculpsit 1644.

translated Van Dyck's fine brushwork into a sophisticated linear design. Interestingly, the sharpness of the engraved lines rendered some details, such as the reflective helmets of Carlo and Ubaldo, more easily distinguishable in the print than in the sketch. The print, in turn, served as a source for later painted copies in colour, where the copyists had to imagine or 'fill in' the colours absent in the print.[10]

It is unclear why it took so long for the print to be made, especially considering that the grisaille was incised with a square grid while the paint was still wet, indicating that it was conceived for transfer to the copper plate from the start.[11] This is supported by the fact that the grisaille and the print are roughly the same size, a common feature of grisailles destined to be translated into prints. Some have wondered whether the grisaille served as a preliminary study for the colour painting or as the final presentation piece for Frederik Hendrik's approval.[12] However, it has been convincingly shown that the panel dates to the period Van Dyck spent in the southern Netherlands in 1634–5, at least two years after the completion of the original.[13]

Like Van Dyck, the great Dutch master Rembrandt van Rijn modelled himself – with an explicit rivalry – on Rubens, especially when it came to self-promotion through prints. During the early 1630s, soon after moving to Amsterdam to establish himself as a history painter, Rembrandt began collaborating with the Leiden printmaker Johannes (Jan) van Vliet (about 1600/10–1668?), who reproduced a number of Rembrandt's paintings in print.[14] This collaboration might seem surprising, since Rembrandt was a great printmaker in his own right. Commissioning a printmaker was, for Rembrandt, critical in establishing his reputation as a successful painter whose work was held in high esteem and elicited great demand.

Rembrandt's *Ecce Homo* (cat. 43) is the only oil sketch of the near dozen by the master that was certainly produced in preparation for a print.[15] Rembrandt's monochrome sketch and van Vliet's print after it (cat. 44) represent the dramatic moment from Saint John's Gospel when Pontius Pilate presented Christ to the Jewish people, who called for his crucifixion. In a highly theatrical way, Rembrandt set the scene on a dais with a canopy and curtain framing the composition on the left. Christ stands in the centre of a mob of soldiers whose open mouths, dynamic poses and gruesome expressions vividly convey their ignorance. The resulting print is the largest ever produced by or after Rembrandt. The costly investment in such a large copper plate and in a specialised engraver attests to Rembrandt's ambitions at the time.

Van Vliet's print reproduces the overall design of Rembrandt's sketch in mirror image and to scale. The oil sketch was made on paper and subsequently

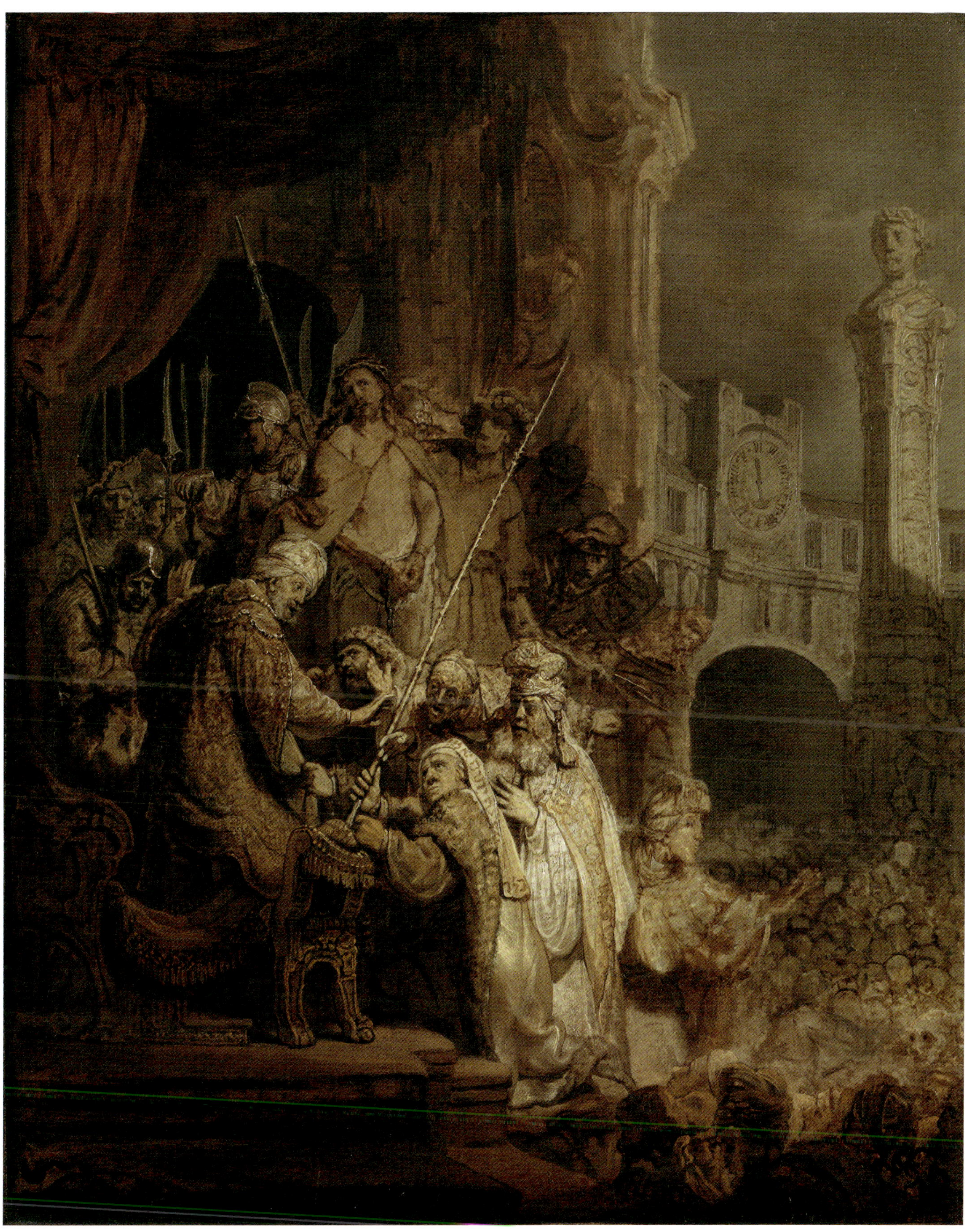

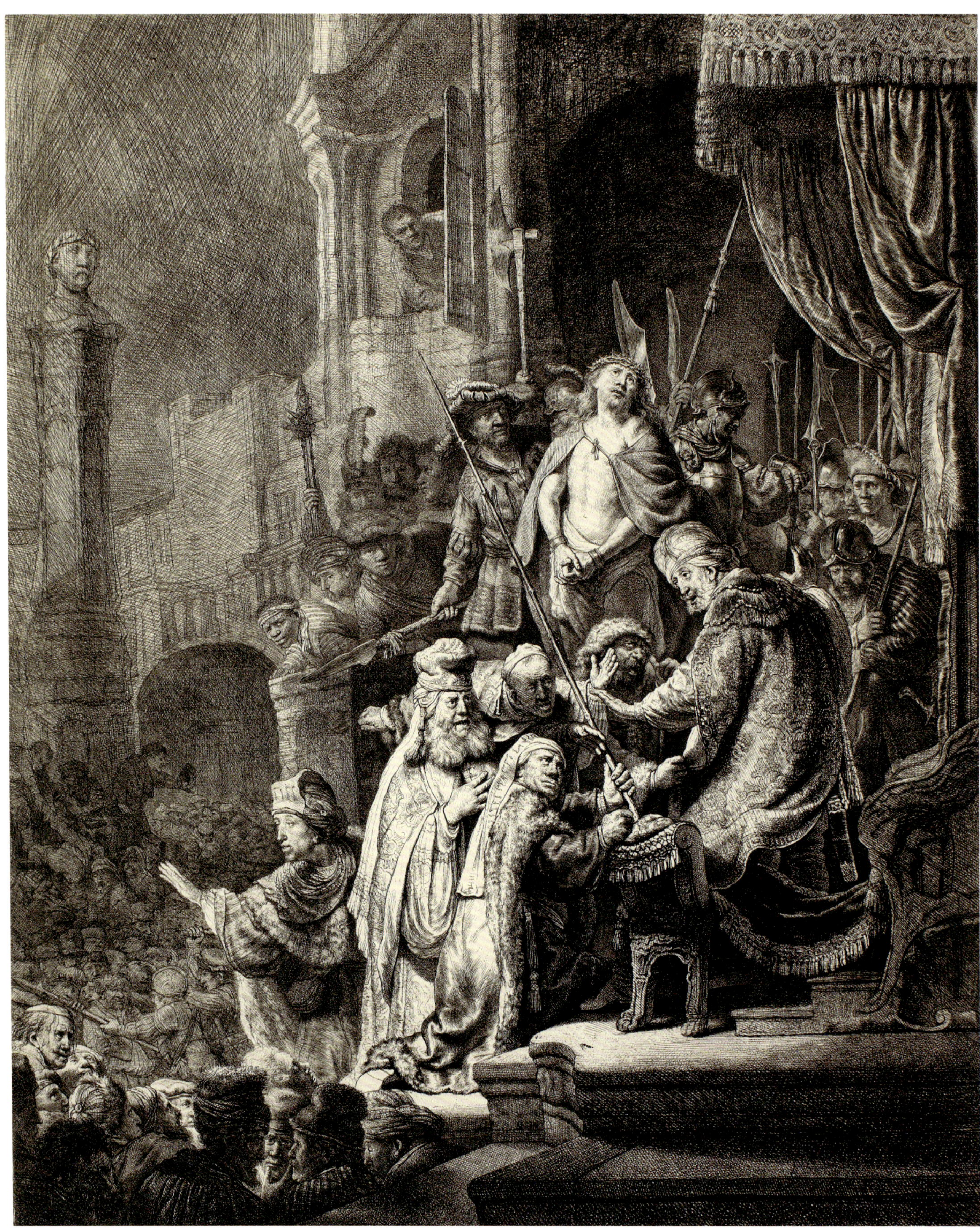

laid down on canvas and varnished. The sketch was incised for transfer to the copper plate in all areas of the composition, even in the most minute details such as Christ's hair.[16] Rembrandt supervised van Vliet closely during the print's production and made corrections in brush and brown oil paint to an initial proof impression of the print.[17] In subsequent states, he even made marks directly on the plate in drypoint, which included adding his own bold signature on the lower edge of the plate. As Rubens did with his own prints, Rembrandt sought a 'privilege' for the print, an early type of copyright, which protected him for a period from copyists.

Rembrandt's repeated interventions during the printmaking process might account for the appearance of the oil sketch itself, which exhibits major discrepancies between highly worked-up areas and roughly indicated, almost indiscernible passages that probably needed further clarification. For example, the group of four priests imploring Pilate to sentence Christ to death is modelled with thick impasto. By contrast, the men to the right of Christ are cursorily sketched in. This variance in handling in Rembrandt's approach can probably be explained as a complex exploration of how to illuminate a scene with light and shadow.

A new genre: pen painting

The rivalry between painting and printmaking is reflected in the Dutch *penschilderij* or pen-painting technique. Tellingly, it was the printmaker Hendrik Goltzius who, at the turn of the seventeenth century, devised this innovative technique which involved drawing in pen and ink on prepared panel or canvas in a manner imitative of engraving.

Born in Germany, Goltzius moved to the Dutch city of Haarlem in 1577 and, by 1582, had established a successful publishing house where he developed a highly innovative engraving style.[18] *The Great Hercules* (1589), designed and engraved by Goltzius on a single, large copper plate, perfectly exemplifies his novel system of deeply cut, swelling and tapering lines (cat. 45). Hercules's exaggerated, bulbous muscles were an opportunity for Goltzius to display his virtuoso manipulation of the burin, creating a printed work that exudes three-dimensionality.

Around the same time, Goltzius began imitating his own novel engraving style in drawings.[19] His famous *Right Hand* (fig. 34) illustrates how the careful pen work parallels the cuts he made to produce stippling and hatching on the copperplate. These experiments encouraged Goltzius to turn next to canvas because, according to Karel van Mander, 'however large the parchments [that he drew on] were, [Goltzius] felt they were still much too small for his grand intentions and talent'.[20] Indeed, Goltzius's pen painting *Without Ceres and*

Cat. 44
Jan van Vliet (about 1600/10–1668?) **after Rembrandt** (1606–1669)
Christ before Pilate (Ecce Homo), 1635–6
Etching and engraving, 54.9 × 44.7 cm
The Syndics of the Fitzwilliam Museum, University of Cambridge, AD.20.15-4

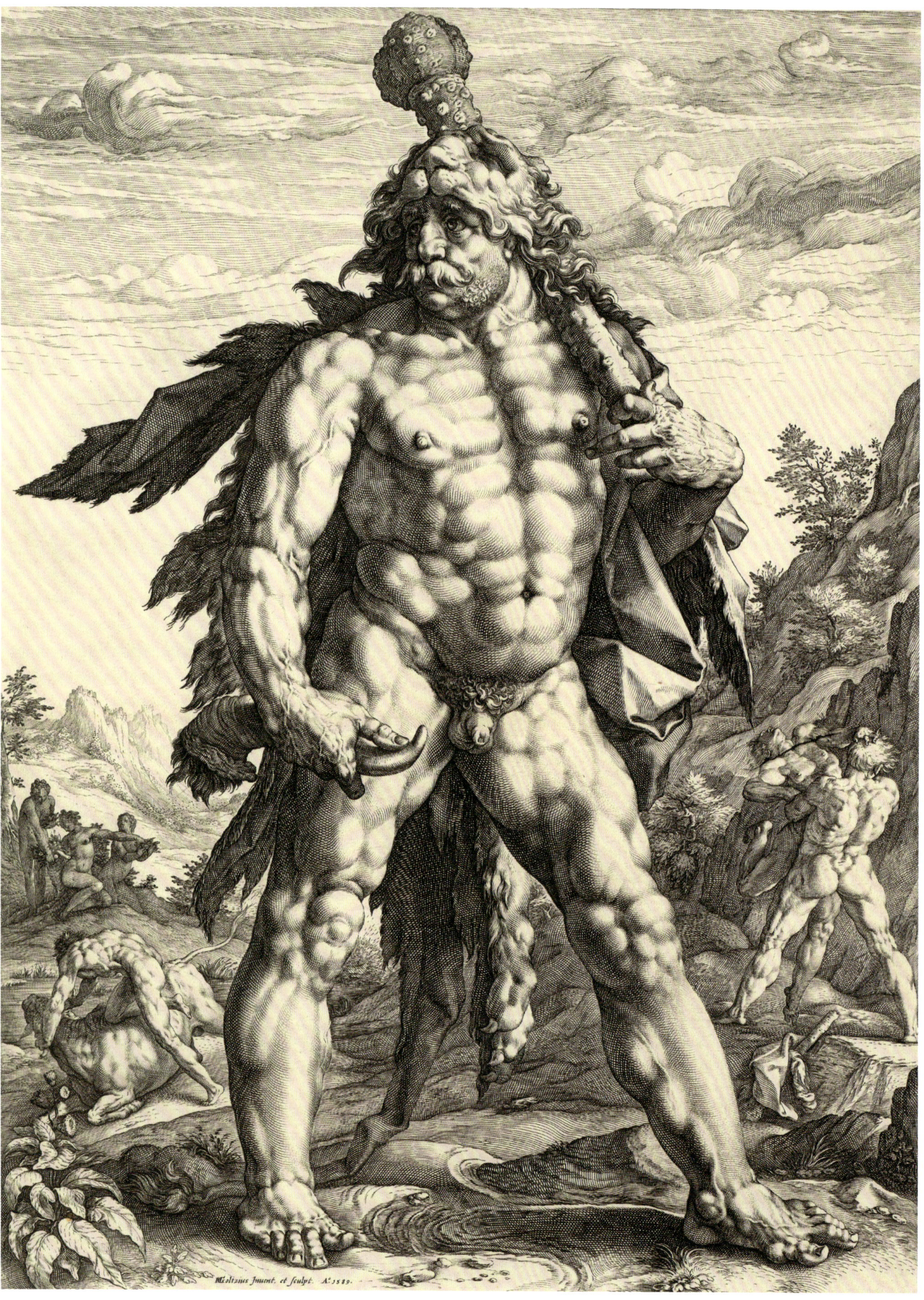

HGoltzius Inuent. et sculpt. A° 1589.

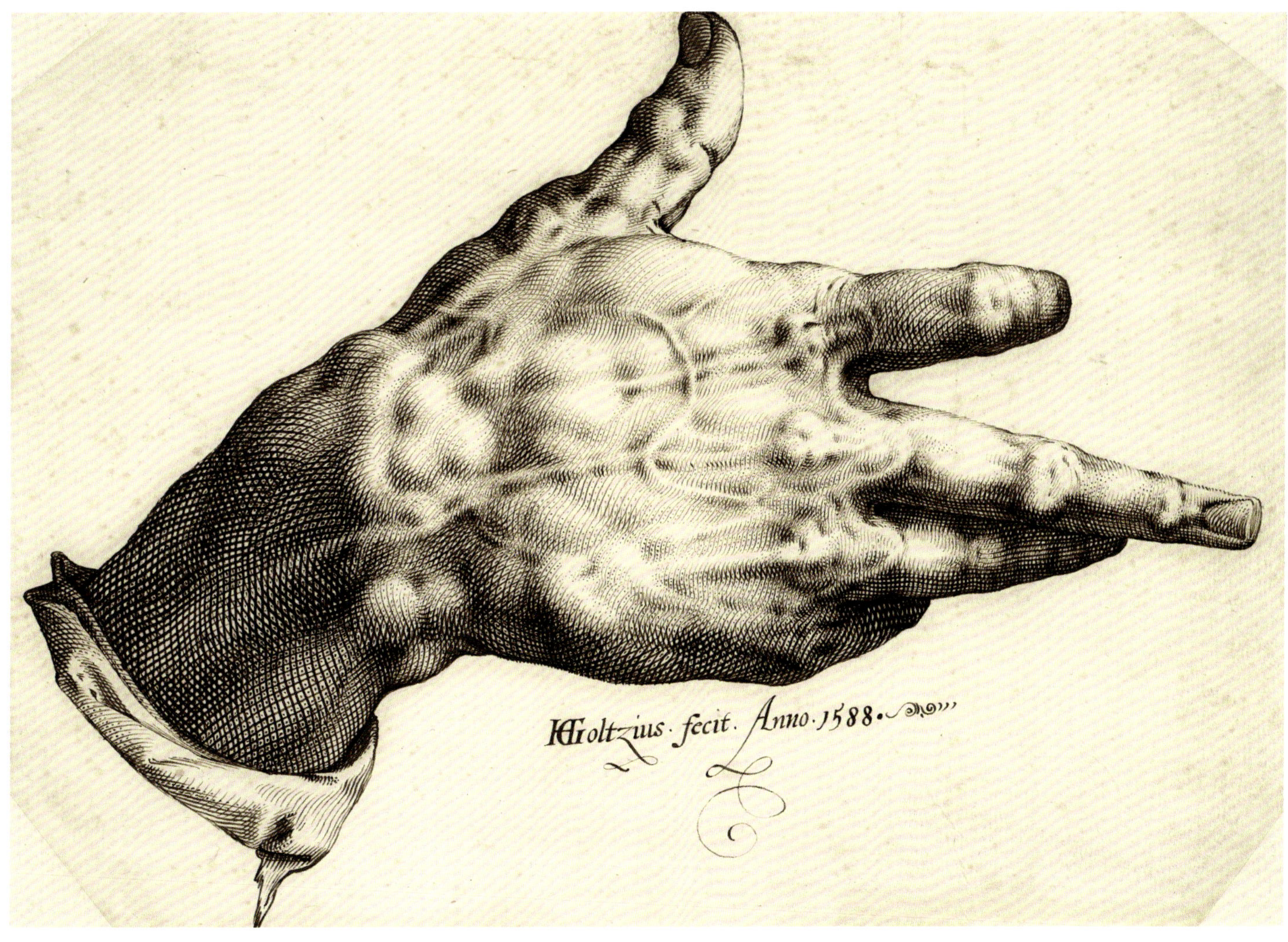

Cat. 45
Hendrik Goltzius (1558–1617)
The Great Hercules, 1589
Engraving, 56.2 × 40.7 cm
Museum Boijmans Van Beuningen, Rotterdam,
BdH 8079 (PK)

Fig. 34
Hendrik Goltzius (1558–1617)
Right Hand, 1588
Pen and ink on paper, 23 × 32.2 cm
Teylers Museum, Haarlem

Bacchus, Venus would Freeze is over two metres high and more than a metre-and-a-half wide, making it the artist's largest pen work on any support (cat. 46). This exceptionally rare canvas illustrates the famous trope from the comedy *The Eunuch* by the ancient Roman dramatist Terence which warns that love grows cold without food and wine. Goltzius drew this colossal image with nearly life-size figures in pen and ink on a prepared canvas, exactly mimicking his own bold engraving style. By using canvas, a support associated with painting, Goltzius created a completely new type of object that demonstrates his ingenuity and technical proficiency whilst blurring clear distinctions among drawing, printmaking and painting.

In 1604, van Mander wrote about this pen painting while it was still a work in progress, anticipating that it would surpass all of Goltzius's previous pen works, which it certainly did.[21] The work was probably commissioned by Emperor Rudolf II (1552–1612), the greatest art patron and collector in western Europe at the time, who owned Goltzius's only other known pen painting,

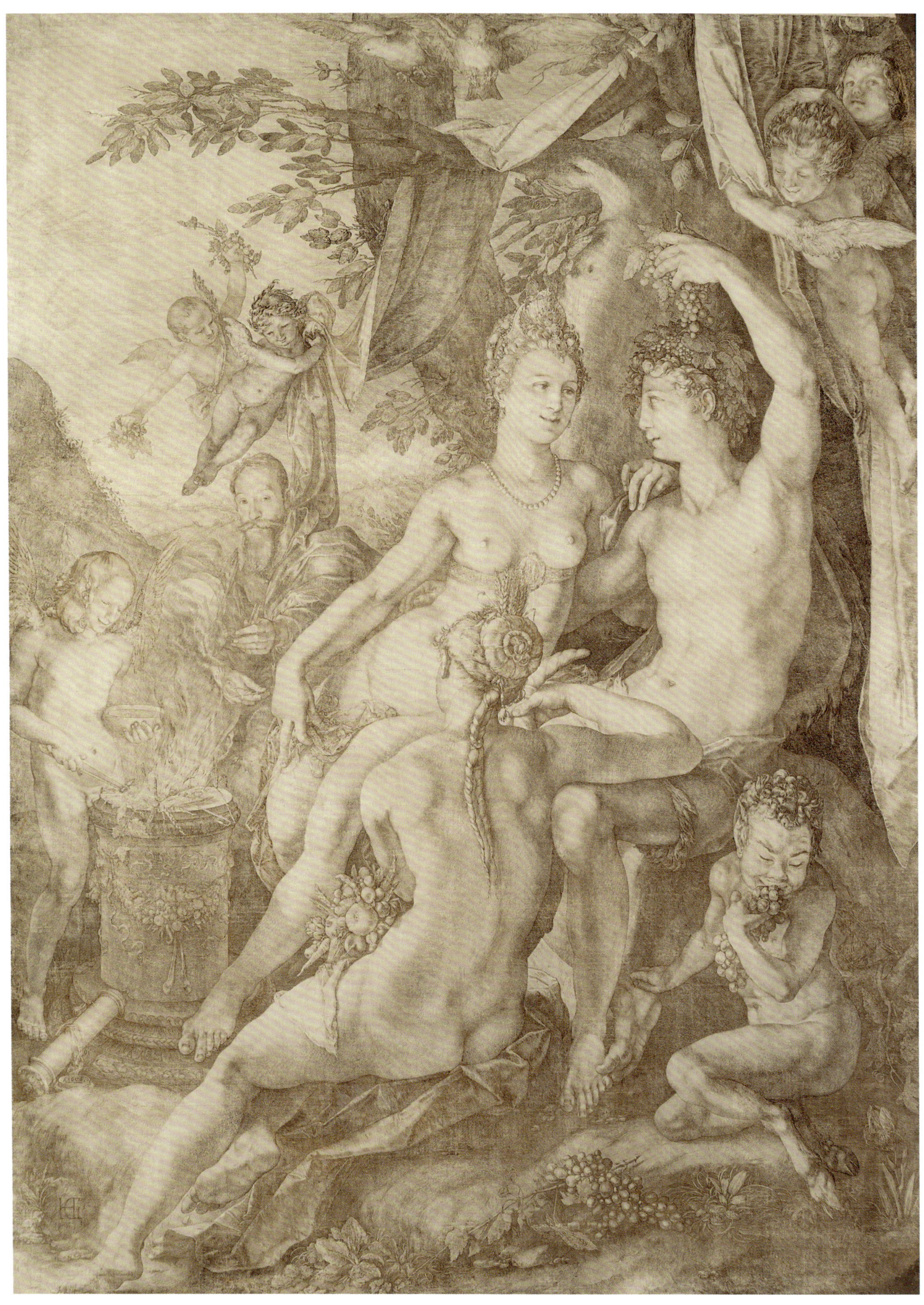

also entitled *Without Ceres and Bacchus, Venus would Freeze* (about 1600–3, Philadelphia Museum of Art).[22] Van Mander recounts how the Emperor was astonished by Goltzius's technique, specifically by 'how it was done, calling in some practitioners of art who were also amazed – for it is very interesting and effective to look upon'.[23] Goltzius further emphasises his manual prowess by including a portrait, to the right of Cupid, of himself holding burins, the very tools he excelled in using in this masterly work of art.

Both of Goltzius's pen paintings were in the possession of Queen Christina of Sweden by the middle of the seventeenth century, when the pen-painting technique was revived in the marine genre.[24] By this time, the Dutch Republic was established as a great seafaring nation, internationally renowned for its superior shipbuilding industry. Van Mander's laudatory passage on Goltzius's pen paintings ensured their fame long after their physical removal from the Dutch Republic, and it is probably to this textual source that Dutch marine pen painters turned for inspiration. Among the earliest and most prolific was the highly gifted draughtsman Willem van de Velde the Elder (1611–1693), who produced numerous pen paintings of naval battles, sea processions and harbours.

During the 1640s, van de Velde, like Goltzius, began by making pen-and-ink drawings on parchment in imitation of engravings, switching to panel and canvas around 1650. *Departure of the Dutch Fleet the 9th of June 1645* (about 1650), a fine, early pen painting by the artist, represents an event that took place five years earlier, when Dutch merchant ships were escorted through the Baltic while Sweden and Denmark were at war (cat. 47). On 9 June 1645, 300 ships set sail under the command and escort of Witte de With, Vice-Admiral of Holland and Westfriesland, whose imposing flagship, the *Brederode*, is represented at the far right of the panel. Van de Velde concentrated on depicting the hustle and bustle of the harbour of Vlieland, where people of all ages gathered to watch this important departure.

Van de Velde laboriously laid down each individual stroke by hand, in a network of parallel and crosshatched lines that convincingly suggest an engraved print. Over the course of the following decade, he began incorporating wash into his technique, probably to speed up production, which made his pen paintings resemble wash drawings more than prints. While the meticulous, exclusively linear technique of this work is as detailed as that of a print, the composition itself is on the scale of a painting, encouraging us to view the object both from up close and from further away. Van de Velde's pen paintings challenged conventional viewing habits, and in doing so, enhanced appreciation of the artist's ingenuity. Van de Velde often sketched *in situ* at sea and had an intimate knowledge of ships. His presence as an eyewitness contributed to

Cat. 46
Hendrik Goltzius (1558–1617)
Without Ceres and Bacchus, Venus would Freeze, 1606
Pen and brown ink over traces of red chalk on prepared canvas, 219 × 163 cm
The State Hermitage Museum, St Petersburg, OP-18983

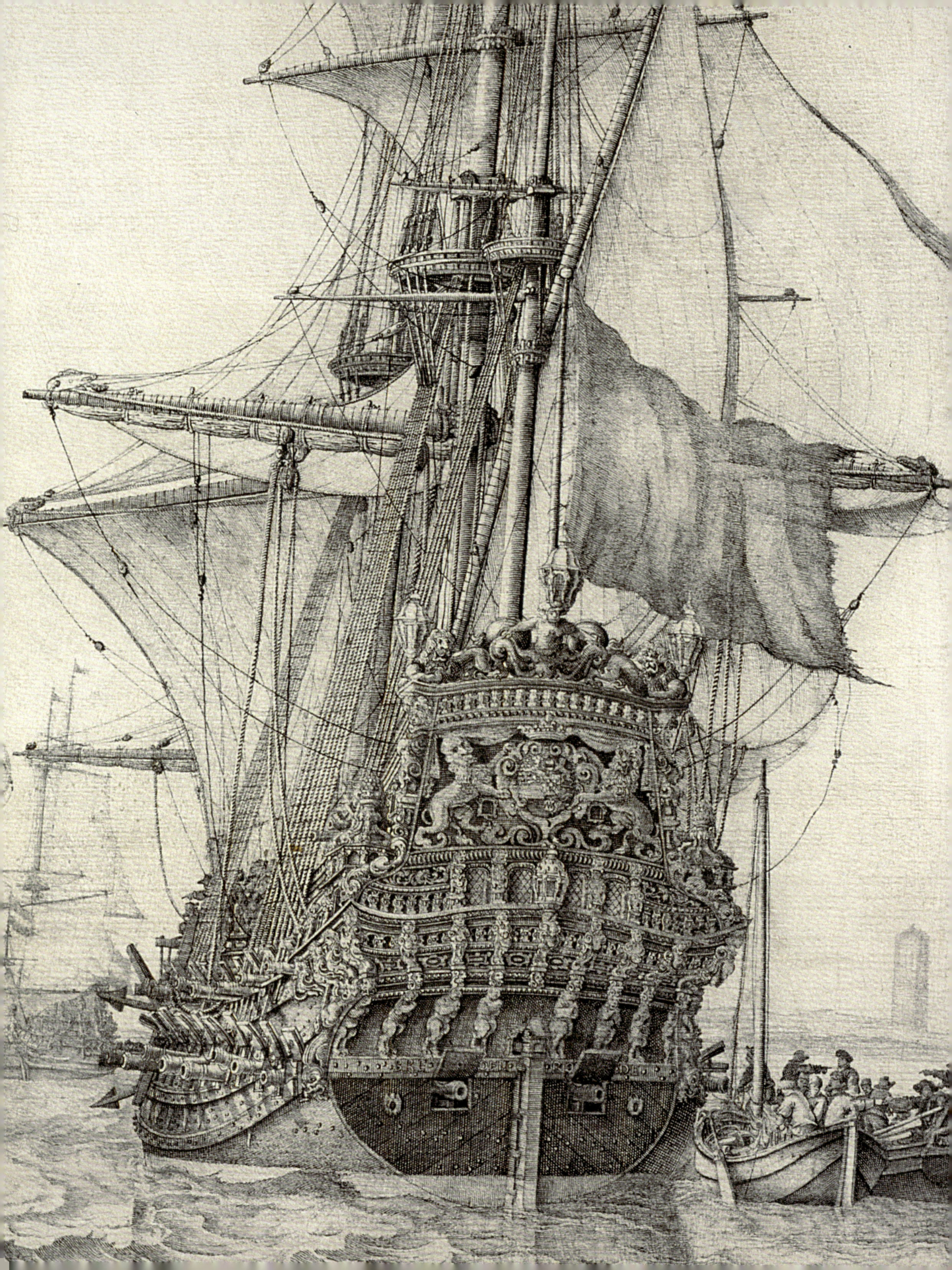

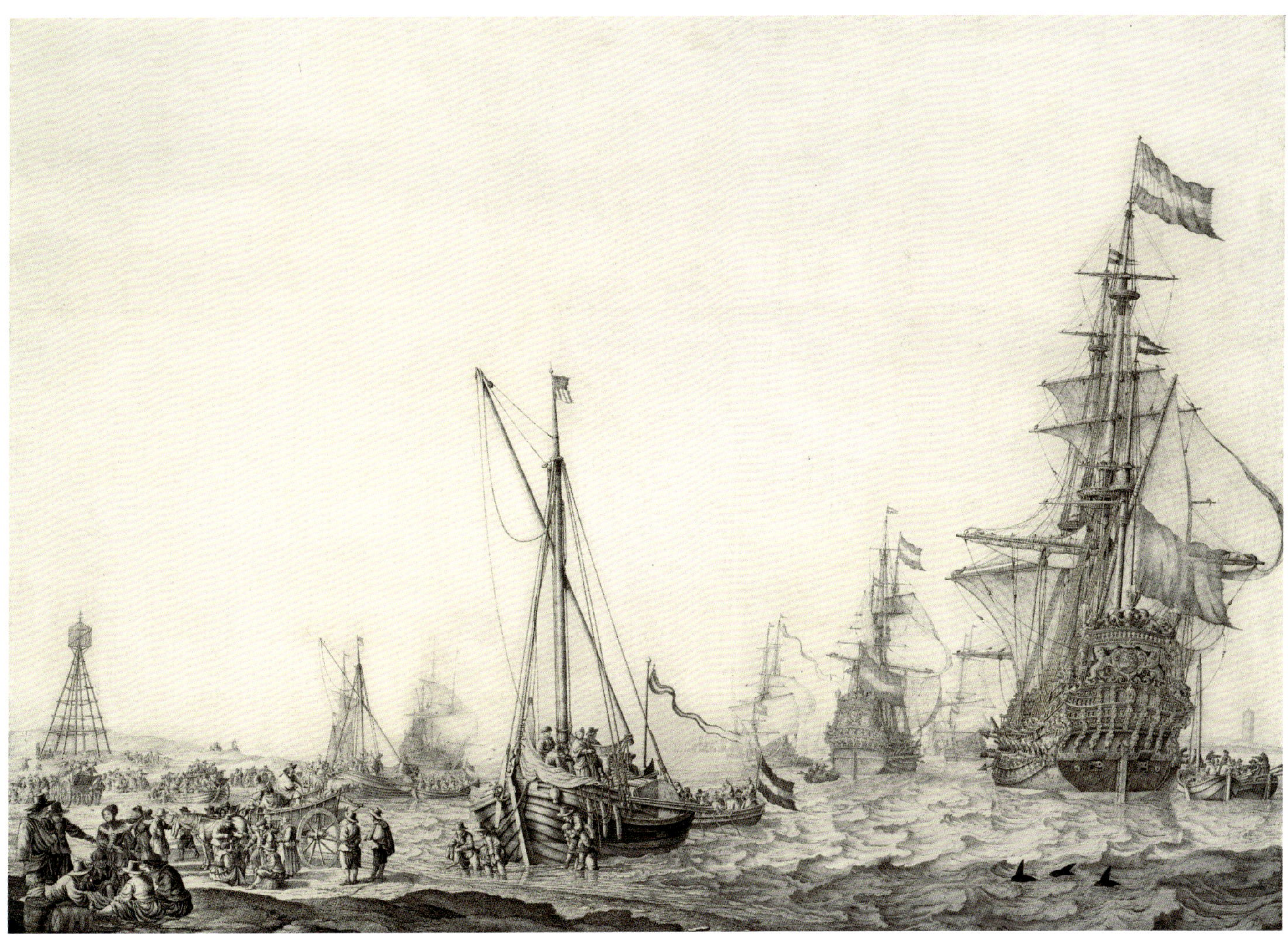

his artistic success, giving credence to the idea that his images were truthful recordings of real events. Working in a print-like manner reinforced this impression of accuracy and documentation.[25]

Monochrome and the *trompe l'oeil* print

Since antiquity, painters have delighted in deceiving their audiences; their viewers, in turn, have long appreciated the painterly deceptions of *trompe l'oeil*. This notion particularly interested painters who sought to create illusions of prints in grisaille, a practice that was especially popular in eighteenth-century France, as seen in the works of Etienne Moulinneuf (about 1720–1789) and Louis-Léopold Boilly.

Moulinneuf's *Back from the Market (La Pourvoyeuse)* (cat. 50) is a convincing painted illusion of a reproductive print after Jean-Siméon Chardin's famous painting of the same name (cat. 48). Chardin's alluring painting, which has long fascinated writers and artists on account of its profound simplicity,

Cat. 47 and detail, left
Willem van de Velde the Elder (1611–1693)
Departure of the Dutch Fleet the 9th of June 1645, about 1650
India ink on prepared panel, 74.3 × 105.4 cm
Museum De Lakenhal, Leiden, S 444

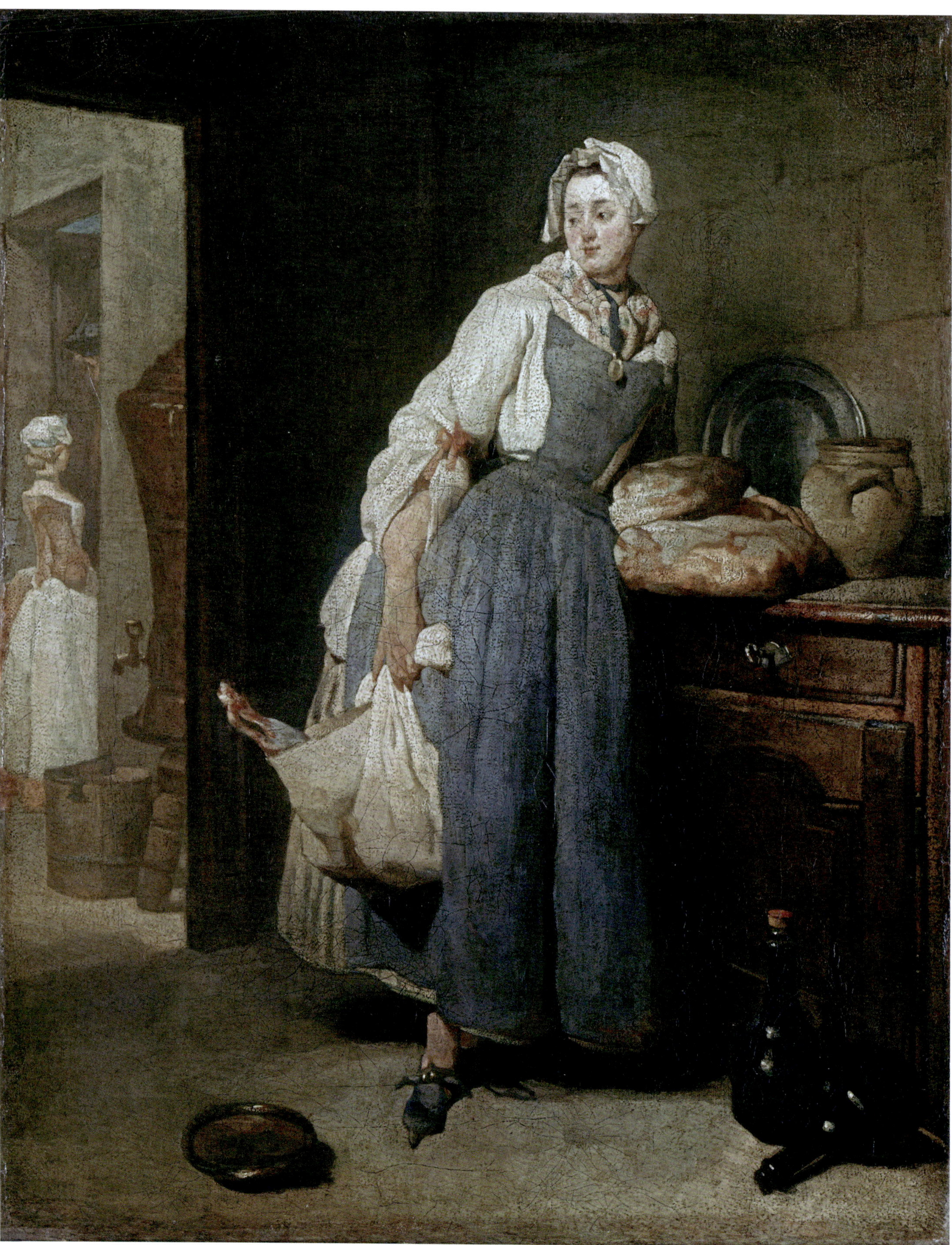

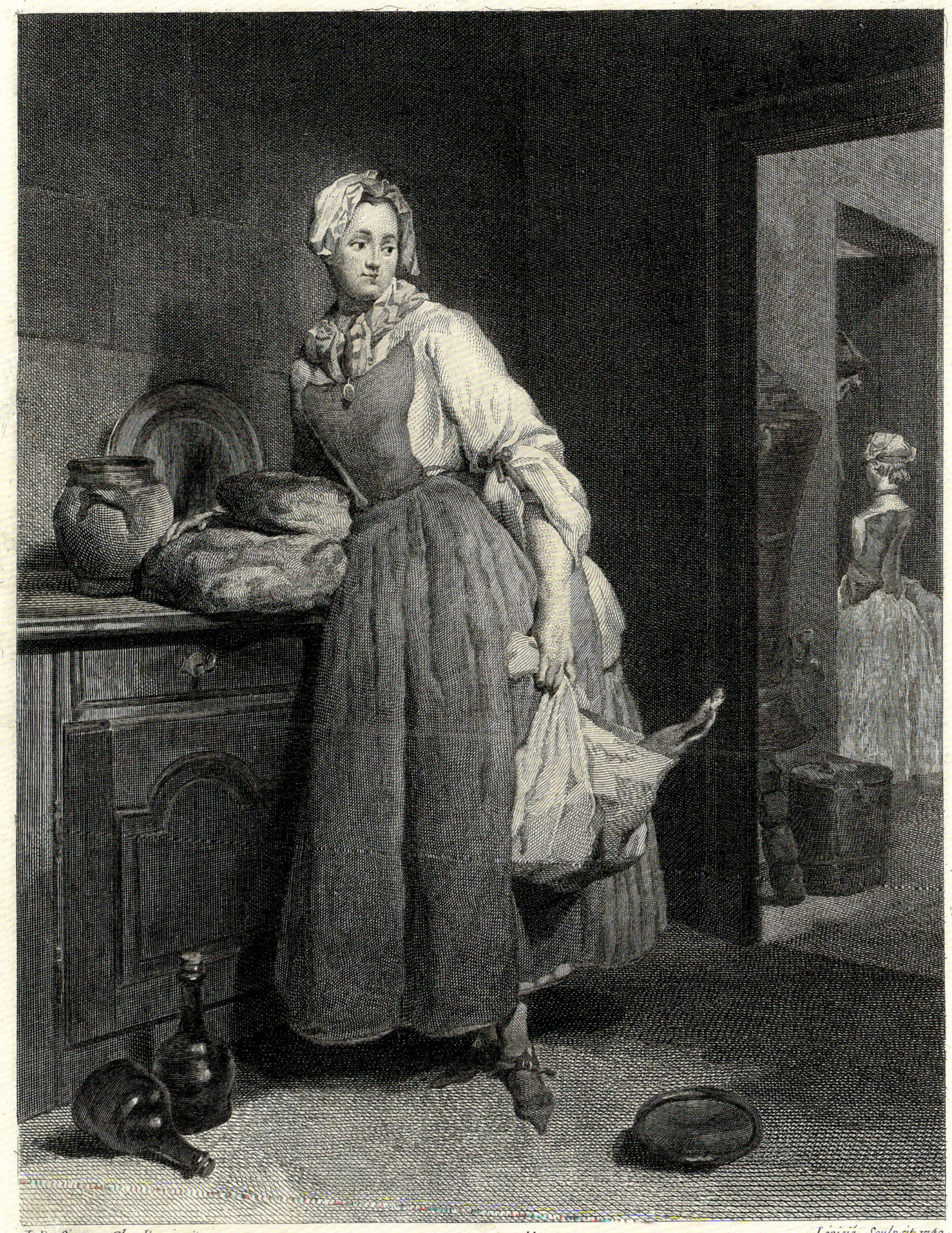

LA POURVOÏEUSE.

A vôtre air j'estime et je pense,   Que vous prenez sur la dépense
Ma chere enfant, sans calculer,   Ce qu'il faut pour vous habiller.

Lepicié

À Paris chez l'Auteur au coin de l'Abreuvoir du Quay des Orfevres.
et chez L. Surugue graveur du Roi, ruë des Noyers, vis a vis le mur de St Yves. Avec Privilege du Roi.

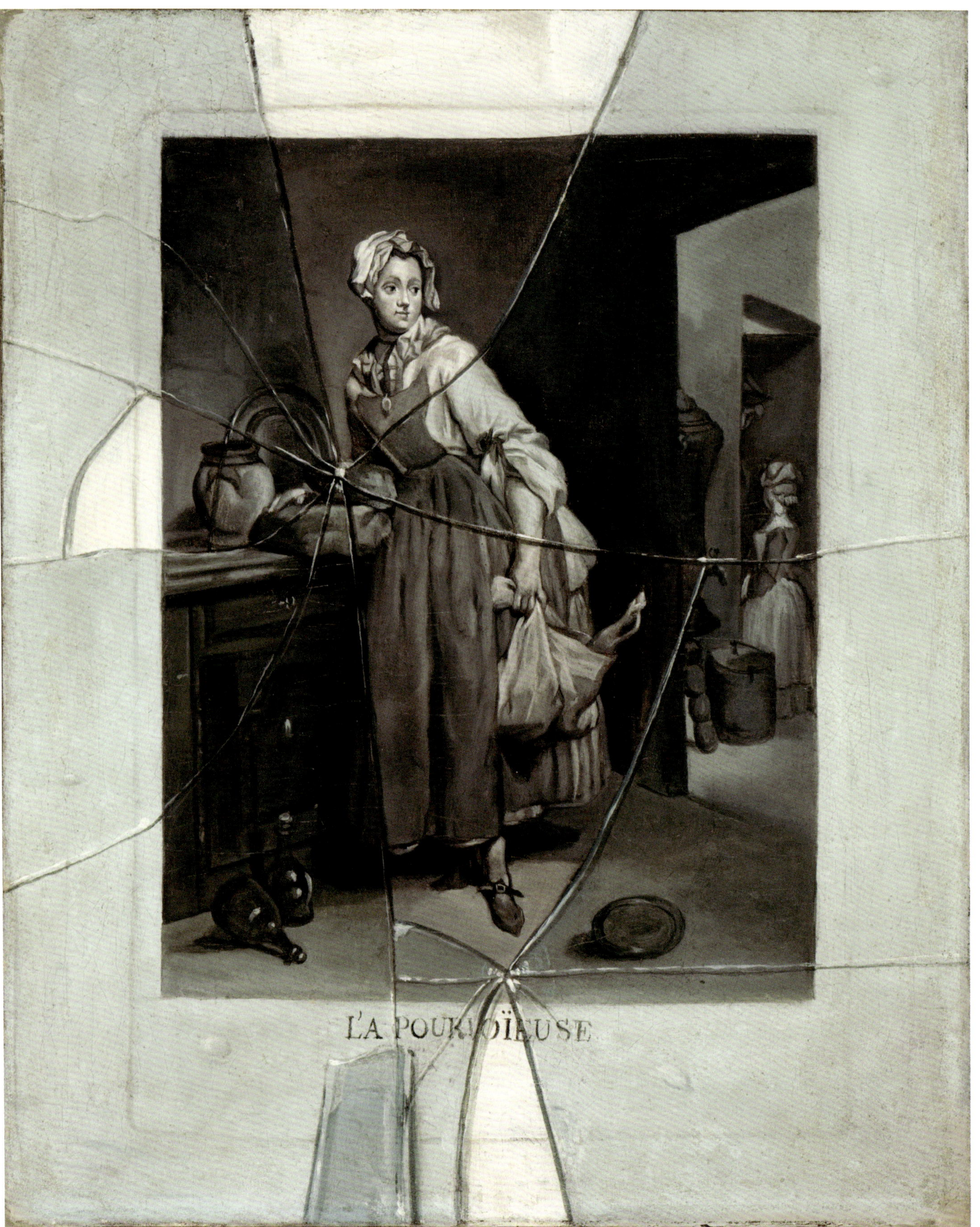

LA POURVOÏEUSE.

represents a servant girl in a moment of repose, having just returned from the market. Taking inspiration from Dutch seventeenth-century genre painters, such as Pieter de Hooch, whose paintings were widely collected in eighteenth-century France, Chardin represented two open doorways through which a maid is seen greeting a male visitor. The painting's success with contemporaries probably led to Chardin's painting at least four versions between 1738 and 1769.[26] The painting's popularity is further illustrated by the fact that François-Bernard Lépicié, Chardin's preferred printmaker, reproduced it in print in 1742 (cat. 49).[27] Lépicié's reproduction is to scale in mirror image, and is probably based on the 1739 version of Chardin's painting now in the Musée du Louvre.[28] With a network of densely spaced parallel and crosshatched lines, Lépicié faithfully translated the subtle details of Chardin's masterly composition into engraved lines, adding a moralising inscription that accuses the girl of stealing from her employer. Lépicié's warning about dishonest servants, difficult to trace back to Chardin's painting, added saleability to the print and reflects the tradition of reading such genre scenes with moral questions in mind.[29]

Basing his clever illusion on Lépicié's print, Moulinneuf created his playful grisaille *trompe l'oeil* a few decades later. As in the print, Moulinneuf reproduced Chardin's original painting in mirror image, to scale. Moulinneuf added a plate mark and seemingly framed the print behind glass, which he has 'shattered', as if symbolically breaking the illusion. By omitting the print's moralising inscription and credit line, he asserted his own authorship over the image. The inclusion of an inscription would have distracted from Moulinneuf's visual narrative about painting's ability to reproduce, as well as rival, prints. Cleverly, Moulinneuf's painting transformed Lépicié's print, which exists in multiple copies, into a single, unique work of art. Moulinneuf's grisaille also demonstrates the feats of deception achievable in monochrome painting and invokes different notions of artistic imitation, transformation and appropriation across media and techniques.

Louis-Léopold Boilly's *A Girl at a Window* (after 1799) uses similar tactics, albeit in a different way (cat. 51).[30] Boilly painted a representation of a mounted reproductive print after a lost colour painting, showing a lavishly dressed young woman who confronts the beholder with her penetrating gaze.[31] The presence of several optical instruments, such as a small monocular and two telescopes, also allude to the act of looking, an implicit subject of this work. Given the absence of lines, Boilly probably meant to imitate a mezzotint, an intaglio print technique that rendered subtle gradations of light and shade without line, making it an especially effective technique for reproducing paintings.[32] By including a mount around the image, Boilly enhanced the illusion of a print.

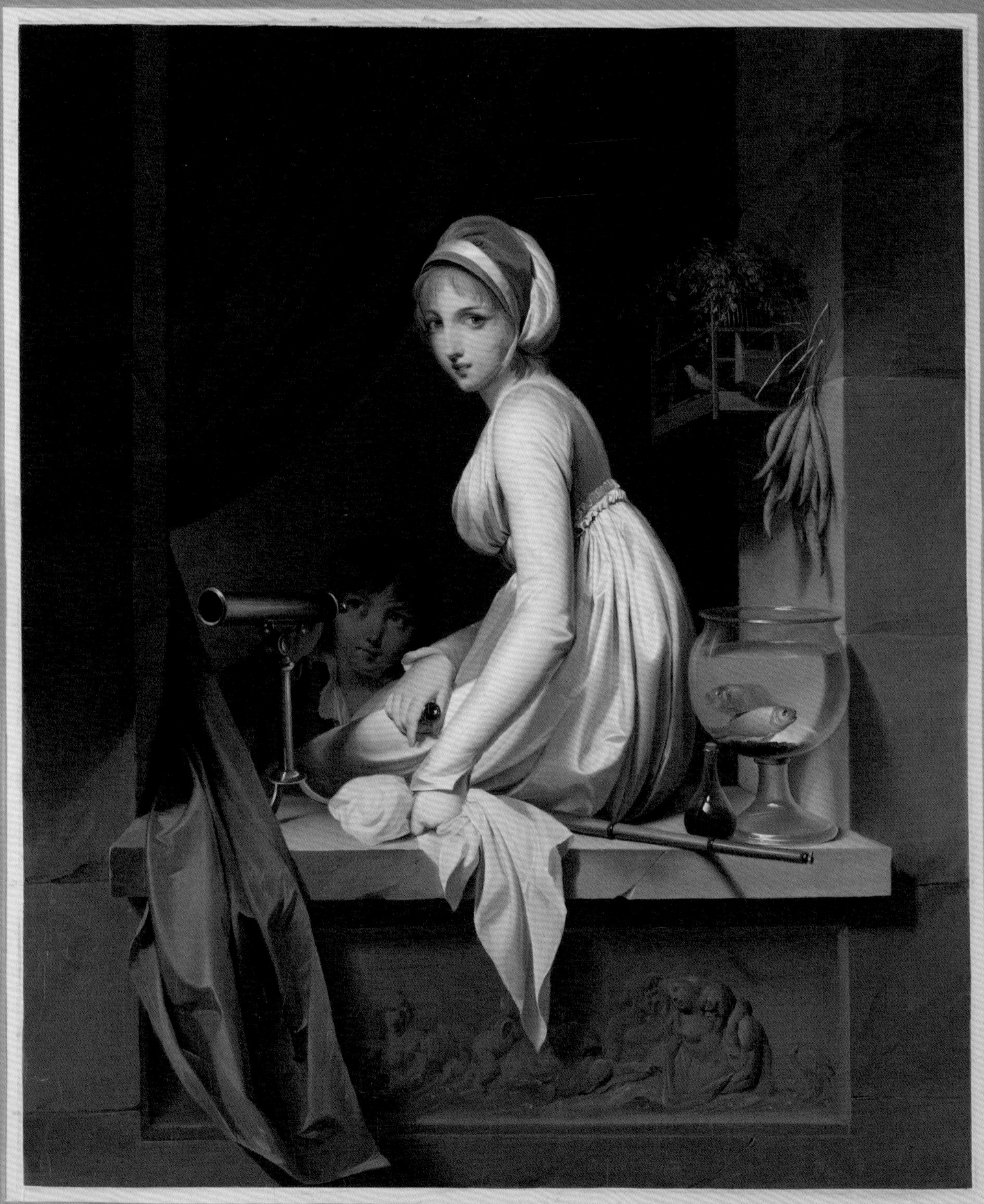

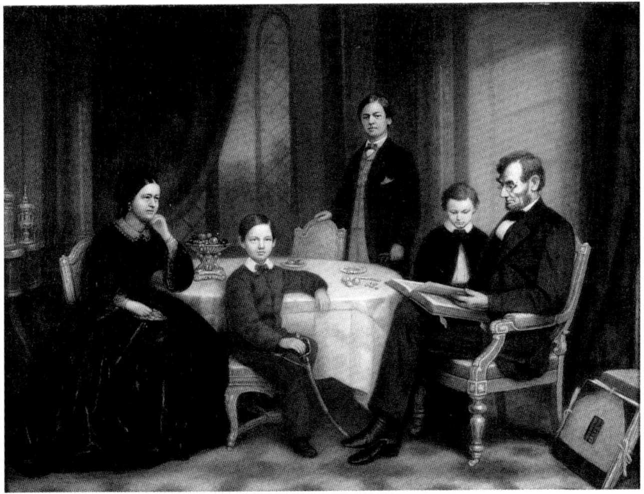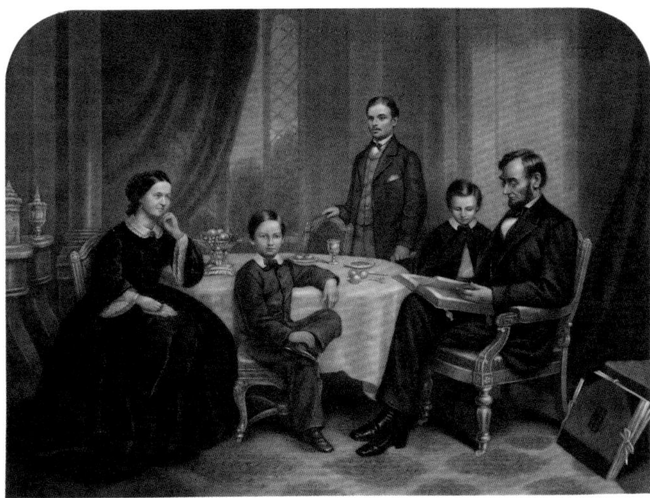

His skill is emphasised not only by his convincing rendering of a wide range of materials, from hard stone to transparent glass to soft silk, but also by his capacity to paint them in a reduced black-and-white palette.

The stone niche, bas-relief, curtain and birdcage, along with the meticulous handling and polished finish bring to mind Dutch seventeenth-century *fijnschilders* (fine paintings), popular in France at the time.[33] By painting the work in black and white, Boilly engaged in a dialogue with, but also went beyond the work of his Dutch predecessors. Painted in monochrome, imitating a print, and including several references to vision, *A Girl at a Window* questions the very act of looking. The beholder is encouraged to reflect on the act of representation in painting, and on how and what he or she sees.

Grisaille paintings continued to be used as preparatory studies for prints into the nineteenth century, but now sometimes together with photographs. Francis Bricknell Carpenter's grisaille of the family of the American president Abraham Lincoln (fig. 35) served as the model for a mezzotint print released two years later (fig. 36). The family never posed together, and Carpenter painted them with the aid of photographs of each sitter. In an 1895 letter, Carpenter stated:

> It was painted in black and white, with the expressed purpose of facilitating the engraving. When that [the engraving] was completed, I fully intended to finish the painting by adding color to the flesh as well as to the draperies. I never considered it finished any farther than as model for the engraving.[34]

In time, with the invention of new, and especially colour, print processes, the use of monochrome painting in preparation for prints diminished, as did the role of engraving as a source of inspiration for black-and-white paintings. The advent of clearer, cheaper and more accessible photography would bring bewildering complexity – but also new creative impetus – to the making of monochrome art.

Cat. 51 and detail overleaf
Louis-Léopold Boilly (1761–1845)
A Girl at a Window, after 1799
Oil on canvas, 55.2 × 45.7 cm
The National Gallery, London, NG 5583

Fig. 35
Francis Bicknell Carpenter (1830–1900)
The Lincoln Family, about 1865
Oil on canvas, 68.6 × 93.3 cm
New-York Historical Society, New York,
Gift of Warren C. Crane, 1909.6

Fig. 36
John Chester Buttre (1821–1893) after
Francis Bicknell Carpenter (1830–1900)
The Lincoln Family, 1867
Mezzotint print, 61.4 × 85.7 cm
The Library of Congress, Washington

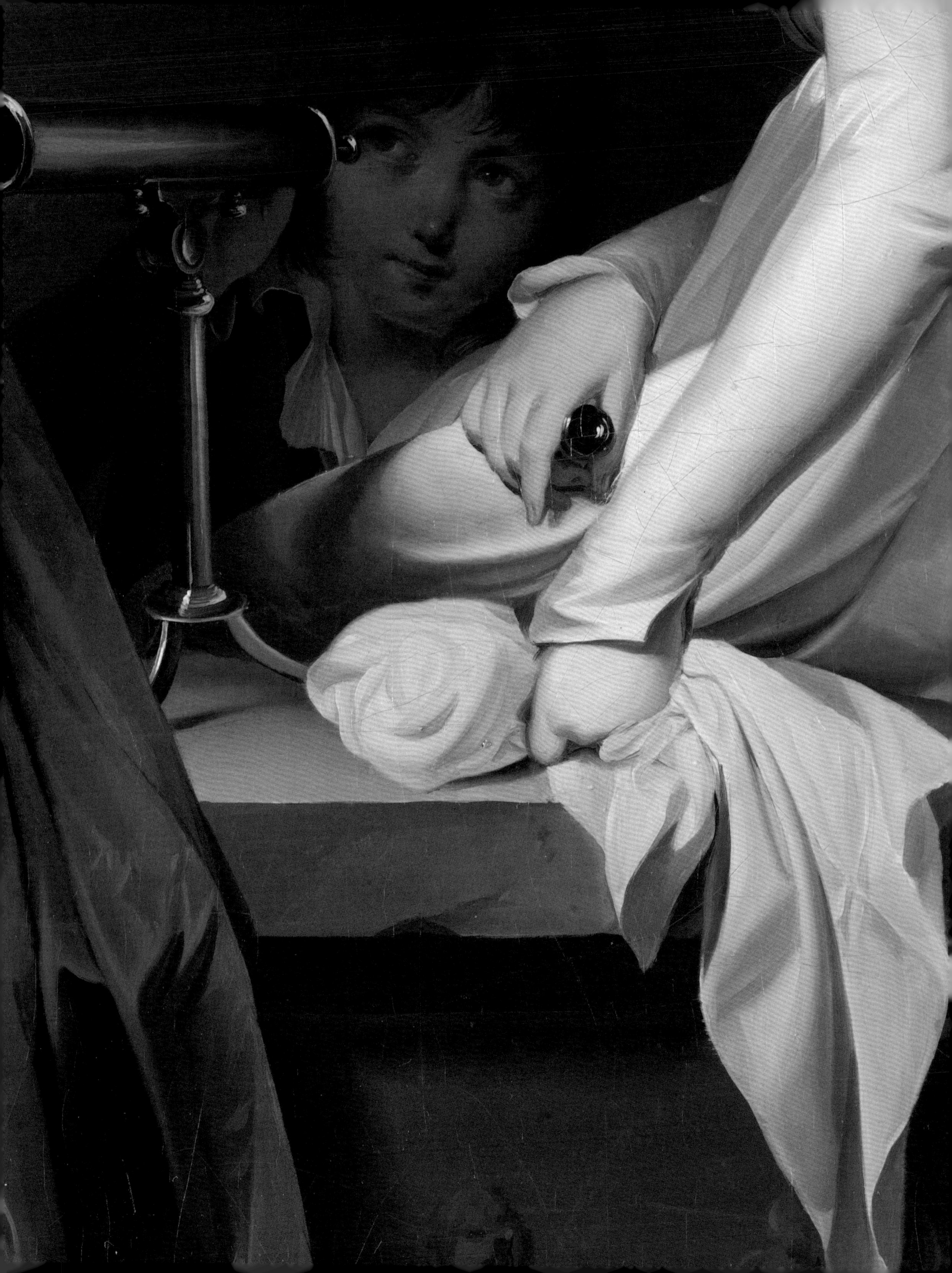

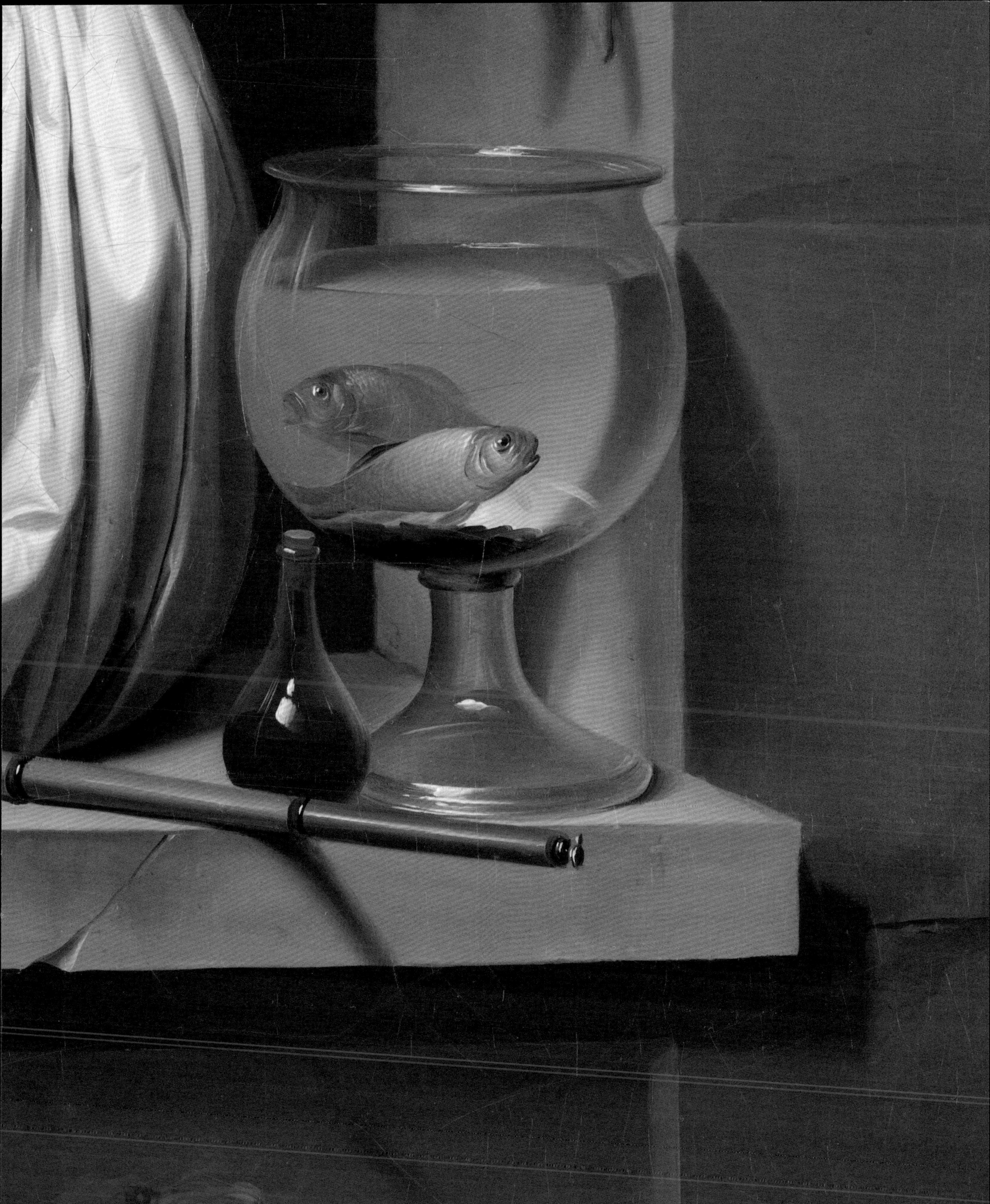

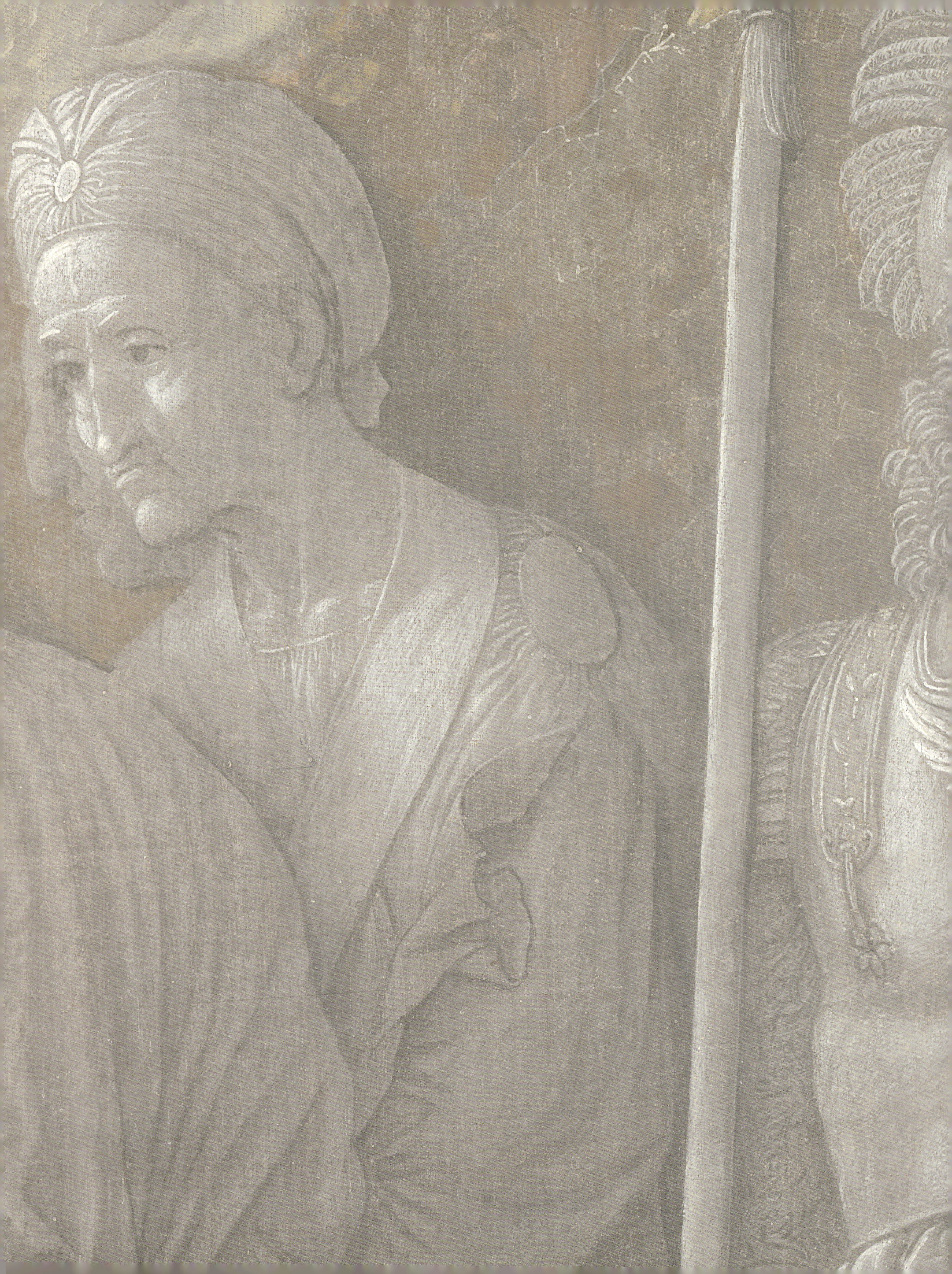

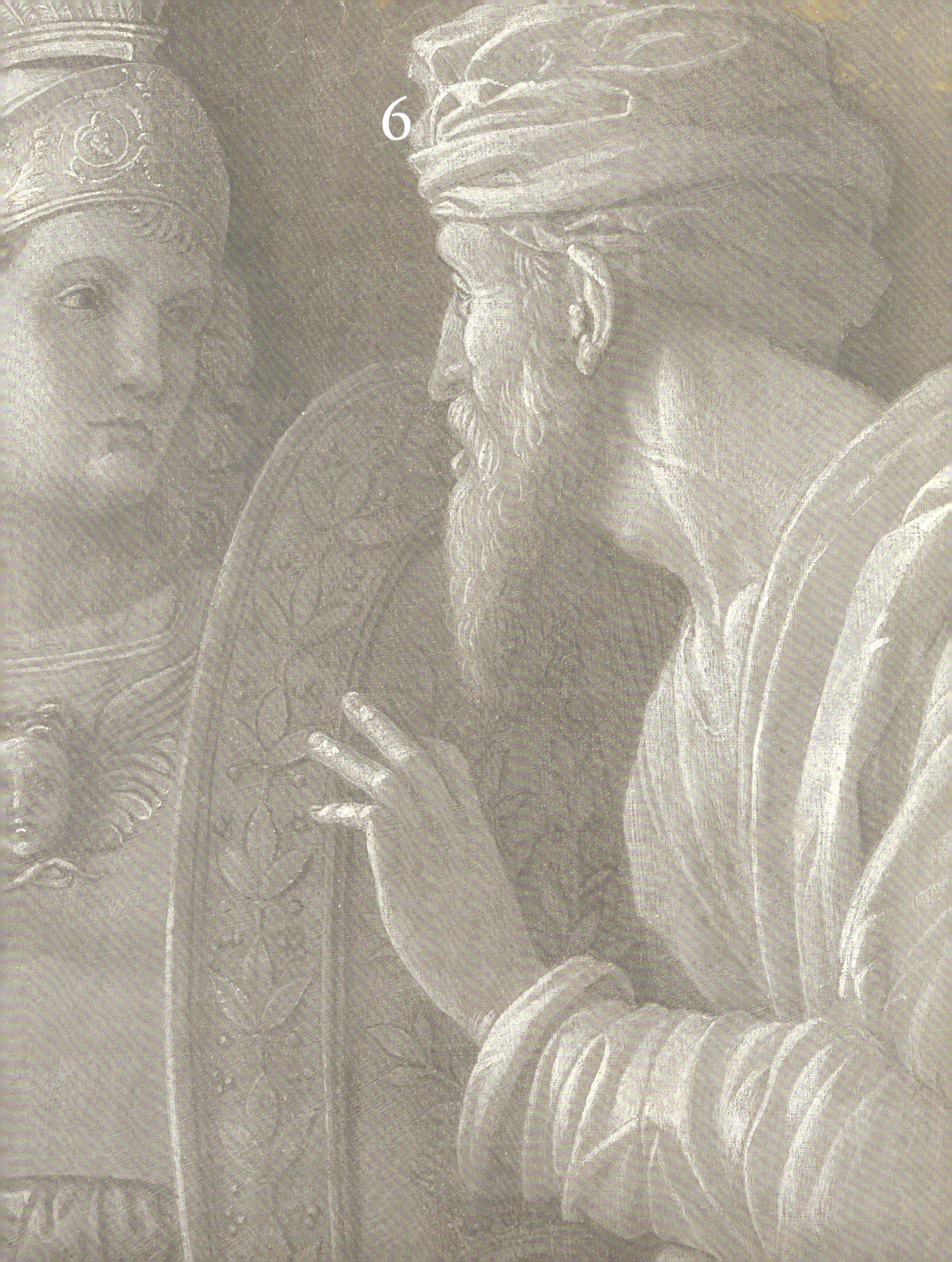
6

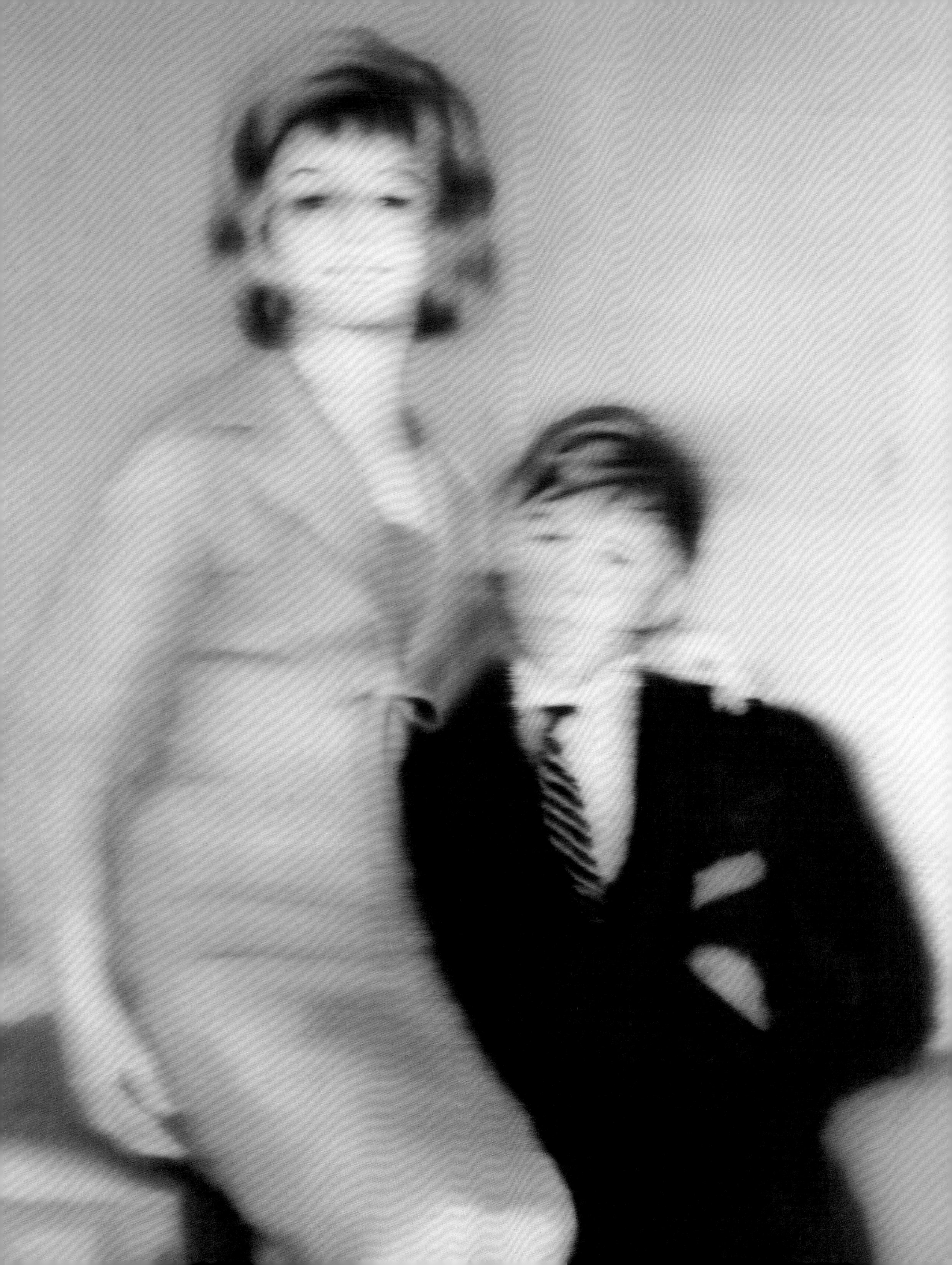

Monochrome Painting in the Age of Photography and Film

Lelia Packer and Jennifer Sliwka

The first photographers, working in the early nineteenth century in black-and-white, often looked to painting as a source of inspiration for their compositions. At the same time, the new medium both stimulated and challenged painters to respond to photography in works in black and white. It is photography's particular use of light and shadow and its perceived association with 'objectivity' that have especially fascinated artists working in paint. Likewise, the invention of black-and-white motion pictures and television in the late nineteenth and early twentieth centuries led to a fundamental transformation in the way many painters saw the world around them. Photography, film and television provided rich and seemingly endless source material for artists who sought to imitate or even rival their distinct qualities in paint, sometimes as a means of commenting on, or drawing attention to, contemporary social and political events.

Drawing with light

The invention of photography, whose name derives from the Greek words meaning 'drawing with light', provided a radical new method of creating images, by capturing the likeness of an object on a light-sensitive support. The new medium combined concepts underlying earlier inventions, such as the *camera obscura* (dark room), with the observation that some substances, such as silver salts, are visibly altered by exposure to light.[1] One of the first photographic processes, the daguerreotype, was invented in 1839 by the Romantic painter Louis Daguerre (1787–1851). It was based on the earlier work of the French scientist Joseph Nicéphore Niépce (1765–1833) and produced clear, finely detailed reproductions of the natural world on a silver-coated copper plate. A second process, introduced by William Henry Fox Talbot (1800–1877) in the same year, enabled photographs to be printed on paper, which became the standard practice from the mid-1840s onwards.

It was Daguerre, an artist who experimented with the manipulation of light and shadow to create atmospheric effects in his paintings, who contributed notably to the development of the photographic medium. Daguerre's stage sets, for example, spectacles known as 'dioramas', were paintings of landscapes that were viewed in a specially designed theatre that subtly manipulated natural light using screens and shutters over the course of a ten- or fifteen-minute show, to create the impression of the gradual passage from day to evening light.[2] His dioramas were a kind of proto-cinema, and his exploration of the effects of light and shade informed both his monochromatic paintings and his first camera photographs. In his painting *The Ruins of Holyrood Chapel*, for example, Daguerre explores the way moonlight breaks through the clouds to project a

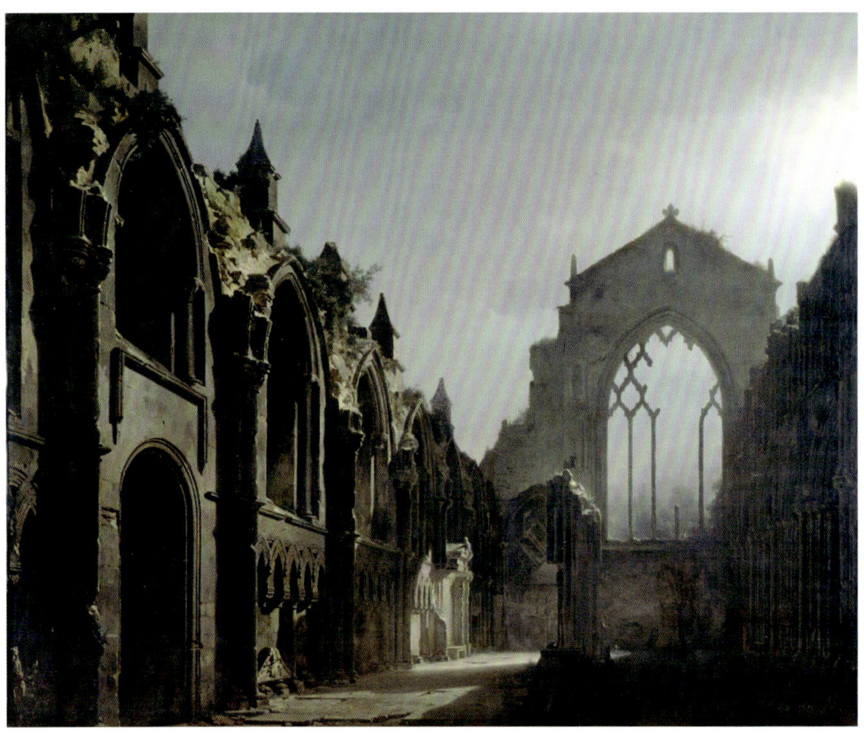

strong beam of light on abandoned ruins, creating dramatic shadows (fig. 37).
Daguerre's scientific and painterly attempts to capture a fleeting moment in
his dioramas and paintings anticipated his subsequent daguerreotypes, which
show architectural views over the city of Paris – such as the *Boulevard du
Temple* (around 1839) – works described in the press as 'an imprint in light
and shade'.[3]

A number of other painters took up photography soon after its invention
and, from the start, each medium had a strong impact on the other.[4] One of
the best-known artists to do this was the Parisian painter Gustave Le Gray
(1820–1884), who produced his first photographs by 1848 and thereafter
became adamant that photography should be considered a valid art form.[5]
He took photography to new heights in his seascapes, which he exhibited in
London and Paris between 1856 and 1858. In his photograph *The Great Wave,
Sète* (*La Grande Vague, Sète*) (cat. 52), for example, he succeeded in producing
dramatic and atmospheric effects of sunlight, clouds and water and revealed
his technical mastery in capturing breaking waves, an impressive achievement
given the long exposure times required. The photograph caused a sensation,
not only for the balanced densities of sea and sky, achieved through an
innovative combination of two negatives, each using a different exposure time,
but also because the resulting poetic effect recalled the works of the greatest
landscape and seascape painters, such as Gustave Courbet.[6] A London critic
remarked on the painterly aspect of Le Grey's photographs, describing them
as successfully imitating the atmospheric effects of J.M.W. Turner's paintings.[7]

Fig. 37
Louis-Jacques-Mandé Daguerre (1787–1851)
Ruins of Holyrood Chapel, about 1824
Oil on canvas, 211 × 256.3 cm
Walker Art Gallery, National Museums
Liverpool

Similarly, a Parisian critic described them as 'tableaux enchantés' ('enchanted paintings') and observed that many talented painters came to the exhibition to admire Le Gray's works.[8] Whether Le Gray's was a conscious imitation of painterly effects or not, these reviews suggest that a comparison between the respective qualities of painting and photography was a subject of discussion in the period. While figures such as Le Gray were making strong cases for the artistic status of photography, some painters expressed concern that this new medium might come to replace painting altogether. Indeed, Le Gray's painting teacher Paul Delaroche, after seeing early examples of the daguerreotype, purportedly said, 'from today, painting is dead'.[9] While this statement, reported in 1874, is probably apocryphal, it nevertheless reveals a growing rivalry between the two arts, one that in some ways recalls the Renaissance *paragone* debate between the relative merits of sculpture and painting.

A question of influence: early photography and painting

The transitory atmospheric effects of Le Gray's seascape photographs capture the energy of a rapidly executed painting such as *The Tempest* (cat. 53), a contemporary work by the Norwegian artist Peder Balke (1804–1887).[10] Inspired by memorable trips along the wild Norwegian coast and the Arctic Circle, Balke often painted scenes of ships hurled about by storm-tossed waves. In the last few decades of his life, when he had largely given up painting to work in urban development, Balke produced between 15 and 20 miniature black-and-white paintings, including *The Tempest*. Unlike earlier works for the art market, these small panels, in which Balke reduced his colours to a minimum and radically simplified his motifs, seem to be personal experiments, which he kept for himself or gave away as gifts.[11] With only a few brushstrokes, Balke evoked a volatile sea and sky in shades ranging from deep black to lead-grey to bright white. The artist used an exceptionally smooth white ground, over which he poured the paint and manipulated its movement using a brush, rags and his fingers, removing paint here and there and exposing the white ground to suggest foam and sea spray.[12] A group of inky-black rocks gives way to churning grey waters and rising swells that toss the boats listing on the waves. Beyond the sea, a strip of unpainted white horizon provides an interval between the waves and the blackening sky, against which a flock of gulls is circling. Although the strict use of an entirely monochromatic palette in such late works is appropriate for these stark, Scandinavian landscapes, Balke's dramatic exclusion of variegated colour and his focus on ephemeral atmospheric effects parallel contemporary developments in black-and-white photography.

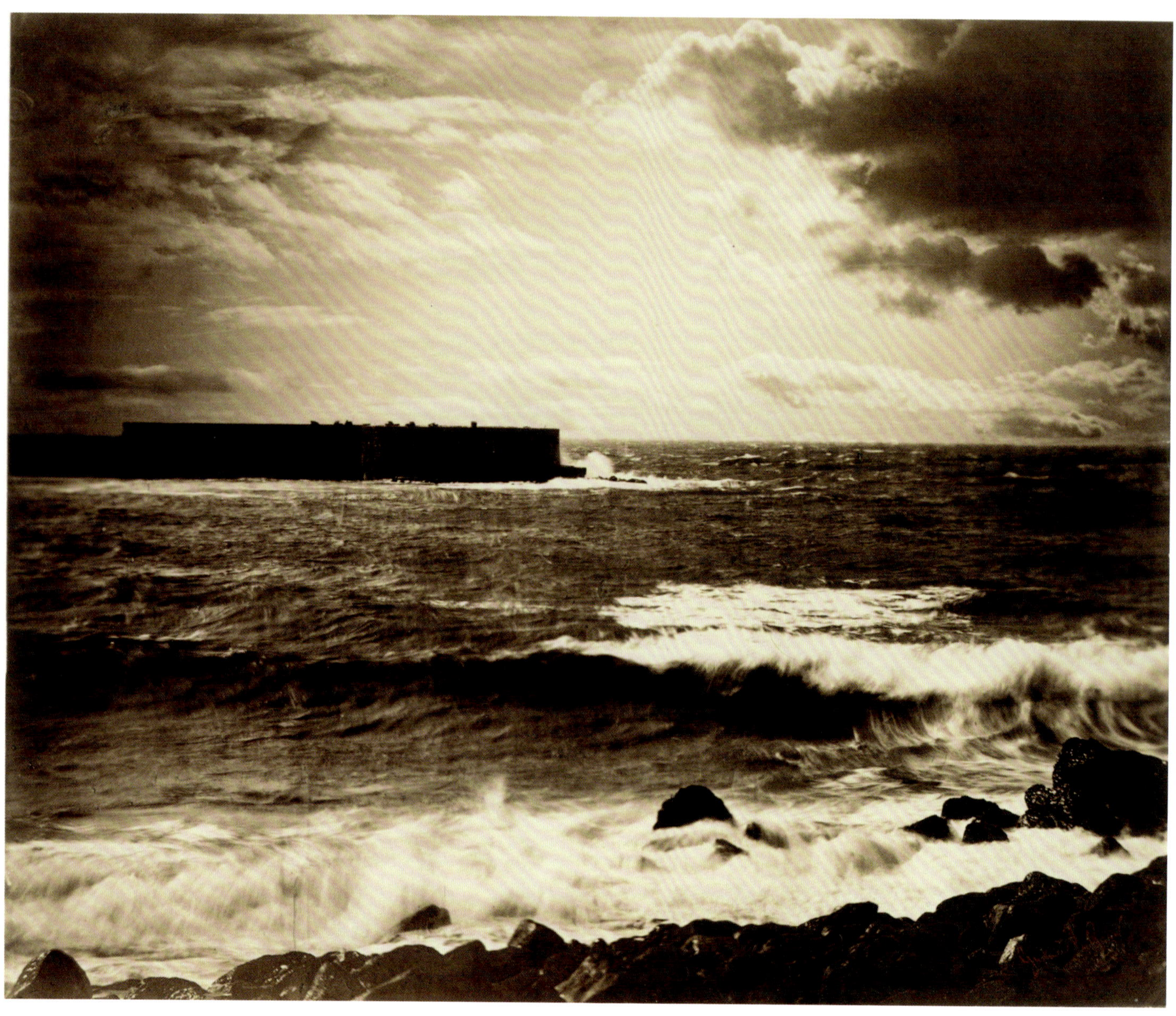

As photographic techniques improved and became more accessible, painters were increasingly inspired to respond to the medium. The monochromatic *Head of a Girl* (cat. 54) by the French painter Célestin Joseph Blanc (1818–1888) reflects traditional modes of portrait painting and appears to refer to contemporary photography.[13] Blanc's little-known works generally consist of elegant narrative or genre scenes in colour. In this rare monochrome, the pale face of the young girl is subtly modelled with diffused light and contrasts dramatically with the velvety black of her dress and grey background. While the formality of her profile pose evokes ancient portraits on coins and medals, as well as early Renaissance portraits, the stiffness of her posture calls

Cat. 52
Gustave Le Gray (1820–1884)
The Great Wave, Sète, about 1857
Albumen print from two collodion-on-glass
negatives, 34.3 × 41.2 cm
Victoria and Albert Museum, London.
Townshend Bequest, 68004

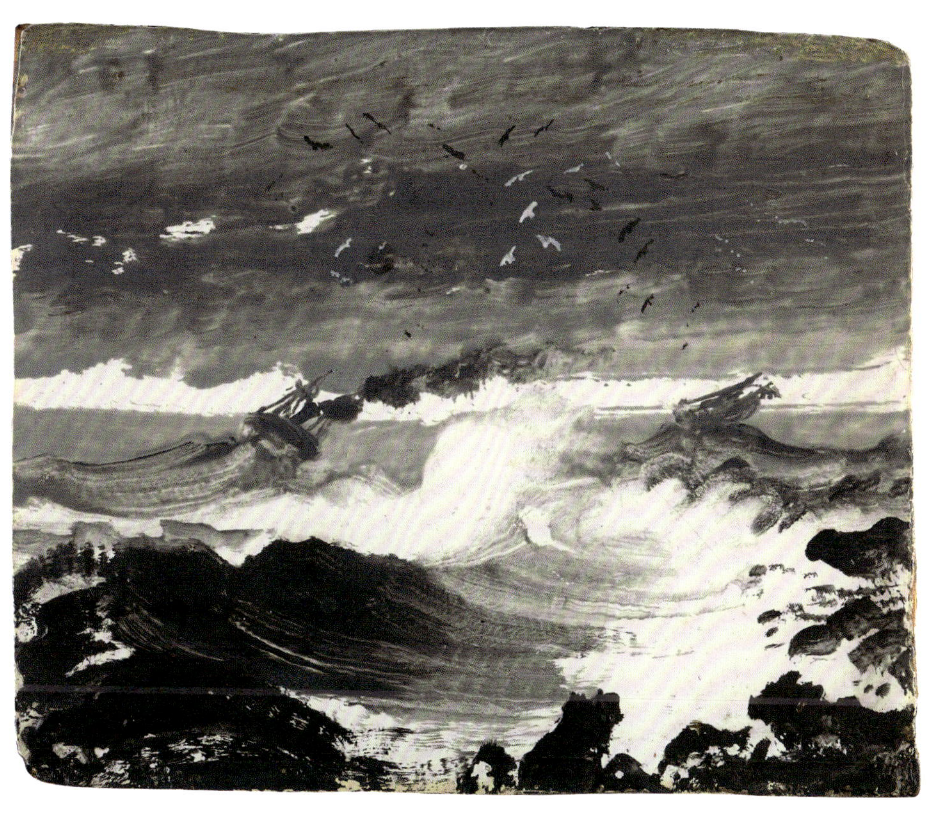

Cat. 53
Peder Balke (1804–1887)
The Tempest, about 1862
Oil on wood panel, 10.3 × 12.2 cm
The National Gallery, London, NG 6614

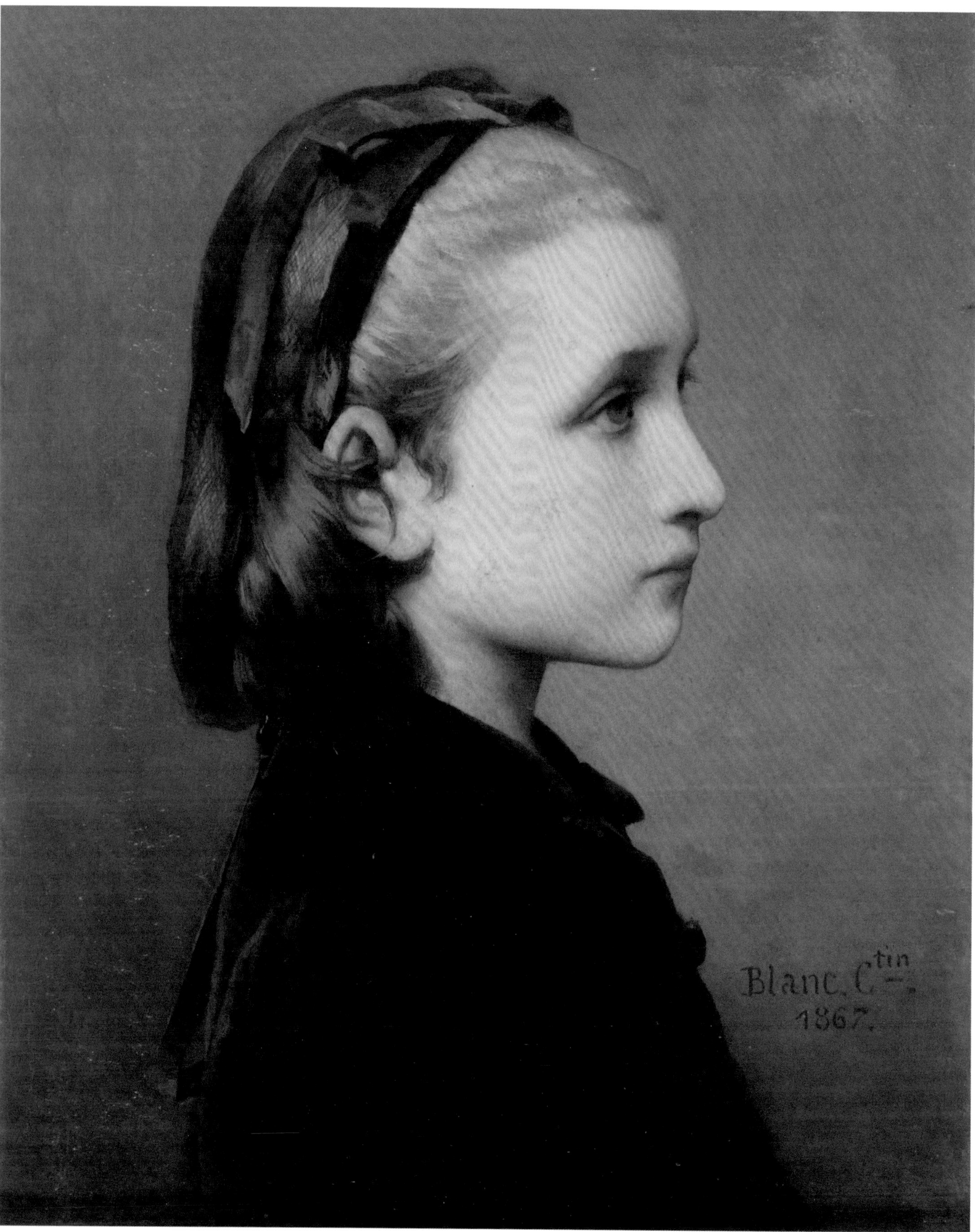

Blanc. C.tin
1867.

to mind early portrait photographs, which required long exposure times that often resulted in a similarly rigid attitude. The painting's monochromatic palette and realism also suggests the *carte de visite*: a contemporary obsession, these small paper portrait photographs of adults and children were mounted on card and exchanged and collected in albums. Blanc's painted portrait, made during photography's early decades, at once imitates the new mechanical technique with its monochrome palette, and challenges it in its convincing realism, achieved by hand with brush and oil on panel. The threat that photography posed to painting was especially felt in the realm of portraiture in precisely this period and was confirmed during the following century, when photographic portraits eventually came to supplant portrait painting.

Black-and-white film, television and painting

With the invention of motion pictures at the end of the nineteenth century, painters and the general public were exposed to larger numbers of black-and-white images than ever before, transforming the way they received and responded to visual information. The earliest films of the 1890s were short and soundless, although innovations, such as the use of artificial lighting and sound, were swiftly introduced. From about 1910 onwards, newsreels provided a popular alternative to newspapers, further transforming the speed and manner in which people received information about contemporary events.

Cat. 54
Célestin Joseph Blanc (1818–1888)
Head of a Girl, 1867
Oil on panel, 26.7 × 21.6 cm
Victoria and Albert Museum, London,
1034-1869

Fig. 38
Pablo Picasso (1881–1973)
The Charnel House, 1944–5
Oil and charcoal on canvas, 199.8 × 250.1 cm
The Museum of Modern Art, New York, Mrs
Sam A. Lewisohn Bequest (by exchange), and
Mrs Marya Bernard Fund in memory of her
husband Dr Bernard Bernard, and
anonymous funds (93.1971)

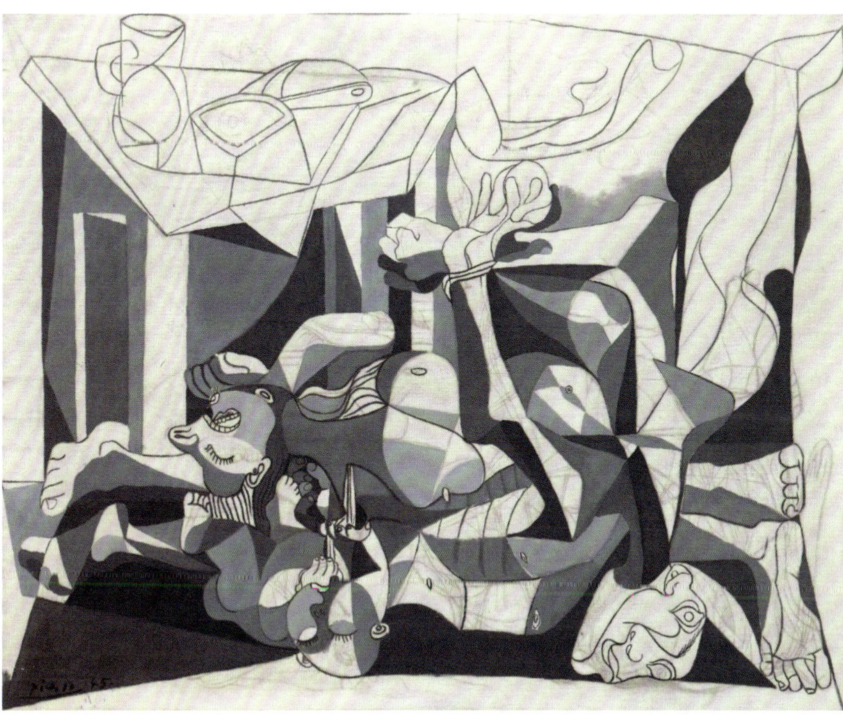

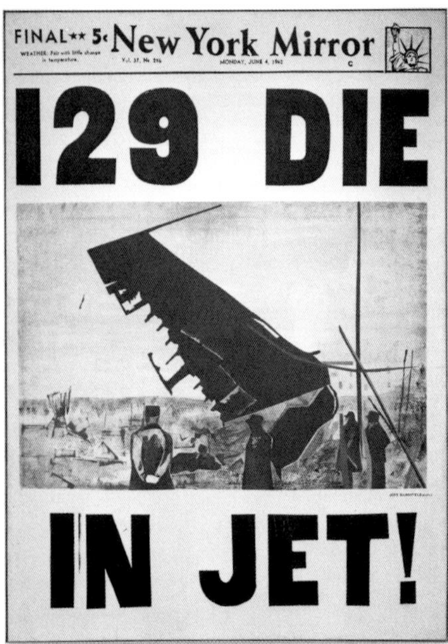

In 1925, the first public demonstration of televised silhouette images in motion took place in London.[14] However, televisions did not become commercially available until after the Second World War. From the post-war period until the introduction of colour television in the mid-1960s, broadcasting was entirely in black and white. For more than half a century, therefore, the western world received a high proportion of its news and entertainment in black and white.[15]

Pablo Picasso was among the first artists to respond in paint to these new technologies. Newspaper accounts and photographs provided both motivation and visual resources for works such as his black-and-white masterpiece, *Guernica* (1937, Museo Reina Sofía, Madrid). Similarly, his *Charnel House* of 1944–5 (fig. 38) was inspired by newspaper photographs of the Spanish Civil War and a black-and-white newsreel of a Spanish Republican family murdered in their kitchen.[16] With its restricted palette and sketch-like quality, enhanced by the charcoal delineations that Picasso purposefully left visible, the painting evokes the grainy look of the source images. The work is composed of a disorientating heap of figures, the murdered family sprawled beneath a dining table, the latter seemingly suspended in mid-air, laid with pots, food and utensils. In using press images and newsreel in this way, and in reducing his palette to reflect the medium by which he received this news, Picasso's painting evokes the documentary function of reportage. Here, as in *Guernica*, Picasso appears to have rejected colour as a means of responding to these atrocities. It has been argued that the absence of colour in Picasso's wartime works became a signifier of pain and deprivation.[17] As he had done when painting *Guernica*, Picasso recorded the process of creating *The Charnel House* in black-and-white photography, a medium long associated with a kind of objective testimony and seriousness, in contrast to colour photography, which was largely used in commercial advertising in magazines.[18]

The American Pop artist Andy Warhol (1928–1987) also employed a strictly black-and-white palette for the depiction of violent tragedies in his famous *Death and Disaster* series from the 1960s.[19] He began the series in the summer of 1962 with *129 Die in Jet!* (fig. 39), a monochrome painting that reproduced the front page of the *New York Mirror*, reporting the details of a tragic plane crash. For subsequent works in the series, including depictions of victims of traffic accidents and execution devices, Warhol extracted images from their original newspaper or magazine context, rendering them largely anonymous and even ambiguous, so that who or what is being portrayed is not immediately apparent. At the same time, he began experimenting with a

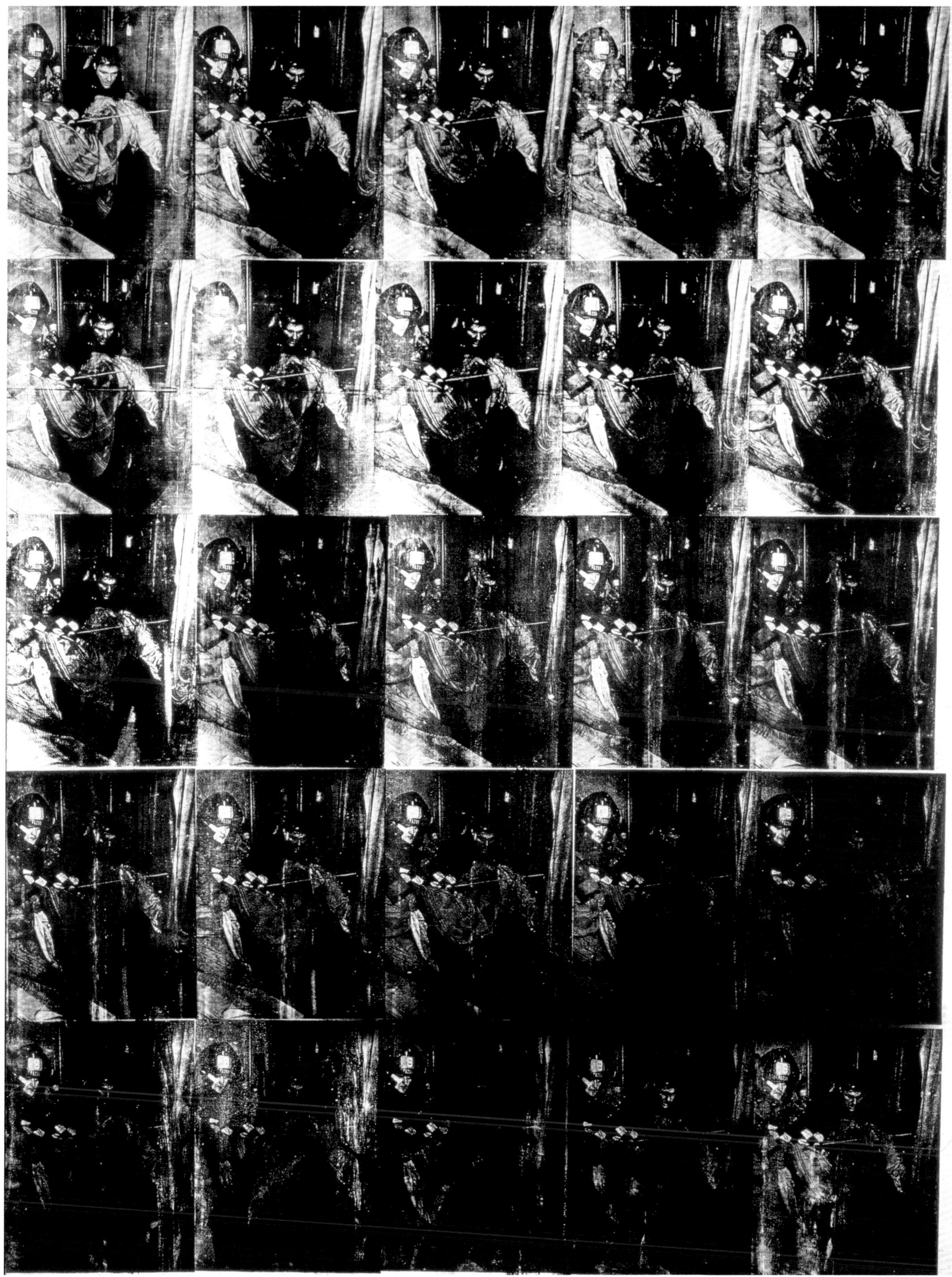

new technique, a photo-silk-screen process, which he hoped would reflect the mechanical reproduction and replication of these images in the press.

In the same year as *129 Die in Jet!*, Warhol produced *Black and White Disaster* from a crude black-and-white newspaper photograph of a fireman cradling a dead body (fig. 40). He first cropped and enlarged the image before transferring it to a series of screens, which he then printed onto the canvas in a densely overlapping grid. The effect of multiplying the image across the canvas makes it resemble an enlarged photographic contact sheet or filmstrip. Indeed, the Swiss filmmaker Peter Gidal has referred to the effect of Warhol's repetition of black-and-white images in this way as 'filmic'.[20] By varying the amount of ink he used, Warhol manipulated light and dark, simulating the effects of an over- or under-exposed black-and-white photograph; in some instances the darkness of the ink renders the image nearly illegible. Warhol's skill lies in creating a work that is simultaneously about the horrific subject represented and the way it is reported by the press: repeated to the point of banality and leaving the viewer disaffected. By replicating and manipulating black-and-white photographic images, Warhol skilfully provokes debate about the relationship between representation and perception.

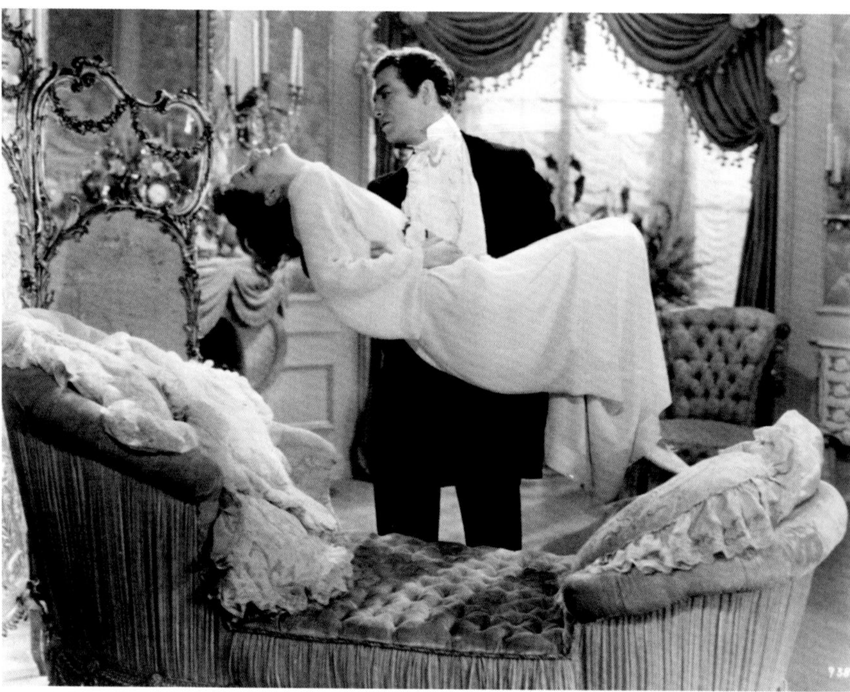

Fig. 41
Still from George Cukor's *Camille*, 1936

Cat. 55
Marlene Dumas (born 1953)
The Image as Burden, 1993
Oil on canvas, 40 × 50 cm
Private collection, Belgium

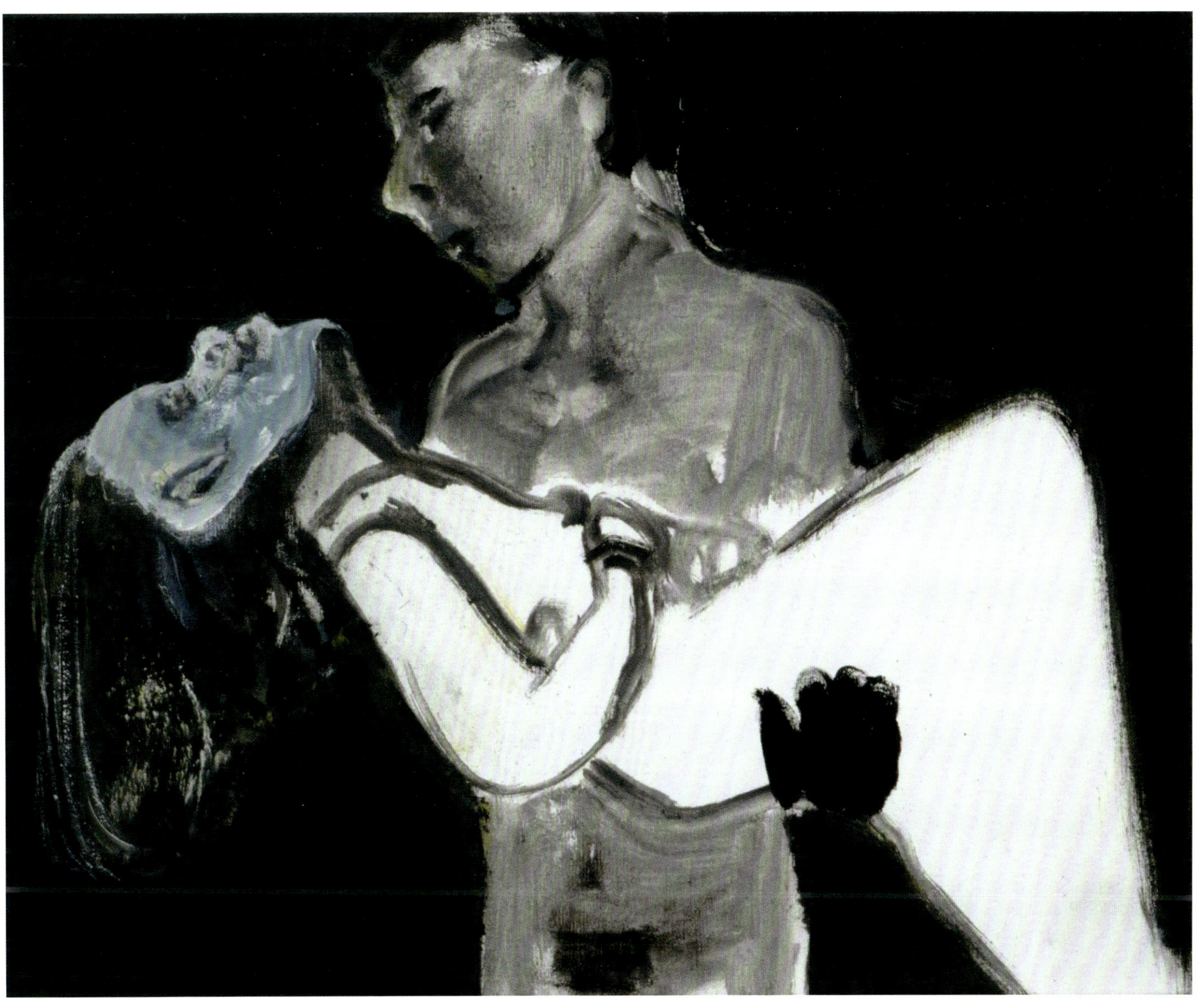

Painting from film

Drawing from her extensive archive of photographic and filmic images, the South African-Dutch painter Marlene Dumas (born 1953) is inspired by what she calls 'second-hand images', which, she asserts, 'can generate first-hand emotions'.[21] Dumas invariably begins with a highly mediated source, a television, film or news item or a photograph, which she then translates into painting, usually using thin washes of white and black watercolour or oil paint which produce an elusive, fugitive effect. The ephemeral appearance of her works appears at odds with the uncompromising nature of her subjects: usually explorations of gender, racism, love, death and shame.

A case in point is *The Image as Burden* (cat. 55), representing a man carrying the unresponsive body of a woman, not unlike the repeated image in Warhol's *Black and White Disaster*. Painted in shades of grey against a black background, Dumas uses the white of the unpainted canvas to represent the woman's dress. The composition derives from a film still from George Cukor's classic 1936 film *Camille* (fig. 41), showing the demise of the star-crossed romantic leads, played by Greta Garbo and Robert Taylor.[22] In translating the black-and-white still into painting, Dumas transformed its appearance and meaning to create a deliberately ambiguous subject. The woman's head is thrown back at an uncomfortable angle, suggesting that she is unconscious or dead. Removed from their narrative context, the respective postures of the figures recall one of the most iconic images in the history of art, the Pietà, in which the Virgin Mary cradles the lifeless body of Christ – only here, the roles are reversed. Alternative or additional readings are suggested by the use of the word 'burden' in the painting's title, which can be variously understood as a reference to the weighty burden of the woman's lifeless body, or perhaps, more broadly, as an allusion to the burden of artistic practice itself.[23] Indeed, Dumas's work often draws attention to the complex relationship between painting and its source image. Tellingly, the artist chose to present a recent exhibition of her works under the same title as her painting, *The Image as Burden*, explaining:

> there is the image (source photography) you start with and the image (the painted image) you end up with, and they are not the same. I wanted to give more attention to what the painting does to the image, not only to what the image does to the painting.[24]

Painterly responses to photographic sources

Three renowned contemporary artists, Gerhard Richter (born 1932), Chuck Close (born 1940) and Vija Celmins (born 1938), began using photographs as source material for their black-and-white paintings during the 1960s. For all three, photography has been a critical source of inspiration throughout their respective, prolific careers, albeit with distinct painterly results.

The German artist Gerhard Richter has used photographs from a variety of sources, such as newspapers, magazines, amateur family snapshots and pictures he took himself. In a 1966 interview, Richter explained that he used photographs as source material because they provide the 'perfect picture' in their ability to convey exact information.[25] He also explained that by painting in black and white he was responding to the media itself, which, at that time, was largely transmitted in those colours.[26] Richter began by painting enlarged copies of black-and-white photographs using only a range of greys, such as the intriguing blurred portrait of *Helga Matura with her Fiancé* (cat. 56). In turning to photography and to the colour grey, Richter sought to endow his paintings with the objectivity often associated with photography. Yet, by electing to blur his source image, he makes the beholder aware that he or she is viewing a mediated image.

Helga Matura with her Fiancé possesses the typical ambiguity of Richter's grey, photo-inspired images. The work depicts the Frankfurt prostitute, Helga Matura, who was brutally murdered and whose story captured the attention of the German media. Richter used the last published photograph of Helga, from *Quick* magazine (February 1966), as a source for this painting (fig. 42). Helga is shown smartly dressed, seated on an armrest next to the boyish Rainer Gutherz.[27] Richter's painterly technique blurs the figures and their surroundings, taking them out of focus, and stands in direct contrast to the crisp representation and purported objectivity of the source photograph.

The painting's composition recalls the practice of using before-and-after photographs in the press to sensationalise such grim stories, in this case representing the victim before her death.[28] In its subdued grey palette, which is for Richter 'the ideal colour for indifference', the painting divorces the image from any sentimentality, creating an emotional distance from Helga's murder.[29] At the same time, the colour grey – often associated with mourning in Christianity – enables Richter to express his profound consciousness of death, which has preoccupied him throughout his career.[30] Like Warhol in his *Death and Disaster* series, Richter used paintings such as *Helga Matura with her Fiancé* to comment on the public's fascination with suffering and on the exploitation of emotions through the use of black-and-white images extracted from their narrative context and repeated in newspapers, magazines or on television.

For Richter, painting from photographs, rather than from life, was advantageous in that it saved time by not having to sketch his subject. While photography provided a means for Richter to convey information about reality, he stated the following about painting: 'I never paint to create a likeness of a person or of an event. Even though I paint credibly and correctly, as if the likeness were important, I am really using it only as a pretext for a picture.'[31] Working in black and white meant that he could remain faithful to the monochromatic palette of his photographic source image, but his manipulation of the oil paint to the point of blurring his image allowed him to create a highly stylised and painterly picture.

While Richter was interested in photography's selective reality, his American contemporary, Chuck Close, uses photography as a source for his paintings in order to enhance the quality of seeing, and he is also a skilled

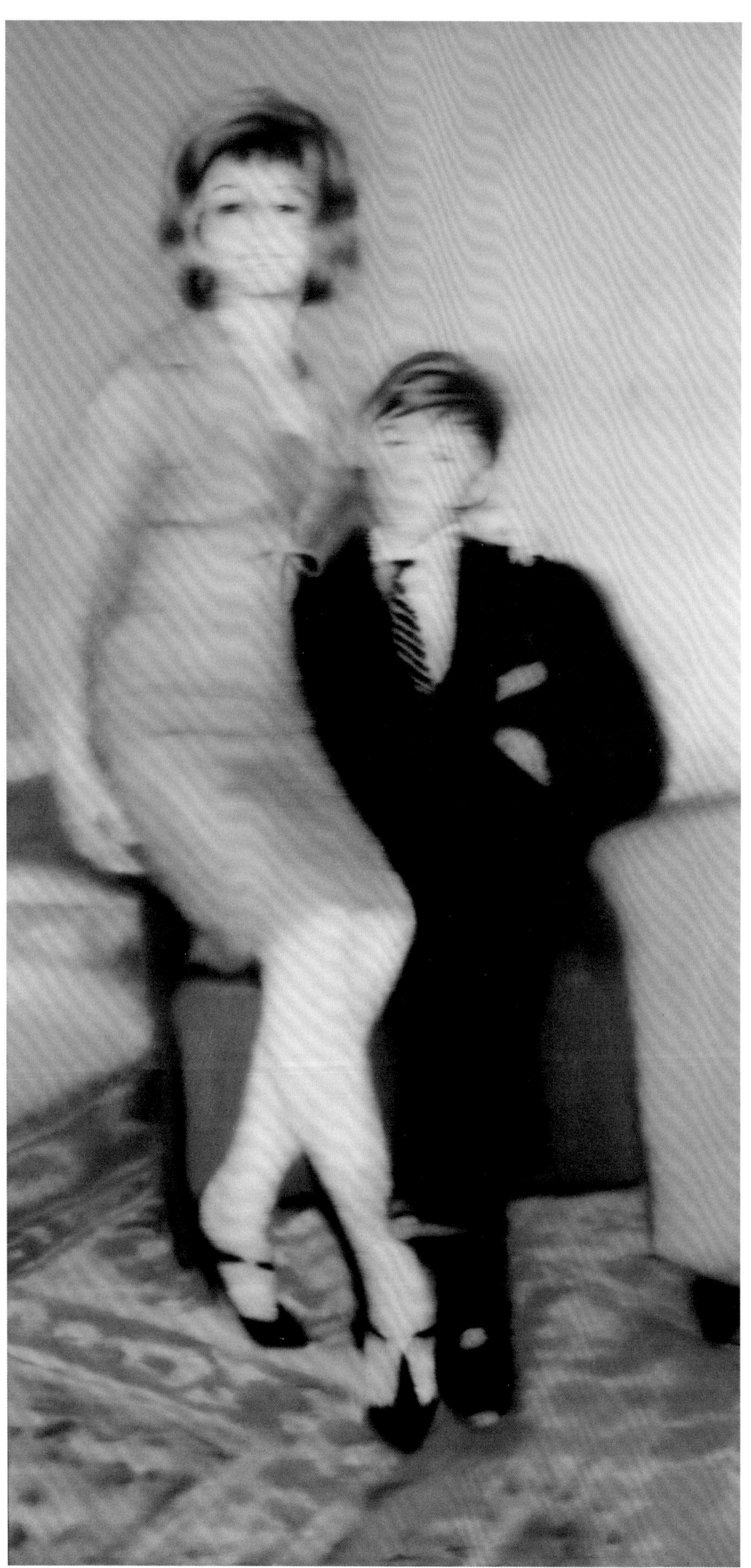

The work of Gerhard Richter is characterised by its focus on the process of painting itself. While his point of departure was often, as in this early 'photo-painting', a figurative motif, Richter distanced himself from his subject by blurring the painting with a wooden stick or a squeegee. *Helga Matura with her Fiancé* is based on a press photograph that illustrated an article documenting the murder of a prostitute. It is barely possible to ignore Helga's tragic story when looking at the painting, yet Richter does not make any pronouncement on it. The photographs that Richter chooses as models for his paintings range from banal subjects, such as a roll of toilet paper, to images that appeal to society's voyeurism, as in the case of Helga Matura.

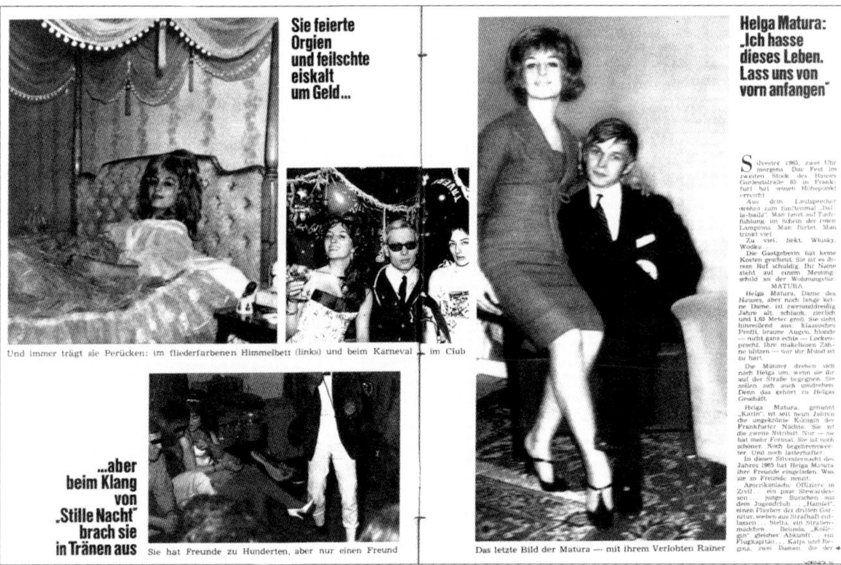

Cat. 56
Gerhard Richter (born 1932)
Helga Matura with her Fiancé, 1966
Oil on canvas, 200 × 100 cm
Museum Kunstpalast, Düsseldorf

Fig. 42
Photograph of Helga Matura with her fiancé in *Quick* magazine, February 1966
Institute for Newspaper Research, Dortmund

photographer in his own right. His early photo-realistic portraits from the late 1960s are massive, blown-up, black-and-white likenesses of fellow artists and friends that expose every wrinkle and blemish of the sitter. After becoming paralysed in 1988, Close devised a new manner of painting. When creating his monumental portrait of the contemporary American sculptor Joel Schapiro (cat. 57), Close began as he always had, by taking a tightly cropped photograph of Joel with a 20- by 24-inch Polaroid camera (cat. 58). Using a grid as an organising device, both on the photograph and on the canvas, he systematically enlarged and transferred the image from photo to painting, one square at a time. With a brush now tied to his wrist, Close filled the grid with concentric rings, with no two units alike. From a distance, the painting appears like a pixelated photograph; up close, Joel's face dissolves into a mosaic of circular shapes. Close confronted photography directly with the painter's tools, albeit in a new way.

Fascinatingly, Close spoke about how studying art through black-and-white reproductions in books inspired him to paint in black and white: 'I made so many black and white paintings because I thought all art was black and white since I had to look at colour paintings in black-and-white reproductions in my formative years.'[32] Moreover, he turned to the camera because it is 'a better way of seeing than [the] naked eye ... [which is] ... more subjective and fallible'.[33] As a result, he replaced the preparatory drawing or worked-up modello of old-master practice with the photograph. Close considers this method more collaborative. He and the sitter together decide on which photograph to employ as model. The restricted black-and-white palette heightens the viewer's awareness of the artist's extraordinary skill.

Works such as *Joel* challenge us to think about the time it takes to create a portrait, and the way it is made. Unlike the Polaroid photograph that Close used as his source, which was taken and developed immediately, Close's canvas took months to produce. It evokes both the snapshot of its genesis and the prolonged

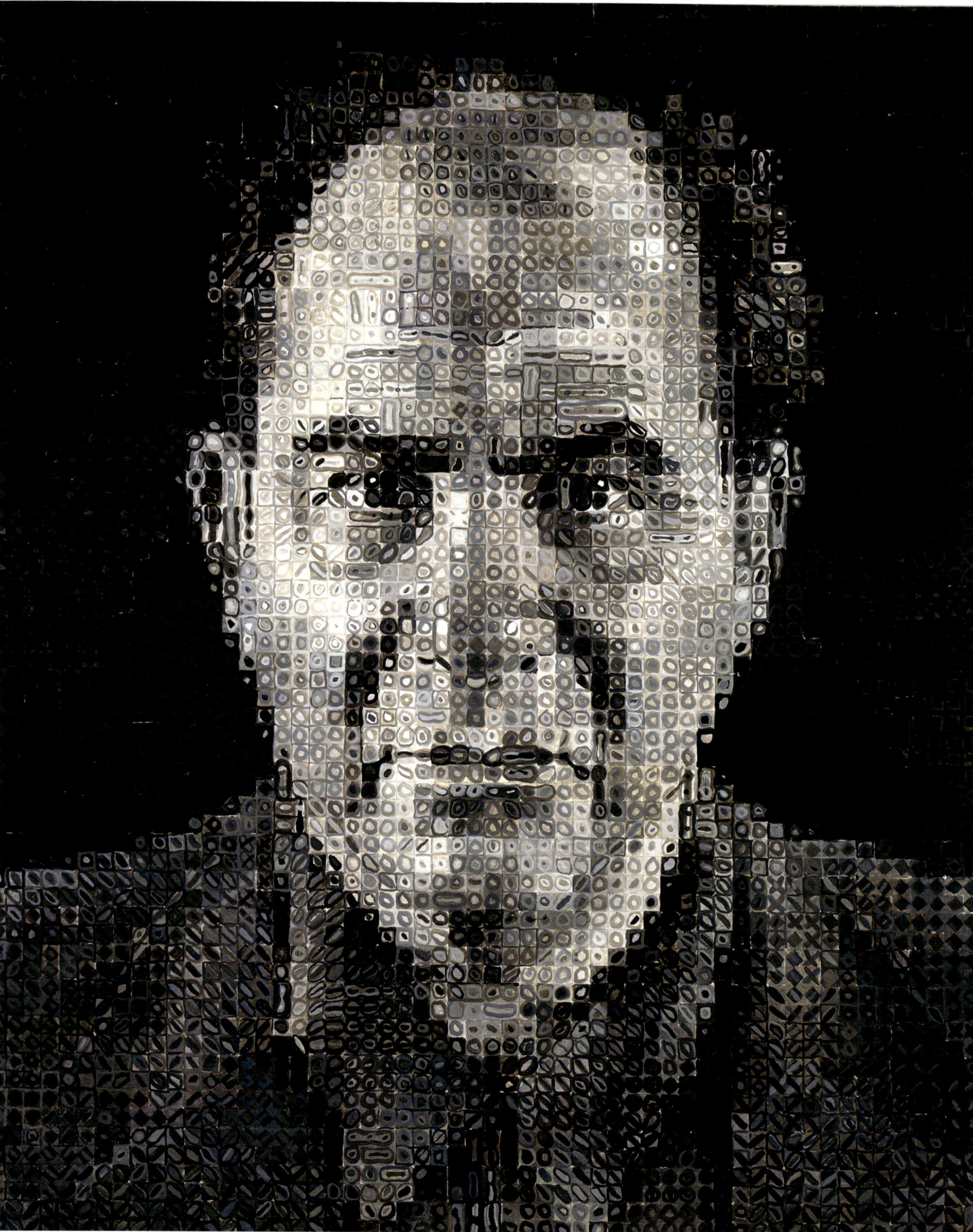

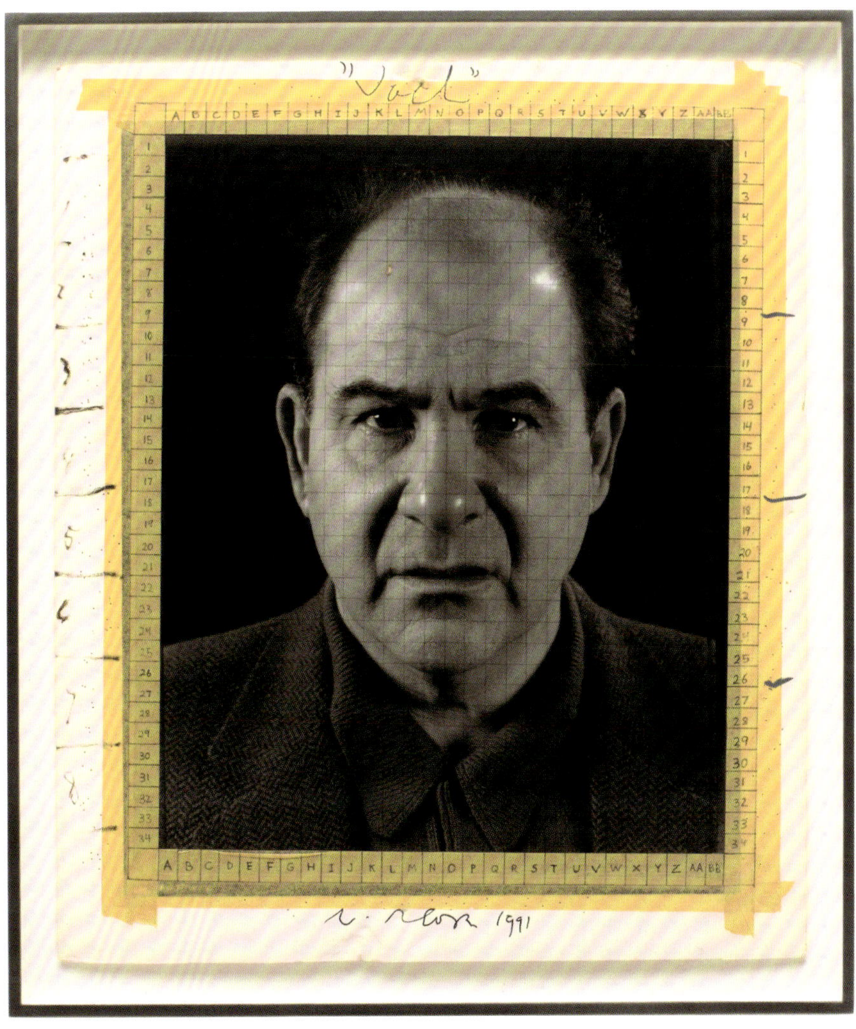

process of its painterly production. And unlike conventional portraitists who rely on their sitters as their models (or on a combination of live observation and photography), Close uses only the photograph, which for him effectively serves as a stand-in, or intermediary, for the live model. When asked by Close what he thought about his portrait, Joel replied: 'I like the painting, it's kind of surprising. I think I was very stern looking, but that's ok.'[34]

Like Close, the Latvian-born American artist Vija Celmins produces paintings that might be understood as 'impossible' photographs. Her captivating monochrome paintings of such natural phenomena as the sea, the desert and the night sky are based on her own photographs, as well as on those published in books, magazines and newspapers. The mesmerising, star-studded *Night Sky no. 3* (cat. 59) is one of a series of works based on American and Russian satellite photographs of the moon and other galaxies. Celmins began working on the series in the 1960s and continues to do so. Her technique is unique: she

creates smooth, velvety effects by applying multiple layers of pigment, sanding each down before adding the next, effectively blurring the visible distinction between photography and painting. Celmins transforms the source photographs into 'meditations on some of the undifferentiated and uninhabited areas of the natural world'.[35]

Celmins's approach is distinct from that of artists like Picasso, Warhol, Richter and Close, who used photographic source material in order to respond to the journalistic reporting of a dramatic event, or to reproduce an aesthetic effect usually associated with photography. In contrast, Celmins's photographic sources enable her to represent vast earthly and otherworldly landscapes, which are otherwise impossible to capture or perceive with the human eye. Celmins has said that for her, 'a photograph is subject matter outside myself'.[36] Counterintuitively, she represents these extensive panoramas on a relatively small, easel-size scale that invites intimacy despite the suggestion of vastness in the image. In her own words:

> I like to work with impossible images, impossible because they are nonspecific, too big, spaces unbound. I make them specific by taking this vast thing and wrestling it into the painting.[37]

Celmins, like other artists discussed in this book, is deeply interested in the illusionistic process of image-making. Her ability to translate predominantly black-and-white photographic images into compelling painterly works in monochrome captivates the imaginations of her viewers.

Like the Renaissance paintings in monochrome that inspired the *paragone* debates discussed in chapter 4, in which painters sought to assert their capacity to challenge or outdo sculpture in painting, black-and-white paintings produced in response to photography, television and film seek to comment on or react to their sources in a variety of fascinating ways. Furthermore, in a period when pigments of every colour are readily available, the persistence of black-and-white painting might be closely associated with the promotion of black-and-white photography after 1960 as something distinct from the colour used in commercial photography. Indeed, the increasing prevalence of colour photography in advertising, for example, helped to establish black-and-white photography's reputation as a more 'artistic' and 'serious' medium – in a similar way that black-and-white painting has been considered as a less 'emotional' and more 'intellectual' genre.[38]

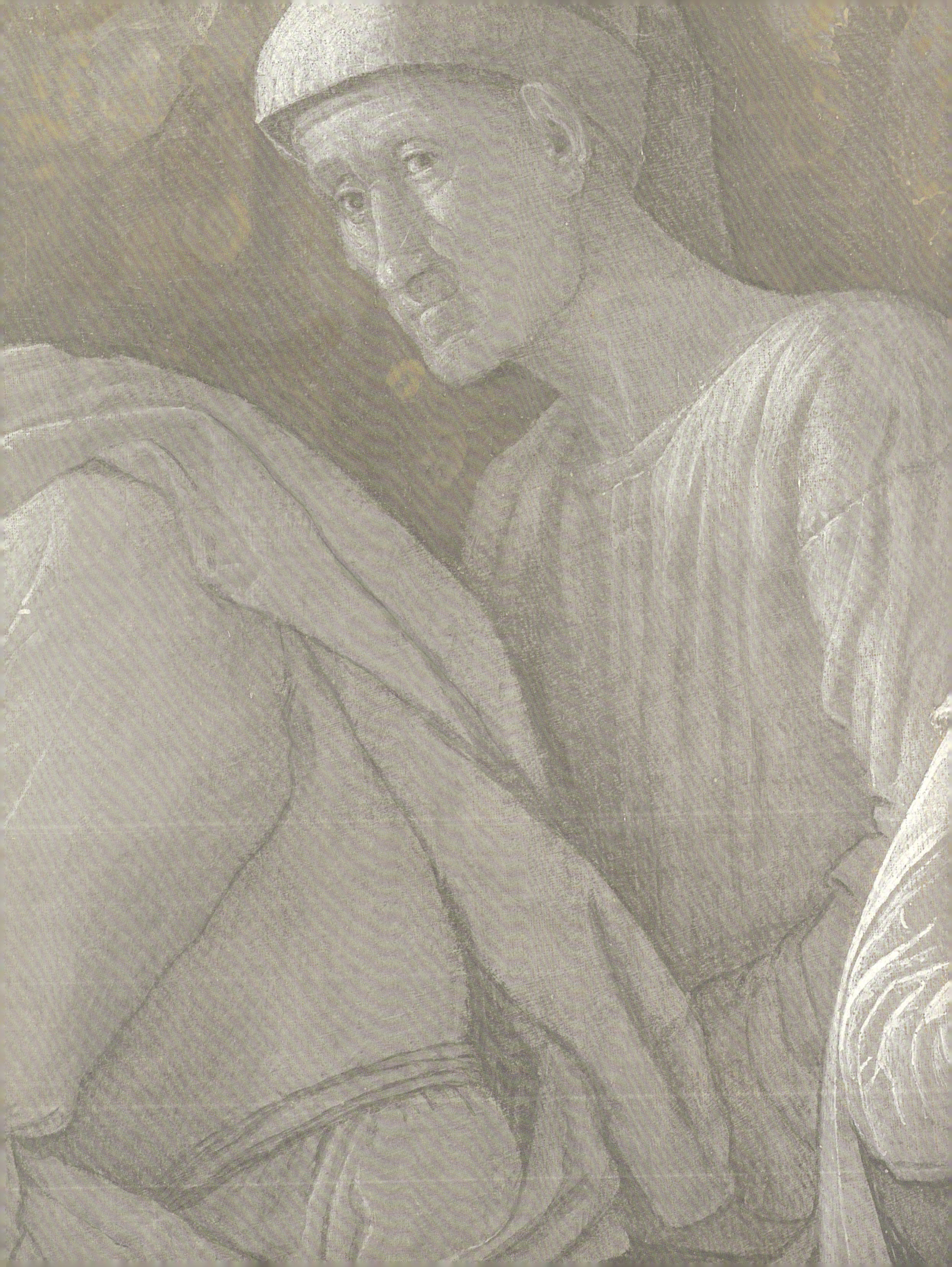

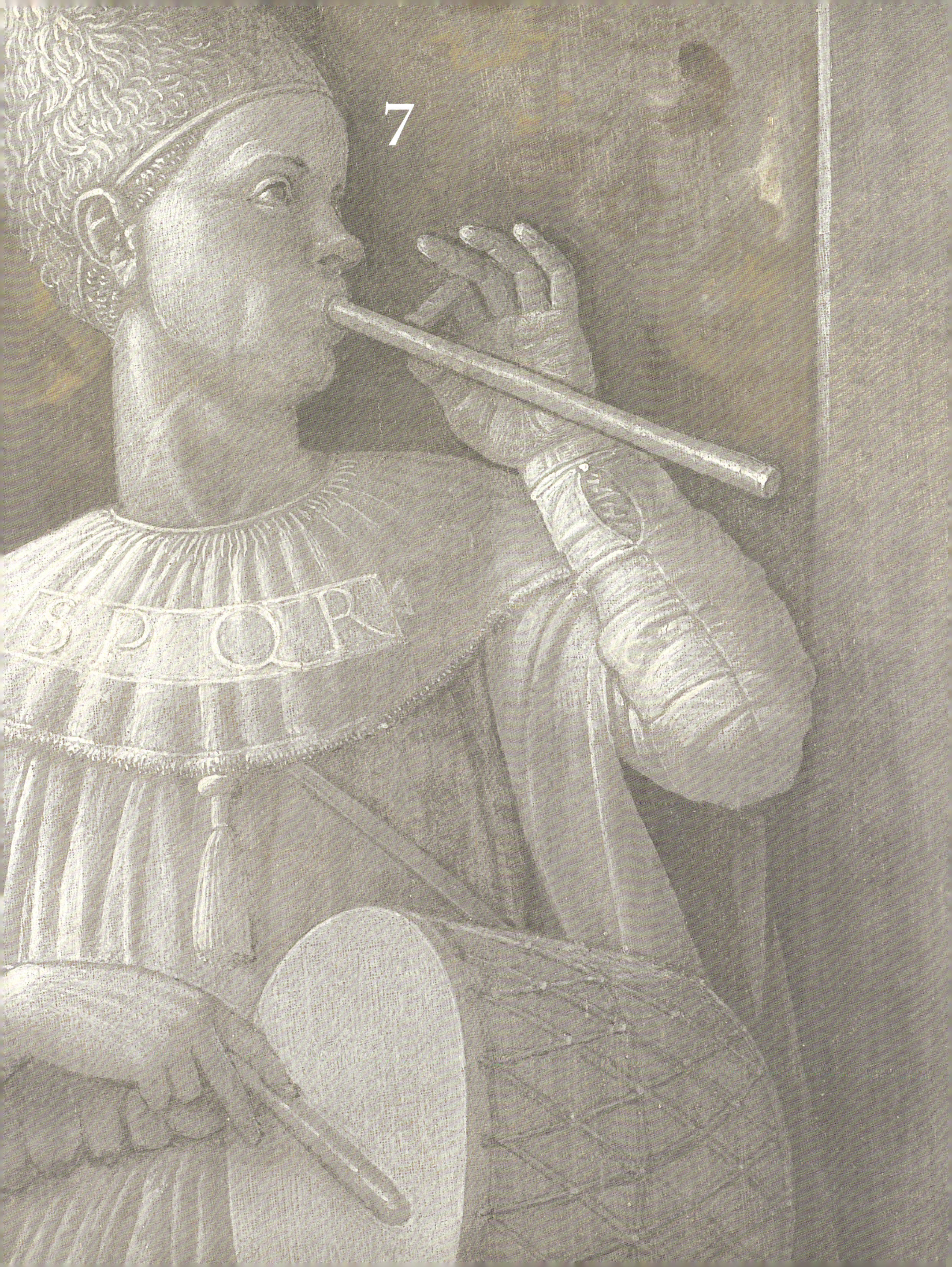
7
SPQR

Abstraction in Black and White

Jennifer Sliwka

Malevich painted his first *Black Square* in 1915 (although he dated it to 1913), and claimed it was 'the face of the new art'. He saw it as the beginning of a new kind of abstract painting. While other artists, including Wassily Kandinsky, had created colourful abstract works shortly before this date, Malevich's exclusively black-and-white, non-figurative painting represented a rupture with the tradition of colourful Russian figurative art and marked a new artistic and political era. Malevich did not consider the *Black Square* a unique work of art and painted four versions between 1915 and 1930. This version was most likely painted in 1929 for his solo exhibition at the Tretyakov Gallery in Moscow, by which time the 1915 square was in poor condition. He had painted it on top of two earlier coloured compositions and its craquelure later revealed seams of colour underneath the black paint.

In 1916, the Kiev-born artist Kazimir Malevich (1878–1935) boldly declared his painting *Black Square* to be the 'face of the new art ... the first step of pure creation'.[1] Malevich considered this revolutionary work, consisting of a black square enclosed within a white painted 'frame', to be the 'zero', or the beginning of non-representational or abstract painting. In a handout for the first public showing of *Black Square* in *The Last Exhibition of Futurist Painting 0,10* in St Petersburg in late 1915, Malevich declared: 'Up until now there were no attempts at painting as such, without any attribute of real life ... Painting was the aesthetic side of a thing, but never was original and an end in itself.'[2] The '0,10' of the exhibition title refers to the point 'zero' from which the *Black Square* was born, and 10 for the number of artists originally meant to participate (ultimately 14 artists were included). In creating this work, Malevich claimed that he was freeing art from 'the dead weight of the real world' by taking refuge in the form of the square, but said very little about his decision to paint in black and white.[3] In a private notebook, however, Malevich describes Suprematism as 'painting in philosophical movement' and 'cognition through colour', a process involving three stages, moving from colour to the 'absence of colour' in black and white.[4] Malevich clearly perceived the 'absence of colour' as the critical end-point in an intuitive and simultaneous process of thinking and creating a work of abstract art. In *Black Square*, he used black and white to establish formal tensions between light and dark and between perceptions of depth and surface. Indeed, read against the black square, the painted white 'frame' might be understood as an absence or void, in contrast to the dark square of pigment which asserts an almost physical presence. Conversely, the white border can be read as a white surface enclosing a black, empty space. It is precisely the challenge to the viewer to fully 'comprehend' this abstract painting that gives it a quality of timelessness and of the otherworldly.

Malevich did not consider *Black Square* a unique work of art and painted four versions of it between 1915 and 1930 (see cat. 60).[5] Although the earliest *Black Square* appears to have been made in 1915, the artist himself dated it to 1913, the year he first used the square form in the design of a stage curtain for an opera. His choice of date suggests it was the conception rather than the execution of the idea that mattered. The libretto of the opera, written by Aleksei Kruchenykh, was composed in 'Zaum', a nonsensical language of signs and sounds. This conceptual approach to language encouraged Malevich to invent 'suprematism', a new painterly idiom in which shapes and colours are given supremacy over figurative representations such as portraits, history or landscape paintings.

Cat. 60
Kazimir Malevich (1878–1935)
Black Square, 1929
Oil on canvas, 80 × 80 cm
Tretyakov Gallery, Moscow

It is worth stressing the novelty that *Black Square* would have had at the time: viewers would never have encountered a work like this before, being more familiar with representational paintings in colour. Malevich painted the 1915 version during the First World War and in a period of huge political unrest that followed the Russian Revolution of 1905, and just two years before the Bolshevik uprising and the October Revolution of 1917. Accordingly, to some, *Black Square* represents a decisive break with the past, marking a new artistic, social and political era.[6]

Black Square is often described as 'iconic', in the sense of its being a famous and representative work of art. However, the painting was also intended as a kind of icon in the more literal sense. When installed at the *Last Exhibition of Futurist Painting 0,10*, Malevich placed the canvas in a distinctive location, high up in a corner straddling two adjacent walls. In the Russian Orthodox tradition, this position was customarily reserved for an icon of Christ or of a saint. By hanging *Black Square* in this way, the work also acquired a spiritual significance. Malevich clearly regarded his minimalistic geometrical forms as the secular equivalent of Russian icons, figurative paintings that present the divine as pure or unmediated reality.[7] He described the *Black Square* as a 'bare icon … for my time.'[8] However, the form should not be understood as possessing a single meaning. As Malevich also indicated, 'the square is not an image, just as a switch or a socket is not yet an electrical current.'[9] The work is therefore an incentive to the viewer to interpret it, perhaps as a symbol of a new era or of revolution, an icon or a combination of these things. Irrespective of its interpretation, *Black Square* became closely identified with the artist: it hung over his deathbed, accompanied him in his hearse and marked his grave.

Joseph Albers: optical effects in black, white and grey

Malevich's use of black and white and geometric shapes for the purposes of abstraction was adopted by other artists, especially in the aftermath of the Second World War. The German-born American artist and teacher Josef Albers (1888–1976) probably knew Malevich's paintings of squares from publications by the Bauhaus, the school of art, architecture and design founded in Weimar, Germany, in 1919, where Albers studied and subsequently taught.[10] Malevich's emphasis on the beauty of the square form and his isolation of it probably inspired Albers's most celebrated works: the *Homage to a Square* series of paintings he began in 1950. Over the following 25 years, Albers produced over a thousand variations on the basic compositional scheme of three or four nested squares painted in varied colours and hues. However, unlike Malevich's reductionist or spiritual use of the square, Albers insisted his choice of the

Cat. 61
Josef Albers (1888–1976)
Study for Homage to the Square, 1965
Oil on Masonite, 61 × 61 cm
Private collection, 1976.1.586

geometric form was devoid of symbolism. Rather, the repeated square appears
to have been a powerful vehicle for exploring the way colours affect one another
and how their juxtaposition or order can cause viewers to perceive different
colours, tones and values.[11] While he is well known for his carefully considered
use of vibrant colour, Albers also produced several black, white and grey
versions of the nested-square compositions.[12] Indeed, his extensive studies in
colour theory often began with an exploration of black and white and the range
of hues available within these 'colours'. In the *Study for Homage to the Square*
(cat. 61) for example, Albers painted in a restricted palette of grey and black
three embedded squares, which he 'framed' within a white-painted border. Here
Albers explores the different effects that shades of black and white can have
on one another. Juxtaposing different tones can create the illusion of volume,
translucency or of flat planes advancing or receding into space.

Albers's experimentation with different hues and tones and with different
artistic techniques, including laying paint directly from the tube using a
palette knife onto Masonite (a type of hardboard made of steam-cooked and
pressure-moulded wood fibres), resulted in a nuanced understanding of how to
create optical effects with a restricted palette.[13] It has been observed that even
when the artist worked exclusively in blacks and dark greys, at least one of the
greys is luminous and the blackest black 'radiant', effectively counteracting
any sense of negativity, heaviness or encumbrance that darker colours might
otherwise suggest.[14] Indeed, despite their dark colour palettes, Albers's works
in black, white and grey all possess an unexpectedly luminous quality. Albers's
prolific artistic output and his many years' teaching, first at the Bauhaus and
subsequently at Black Mountain College and Yale University in the United
States, were particularly important for the next generation of abstract artists
who drew on his use of pattern, colour theory and visual perception.[15]

From Abstract Expressionism to Minimalism

In the United States, around the middle of the twentieth century, a new
generation of painters became interested in a kind of abstract art that drew
attention to the expressionistic gesture and the act of painting itself. These
artists became known as the Abstract Expressionists, following the coinage of
the term in 1946, and, although they worked in both colour and monochrome,
many produced series of works exclusively in black and white, and regularly
returned to this palette throughout their careers.[16] Jackson Pollock (1912–1956),
a major figure in this movement, often worked in black and white as a means of
exploring new ideas and approaches to painting. Introduced to the use of liquid
paint in 1936 at an experimental workshop in New York, Pollock began using

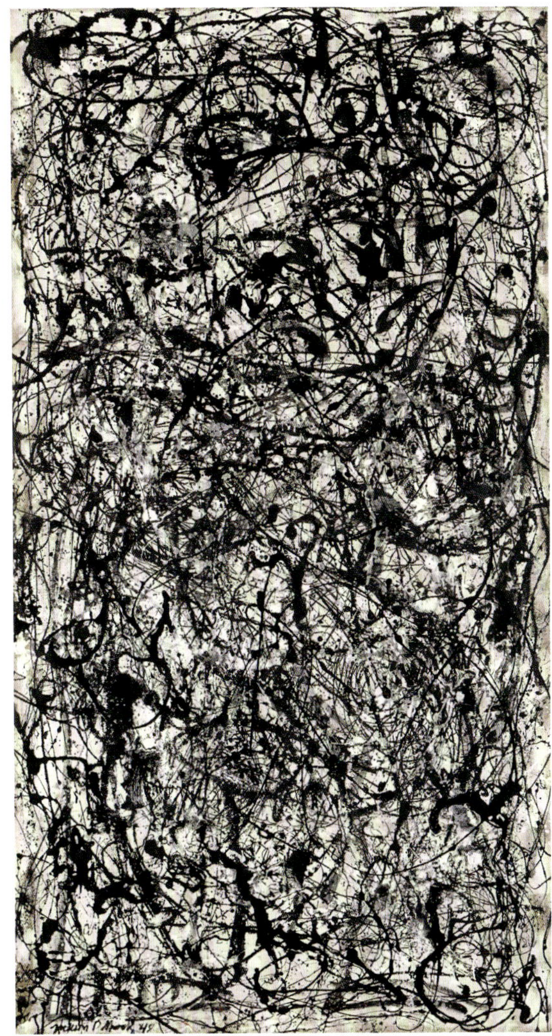

paint-pouring as one of several techniques in his canvases of the early 1940s. In 1945, he began laying his canvases on the studio floor, which facilitated his development of what would become his signature 'drip' technique.

Using cheaper and more readily available household paints – synthetic resin-based paints called alkyd enamels – Pollock experimented with different tools for applying them, using everything from hardened brushes or sticks to basting syringes. He soon developed a technique of pouring and dripping paint from all directions onto the canvas, an approach termed 'action painting' by Harold Rosenberg in 1952, in which paint is spontaneously dribbled, splashed or smeared onto the canvas in order to emphasise the physical act of painting.[17] The predominant colours of Pollock's 'drip' paintings from 1947 and in his later 'syringe' paintings from around 1951 onwards are black and white, although most contain splashes of yellow, red, blue or silver paint that immediately draw the eye.[18] *Number 26 A, Black and White, 1948*

Fig. 43
Jackson Pollock (1912–1956)
Number 26 A, Black and White, 1948, 1948
Enamel on canvas, 205 × 121.7 cm
Centre Georges Pompidou, Paris, Musée
national d'art moderne, AM 1984-312

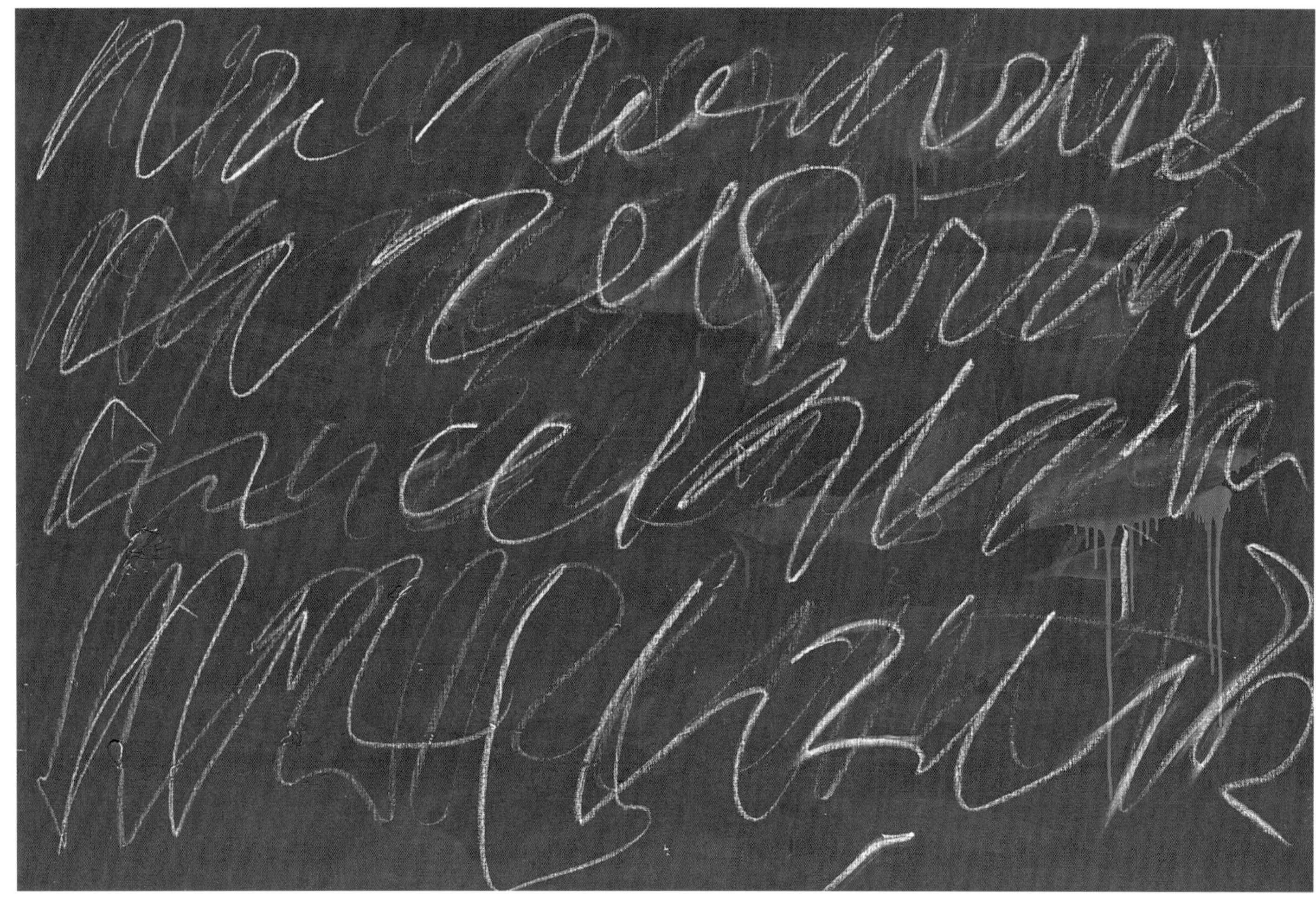

(fig. 43) occupies a special place in Pollock's oeuvre as one of the earliest
of his iconic drip paintings to be executed on canvas instead of paper and it
contains little other colour than black and white. Here the absence of colour
gives greater attention to the layered and relief-like effects of the work and
to the subtle tonal distinctions created between paint that has been diluted
or absorbed into the canvas and the stronger, denser pools and splashes of
pigment. Pollock developed his radical and unorthodox technique in precisely
these years (1947–8) and the effect was one that produced calligraphic visual
rhythms and sensations that alternate between light and dark, thick and thin
and horizontal and vertical in a way that blurred the distinction between
painting and drawing.[19] Pollock's shifting, almost animate surfaces anticipate
visual effects subsequently exploited by optical artists (discussed below) who
similarly experimented with line and space in monochrome to manipulate visual
perception and produce optical illusions.

Edwin Parker 'Cy' Twombly (1928–2011) was part of a younger
generation of American artists who took up the Abstract Expressionists'

Cat. 62
Cy Twombly (1928–2011)
Untitled [Rome], 1970
Oil-based house paint, wax crayon on canvas,
96 × 145 cm
Private collection

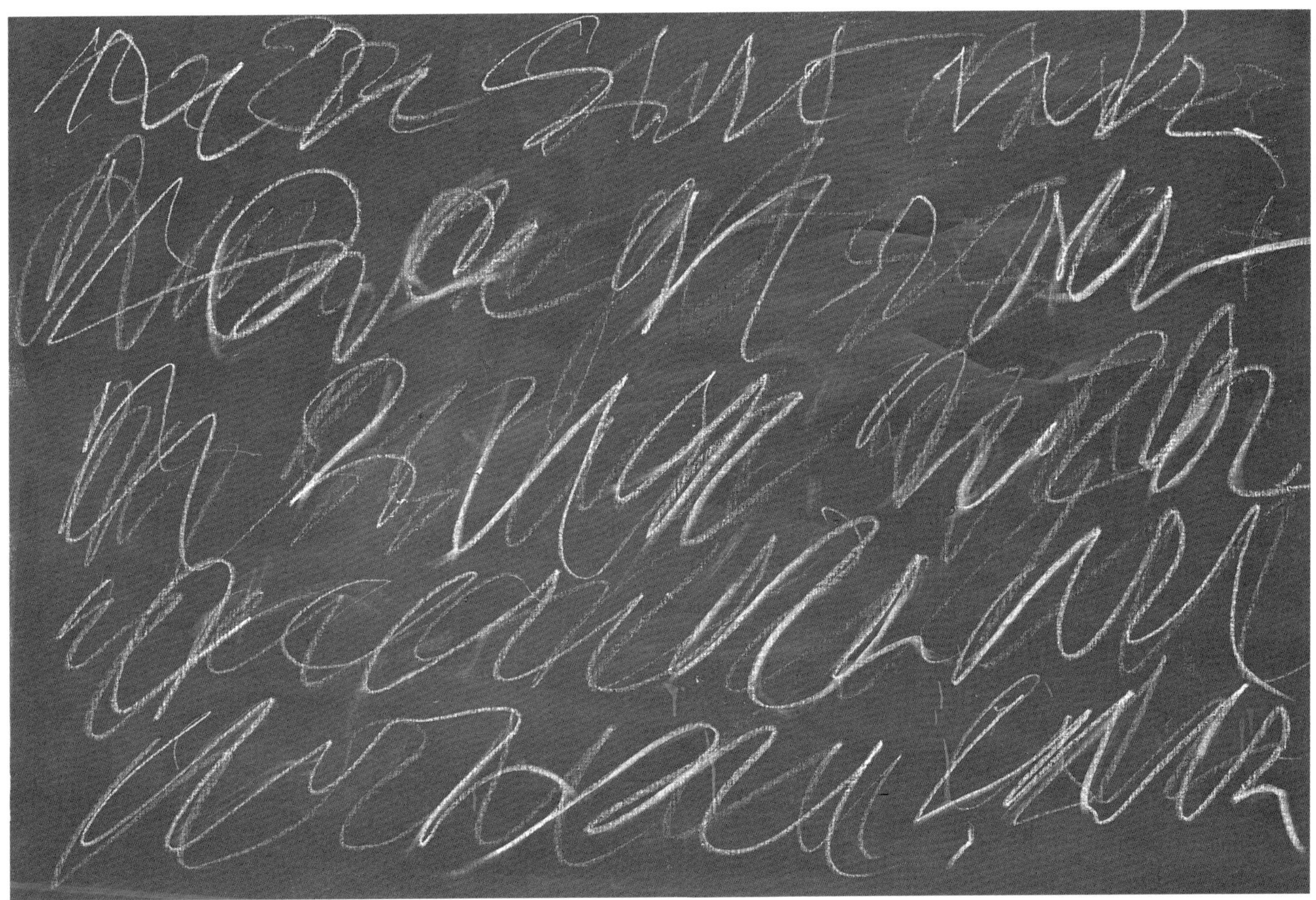

interest in recording gesture and transformed it into a new kind of pictorial language. In Twombly's case, aspects of these 'gestures' often deliberately evoke the written language. His mesmerising *Untitled* paintings of 1970, for example, two of the last of the famous series of 'blackboard' paintings he made between 1966 and 1971, are painted with a dark grey ground over which the artist layered loosely scrawled looping rows of illegible 'script' using a white wax crayon (cats 62 and 63).[20] So named because their dark ground resembles the slate of a classroom blackboard while the white wax crayon loops recall handwritten chalk script, these compelling monochromatic works suggest an increased interest in drawing, language and the line as expressions of human creativity and learning.

Marking a departure from his earlier, predominantly coloured pictures on a white ground inspired by the history and mythology of the Mediterranean landscape, the indecipherability of Twombly's fluid 'script' situates his 'blackboard' series between painting and drawing, writing and abstraction. In these works, ground and 'text' appear to overlap in places where Twombly

Cat. 63
Cy Twombly (1928–2011)
Untitled [Rome], 1970
Oil-based house paint, wax crayon on canvas,
97 × 145 cm
Private collection

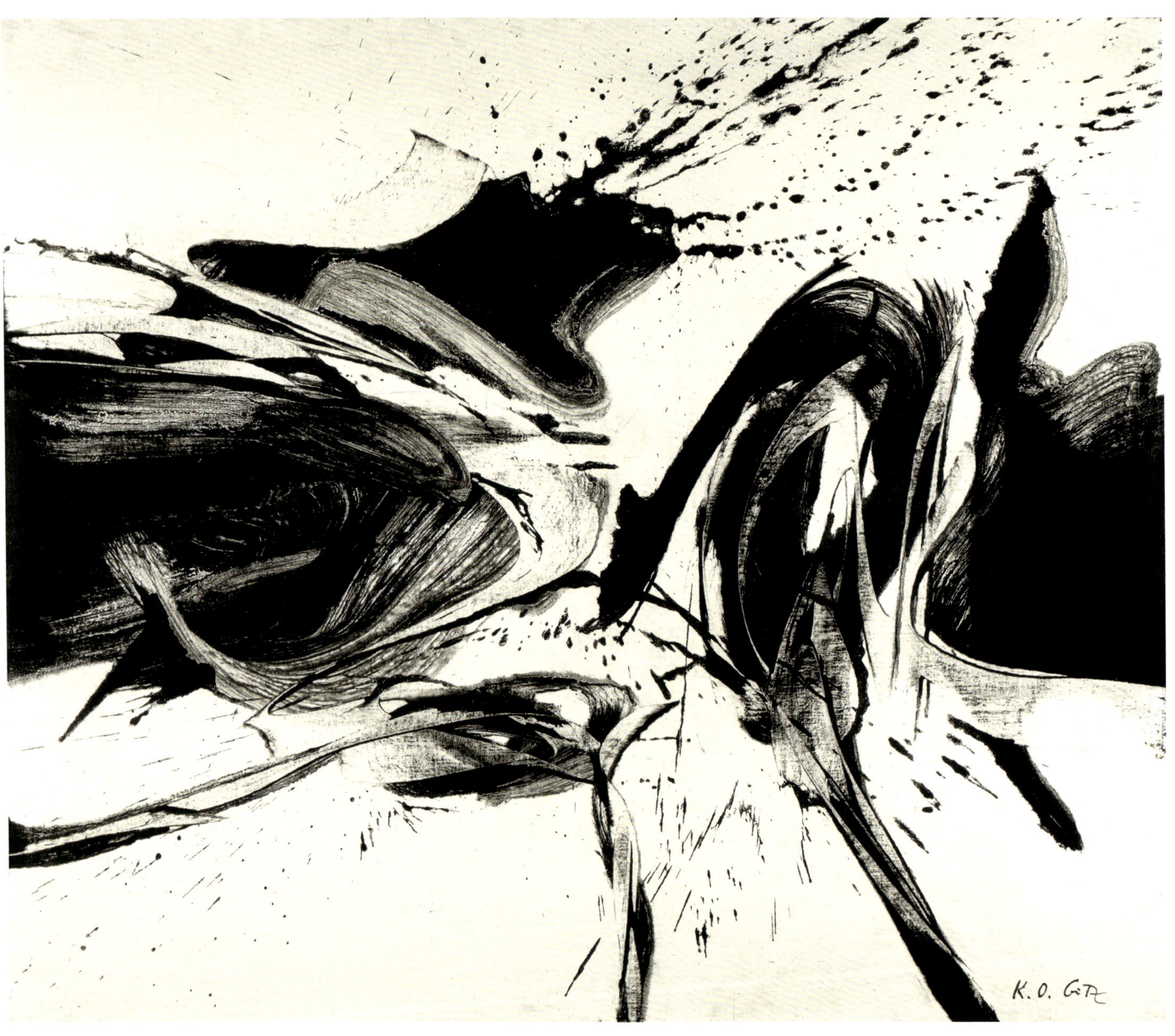

nearly obscures his earlier gestural white 'writing' by painting over it before subsequently adding further layers of lines, which simultaneously appear to emerge from, and dissolve into, the painting's dark, monochromatic ground. The work appears to invite the viewer to try to interpret the indecipherable 'script' and yet stands at a remove, forming an abstract but energised canvas full of graphic activity that explores both the capacity and the limits of language and art to communicate meaning. Accordingly, Twombly's two paintings also suggest the moment or place where the graphic arts of writing and drawing begin to fuse into and become painting.

Cat. 64
Karl Otto Götz (1914–2017)
Toro, 1964
Mixed techniques on canvas, 145 × 175 cm
Museum Kunstpalast, Düsseldorf
Exhibited Düsseldorf only

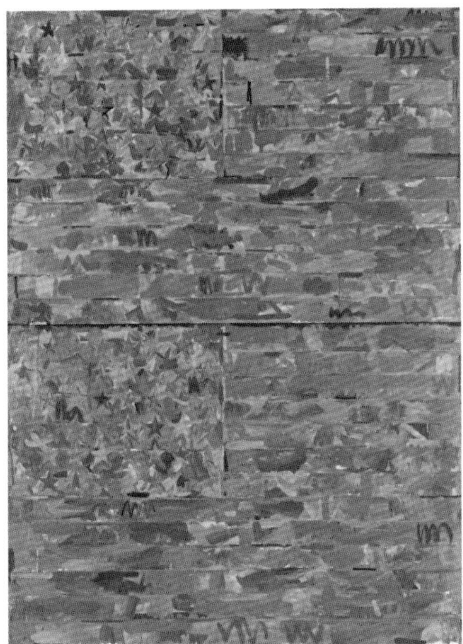

The European equivalent of American Abstract Expressionism is known as Art Informel and was practised at around the same time by such artists as the German painter Karl Otto Götz (1914–2017) who, in 1952, developed a new painting technique in which he first applied glue to the canvas before adding a layer of gouache paint, which he then partially removed with a squeegee before applying another paint layer.[21] This approach is evident in works such as *Toro* (cat. 64), which Götz executed swiftly with the canvas placed on the floor of his studio, playing with the strong contrast of the black paint against a white background. His gestural markings nevertheless avoid any suggestion of the figurative, adhering to the artist's motto that 'abstract is more beautiful'.[22]

By contrast, the paintings of Jasper Johns (born 1930), which reveal a preoccupation with perception, colour and phenomenology (that is, the study of structures of consciousness as experienced from the first-person point of view), are often seen as a reaction to Abstract Expressionism and a bridge to 1960s and 1970s Minimalism.[23] Indeed, rather than gesture and the act of painting, Johns reinforces the physical objecthood of his paintings by using media such as encaustic, a combination of pigment and wax that has highly tactile and plastic values. Johns, who has produced works in a monochromatic grey palette throughout most of his career, often blurs the distinction between representation and abstraction in his paintings by removing recognisable objects from their referential contexts and by eliminating their traditional colours. He is best known for his paintings incorporating images from popular culture, such as flags, maps, targets, letters and numbers, in which he re-presents these familiar subjects in unexpected and unorthodox ways. His *Gray Flag* (Ohara Museum of Art) and *Two Flags* (fig. 44), for example, take the American flag as a starting point but are painted entirely in shades of grey. Johns made his grey flags after his coloured *American Flag* paintings (for example, *Flag*, 1954–5, The Museum of Modern Art, New York) and attributes his desire to produce grey monochrome versions of his own coloured works in part to Ingres's *Odalisque in Grisaille* (cat. 28), a work he regularly visited at New York's Metropolitan Museum.[24]

In Johns's case, the effect of translating his coloured paintings into grey is often that of abstraction. Although the subject might appear well known to the viewer, the use of grey defamiliarises and counteracts the meanings a symbol usually holds. When asked about his grey flags and targets, Johns said: 'I was concerned with the invisibility those images had acquired, and the idea of knowing an image rather than just seeing it out of the corner of your eye. I wanted to make the flags and targets very concrete, to see them as objects.'[25] In viewing such works, 'seeing becomes thinking'.[26] Like his flags and targets,

Fig. 44
Jasper Johns (born 1930)
Two Flags, 1959
Acrylic on canvas, 203 × 148 cm
mumok, Museum moderner Kunst Stiftung
Ludwig Wien, L 112/0

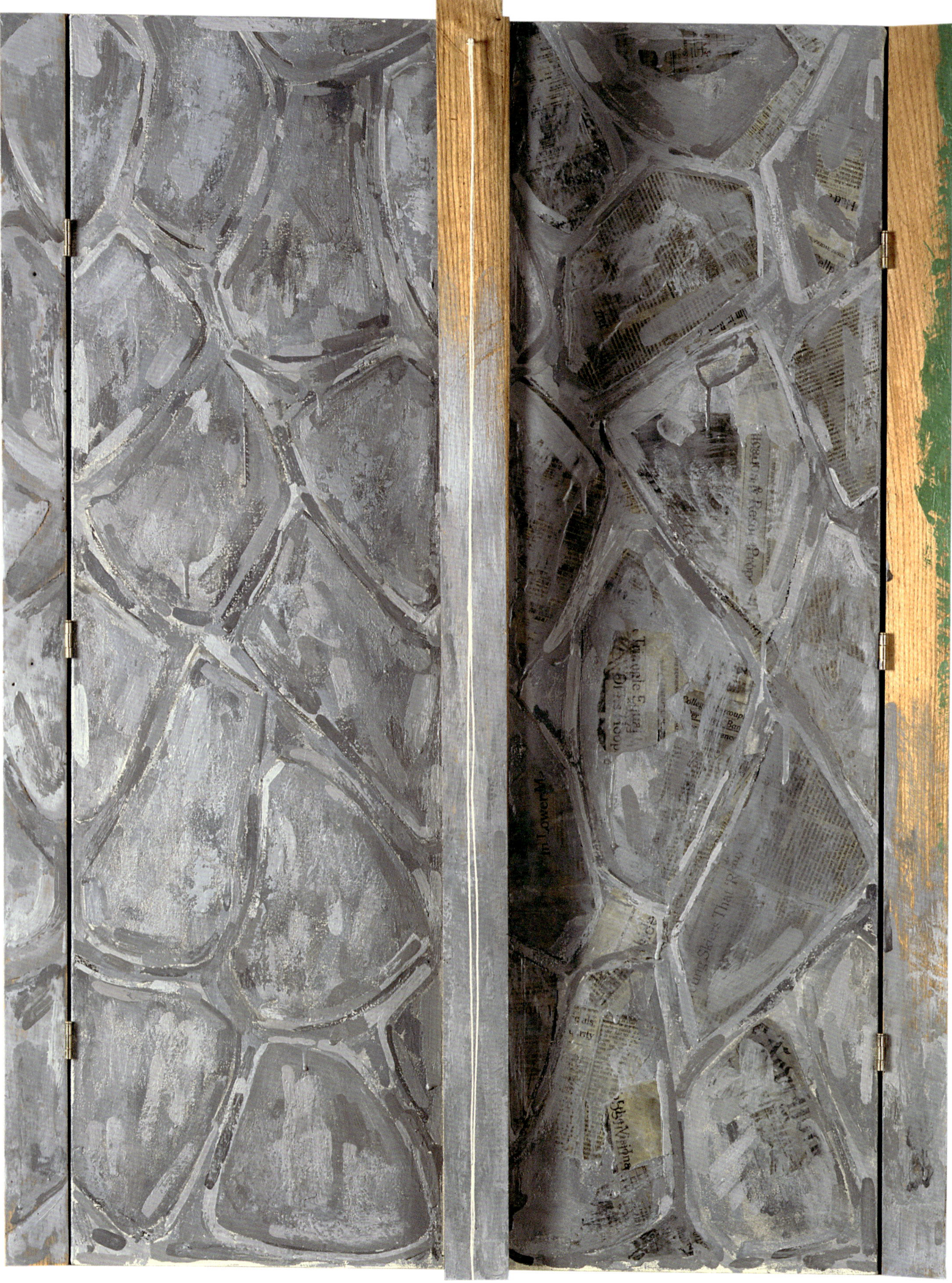

Untitled (cat. 65) is not strictly abstract. It combines a painted grey flagstone
motif with a slat-and-string construction, which nearly obscures the 'subject'
of the work.[27] The wooden hinged slats on either side of *Untitled* and the
central slat from which the string hangs imply movement and suggest that
this painted flagstone 'wall' or 'barrier' may be manipulated or opened like a
shutter or diptych to reveal something beyond. Barely discernible between
the painted stones on the right side are collaged newspaper fragments that
are rendered nearly illegible through the application of paint on top. This
treatment raises questions about the relationship between the two halves of
this work and between the actual wall on which the painting hangs versus
the simulated, painted wall it both represents and subverts. The seemingly
haphazard application of bright green paint on the far right provides a startling
contrast to the shades of grey in the newsprint and painted flagstones. The
flash of colour recalls the medieval and Renaissance tradition of painting the
exterior shutters of winged altarpieces in grisaille to simulate stone, shutters
that would then be opened at key moments in the liturgy to reveal the brilliant
polychrome image concealed inside. Here, using only a simple black-and-white
palette, the artist transforms a familiar, banal subject into a conceptual exercise
about representation. Johns has continued to work in shades of grey throughout
his career and his affinity for grey has been attributed to the colour's ability to
mediate between the extremes of black and white and to connote ambiguity and
a deliberate 'indeterminacy of meaning'.[28]

Like Johns's paintings, the works of the French-born Polish painter Roman
Opałka (1931–2011) straddle the worlds of figuration and abstraction. From
1965 until his death, Opałka painted numbers, starting with the number one and
working his way, with monastic discipline, towards infinity. Starting in the top
left-hand corner of the canvas and finishing in the bottom right-hand corner,
he painted tiny numbers in horizontal rows. Each time he began a new canvas,
which he called a 'detail' (all measuring roughly 197 x 136 cm, the dimensions
of his studio door), Opałka continued counting where he had left off. His series
began with white numbers on a grey canvas, and, from 1972 onwards, he added
one per cent more white to the ground of each new canvas, so that his paintings
became increasingly lighter.[29] Painted in the first year of his project, *Detail
612464–638092* (cat. 66) is still fairly grey, but the tiny compact numbers are
only just discernible and appear more like an abstract repeated pattern across
the surface of the canvas. Towards the end of his life, however, Opałka was
painting white numbers on an almost white support, his paintings becoming
nearly invisible – a poetic transformation that may be read as a metaphor for
a life that is gradually extinguishing. The strict use of a white-and-grey colour

Cat. 65
Jasper Johns (born 1930)
Untitled, 2007
Encaustic and collage on canvas
and encaustic on wood, with objects,
94 × 71.5 cm
Collection of the artist

palette and the austerity of the canvases underscore the philosophical and spiritual aspects of Opałka's exercise.

Minimalism

The spontaneity and gesture in the work of Abstract Expressionist painters such as Pollock provoked Frank Stella and Ellsworth Kelly to create alternative kinds of abstract paintings that emphasised the 'flatness' of a surface, in what was to become known as Minimalist painting. As a student at Princeton University in the 1950s, Frank Stella (born 1936) frequently visited New York art galleries to study the works of Pollock and other Abstract Expressionists such as Franz Kline, who worked almost exclusively in black and white. After graduating in

Cat. 66
Roman Opałka (1931–2011)
Opałka 1965/1–∞, Detail 612464–638092,
1965
Oil on canvas, 197 × 136 cm
Museum Kunstpalast, Düsseldorf
Exhibited Düsseldorf only

Cat. 67
Frank Stella (born 1936)
Tomlinson Court Park I, 1959
Matt black enamel paint on canvas,
220 × 280 cm
Museum Folkwang Essen, inv. G 394

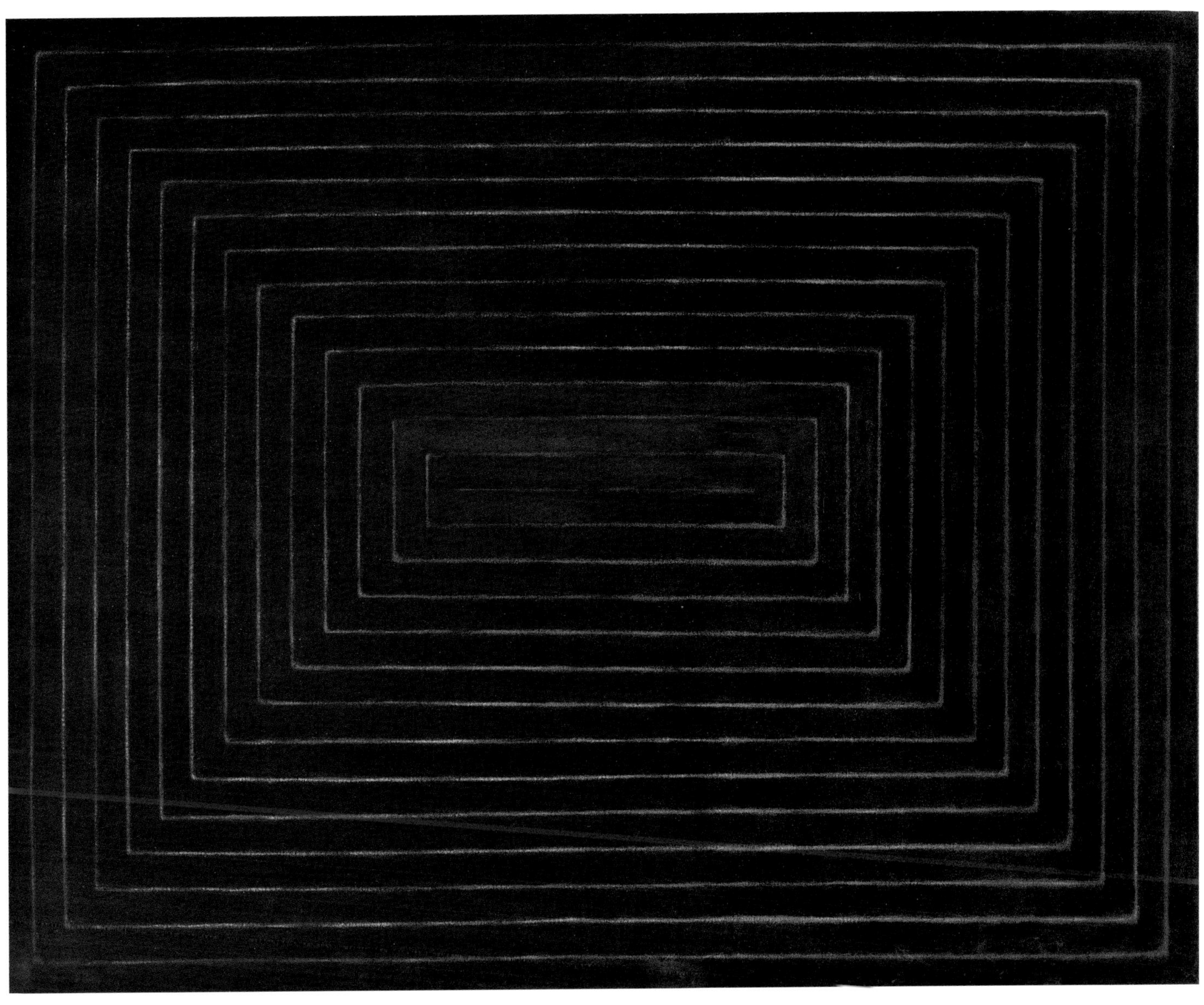

1958, Stella moved to New York, where he found work as a house painter to supplement his income and, soon after, began painting with the commercial black enamel he had to hand.[30]

Tomlinson Court Park I (cat. 67) is a result of these early experimentations and one of the first of Stella's 'Black Paintings', a series of 24 works in varying sizes, shapes and patterns that otherwise adhere to the same aesthetic and design principles.[31] The series marks a watershed, both in Stella's career and in painting at the time. He restricted himself to simplified compositions in black enamel paint in order to concentrate on the design and structure of his works. Each painting is composed of a series of parallel bands of black enamel paint measuring 2.5 inches (6.35 cm) wide and placed at a slight distance from one

another, allowing a very narrow strip of unpainted white canvas to show in-between. In *Tomlinson Court Park I*, Stella began painting from the edge of the rectangular canvas and worked his way inwards, creating a series of concentric rectangles that parallel the shape of the canvas.

Together, the pattern and reduced palette of *Tomlinson Court Park I* produce extraordinary optical effects, so that viewers often read the unpainted areas as white lines painted on a black ground rather than an absence of paint between the painted bands.[32] Rather than direct observation of the object in front of them, the viewer's perception is swayed by expectation and habit to perceive black shapes as the shadow of forms. When contemporary art critics mistakenly described Stella's Black Paintings as having 'white pin-stripes', Stella responded by insisting that this section was deliberately not drawn with the brush, as a means of distinguishing it from the gestural practice so popular with contemporary Abstract Expressionists. Stella eliminated gesture and developed an almost mechanical method of working in order to suggest flatness, an effect he described as 'forcing illusionistic space out of the painting at constant intervals by using a regular pattern'.[33]

It is not only the appearance of the Black Paintings that is dark but also their implied 'subjects', as suggested by the spectrum of human sorrows alluded to in their titles, from New York tenements, to a London insane asylum and the Nazi concentration camp at Auschwitz.[34] In *Tomlinson Court Park I*, Stella referred to the Bedford-Stuyvesant area of Brooklyn, New York, described by him at the time as 'downbeat' and 'politically depressed'.[35] Stella's response when asked how these abstract paintings should be read was 'what you see is what you see', suggesting that the viewer should suppress his or her habit of looking beyond the surface and instead focus on the immediate visual experience, accepting the painting simply for what it is. In developing this innovative approach to image-making, Stella established the foundation for a new kind of art, one that eventually formed the core of 1960s Minimalism, an artistic style characterised by the use of simple, massive forms based on the square and the rectangle.

Ellsworth Kelly (1923–2015), an American abstract artist associated with Minimalism, embraced a similar approach to painting, emphasising the 'flatness' of the surface of his canvases by painting them in a single colour or with simple geometric forms. Inspired by how light dispersed on the surface of the river Seine in Paris, Kelly painted *Seine* (fig. 45), an arrangement of black-and-white rectangles and one of his earliest non-figurative paintings. With this work, he began his practice of extracting an object or a scene from the world around him and rendering it in only its most basic outlines.

From the mid-1950s onwards, Kelly created multi-panel canvas paintings inspired by direct observations from nature, such as the shadows cast by trees or the spaces between architectural forms. In these works, which he continued to produce throughout the 1960s, each canvas is evenly painted in a single colour, creating a sense of 'flatness' rather than depth. Initially, Kelly executed the works in bright, primary colours but later also began painting them in black and white. Moving to Spencertown in upstate New York in 1970, Kelly began creating duo-panelled paintings inspired by the vistas and architecture of his new home. *Black with a Red Bar*, 1970 (Private collection), for example, was

inspired by a cantilevered structure he had seen locally.[36] These cantilevers –
usually a long beam or girder projecting from a wall to support a balcony or
cornice – were of particular interest to the artist. He painted another version
of the same composition, *Black and White Bar I* (cat. 68), the same year, in
a restricted palette. Here, Kelly painted a long, horizontal canvas in white,
pairing it with a smaller, rectangular canvas painted in black, which he centered
and affixed below the larger canvas. The creation of two versions of this
composition in the same year reveals Kelly's practice of testing new ideas by
creating black-and-white iterations usually in tandem with, or sometimes in
anticipation of, a work in colour.[37] The black-and-white versions, roughly a third
of his opus, enabled the artist to concentrate on the form and profile of a new
work without the distraction of the 'emotional' values of the colours.[38]

Kelly described the process of changing and refining his compositions
as a series of highly intuitive and aesthetic decisions, which ultimately rely on
vision, declaring, 'I don't know what I want, my eye does.'[39] With this practice
in mind, Kelly's *Black and White Bar I* appears like a cantilever with a cast
shadow and recalls the artist's close observations of shadows cast by buildings
or of spaces between architectural elements. The particular appeal of the
painting is that it simultaneously suggests a certain three-dimensionality and a
kind of flatness, implying both the presence of architecture in the form of the
cantilever and its absence as a void or shadow.

Op art

A restricted palette of black and white has long been used by artists working in
both figurative and abstract modes to create illusion. This was an effect taken
to new heights in Optical art – better known as 'Op art'– painting in the 1960s.
It combined a purely geometric pictorial language with colour theory and an
understanding of the physiology and psychology of perception to create optical
effects, ranging from the subtle to the disorientating.[40] While some Op art
works were painted in colour, the majority were painted in black and white and
the psychophysiological effects they create are normally those of movement,
with forms often appearing to vibrate, swell or warp. Op art was introduced
to the broader public in the exhibition *The Responsive Eye* held in 1965 at the
Museum of Modern Art, New York. It showcased two main types of works:
those in which perceptual ambiguity was created through coloured surfaces,
and those that suggested movement through the arrangement of lines and
patterns in black and white.

One of the artists featured in *The Responsive Eye* was the British abstract
artist Bridget Riley (born 1931). Riley explores ideas of perception in her

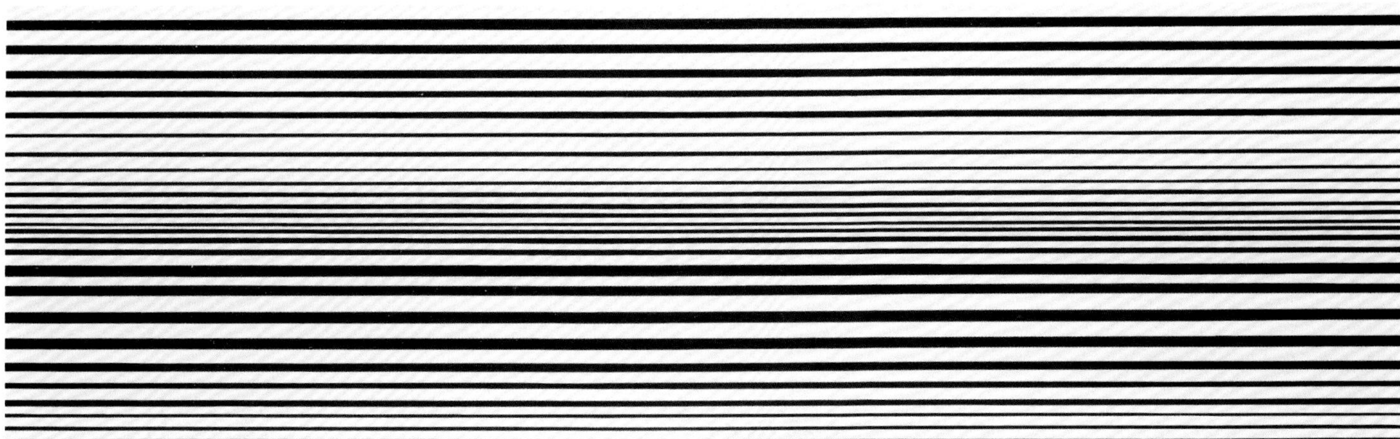

paintings through the use of repeating colours and shapes to generate and manipulate complex visual effects. In addition to a nuanced understanding of colour and colour theory, her work also demonstrates a sustained interest in a restricted black-and-white palette, to which she has returned at different points in her career. Riley has used an array of geometrical forms in her Op art works, from squares to triangles and circles, which are repeated and arranged so as to create both rhythms and distortions.

In addition to a monochromatic palette, stripes are a consistent motif in Riley's oeuvre. One of her earliest black-and-white striped works is *Horizontal Vibration* (cat. 69), which pre-dates the coinage of the term 'Op art' and marks the year she abandoned figurative painting altogether. Here, on a horizontal support, Riley painted black horizontal lines of varying thicknesses and proximities to one another so that they appear to swell and constrict hypnotically against the white ground. The vibrations alluded to in the title are the resultant effect on the eye as it attempts to read the negative (white) space between the positive (black) painted stripes. For the viewer, unable to rest his or her gaze on any single section of the composition, the overall sensation is destabilising and somewhat dizzying.

Riley worked exclusively in black and white throughout the 1960s before moving to colour. However, she has recently revisited monochrome in a new way. In *Rustle* (2015), for example, she returns to a series of variations on the triangle that had previously been explored in *Tremor* (1962). Here, she had arranged equilateral, convex and concave black-and-white triangles to form a dense field of optical vibration that creates an almost hallucinatory effect in the viewer. In contrast, the triangles in *Rustle* are arranged on a much more assertive grid and use proportionally larger shapes and less diverse combinations so that, in distinction to her earlier works, the viewer never loses sight of the clear structure of the painting and of its component units.[41] Unlike the optical effects of rupture and agitation in *Tremor*, the triangles in *Rustle* afford a continuous view that slowly and harmoniously changes as the forms appear to compose themselves into different geometric arrangements.

Cat. 69
Bridget Riley (born 1931)
Horizontal Vibration, 1961
Emulsion on board, 44.5 × 141 cm
Private collection, Nottingham

Between abstraction and figuration: Gerhard Richter's *Mirror Painting*
While Gerhard Richter alternates between figurative and abstract works, the colour grey has been an important recurring motif throughout his artistic career. He began using grey in his paintings in conspicuous ways from the early 1960s. In the grey photorealist painting *Table*, 1962 (Private collection), for example, he almost entirely suppressed the image by scraping sections off and adding swirls of grey paint over the top, rendering the work all but abstract.[42] A few years later, in 1969, he produced his first set of grey monochrome canvases, which are differentiated only by the textures resulting from different methods of paint application with either a roller or a brush.

Cat. 70
Gerhard Richter (born 1932)
Grey Mirror – 765, 1992
Pigment on glass, 220 × 176 cm
Statens Museum for Kunst, Copenhagen,
KMS7642

Writing in 1975, Richter mused about his use of grey in these works:

> When I first painted a number of canvases grey all over ... I did so because I
> did not know what to paint, or what there might be to paint: so wretched a
> start could lead to nothing meaningful. As time went on, however, I observed
> differences of quality among the grey surfaces – and also that these betrayed
> nothing of the destructive motivation that lay behind them. The pictures
> began to teach me. By generalizing a personal dilemma, they resolved it.[43]

Richter's words capture something of the challenge any artist faces in producing
a painting in monochrome and reveal how the creation of such works encourages
greater attention to subtle detail and a nuanced appreciation of texture.

At around the same time as he began producing his grey canvases,
Richter also began to use glass in his work. The earliest of these use only clear
glass, but he later began to experiment with coloured glass – until 1981, when
he produced his first monumental transparent mirror paintings. Thereafter,
mirrors appear relatively frequently in his works and seem to play on painting's
more traditional form as a representation of a real or imagined subject matter,
or on the notion of the painting as a window onto a fictive reality.[44] One of the
most striking of these works is *Grey Mirror – 765* of 1992 (cat. 70). Richter's
'mirror' was created by painting grey pigment on one side of a sheet of highly
reflective glass. As in many monochrome works, the distinctions between
different media become indistinct: *Grey Mirror* is simultaneously painting
and mirror. However, rather than reflect the world as it is, the surface of this
'mirror' shows an alternative world in greyscale. This realm, removed of colour,
has a destabilising effect as it renders the familiar unfamiliar, much like Johns's
grey flags and targets. Both Richter and Johns explore different kinds of visual
perception, attention and expectation in their monochromatic works. It is
tempting to also consider Richter's *Grey Mirror* an interactive work of sorts,
one that is 'activated' by the presence of the viewer standing or passing before
it. The viewer may be seen as both animating and transforming the painting
from an abstract into a figurative work of art. This poetic and engaging work
encourages a consideration in the viewer of the meanings and effects of colour
and 'colourlessness' of the kind that has long preoccupied the artist himself.

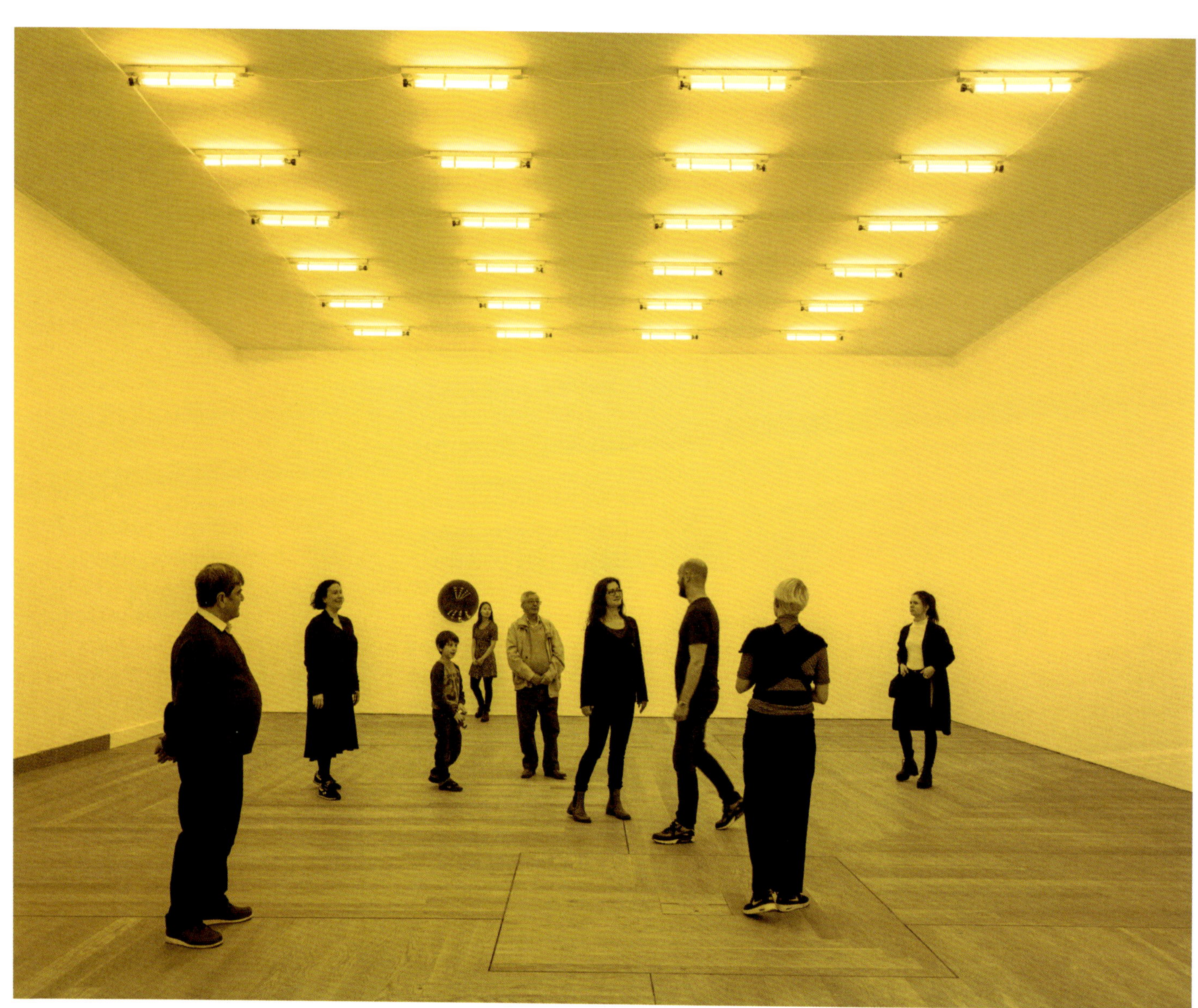

Beyond Painting: Monochrome and Installation Art

Jennifer Sliwka

Olafur Eliasson is known for his large-scale art installations that create immersive environments and intense experiences. In *Room for one colour*, he uses single-frequency monochromatic sodium-yellow lights that suppress all other colours in the spectrum, transforming the objects and occupants of his exhibition space into shades of grey, black and white. The sensation experienced in this room is one of stepping into a black-and-white photograph or film where, in the absence of other colours, the eye registers the fine detail of line, shade and contour and detects many more shades of grey in the scale of black to white. The effect is a kind of enhanced vision that heightens our awareness and perception of the space, people and objects around us.

The Danish-Icelandic artist Olafur Eliasson (born 1967) is known for his large-scale art installations that often use or evoke the elements – light, water, earth and air – to create immersive and often transcendent experiences. Working primarily with lightbulbs, gels and filters rather than paints and pigments, Eliasson has an exceptionally deep understanding of light and colour and how these manipulate visual perception. In his 2006 essay 'Some Ideas About Colour', he states:

> Colour, in its abstraction, has an enormous psychological and associative potential ... our experience of the colours of specific objects is often constant despite significant changes in ambient light ... we perceive an object as the same over time, but actually a large number of micro-transformations occur that continually negotiate the object's relationship to its surroundings ... if we become aware of this constant movement, we may be able to understand the world as a much more open, negotiable space than we usually think it is.[1]

Eliasson's profound interest in colour theory and in how different colours, in varying degrees of light, can transform our perception of the world around us, led him to develop a light installation entitled *Room for one colour* in 1997 (cat. 71), which effectively cancels out colour. Using single-frequency, sodium-yellow lights that suppress every other colour in the spectrum, Eliasson transforms the occupants of his exhibition space, usually a simple white room, into shades of black and white. The effect of this is, in Eliasson's words,

> Like a black-and-white image with shades of grey in between ... [in which] our brain has to handle or digest less visual information, because of the lack of other colours, we feel that we see details more easily than we usually do. This means that our eyes can detect more shades of grey in a black-and-white photograph than shades of colour in a colour image. We have, in other words, in this monochrome space, a sort of hyper-vision that gives us the feeling of having a particularly sharp ability to perceive the space and people around us.[2]

In *Room for one colour*, therefore, the 'suppression' of visual information tends to result in a heightened sensitivity to line, shade and contour. In this space, the mind is quietened and able to focus on details in a meditative way, recalling the simplified interiors of Cistercian monastic buildings, in which colour was prohibited and deemed unnecessarily stimulating to the senses and art works were rendered exclusively in shades of black and white (see chapter 1). As the artist's observations remind us, our perception of the colours of objects – and

Cat. 71
Olafur Eliasson (born 1967)
Room for one colour, 1997
Installation view at Moderna Museet, Stockholm, 2015
Courtesy of the artist; Tanya Bonakdar Gallery, New York; neugerriemschneider, Berlin

here we should include works of art – is generally and misleadingly constant, despite their continual transformation according to changes in their immediate environment. The artistic practice of removing colour, therefore, can be seen as a kind of 'jump start' that reboots the sluggish motor of the mind, forcing it to rethink old habits and compelling the eyes to look anew.

Similarly, the installations of the Belgian artist Hans Op de Beeck (born 1969) often transform everyday objects and spaces into unsettling environments devoid of colour.[3] *The Collector's House* (cat. 72), for example, is a monumental, immersive installation measuring 250 square metres. Composed entirely in shades of grey, black and white, it is only the visitors who enter the room that provide any colour. The work is a large reception area occupied by a sculpted grand piano, a library, display cases filled with trinkets, tables piled with objects reminiscent of *memento mori* or still-life paintings, life-size sculpted figures as well as paintings and stuffed animals. A sculptural interpretation of a large lily pond fills the centre of the space.

The eclectic grey art collection contains sculptures inspired by the classical, the modern and the contemporary, interspersed with kitsch, and wittily suggests that the fictional collector alluded to in the title might be a megalomaniac naively attempting to creat a sense of architectural grandeur through a use of symmetry and neoclassical elements. Strewn amongst the works of art are what appears to be the remains of a party: empty pizza boxes, beer bottles, ashtrays filled with cigarette butts, and scattered laptops and mobile phones.

The stillness and overall grey tonality of *The Collector's House* gives it an almost petrified appearance and raises questions about how we live and present our surroundings, possessions and selves to others, perhaps feigning status or a particular identity. The minimal grey palette transforms everyday items into something curious, almost otherworldly, compelling the viewer to consider the relationship between reality and representation, between a work of art and a banal object.

Cat. 72
Hans Op de Beeck (born 1969)
The Collector's House, 2016
Sculptural installation, mixed media,
4 × 12.5 × 20 m
Studio Hans Op de Beeck
Exhibited Düsseldorf only

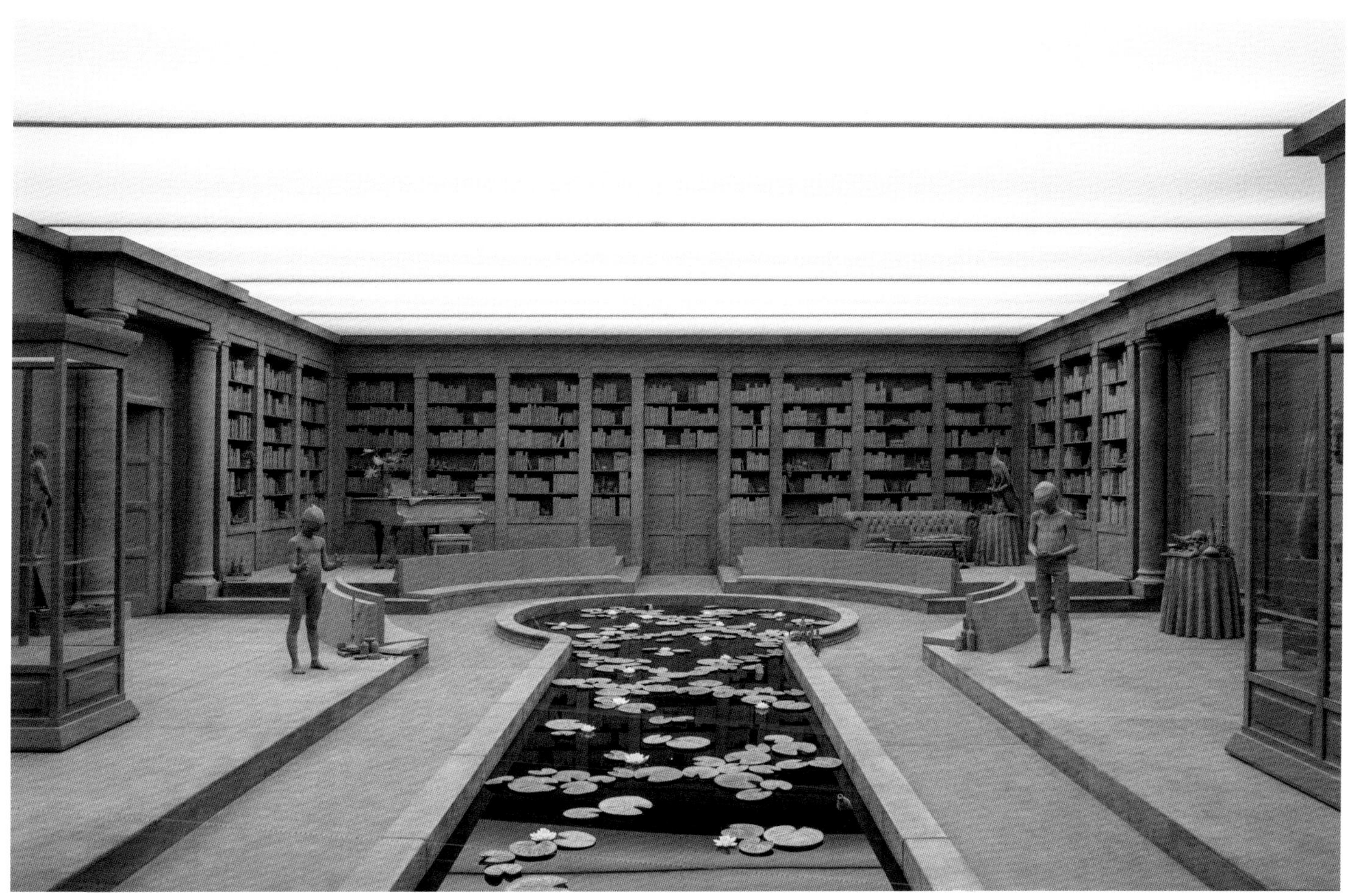

Your monochromatic listening
Olafur Eliasson

Emotions and reason, concrete and abstract thought – all come into play in how we perceive, understand and even create our world. In my artistic practice, I spend much of my time exploring the connections between an abstract feeling and the world. I believe, for instance, that we can better grasp a complex, data-driven topic like climate change through haptic experience – by directly touching melting blocks of glacial ice – and that participating in collaborative work can encourage empathy and compassion and a willingness to engage with 'the Other'. While acknowledging the crucial roles that science and reason play, I trust people's emotions and emotion-driven engagement. And sometimes I feel it is important simply to have confidence in abstraction, to trust people's ability to live with and make use of complexity and uncertainty.

By far the most radical form of abstraction is the monochrome. By reducing an artwork to only one colour, you eliminate narrative entirely, even compositional narrative. This makes it possible to pay attention not only to the monochromatic matter in front of you but also to the conditions in which your experience takes place, to the peripheral stimuli and noise that surround it, to the emotional state you are in when you encounter the work, and to the nature of perception itself. It is not the monochrome itself – the abstraction – that is the subject matter, but your perception and experience, at once abstract and very close.

Although monochrome is often seen as having an aura of exclusivity about it – as being hermetic, sealed off, mystical even (think Kazimir Malevich) – I see the monochrome as actually being about inclusion. It can be open and hospitable once we trust ourselves to step into it. The 'mono' in monochrome does not mean the elimination of complexity; rather, the monochromatic space holds plurality in it – it welcomes multidimensionality and offers it to us as viewers. Some art seems to tell you what to think, and it may even make you feel inadequate and that you don't fit in. Or else it simply ignores you. Other artworks address you as a subject and urge you to become active in making the experience your own. Monochrome is the latter. It allows you to be in charge of defining who you are and of assuming authorship of your own experience.

This idea of assuming authorship has long been crucial to me. I worked with it explicitly in an app called *Your exhibition guide*, which I created in 2014 for K20, Kunstsammlung Nordrhein Westfalen in Düsseldorf, to accompany an exhibition there of paintings by Malevich, Wassily Kandinsky and Piet Mondrian. In the app, I led people through eleven exercises, each focusing on a separate topic: *welcome, panoramic awareness, time, uncertainty, your other self, asteroids, light and darkness, movement, non-art, empathy* and *abstraction*. Visitors were invited to do the exercises while walking through the actual exhibition. They could 'float like an asteroid' past a Malevich or approach a Mondrian and 'greet it as if it were a long-distance traveller come from afar'. These were just suggestions, of course, and visitors could think most anything – what matters is being open to the vast field of imagination and abstraction that the once avant-garde paintings hold.

Another type of exercise that I have engaged in involves depriving people of the sense of vision as we know it. In the installation *Din blinde passager* (Your blind passenger, 2010), visitors enter a long, narrow tunnel of fog infused with varying hues of white and yellow light. Inside this space you feel blinded at first, but it only takes about ten seconds to reorganise your navigational toolbox. You start focusing on detecting sounds in the tunnel around you to estimate your distance from other visitors, and you begin to 'see' with your hands instead of your eyes. It is extraordinary how quickly we are able to adjust our sensory apparatus to our surroundings.

In seeking to engage viewers in assuming some authorship of their experiences, I have also worked a number of times with what I call the 'monochromatic listening phenomenon'. Viewing a monochrome or an object or scene in monochromatic light stimulates a certain activity in your eye and brain – it activates them in a different way from how they are activated by the full spectrum of colours. It is as if the monochrome material had the ability to host and listen to your not-yet-verbalised or not-yet-conscious emotional need. This can be a comfortable sensation or an uncomfortable one, depending on what emotional luggage you bring to this encounter.

In *Room for one colour* (1997), the entire space is bathed in light from monofrequency lamps that emit light of around 589 nanometres in wavelength, in the yellow region of the visible spectrum. At first you see only a saturated yellow light that makes all colours appear to be shades of yellow, grey and black. Once you become comfortable with this situation, with the degree of abstraction it entails, you can start to pay attention to what is actually happening with your vision as such. The experience may vary, but the most obvious impact of the yellow light is the realisation that reality outside is very much conditioned by our perception of it: vision itself is not objective, and this realisation can help us begin to see ourselves and our world in a different light.

A very clear example of this is how the brain adjusts the colour of known objects to make them appear the same colour in radically different lighting conditions: experiments have shown that if we look at a desaturated image of a bunch of bananas, for instance, our brain corrects what we see according to what we know, tinting the bananas yellow. Colour and consciousness of colour are not fixed things, set in stone; like all aspects of our reality, they are relative.

If our perceptive apparatus were altered, the world would appear different to us. Imagine, for example, if we could see infrared or ultraviolet light in addition to the spectrum that we can perceive. Research into colour perception in animals and the colour-blind has shown us the importance of colour for how we grasp and relate to the world. The late Francisco Varela, whose work on empathy and embodiment has been deeply influential to me as well as to many scientists and philosophers, argued that the gulf between what we humans experience of colour and what birds experience is so great that we cannot even imagine it; it is like telling someone who only perceives the world in two dimensions that there is a third.

The experience of monochromatic light offers us an opportunity of imagining another perspective, of viewing the world with a recalibrated perceptual apparatus. It makes us aware of the limits of our senses and helps us to see the relativity of our colour perception. Understanding how we see colour can make us reconsider how we constitute the world. By reducing experience to the minimum, the monochrome allows us to reflect on what is happening when we perceive something, on how perception is also a type of world-making. For a moment, we can imagine what it might be like to become colour-blind or another species of animal or even more radically other. What strange, new worlds might emerge then?

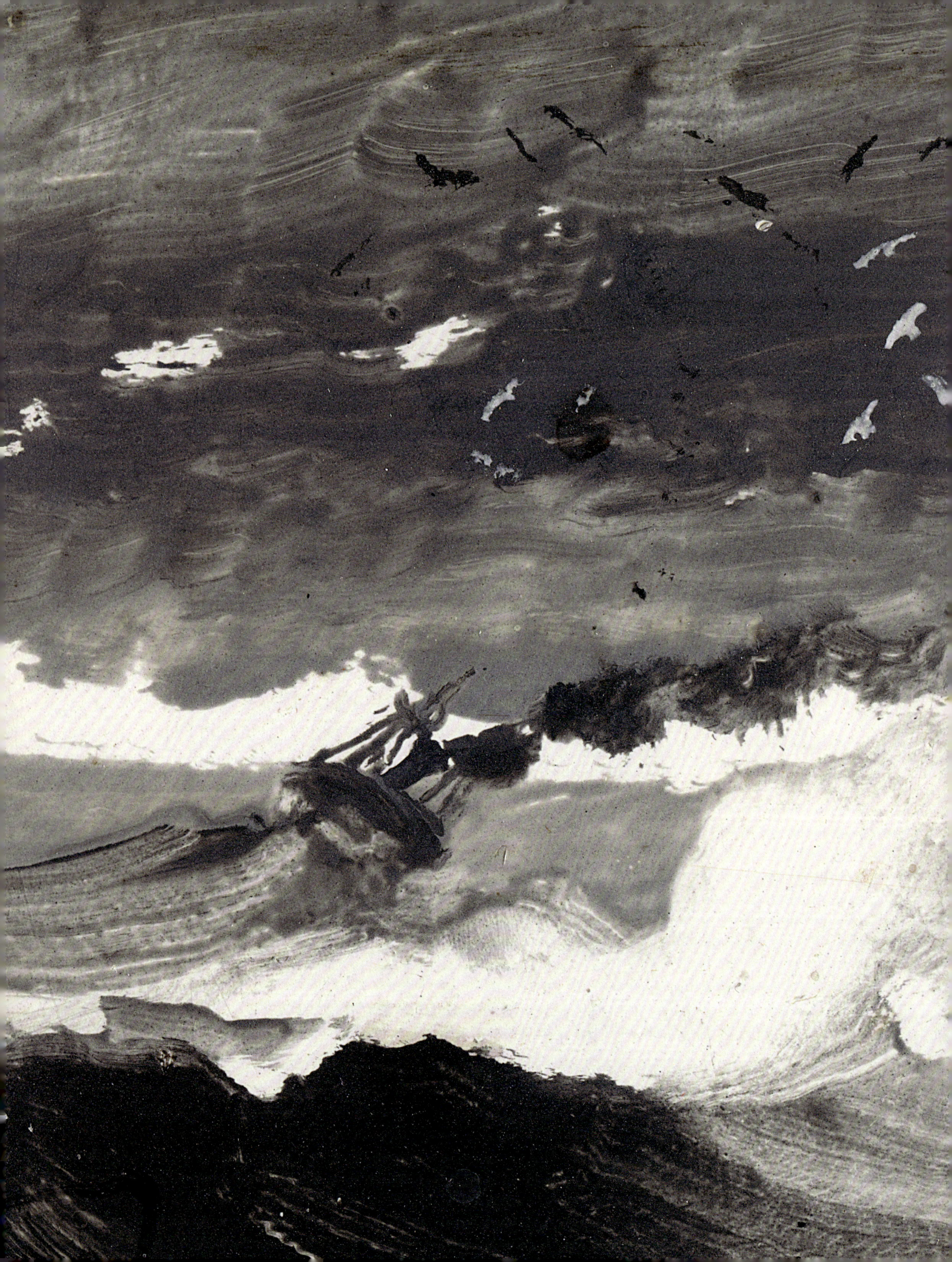

Notes

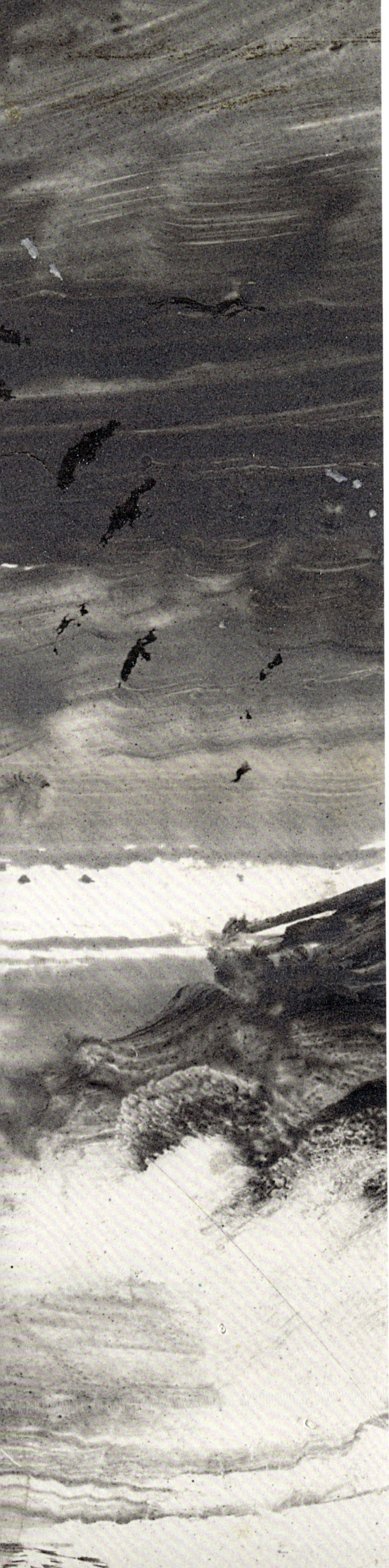

Introduction

1 Interview with Christiane Vielhaber, 1986, in Richter 2009, p. 191.
2 For Pliny's discussion of monochrome, see Pliny, *Naturalis Historia*, 35.5.
3 Although no *skiagraphia* panel paintings by Apollodorus survive, the technique is found on contemporary white-ground pottery and is described by Pliny, *Naturalis Historia*, 35.60. An example of *skiagraphia* technique can be found on the drinking cup attributed to the Sotades Painter at the British Museum (inv. 1892,0718.2). On the technique, see Stansbury-O'Donnell 2015, pp. 255–6.
4 Pliny traces the origins of painting to the outline of a man's shadow on a wall using a single colour. See Pliny, *Naturalis Historia*, 35.5. On the discussion of '*lumen et umbras*', see ibid., 35.46.
5 For a discussion on the origins of the term, see Folena 1951, pp. 51–63.
6 Cited in Teasdale Smith 1959, pp. 51–2.
7 Cited in Van der Meulen 1994, vol. II, p. 192. The result of that commission is Peter Paul Rubens's *The 'Apotheosis of Germanicus': Copy after an Antique Cameo (The 'Gemma Tiberiana')*, oil on canvas, 100.7 x 78 cm, Ashmolean Museum, Oxford, inv. A1169. See also Krieger 1995, pp. 3–6, on the early history and uses of the term.
8 The film is discussed in Bain 2012, pp. 5–6.
9 On grey's qualities of quietness and indifference, see Richter's interview with Jan Thorn-Prikker, 2004, cited in Richter 2009, p. 478.
10 Ibid.
11 On Richter's description of grey's capacity to mediate, see his letter to Edy de Wilde, 23 February 1975, cited in Richter 2009, p. 91.

Chapter 1
Painting the Sacred

1 Rudolf 1987, pp. 1–45.
2 These statutes, numbered 10 and 20, prohibited excess in liturgical vestments and vessels and limited the amount of sculpture and painting in the monastery. See ibid., p. 2.
3 The statute (known as number 80) indicated that manuscripts were to be made of one colour only and that windows were to be made white, without crosses or pictures. The precise year this statute was added has been debated, and it could have been written at any time between 1119 and 1152 but is generally dated to 1134. See ibid., pp. 21ff; Burton and Kerr 2011, p. 76.
4 Kinder 2002, pp. 141–61.
5 Burton 2008, p. 157.
6 Park in Norton and Park 2012, pp. 181–210; Norton in Norton and Park 2012, pp. 228–55; Cothren in Lillich 1982, vol. 1, pp. 112–29.
7 Arnold 1913, pp. 115–16; Marks in Norton and Park 2012, pp. 211–27. Other surviving examples of Cistercian glass may be seen at the Abbey of La Bénisson-Dieu in the Loire Valley.
8 It remains unclear whether the Cistercians invented this technique to serve their spiritual and aesthetic needs or whether they adopted glazing types that already existed. Regardless, the technique clearly became closely associated with the Order at an early date and the technique is still known today as 'Cistercian glass'.
9 The glass appears to have been removed during the French Revolution in the eighteenth century and survives as a series of six fragments dispersed in collections across the Britain, France and the America. Saint-Denis was closed by the French revolutionary government in the 1790s; the stained-glass windows were removed and eventually found their way into public collections. On the associated fragments, see Hayward 1992, pp. 303–25, figs 1, 2a, 2b.
10 Doublet 1625, p. 287, and Félibien 1706, p. 277, both describe a profusion of fleurs-de-lis throughout the church.
11 On the tradition of Netherlandish stained glass see New York 1995.
12 For a broader discussion of marginal imagery in illuminated manuscripts see Camille 1992.
13 Holcomb in Madrid 2009, pp. 254–60.
14 Krieger 1995, pp. 1, 4, 6–36, 43, 120–69, 172–7, 182, figs 6–17, 119, pls I–VIII.
15 Brussels and Paris 2012, cat. 50, pp. 252–3.
16 The work may have especially appealed to Boilly since he was a painter of grisailles; his work is discussed in Chapter 5.
17 As Susie Nash has demonstrated, the term 'cendré' or 'ashen' is used in the inventory of

the French King Charles V to describe the grey colour of his Lenten altar hangings and is also associated with ashes, and hence with liturgical rites on Ash Wednesday, in the 1404 inventory of the noble house of Burgundy. See Nash 2000, pp. 77–87. On liturgical practices during Lent, see the *Roman Missal*, 2011.

18 The practice of veiling images of Christ (and of the saints for reasons of decorum) is described by William Durandus in his treatise on the liturgy and its symbolism, the *Rationale divinorum officiorum* of 1286. See Durandus 1906, pp. 56–7.

19 Thurston 1904, p. 101, argues that records of Lenten cloths exist as early as the tenth century. Other authors, such as Bond 1916, pp. 104–5, note examples from 1220 until the sixteenth century in Salisbury. Lenten coverings today are usually violet in colour.

20 Nash 2000, p. 78.

21 The scenes represented are the Arrest, the Flagellation, the Crucifixion, the Harrowing of Hell and the *Noli me tangere*.

22 Markschies in Madrid 2009, p. 273.

23 The association was first made by Stirling 1938, p. 29.

24 Madrid 2009, p. 323.

25 The inventory dates to 1480 and was first published by Vidier 1910, pp. 185–369, esp. p. 188; for further discussion of the mitre, see Madrid 2009, cat. 18, pp. 322–4.

26 See Teasdale Smith 1959, p. 43; Nash 2000, p. 79.

27 Another surviving example is a grisaille painting on cloth of a Madonna holding the Christ Child, from the Cathedral of Huesca, Spain, of around 1400. See Ricart 1956, p. 158. A larger fragment of a Spanish Lenten cloth of the Virgin Annunciate painted in grisaille on linen around 1500 in Valencia, which probably served as an organ cover, is now in the Victoria and Albert Museum (inv. P.19-1928). See Kauffmann 1973, cat. 348, pp. 283–4.

28 For an example of white-painted Lenten cloths, see Weigert 2003, pp. 199–229. On Genoa blue and its use for these monochrome cloths, see Cataldi Gallo 2008. Our modern word 'jeans' comes from the French *Gênes*, for Genoa.

29 Harris 2005; Cataldi Gallo 2008; Cataldi Gallo in Boggero and Sista 2013, pp. 36–42;

Martini in Boggero and Sista 2013, pp. 44–8.

30 Ibid.

31 Laurent de la Hyre, for example, decorated the refectory of the convent of the Minims on the Place Royale in Paris in 1649 with 18 prophets and saints and 14 landscapes, all executed in grisaille. The decoration, lost when the convent was demolished in 1926, is known through a series of small-format grisaille studies in the Musée du Louvre, Paris. See Grenoble, Rennes and Bordeaux 1989–90, pp. 310–15.

32 For more on Giotto see Chapter 4.

33 There has been a great deal written on the entire programme of the chapel. Two recent accounts are Derbes and Sandona 2008 and Frugoni 2008.

34 On Raphael's grisaille Theological Virtues (Vatican Museums) and their physical and thematic relationship to the rest of the altarpiece, see Meyer Zur Capellen 2001, vol. 1, cat. 31, pp. 233–46.

35 Bain 2012, pp. 5–20.

36 This artistic metaphor seems to derive from a passage in the Epistle to the Hebrews (10: 1) describing the Old Testament as but a shadow of the good things to come; see the discussion in Kessler 1994, pp. 74ff; Kessler 2000, p. 45. On the use of black and white for Old Testament subjects, see also Schoell-Glass 1999, pp. 197–204.

37 John of Damascus in Louth 2003, p. 49.

38 On the panel, see Upton 1975, pp. 49–79, figs 1, 8–9, 17–18, 22–3; Hand and Wolff 1986, pp. 41–9.

39 Teasdale Smith 1959, pp. 43–54.

40 On the history of the winged altarpiece, see Baxandall 1980, pp. 9–26; 50–93; Kemperdick 2009, pp. 125–46; Ehresmann 1982, pp. 359–69.

41 These fragments are now preserved in the Gemäldegalerie, Berlin, and in the National Gallery, London. See Campbell 1998, pp. 300–9.

42 Similarly, the Prophets and Evangelists flanking the *Annunciation* bear scrolls alluding to their prophesies or gospels on the coming of Christ or episodes from his life and are therefore also represented in grisaille.

43 Teasdale Smith 1959, pp. 49–51.

44 On the altarpiece see Campbell 1998, pp. 374–91; Jacobs 2011, p. 157.

45 Donne's parents obtained a papal
indulgence enabling them to have a portable
altar, suggesting that Donne himself had
the same. See discussion in Campbell 1998,
p. 387.

46 On the altarpiece, its reconstruction and
restoration, see Stuttgart 2010.

47 Beutler and Thiem 1960, p. 41. Although the
document cited by Beutler and Thiem
about Erhart's stone crucifix cannot be
conclusively tied to the *Grey Passion*, the
original carved element at the centre of
the altarpiece probably shared the same
monochromatic colour scheme. This theory
was recently reiterated in Taubert 2015, p.
88.

48 Examples of such works can be found in Los
Angeles and London 2003–4, such as cat.
125 by the so-called Flemish Master of
James IV of Scotland, 1515–25.

Chapter 2
Studies in Light and Shadow

1 These works were brought together in
seminal exhibition held at the Musée du
Louvre in 1989. See Paris 1989.

2 Vasari 1906, vol. IV, p. 20; for the English
translation, see Popham 1945, p. 11.

3 On the attributions of the linen studies, see
Paris 1989; Brown 1998, pp. 79–80, 94;
Cadogan 1983, pp. 27–62; Fiorani 2013, pp.
267–73, 840–1.

4 The practice is discussed in Book 24 of
Filarete's *Trattato di architettura*. See Filarete
1965.

5 This point was observed by Christiansen
1990, pp. 572–3.

6 In this way they are similar to the workshop
'model-books' used in the medieval and
Renaissance workshops.

7 Alberti 1972, pp. 75, 79–87.

8 Paris 1989, cat. 9 (as Leonardo); Cadogan
1983, pp. 27–62 (as Ghirlandaio, following
Suida 1929, Fahy 1969 and Dalli Regoli
1976).

9 On this study, see Washington, Munich,
London and New York 2013, cat. 104, p. 259;
for Dürer's personal account of his travels,
see Dürer in Troutman 1971.

10 Beccafumi's earliest surviving monochrome
oil studies are for his *Mystic Marriage of*

Saint Catherine altarpiece (Chigi Saraceni
collection, Siena), which was completed and
installed in the church of Santo Spirito, Siena,
in March 1528. On his oil sketches more
generally, see Sanminiatelli 1955, pp. 35–41.

11 See Torriti 1998, p. 307, no. D117.

12 See Chapter 5.

13 Sutton in Greenwich, Berkeley and Cincinnati
2005, p. 17.

14 A rare etching by Jacob Neefs, however,
reproduces the basin together with a ewer,
and its inscription indicates that the Antwerp
goldsmith Theodore Rogiers (also known
as de Rasières) made both of these in silver
for Charles I of England. Unfortunately, the
objects, if made, no longer survive, and there
is no record of them in the royal inventories.
See discussion in Martin 1970, pp. 187–93,
and Held 1980, vol. I, cat. 256, pp. 355–8. On
the possible commission of the basin for
Princess Mary (b. 1631), see Braham 1973,
no. 8.

15 On Rembrandt's oil sketches, see Baer in
Boston and Chicago 2003, pp. 29–44.

16 For an in-depth technical discussion of the
work, see Bomford 2006, pp. 100–9.

17 Before about 1730, the grisaille was altered
again, possibly by Rembrandt's pupil
Ferdinand Bol, with the addition of extra
strips of canvas, which converted the
horizontally orientated picture into a vertical
format. The attribution of the additions to
Bol was first made by J.G. van Gelder in Van
Gelder 1973, pp. 100–4; see also Bomford
2006, pp. 100–9.

18 Bruyn 1989, vol. 3, no. 107, p. 94.

19 See Boston and Chicago 2003, p. 111.

20 Bruyn 1989, vol. 3, no. A107, pp. 96–7.

21 See Hinterding in London and Amsterdam
2014, pp. 153–63, especially p. 157.

22 Saragossa 1996, pp. 244–5; Morales y Marín
1995, p. 128.

23 The fact that the pencil lines are below the
paint layer indicates that they were used to
transfer an earlier drawing to this canvas
rather than for the process of transferring
this design to the final, finished work, as is
the case, for example, in Van Dyck's *Rinaldo
and Armida*, 1634–5 (NG 877.2), which has
been squared up by the engraver to facilitate
the transfer of the design to his engraving
plate.

24 See, for example, the colour and

monochrome oil sketches for the decoration of the cupola of Saint Pillar, Saragossa, now in the Museo Diocesano, Saragossa. Discussed in Morales y Marín 1995, nos 140–1, pp. 81, 84, 103.

25 On these murals and their cartoons, see Ormond 1975.

26 A letter dated 12 August 1747 from Jean-Baptiste Oudry, co-director of the Beauvais tapestry manufactory (together with Nicolas Besnier), indicates that Boucher was working on a series of designs for the Loves of the Gods tapestries at this time. See letter cited in Standen 1986, p. 65.

27 One of the coloured oil sketches is signed and dated 1757 (Musée du Louvre, Paris, inv. 2707 bis); the other is in the Sterling and Francine Clark Art Institute, Williamstown (inv. 1983.29). The coloured painting dates to 1747 and is in the Musée du Louvre, Paris (inv. MI 1022).

28 New York, Detroit and Paris 1986–7, p. 276.

29 This seems to be the case for two additional sketches made by Boucher for the *Fêtes Vénitiennes* and the *Fêtes de Thalia*, which were never made into tapestries. See ibid., p. 276.

30 For the provenance of the work in the Musée des Arts Décoratifs see ibid., p. 272.

31 Large groups of oil sketches are found in estate inventories of artist-dealers active in seventeenth-century Antwerp, for example. See Greenwich, Berkeley and Cincinnati 2005, p. 47.

32 The Marquis de Marigny persuaded King Louis XV to commission a set of four tapestries depicting the Loves of the Gods, each designed by a different artist: François Boucher, Louis Michel van Loo (1707–1771), Jean-Baptiste Pierre (1714–1789) and Joseph-Marie Vien (1716–1809).

33 The Mobilier National also owns a version woven in 1774–5 for the Comtesse du Barry. Another version, apparently once belonging to the Princesse de Sagan, is in the Walters Art Gallery, Baltimore.

34 On the early practice of underdrawing, see Bomford 2002.

35 Ibid., p. 73.

36 Cennini 1982, pp. 75 and 126–7.

37 One exception to this is Van Hout 2010.

38 See discussion of 'dead-colouring' in Van Hout 2010; Van de Wetering 2000, pp. 30–3;

Woordenboek der Nederlandsche taal, III-2, col. 2881–2883.

39 Mannings 2000, vol. I, cat. 1863, p. 468.

40 Paris and London 1985–6, pp. 55–70.

41 Toulouse 2008, cat. 55.

42 On Moreau's visual sources for these works, see Rouen 2000.

Chapter 3
Independent Paintings in Grisaille

1 The practice of underdrawing is also discussed in Chapter 2.

2 On van Eyck's underdrawings, see Billinge in Foister, Jones and Cool 2000.

3 On van Eyck's frames, see Verougstraete and Van Schoute in Foister, Jones and Cool 2000. It has also been suggested that the frame resembles dark red jasper. New York 2016a, p. 287.

4 Van Hout 2012, p. 36.

5 For example, ibid., p. 36, and Madrid 2009–10, pp. 280–1, consider it an unfinished painting; Billinge, Verougstraete and Van Schoute in Foister, Jones and Cool 2000, pp. 46–7, consider it a finished drawing; Belting and Kruse 1994 regard it as a conscious decision on van Eyck's part to create the illusion of an unfinished painting; Van Asperen de Boer 1992, p. 18, argues that there was a change of project during the course of the work from an underdrawing to a pen painting in its own right.

6 Van Mander 1994–9, vol. 1, p. 66–9, fols 202r–202v. For more on dead colour, see Chapter 2.

7 For example, Robertson 1968, p. 118, considered it an underdrawing of an incomplete painting; Humfrey 2004, p. 206, discussed it as an independent grisaille.

8 On Bruegel's grisailles, see Grossmann 1952 and London 2016a.

9 On the painting's provenance, see London 2016a, pp. 30, 36–7.

10 On Goltzius as a printmaker, see Chapter 5.

11 Amsterdam, New York and Toledo 2003–4, p. 230.

12 Reznicek 1961, vol. 1, pp. 287–8; Washington and New York 1986–7, pp. 171–3.

13 Nichols 1992, p. 27.

14 An excellent account of van de Venne's

grisailles is provided by Westermann 1999; see also Bol 1989, pp. 77–111 and Buijsen 2015.

15 On how van de Venne anticipated and steered market demand for his grisailles, see Westermann 1999, pp. 249–52.

16 Lammertse 1998, p. 179.

17 London, Paris and Washington 1994–5, p. 143.

18 Other examples include *Arrangement in Black, No. 2: Portrait of Mrs Louis Huth* (1872–3), catalogued in ibid., pp. 148–9.

19 Geffroy 1892, pp. VII–VIII.

20 See London 2015–16.

21 Schneider 2008, p. 79.

22 London 2015–16, pp. 30–1.

23 See Leuschner 2008 on the De Backer Group, which produced a number of grisaille variations or repetitions of their own paintings in colour.

24 For copying practices in the workshop of Pieter Brueghel the Younger, see Maastricht and Brussels 2001–2.

25 See London 2016a, pp. 30, 36–7, 40, 44.

26 Essen, Vienna and Antwerp 1997–8, pp. 80–5.

27 Ibid., cats 18 and 20.

28 The painting formerly in Potsdam is catalogued in Gaehtgens 1987, p. 265, no. 42.

29 See Chapter 4. Van der Werff included a variety of busts, statuary and fragments of friezes in his paintings to give authenticity to the setting. See Franits 2004, p. 255.

30 Paris 2012 suggested that this painting is a *ricordo*.

31 A good discussion of all three versions of the composition is provided in Paris, Ottawa and New York 1988–9, pp. 225–9.

32 See Chapter 2.

33 See London 2009.

34 For a discussion of the series, see Madrid 2006, pp. 300–17.

35 Munich, London and New York 2012–13.

Chapter 4
Monochrome Painting and Sculpture

1 Borchert in Madrid 2009, pp. 239, 252 note 2.

2 Alberti 2004, p. 82.

3 Vasari 1907, pp. 240–1.

4 '… grisailles, en effet, forment si parfaitement la sculpture … que souvent l'oeil le plus connaisseur y est trompé.' La Font de Saint-Yenne, *Discours sur la peinture et l'architecture*, 1758, cited in Michel 1993, p. 360.

5 Baxandall 2006, p. 55. Petrarch's writings on painting and sculpture derive from his book of practical philosophy, *De remediis utriusque fortunae* (1354–66), a collection of 254 Latin dialogues.

6 Alberti 2004, pp. 61, 63.

7 Leonardo argued for the supremacy of painting over poetry, music and sculpture in writings known today as the *Paragone*, compiled in notebooks around the middle of the sixteenth century. See Da Vinci 1949, and Farago 1992, especially pp. 92–5.

8 The lectures and letters are transcribed in Barocchi 1998, pp. 7–84. See also Mendelsohn 1982; Quiviger 1987.

9 Da Vinci 1949, p. 91.

10 Collareta 2008, p. 67.

11 Steiner 1990, pp. 75, 81; Markschies in Madrid 2009, p. 272 concurs with this assessment.

12 Holcomb in Madrid 2009, p. 258. Balas 1982 suggested that Pucelle was influenced by thirteenth-century French cathedral sculpture, but made claims that require further investigation. It is also plausible that Pucelle was influenced by Giovanni Pisani's marble pulpit in the church of Sant' Andrea in Pistoia, completed in 1301. See Ferber 1984, pp. 67–72. The idea that Pucelle's primary concern was to produce material surrogates has been questioned by Borchert in Madrid 2009, p. 242. See Chapter 1 for more on this manuscript.

13 Robert Campin's *Throne of Mercy* (1425–35, Städel Museum, Frankfurt) constitutes one of the earliest convincing examples of grisaille-painted sculpture on a monumental scale. For this and the two surviving polychromed panels from the same programme, see Frankfurt and Berlin 2008–9, pp. 206–14.

14 On van Eyck's workshop, see Campbell 1998, p. 174; Kemperdick in Frankfurt and Berlin 2008–9, pp. 120–1.

15 Chapuis in Madrid 2009, p. 265.

16 Markschies in Madrid 2009, pp. 267–8. Bosshard 1992, p. 7, considered that the

figures were composed of unpainted limestone set before black polished limestone. Chapuis in Madrid 2009, p. 263 was unclear whether the exterior is intended to represent porphyry or simply depicts a coloured marble.

17 Panofsky 1953, vol. 1, p. 162.
18 Ibid.
19 Chapuis in Madrid 2009, pp. 262–5.
20 Kemperdick in Frankfurt and Berlin 2008–9, p. 122.
21 Grünewald's panels are discussed in Stuttgart 2010, pp. 228–39. On the Heller Altarpiece, see Frankfurt 2013, pp. 218–33; Karlsruhe 2007–8, pp. 127–30; Ziermann 2001, pp. 48–62; Decker 1985. Like many other multi-panelled retables of this kind, the altarpiece was later dismantled and the panels separated. A convincing reconstruction is provided in Karlsruhe 2007–8, p. 135.
22 Stechow 1999, p. 92.
23 On Mantegna's grisailles, see Lightbown 1986, pp. 210–18, and Christiansen in London and New York 1992, pp. 294–400.
24 See, for example, the right-hand background of Mantegna's *Man of Sorrows with a Seraph and a Cherub* (about 1485–90, Statens Museum for Kunst, Copenhagen).
25 Vasari 1912–15, vol. 3, p. 281.
26 See Howe et al. 2012.
27 Ibid., p. 49.
28 Schmitter 2002, p. 133.
29 Armenini 1977, p. 270.
30 Vasari 1907, p. 240.
31 In parallel, artists painted murals in grisaille without necessarily imitating sculpture, such as Francesco di Giorgio Martini's frescoes of the Nativity and the Birth of the Virgin (1488–94) in Sant'Agostino, Siena, and Andrea del Sarto's fresco cycle representing the Life of Saint John the Baptist (1513–26) in the Chiostro dello Scalzo, Florence.
32 Marabottini 1969, vol. 1, p. 105.
33 Vasari 1912–15, vol. 5, p. 176.
34 The facade decoration of the Palazzo Ricci in Rome is one of few surviving examples and has been extensively repainted. See Los Angeles 2007–8, pp. 73–4.
35 Vasari mentioned several *sgraffito* facades realised by Polidoro and Maturino, in Vasari 1912–15, vol. 5, p. 177. See Vasari 1907, pp. 243–4, for a discussion of *sgraffito*. On non-figurative *sgraffito* facades popular in Florence, see Payne 2013 and Payne 2016.
36 This drawing is part of a series of 20 extraordinary sheets, today at the J. Paul Getty Museum, Los Angeles illustrating episodes from the early life of Taddeo Zuccaro. See Los Angeles 2007–8, pp. 6–35.
37 A number of Tiepolo's frescoes from this palace are preserved at the Metropolitan Museum of Art, New York. See, for example, *Virtue and Abundance*, 1760 (inv. 43.85.12).
38 A reconstruction of the position and arrangement of the frescoes was done by Forssman 1973, pp. 65–6.
39 Menegozzo 1990, p. 119.
40 Hull 2002, pp. 102–3. On De Wit, see Amsterdam 2000. A precursor to De Wit was Gerard de Lairesse, who painted decorative grisailles at the turn of the eighteenth century. See Snoep 1970, pp. 177–89.
41 Between 1775 and 1790 in France, paintings imitating sculptural reliefs became an independent pictorial genre and were produced in great numbers. See Michel 1993.
42 Duquenne 2008.
43 Michel 1993, pp. 362–3.
44 See, for example, Pierre-Paul Prud'hon, *The Monument to Clement XIV, Executed by Canova*, 1787, oil on canvas, 90.5 x 60 cm, Musée du Louvre, Paris.
45 On Canova and printmaking, see Rome and Bassano del Grappa 1993.
46 Bassano del Grappa and Possagno 2003, pp. 329–43.

Chapter 5
Monochrome Painting and Printmaking

1 On the varied uses of monochrome oil sketches, see Chapter 2.
2 Dirck Barendsz. made 40 chiaroscuro oil sketches with scenes from the Passion, some of which were used as designs for prints.
3 On Rubens's use of the oil sketch, see Chapter 2, and Greenwich, Berkeley and Cincinnati 2004–5.
4 Rubens also commissioned drawings on paper after his paintings as designs for prints.
5 Cambridge 1990.
6 Antwerp and Amsterdam 1999–2000, pp. 43–55.

7   Numerous prints were released after Van
    Dyck's paintings. However, the degree to
    which Van Dyck was involved in some of
    them, if at all, is not always clear. See ibid.,
    p. 219.
8   Spicer 1994; Antwerp and Amsterdam
    1999–2000, pp. 73–91; New York 2016a,
    pp. 21–9, 135–91.
9   Barnes 2004, p. 297.
10 Antwerp and Amsterdam 1999–2000,
    pp. 316–17.
11 Roy 1999, p. 68.
12 Antwerp and Amsterdam 1999–2000, p. 314.
13 Roy 1999, p. 68.
14 Amsterdam 1996; Hinterding 2006, vol. 1,
    pp. 83–92.
15 Boston and Chicago 2003–4, pp. 29–44;
    Amsterdam and London 2000–1, pp. 36–63;
    Hinterding 2006, vol. 1, pp. 88–92.
16 Bomford 2006, pp. 78–80.
17 British Museum, London, inv. F,4.181.
    Rembrandt cut back the canopy, raised the
    arch behind Christ, darkened the figures
    in the lower left foreground and added
    emphasis to some of the architecture.
18 Filedt Kok 1993.
19 These are known as *pen-wercken* (pen
    works), a term van Mander used to describe
    them. Van Mander 1994–9, vol. 1, p. 401, fol.
    285v. On Goltzius's pen works, see Reznicek
    1961, vol. 1, pp. 76–9, 101–5, 128–30;
    Amsterdam, New York and Toledo 2003–4,
    pp. 235–63; Packer 2012, pp. 118–68.
20 Van Mander 1994–9, vol. 1, p. 398, fol. 285r.
21 Ibid., p. 401, fol. 285v.
22 Van Mander mentioned three pen paintings
    by Goltzius in his biography of the artist, but
    only two are known today.
23 Ibid., p. 398, fol. 285r.
24 Both appear in the Queen's inventories of
    1648 and 1652 respectively. For
    provenances, see Nichols 1992, pp. 17–19.
25 Packer 2017, p. 52.
26 The first two versions, painted in 1738, are at
    the National Gallery of Ottawa and the
    Stiftung Preussische Schlösser und
    Gärten, Schloss Charlottenburg, Berlin. The
    fourth, now destroyed version was painted
    some time later and exhibited at the 1769
    Salon. The latter was in the collection
    of Baron Henri de Rothschild during the
    Second World War, and is known through
    a drawing by Gabriel de Saint-Aubin and a

photograph. On the different versions, see
Paris, Cleveland and Boston 1979, pp. 252–7;
and Paris, Düsseldorf, London and New York
1999–2000, pp. 232–7.

27 Lépicié produced ten engravings after
    Chardin's most important Salon paintings
    between 1739 and 1744. Paris, Düsseldorf,
    London and New York 1999–2000, pp. 66–8.
28 Paris, Cleveland and Boston 1979, p. 256;
    Paris, Düsseldorf, London and New York
    1999–2000, p. 234.
29 On whether the verses offer a key to
    understanding Chardin's composition or
    impoverish his intentions, see ibid., p. 61.
30 The painting is catalogued in Humphrey
    Wine, *National Gallery Catalogues: The
    Eighteenth-Century French Paintings*,
    forthcoming 2018.
31 Wine in Lille 2011, no. 186. Boilly's colour
    version was listed as no. 28 in the 1799 Salon
    livret.
32 On the mezzotint, see Wuestman 1995; Wax
    1990.
33 Washington, London and The Hague
    2000–1; Bonfait 2008, p. 85.
34 http://www.nyhistory.org/exhibit/lincoln-
    family. Accessed 28 February 2017.

Chapter 6
Monochrome Painting in the Age of
Photography and Film

1   The term was coined in 1839 by John
    Herschel. See Schaaf 1979; for a general
    history of the medium, see Watson and
    Rappaport 2013.
2   On Daguerre's dioramas, see Watson and
    Rappaport 2013, pp. 48 ff.
3   A paragraph by an unknown author was
    added to the end of a review of one of
    Daguerre's diorama spectacles in the
    Journal des artistes on 27 September 1835
    and describes Daguerre's photograph as
    'une empreinte en clair et en ombre'. See
    Anon. 1835, pp. 202–3. Unfortunately, the
    Boulevard du Temple daguerrotype suffered
    damage during wartime bombing and from
    subsequent over-cleaning and no longer
    survives.
4   On this subject, see de Font-Réaulx 2007;
    Jacobi in London 2016b, pp. 11–21.
5   On Le Gray, see Aubenas 2002; Le Gray

made this desire clear in his treatises on
photography: Le Gray 1852, pp. 70–1.

6 London 2012, p. 169; the comparison
between Le Gray and Courbet is made in
de Font-Réaulx 2007.

7 See the unnamed reviewer in Anon. 1857,
p. 170; source cited in London 2012, p. 168.

8 Anon. 1857, p. 213.

9 This apocryphal tale, promoted by Gaston
Tissandier in 1874, is discussed in Bann
1997, pp. 17, 226, 264.

10 London 2012, p. 169.

11 London 2014a, p. 40.

12 On Balke's technique, see Lange in ibid.,
p. 29.

13 For more on the painting, see Kauffmann
1973, vol. II, p. 6, cat. 14.

14 Burns 1998; on this first demonstration in
London, see also Anon. 1925, pp. 505–6.

15 Although advances were made in colour
cinematography from the beginning of the
twentieth century, film possessed a limited
range of colour until the introduction of
Technicolor in 1932. The dramatically high
costs of filming and printing in colour film,
about three times as much as black-and-
white, made it still relatively rare until new,
cheaper processes were developed in the
1950s and 1960s.

16 Daix 1993, p. 281; New York and Houston
2012, p. 62.

17 Nash 1998, p. 17.

18 New York and Houston 2012, p. 73.

19 On the series, see Printz and Guidieri 1988;
Bastian 2014.

20 Gidal noted this effect in Warhol's
black-and-white *Saturday Disaster*, 1963
(Rose Art Museum, Brandeis University,
Waltham, Massachusetts). See Gidal 2000,
pp. 19–28.

21 Dumas 1993 and republished in Dumas
1998.

22 Amsterdam and London 2014–15, pp. 7,
63–5.

23 Ibid.

24 Ibid., p. 7.

25 Richter 1995, pp. 56–8.

26 Interview with Babette Richter, 2002. See
Richter 2009, p. 442.

27 This is one of two paintings Richter
produced of Helga in 1966. The other (*Helga
Matura*, 1966, oil on canvas, 180 x 110 cm,
Art Gallery of Ontario, Toronto), represents

Helga alone.

28 New York, Chicago, San Francisco and
Washington 2002–3, p. 39.

29 Interview with Jan Thorn-Prikker 2004, cited
in Richter 2009, p. 478.

30 New York, Chicago, San Francisco and
Washington 2002–3, p. 38.

31 Richter 1995, p. 58.

32 New York, Chicago, Washington, Seattle and
London 1998–9, p. 87.

33 Westerbeck 2014, p. 122.

34 Kesten 1997, p. 579.

35 Chicago 1995, p. 155.

36 Parkett Series 1995, no. 44, p. 42.

37 Ibid., p. 40.

38 These associations are discussed in greater
depth in Chapter 7 in the context of abstract
and Minimalist painting.

Chapter 7
Abstraction in Black and White

1 Malevich in Golding 1994, p. 177; for an in
depth study of the painting see Shatskikh
2012.

2 Malevich 1980, pp. 107–10.

3 Malevich 2003.

4 Malevich in Drutt 2003, p. 34.

5 On the different versions see London 2014b,
p. 28.

6 See ibid., pp. 24–9.

7 On the history of the icon, see Belting 1994.

8 Malevich cited in London 2014b,
p. 29.

9 Translation taken from http://www
tretyakovgallery.ru/en/collection/_show/
image/_id/378.

10 Fox Weber in New York 1988, p. 45.

11 New York 1964, n.p.

12 See *Josef Albers: Black and White*, exhibition
sales catalogue, Waddington Custot
Galleries, London 2014.

13 Fox Weber in New York 1988, p. 46.

14 Ibid., p. 38.

15 Albers's theories on colour were also widely
disseminated through his influential treatise
Interaction of Color (1963).

16 The term 'Abstract Expressionism' was
coined by the art critic Robert Coates in
the *New Yorker* in 1946, applying it to the
canvases of Hans Hofmann.

17 Rosenberg 1952, p. 22; revised and

republished in Rosenberg 1959, pp. 28–30.

18 See for example the recent exhibition catalogue Liverpool and Dallas 2015.

19 New York and London 1998, cat. 136, p. 240.

20 Bastian 1992–5, p. 223, nos. 105, 106.

21 Berlin, Duisburg and Cologne 2013.

22 See for example Klant and Zuschlag 1994.

23 On the notion of phenomenology see Merleau-Ponty 1965.

24 Chicago and New York 2007–8, p. 91. On the Ingres and workshop painting see Chapter 3.

25 Glueck 1966, p. 26; reprinted in Varnedoe 1996, p. 128.

26 Steinberg 1962; revised and reprinted in Steinberg 1972, pp. 17–54.

27 Bernstein 2017.

28 Rondeau in Chicago and New York 2007–8, p. 33.

29 New York 2016b.

30 Rosenblum in Rubin and Rosenblum 1986, p. 11.

31 Rubin and Rosenblum 1986, cat. 41, p. 74, illustrated.

32 New York 1970, pp. 15–18.

33 Cited in ibid., p. 23.

34 Rosenblum in Rubin and Rosenblum 1986, p. 11. On this theme more broadly see Godfrey 2007.

35 Rubin and Rosenblum 1986, p. 44.

36 Paik 2015, p. 199.

37 See discussion in Munich 2011.

38 Ibid.

39 Paik 2015, p. 200.

40 The term 'Op art' was coined by an author in an unsigned article in *Time* magazine (23 October 1964) in response to Julian Stanczak's show 'Optical Paintings at the Martha Jackson Gallery', to refer to a form of abstract art that uses optical illusions.

41 On Riley's recent return to black and white see Paris 2015, pp. 27–30.

42 On *Table*, see London, Berlin and Paris 2011, pp. 29, 38–9, 74, 247, 283, 296.

43 From a letter to Edy de Wilde, 23 February 1975, cited in Richter 2009, p. 91.

44 On these works, see Brill in London, Berlin and Paris 2011, pp. 245–54.

Beyond Painting: Monochrome and Installation Art

1 Eliasson in Glenside 2006, p. 76.

2 Ibid., p. 75.

3 Wolfsburg 2017.

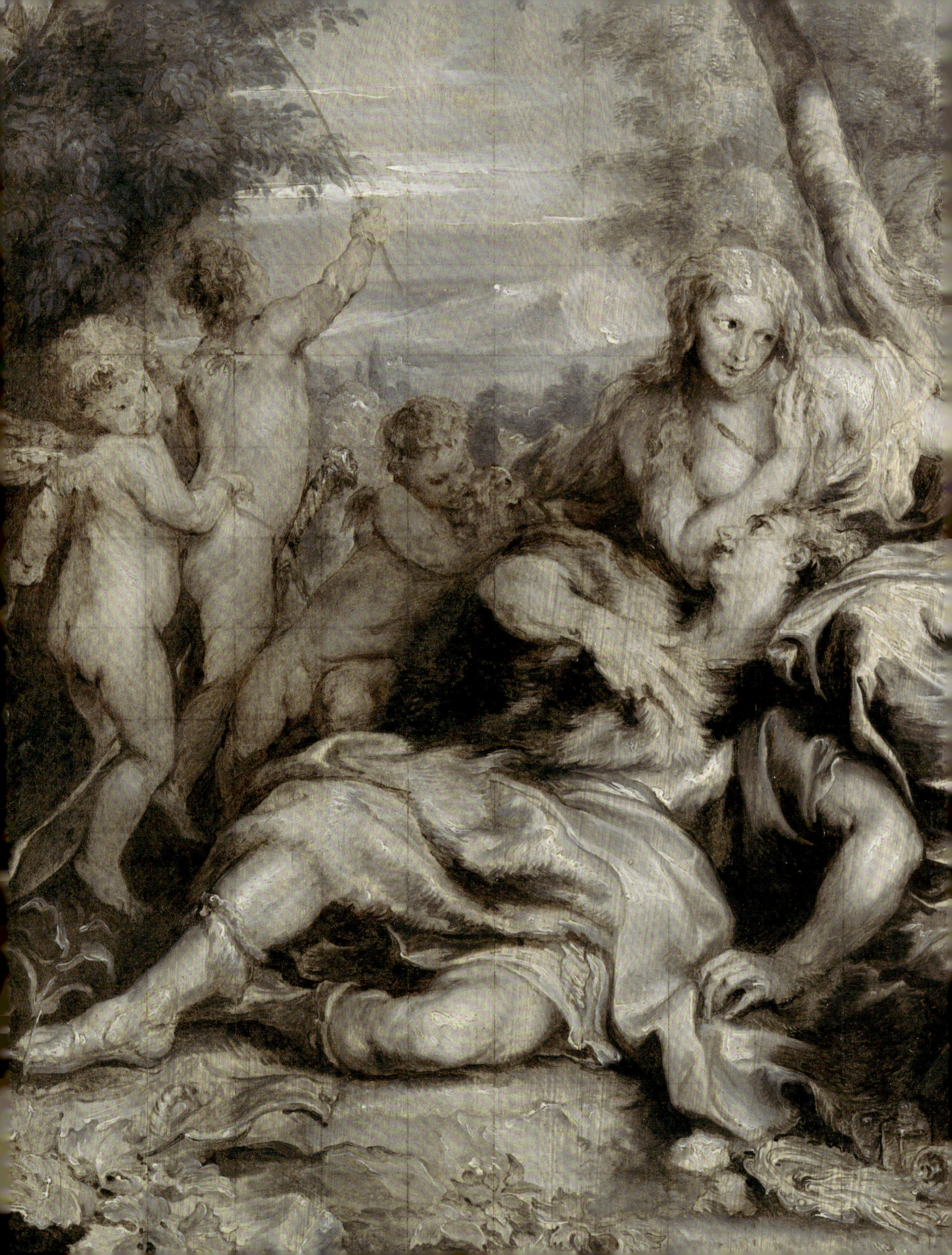

Bibliography

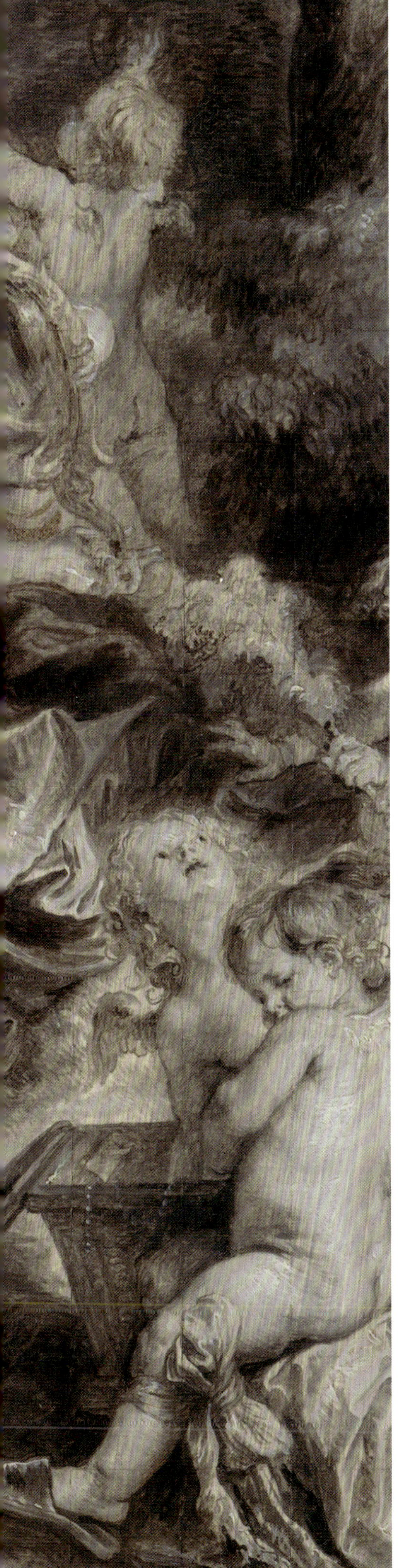

Alberti 1972
Leon Battista Alberti, *On Painting and On Sculpture* [1439–41; 1462], ed. and trans. C. Grayson, London 1972

Alberti 2004
Leon Battista Alberti, *On Painting* [1439–41], trans. C. Grayson, London and New York 2004

Anon. 1925
Anonymous, 'Current Topics and Events', in *Nature: The International Weekly Journal of Science*, vol. 115 (4 April 1925), pp. 505–6

Anon. 1835
Anonymous, [Review of Daguerre's exhibition of photographs], *Journal des artistes*, no.13, vol. II (1835), pp. 202–3

Anon. 1857a
Anonymous, [Review of Daguerre's exhibition of photographs in London], *The Liverpool and Manchester Photographic Journal*, 1857, p. 170

Anon. 1857b
Anonymous, [Review of Daguerre's exhibition of photographs in Paris], *La Revue Photographique*, no. 16 (5 February 1857), p. 213

Amsterdam 1996
C. Schuckman, M. Royalton-Kisch and E. Hinterding, *Rembrandt and Van Vliet: A Collaboration on Copper*, exh. cat., Amsterdam 1996

Amsterdam 2000
J. Boonstra and G. van de Hout (eds), *In de wolken: Jacob de Wit als plafondschilder*, exh. cat., Amsterdam 2000

Amsterdam and London 2000–1
E. Hinterding, G. Luijten and M. Royalton-Kisch, *Rembrandt the Printmaker*, exh. cat., Amsterdam 2000–1

Amsterdam and London 2014–15
L. Coelewij, H. Sainsbury and T. Vischer (eds), *Marlene Dumas: The Image as Burden*, exh. cat., Amsterdam and London 2014

Amsterdam, New York and Toledo 2003–4
H. Leeflang and G. Luijten (eds), Hendrick Goltzius (1558–1617): *Drawings, Prints and Paintings*, exh. cat., Amsterdam, New York and Toledo 2003

Antwerp and Amsterdam 1999–2000
C. Depauw and G. Luijten, *Anthony van Dyck as a Printmaker*, exh. cat., Antwerp and Amsterdam 1999

Armenini 1977
G.B. Armenini, *On the True Precepts of the Art of Painting*, ed. and trans. E.J. Olszewski, New York 1977

Arnold 1913
H. Arnold, *Stained Glass of the Middle Ages in England and France*, London 1913

Aubenas 2002
S. Aubenas, *Gustave Le Gray, 1820–1884*, Los Angeles 2002

Aubenas 2003
S. Aubenas, *Gustave Le Gray*, London and New York 2003

Baccheschi 1977
E. Baccheschi, *L'opera completa del Beccafumi*, Milan 1977

Bain 2012
J. Bain, 'Signifying Absence: Experiencing Monochrome Imagery in Medieval Painting', in L. Bourdua and R. Gibbs (eds), *A Wider Trecento: Studies in Thirteenth- and Fourteenth-century European Art*, 2012, pp. 5–20

Balas 1982
E. Balas, 'Jean Pucelle and the Gothic Cathedral Sculptures: A Hypothesis', *Gazette des Beaux-Arts*, vol. 99 (1982), pp. 39–44

Bann 1997
S. Bann, *Paul Delaroche: History Painted*, London 1997

Barnes 2004
S.J. Barnes et al., *Van Dyck: A Complete Catalogue of the Paintings*, New Haven and London 2004

Barocchi 1998
P. Barocchi, *Pittura e Scultura nel Cinquecento*, Livorno 1998

Bassano del Grappa and Possagno 2003–4
S. Androsov, M. Guderzo and G. Pavanello, *Canova*, exh. cat., Milan 2003

Bastian 1992–5
H. Bastian (ed.), *Cy Twombly: Catalogue Raisonné of the Paintings*, 4 vols., Munich 1992–5.

Bastian 2014
H. Bastian, *Andy Warhol: Death and Disaster*, trans. P. Cumbers, Bielefeld 2014

Baumgärtel 2005
B. Baumgärtel with K. Bürger, *Ein Fest der Malerei. Die niederländischen und flämischen Gemälde des 16.–18. Jahrhunderts. Bestandskatalog der Gemäldesammlung museum kunst palast – Sammlung der Kunstakademie Düsseldorf*, Leipzig 2005

Baxandall 1980
M. Baxandall, *The Limewood Sculptors of Renaissance Germany*, New Haven and London 1980

Baxandall 2006
M. Baxandall, *Giotto and the Orators* (1971), reprinted Oxford 2006

Belting 1994
H. Belting, *Likeness and Presence: A History of the Image before the Era of Art*, trans. E. Jephcott, London *c*.1994

Belting and Kruse 1994
H. Belting and C. Kruse, *Die Erfindung des Gemäldes: das Erste Jahrhundert der niederländischen Malerei*, Munich 1994

Berlin and Amsterdam 2015
D.Pörschmann and M. Schavemaker (eds), *ZERO*, exh. cat., Berlin and Amsterdam, Cologne 2015

Berlin, Duisburg and Cologne 2013
J. Jäger, U. Kittelmann, A. Klar and W. Smerling (eds), *K.O. Götz*, exh. cat., Berlin, Duisburg and Cologne 2013

Bernstein 2017
R. Bernstein, with H. Colsman-Freyberger, C. Sweeney and B. Stepina Zinn, *Jasper Johns: Catalogue Raisonné of Painting and Sculpture*, New Haven and London 2017

Beutler and Thiem 1960
C. Beutler and G. Thiem, *Hans Holbein der Ältere: Die spätgotische Altar- und Glasmalerei*, Augsburg 1960

Boggero and Sista 2013
F. Boggero and A. Sista (eds), *Il Teatro dei Cartelami: effimeri per la devozione in area mediterranea*, Genoa 2013

Bol 1989
L.J. Bol, *Adriaen Pietersz. Van de Venne: Painter and Draughtsman*, Doornspijk 1989

Bomford 2002
D. Bomford (ed.), *Underdrawings in Renaissance Paintings*, London 2002

Bomford 2006
D. Bomford et al., *Art in the Making: Rembrandt* (1988), rev. edn, London 2006

Bond 1916
F. Bond, *The Chancel of English Churches*, London 1916

Bonfait 2008
O. Bonfait, 'Du Genre au genre á Paris autour de 1800: "moelleux fini" et "velouté du satin" de Gerrit Dou á Marguerite Gérard', in P. Costamagna and O. Bonfait (eds), *La Peinture de genre au temps du Cardinal Fesch, actes du colloque, Ajaccio, 15 juin 2007*, Paris 2008, pp. 81–91

Bosshard 1992
E. Bosshard, 'Revealing van Eyck: The Examination of the Thyssen-Bornemisza Annunciation', *Apollo*, vol. 136, no. 365 (July 1992), pp. 4–11

Boston and Chicago 2003–4
R. Baer, T.E. Rassieur and W.W. Robinson, *Rembrandt's Journey: Painter, Draughtsman, Etcher*, exh. cat., Boston 2003

Braham 1973a
A. Braham, 'A Reappraisal of "The Introduction of the Cult of Cybele at Rome" by Mantegna', *The Burlington Magazine*, vol. 115, no. 844 (July 1973), pp. 457–63

Braham 1973b
A. Braham, *Rubens, Themes and Painters in the National Gallery*, London 1973

Brown 1998
D.A. Brown, *Leonardo da Vinci: Origins of a Genius*, New Haven and London 1998

Brussels 1986
P. Cockshaw, *Miniatures en grisaille: Bibliothèque royale Albert Ier, Bruxelles*, exh. cat., Brussels 1986

Brussels and Paris 2012
B. Bousmanne and T. Delcourt (eds), *Miniature Flamandes: 1404–1482*, exh. cat., Brussels and Paris 2012

Bruyn 1989
J. Bruyn et al., *A Corpus of Rembrandt Paintings*, vol. 3, The Hague and London 1989

Buijsen 2015
E. Buijsen, 'De Sinne-cunst van Adriaen van de Venne in theorie en praktijk', *Oud Holland*, vol. 128, issue 2/3 (2015), pp. 83–124

Burns 1998
R.W. Burns, *Television: An International History of the Formative Years*, London 1998

Burton 2008
J. Burton, *Monastic and Religious Orders in Britain, 1000–1300*, Cambridge 2008

Burton and Kerr 2011
J.E. Burton and J. Kerr, *The Cistercians in the Middle Ages*, Suffolk 2011

Cadogan 1983
J.K. Cadogan, 'Linen Drapery Studies by Verrocchio, Leonardo and Ghirlandaio', *Zeitschrift für Kunstgeschichte*, vol. 46, part 1 (1983), pp. 27–62

Caianiello and Visser 2015
T. Caianiello and M. Visser (eds), *The Artist as Curator: Collaborative Initiatives in the International ZERO Movement, 1957–1967*, Ghent 2015

Camille 1992
M. Camille, *Image on the Edge: The Margins of Medieval Art*, London 1992

Campbell 1998
L. Campbell, *National Gallery Catalogues: The Fifteenth-Century Netherlandish Paintings*, London 1998

Cambridge 1990
C. Hartley (ed.), *Rubens and Printmaking*, exh. cat., Cambridge 1990

Cataldi Gallo 2008
M. Cataldi Gallo, *Passione in blu. I teli con storie della passione del XVI secolo a Genova*, Genoa 2008

Cennini 1954
C. Cennini, *Il Libro dell'Arte, The Craftsman's Handbook*, ed. D.V. Thompson, New York and London 1954

Cennini 1982
C. Cennini, *Il Libro dell'Arte*, with commentary and annotations by F. Brunello, Vicenza 1982

Chicago 1995
M. Grynsztejn, *About Place: Recent Art of the Americas. The 76th American Exhibition, The Art Institute of Chicago*, exh. cat., Chicago and New York 1995

Chicago and New York 2007–8
J. Rondeau and D. Druick, *Jasper Johns: Gray*, exh. cat., Chicago 2007

Christiansen 1990
K. Christiansen, 'Leonardo's Drapery Studies', *The Burlington Magazine*, CXXXII (1990), pp. 572–3.

Collareta 2008
M. Collareta, 'From Colour to Black and White, and Back Again: The Middle Ages and Early Modern Times', in R. Panzanelli, E. Schmidt and K. Lapatin (eds), *The Color of Life: Polychromy in Sculpture from Antiquity to the Present*, Los Angeles 2008, pp. 62–74

Daix 1993
P. Daix, Picasso: *Life and Art*, London 1993

Dalli Regoli 1976
G. Dalli Regoli, 'Il piegar de' panni', *Critica d'arte*, XXII, new series, issue 150 (1976), pp. 35–48

Decker 1985
B. Decker, 'Notizen zum Heller-Altar', *Städel Jahrbuch* (1985), pp. 179–92

Derbes and Sandona 2008
A. Derbes and M. Sandona, *The Usurer's Heart: Giotto, Enrico Scrovegni and the Arena Chapel in Padua*, Pennsylvania 2008

De Zegher and Teicher 2005
C. de Zegher and H. Teicher (eds.), *3x an Abstraction: New Methods of Drawing by Hilma Af Klint, Emma Kunz and Agnes Martin*, New Haven 2005

Doublet 1625
D.J. Doublet, *Histoire de l'abbaye de Saint Denis en France contenant les antiquités d'icelle …*, Paris 1625

Dresden 2014
I. Mossinger, K. Drechsel and C. Krell (eds), *K.O. Gotz zum 100. Geburtstag, Bestands- und Ausstellungskatalog / K.O. Gotz on his 100th Birthday: Collection and Exhibition Catalogue*, Dresden 2014

Drutt 2003
M. Drutt, *Kasimir Malevich: Suprematism*, New York 2003

Dumas 1993
M. Dumas, 'Blind Dates and drawn Curtains', in *Marlene Dumas*, Philadelphia 1993

Dumas 1998
M. Dumas, *Sweet Nothings: Notes and Texts,* Cologne 1998

Duquenne 2008
X. Duquenne, 'Marten Geeraerts (1707–1791) peintre d'Anvers, maître du trompe l'oeil', in *Actes du Colloque autour de Bayar / Le Roy*, ed. J. Toussant, Société Archéologique de Namur, Namur 2008, pp. 319–24

Durandus 1906
William Durandus, *Rationale Diviniorum Officiorum*, Book I [c.1258], trans. J.M. Neale and B. Webb as *The Symbolism of Churches and Church Ornaments*, London 1906

Düsseldorf 2010
K. Heymer, S. Rennert, B. Wismer, *Le grand geste! Informel und Abstrakter Expressionismus 1946–1964*, exh. cat., Düsseldorf 2010

Düsseldorf and Saint-Etienne 2006
ZERO: Internationale Künstler-Avantgarde der 50er/60er Jahre, exh. cat., Düsseldorf and Saint-Etienne, Ostfildern 2006

Ehresmann 1982
D.L. Ehresmann, 'Some Observations on the Role of Liturgy in the Early Winged Altarpiece', *The Art Bulletin*, vol. 64, no. 3 (1982), pp. 359–69

Essen, Vienna and Antwerp 1997–8
K. Ertz and C. Nitze-Ertz (eds), *Pieter Breughel le Jeune (1564–1637/8), Jan Brueghel l'Ancien (1568–1625): une famille des peintres flamands vers 1600*, exh. cat., Lingen 1998

Fahy 1969
E. Fahy, 'The Earliest works of Fra Bartolommeo', *The Art Bulletin*, LI (1969), pp. 152–4

Farago 1992
C.J. Farago, *Leonardo da Vinci's Paragone: A Critical Interpretation with a New Edition of the Text in the Codex Urbinas*, Leiden and New York 1992

Félibien 1706
D.M. Félibien, *Histoire de l'abbaye royale*, Paris 1706

Ferber 1984
S.H. Ferber, 'Jean Pucelle and Giovanni Pisano', *The Art Bulletin*, vol. 66, no. 1 (Mar. 1984), pp. 65–72

Filarete 1965
Filarete, *Filarete's treatise on architecture, being the treatise by Antonio di Piero Averlino, known as Filarete* [c.1464], trans. with an introduction and notes by J.R. Spencer, New Haven and London 1965

Filedt Kok 1993
J.P. Filedt Kok, 'Hendrick Goltzius: Designer and Publisher 1582–1600', *Nederlands Kunsthistorisch Jaarboek*, vol. 42–3 (1993), pp. 159–211

Fiorani 2013
Francesca Fiorani, 'The Genealogy of Leonardo's Shadows in a Drapery Drawing', in M. Israel and L. Waldman (ed.), *Renaissance Studies in Honor of Joseph Connors*, Cambridge, MA 2013

Foister, Jones and Cool 2000
S. Foister, S. Jones and D. Cool (eds), *Investigating Jan van Eyck*, Turnhout 2000

Folena 1951
G. Folena, 'Chiaroscuro leonardesco,' in *Lingua nostra*, no. 12 (September 1951), pp. 51–63

Font-Réaulx 2007
Dominique de Font-Réaulx, 'Parallel Lines: Gustave Courbet's "Paysages de Mer" and Gustave Le Gray's Seascapes 1856–70', in M. Morton (ed.), *Looking at the Landscapes: Courbet and Modernism, Papers from a symposium held at the J. Paul Getty Museum on March 18, 2006*, Los Angeles, published online 2007, pp. 35–45

Forssman 1973
E. Forssman, *Il Palazzo da Porto Festa di Vicenza, Corpus Palladianum*, vol. 8, Vicenza 1973

Franits 2004
W. Franits, *Dutch Seventeenth-Century Genre Painting: Its Stylistic and Thematic Evolution*, New Haven and London 2004

Frankfurt 2013
J. Sander (ed.), *Albrecht Durer: His Art in Context*, exh. cat., Munich 2013

Frankfurt and Berlin 2008–9
S. Kemperdick and J. Sander (eds), *The Master of Flémalle and Rogier Van der Weyden*, exh. cat., Frankfurt and Berlin 2009

Frugoni 2008
C. Frugoni, *L'affare migliore di Enrico: Giotto e la cappella Scrovegni*, Turin 2008

Gaehtgens 1987
B. Gaehtgens, *Adriaen van der Werff 1659–1722*, Munich 1987

Geffroy 1892
G. Geffroy, *La Vie artistique*, Paris 1892–1903

Gidal 2000
P. Gidal, 'Once is never: Warhol's Saturday Disaster & Blowjob', in E. Beyeler et al., *Andy Warhol: Series and Singles*, Basel 2000, pp. 19–28

Glenside 2006
Olafur Eliasson, 'Some Ideas About Colour', in I. Soyugenc and R. Torchia (eds), *Olafur Eliasson: Your Colour Memory*, exh. cat., Glenside 2006, pp. 75–83

Glueck 1966
G. Glueck, 'No Business like No Business', *New York Times*, 16 Jan., section 2 (1966), p. 26

Godfrey 2007
M. Godfrey, *Abstraction and the Holocaust*, New Haven and London 2007

Golding 1994
Kasimir Malevich, 'From Cubism and Futurism to Suprematism: The New Realism in Painting (November 1916)', in J. Golding, *Visions of the Modern*, Berkeley and Los Angeles 1994, p. 177
Greenwich, Berkeley and Cincinnati 2004–5
P.C. Sutton, M.E. Wieseman and N. van Hout, *Drawn by the Brush: Oil Sketches by Peter Paul Rubens*, exh. cat., Greenwich, Berkeley and Cincinnati 2004

Grenoble, Rennes and Bordeaux 1989–90
P. Rosenberg and J. Thuillier, *Laurent de La Hyre, 1606–1656: l'homme et l'oeuvre*, exh. cat., Geneva 1988

Grossmann 1952
F. Grossmann, 'Bruegel's "Woman Taken in Adultery" and Other Grisailles', *The Burlington Magazine*, vol. 94, no. 593 (Aug. 1952), pp. 218–27 and 229

Gustavson 2009
T. Gustavson, Camera: *A History of Photography from Daguerreotype to Digital*, New York 2009

Hamburg and Munich 2011
O. Westheider and M. Philipp, *Gerhard Richter. Bilder einer Epoche*, exh. cat., Hamburg and München 2011

Hand and Wolf 1986
J.O. Hand and M. Wolff, *Early Netherlandish Painting: The Collections of the National Gallery of Art Systematic Catalogue*, Washington 1986

Harris 2005
J. Harris, 'The Monochrome Passion Cycle of San Nicolò del Boschetto in Genoa: Contexts, Contents and Contemplation', unpublished MA thesis, Courtauld Institute of Art, London 2005

Hayward 1992
J. Hayward, 'Two Grisaille Glass Panels from Saint-Denis at The Cloisters', in E.C. Parker (ed.), *The Cloisters: Studies in Honor of the Fiftieth Anniversary*, New York 1992, pp. 303–25, figs 1, 2a, 2b

Held 1980
J. Held, *The Oil Sketches of Peter Paul Rubens: A Critical Catalogue*, vol. I, Princeton 1980

Hinterding 2006
E. Hinterding, *Rembrandt as an Etcher*, 3 vols., trans. M. Hoyle, in *Studies in Prints and Printmaking*, vol. 6, Ouderkerk aan den Ijssel 2006

Houston 1974
P. Marandel, *Gray is the Color: An Exhibition of Grisaille Painting, XIIIth–XXth centuries*, exh. cat., Houston 1974

Howe 2012
E. Howe et al., *Wall Paintings of Eton*, London 2012

Hull 2002
C. Wright, *From Medieval to Regency: Old Masters in the Collection of the Ferens Art Gallery*, exh. cat., Hull 2002

Humfrey 2004
P. Humfrey, *The Cambridge Companion to Giovanni Bellini*, New York 2004

Jacobs 2011
L.F. Jacobs, *Opening Doors: The Early Netherlandish Triptych Reinterpreted*, Pennsylvania 2011

Judey 1932
J. Judey, *Domenico Beccafumi*, Freiburg 1932

Karlsruhe 2007–8
J. Mack-Andrick et al. (eds), *Grünewald und seine Zeit*, exh. cat., Munich and Karlsruhe 2007

Kauffmann 1973
C.M. Kauffmann, *Catalogue of Foreign Paintings, vol. I, Before 1800: The Victoria and Albert Museum*, London 1973

Kemperdick 2009
S. Kemperdick, 'Altar Panels in Northern
Germany, 1180–1350', in J.E.A. Kroesen
and V.M. Schmidt (eds), *The Altar and its
Environment, 1150–1400*, Turnhout 2009

Kessler 1994
H.L. Kessler, *Studies in Pictorial Narrative*,
London 1994

Kessler 2000
H.L. Kessler, *Spiritual Seeing: Picturing God's
Invisibility in Medieval Art*, Philadelphia 2000

Kesten 1997
J. Kesten (ed.), *The Portraits Speak: Chuck
Close in conversation with 27 of his subjects*,
New York 1997

Kinder 2002
T.N. Kinder, *Cistercian Europe: Architecture
of Contemplation,* Grand Rapids, MI 2002,
pp. 141–61

Klant and Zuschlag 1994
M. Klant and C. Zuschlag (eds), *Karl Otto Götz
im Gesprach: 'Abstrakt is schöner'*, Stuttgart
1994

Krieger 1995
M. Krieger, *Grisaille als Metapher: zum
Entstehen der Peinture en Camaieu im frühen
14. Jahrhundert*, Vienna 1995

Kuhn 1991
A. Kuhn, *Zero: Eine Avantgarde der der
sechziger Jahre*, Frankfurt and Berlin 1991

Lammertse 1998
F. Lammertse, *Dutch Genre Paintings of
the Seventeenth Century, Collection of the
Museum Boijmans van Beuningen*, Rotterdam
1998

Le Gray 1852
G. Le Gray, *Nouveau traité theoretique et
pratique de photographie sur papier et sur
verre*, Paris 1852

Leuschner 2008
E. Leuschner, 'A Grisaille Oil Sketch from the
"De Backer Group" and Workshop Practices
in Sixteenth-Century Antwerp', *Metropolitan
Museum Journal*, vol. 43 (2008), pp. 99–110

Lightbown 1986
R.W. Lightbown, *Mantegna: With a Complete
Catalogue of the Paintings, Drawings and
Prints*, Oxford 1986

Lille 2011
A. Scottez-De Wambrechies and F. Raymond,
Boilly (1761–1845), exh. cat., Lille and Paris
2011

Lillich 1982
M. Cothren, 'Cistercian Tile Mosaic Pavements
in Yorkshire: Context and Sources', in M. P.
Lillich (ed.), *Studies in Cistercian Art and
Architecture*, vol. 1, Michigan 1982, pp. 112–29

Liverpool and Dallas 2015
G. Delahunty, *Jackson Pollock: Blind Spots*,
exh. cat., London 2015

London 2009
E. Cowling et al., *Picasso: Challenging the Past*,
exh. cat., London 2009

London 2011
A. Gingeras, *Grisaille*, exh. cat., Luxembourg
and Dayan, London 2011

London 2012
H. Kingsley and C. Riopelle, *Seduced by Art:
Photography Past and Present*, exh. cat.,
London 2012

London 2014a
A. Borchardt-Hume (ed.), *Malevich*, exh. cat.,
London 2014

London 2014b
M. Ingeborg Lange, K. Ljøgodt and C. Riopelle,
Paintings by Peder Balke, exh. cat., London
2014

London 2015–16
P. Moorhouse, *Giacometti: Pure Presence*,
exh. cat., London 2015

London 2016a
K. Serres, *Bruegel in Black and White: Three
Grisailles Reunited*, exh. cat., London 2016

London 2016b
C. Jacobi, 'Painting with Light', in *Painting
with Light: Art and Photography from the
Pre-Raphaelites to the Modern Age*, exh. cat.,
London 2016

London and Amsterdam 2014
J. Bikker and G. Weber (eds), *Rembrandt: The
Late Works*, exh. cat., London and Amsterdam
2014

London, Berlin and Paris 2011–12
M. Godfrey and N. Serota (eds), *Gerhard
Richter: Panorama. A Retrospective*, exh. cat.,
London 2011

London, Madrid, Winterthur and Frankfurt 1996–7
J. Lingwood (ed.), *Vija Celmins*, exh. cat., London 1996

London and New York 1992
J. Martineau (ed.), *Andrea Mantegna*, exh. cat., London and New York 1992

London, Paris and Washington 1994–5
R. Dorment and M.F. MacDonald, *James McNeill Whistler*, exh. cat., London 1994

Los Angeles 2007–8
J. Brooks, *Taddeo and Federico Zuccaro: Artist-brothers in Renaissance Rome*, exh. cat., Los Angeles 2007

Los Angeles and London 2003–4
T. Kren and S. McKendrick (eds), *Illuminating the Renaissance: The Triumph of Flemish Manuscript Painting in Europe*, exh. cat., Los Angeles and London 2003

Louth 2003
John of Damascus, *Three Treatises on the Divine Images*, trans. Andrew Louth, Crestwood, New York 2003

Maastricht and Brussels 2001–2
P. van der Brinck (ed.), *Brueghel Enterprises*, exh. cat., Masstricht and Ghent 2001

Mack 2011
H. and U. Mack, *Heinz Mack: Leben und Werk – Life and Work*, Cologne 2011

Madrid 2006
C. Giménez and F. Calvo Serraller, *Picasso: Tradition and Avant-Garde*, exh. cat., Madrid 2006

Madrid 2009
T-H. Borchert et al., *Jan van Eyck: Grisallas*, exh. cat., Madrid 2009

Malevich 1980
K. Malevich, 'From Cubism to Suprematism in Art, to the New Realism of Painting to Absolute Creation' [1915], trans. in Charlotte Douglas, *Swans of Other Worlds: Kazimir Malevich and the Origins of Abstraction in Russia*, Ann Arbor 1980, pp. 107–10

Malevich 2003
K. Malevich, *The Non-Objective World: The Manifesto of Suprematism* [1926], Mineola 2003

Mannings 2000
D. Mannings, *Sir Joshua Reynolds: A Complete Catalogue of his Paintings*, 2 vols, New Haven and London 2000

Marabottini 1969
A. Marabottini, *Polidoro da Caravaggio*, 2 vols, Rome 1969

Martin 1970
G. Martin, *National Gallery, The Flemish School: c.1600–c.1900*, London 1970

Mathieu 1977
P.-L. Mathieu, Gustave Moreau: *Complete Edition of the Finished Paintings, Watercolours and Drawings*, Oxford 1977

Mendelsohn 1992
L. Mendelsohn, *Paragoni. Benedetto Varchi's 'Due Lezzioni' and Cinquecento Art Theory*, Ann Arbor 1982

Menegozzo 1990
R. Menegozzo, *Nobili e Tiepolo a Vicenza: l'artista e i committenti*, Vicenza 1990

Merleau-Ponty 1965
M. Merleau-Ponty, *Phenomenology of Perception* [1945], trans. Colin Smith, London 1965

Van der Meulen 1994
M. van der Meulen, *Rubens Copies after the Antique. Corpus Rubenianum Ludwig Burchard XXIII*, ed. A. Balis, London 1994

Meyer Zur Capellen 2001
J. Meyer zur Capellen, *Raphael: A Critical Catalogue of his Paintings*, vol. 1, Munster 2001

Michel 1993
M.R. Michel, 'Mode ou imitation: sculpture et peinture en trompe-l'oeil au XVIIIe siècle', in G. Scherf (ed.), *Clodion et la sculpture française de la fin du XVIIIe siècle: actes du colloque organisé au musée du Louvre par le service culturel les 20 et 21 mars 1992*, Paris 1993

Morales y Marín 1995
J.L. Morales y Marín, *Francisco Bayeu: vida y obra*, Saragossa 1995

Munich 2011
U. Wilmes, *Ellsworth Kelly: Schwartz and Weiss/Ellsworth Kelly: Black and White*, exh. cat., Ostfildern 2011

Munich 2014
S. Dupré, D. von Kerssenbrock-Krosigk and B. Wismer, *Kunst und Alchemie. Das Geheimnis der Verwandlung*, exh. cat., Munich 2014

Munich and Cologne 2002
E. Mai and K. Wettengl, *Wettstreit der Künste: Malerei und Skulptur von Dürer bis Daumier*, Munich and Cologne 2002

Munich, London and New York 2012–13
C. Giménez (ed.), *Picasso Black and White*, exh. cat., Munich, London and New York 2012

Nash 1998
S. Nash, *Picasso and the War Years*, New York 1998

Nash 2000
S. Nash, 'The Parement de Narbonne: Context and Technique', in Caroline Villiers (ed.), *The Fabric of Images: European Paintings on Textile Supports in the Fourteenth and Fifteenth Centuries*, London 2000, pp. 77–87

New York 1964
Josef Albers, 'The Color in My Paintings', in K. McShine (ed.), *Josef Albers: Homage to the Square*, exh. cat., New York 1964

New York 1969
B.H. Friedman, 'An Interview with Lee Krasner Pollock', in *Jackson Pollock: Black and White*, exh. cat., New York 1969

New York 1988
N. Fox Weber et al., *Josef Albers: A Retrospective*, exh. cat., New York 1988

New York 1970
W.S. Rubin, *Frank Stella*, exh. cat., New York 1970

New York 1995
T.B. Husband et al., *The Luminous Image: Painted Glass Roundels in the Lowlands, 1480–1560*, exh. cat., New York 1995

New York 2014
Roman Opalka, *Painting [Infinity]*, exh. cat., New York 2014

New York 2016a
S. Alsteens and A. Eaker, *Van Dyck: The Anatomy of Portraiture*, exh. cat., New York and New Haven 2016

New York 2016b
L. Hegyi and C. Wylie, *Roman Opalka. Painting*, New York 2016

New York, Chicago, San Francisco and Washington 2002–3
R. Storr, *Gerhard Richter: Forty Years of Painting*, exh. cat., New York 2002

New York, Chicago, Washington, Seattle and London 1998–9
R. Storr, *Chuck Close*, exh. cat., New York 1998

New York, Detroit and Paris 1986–7
A. Laing et al., *François Boucher*, exh. cat., Paris 1986

New York and Houston 2012
C. Giménez (ed.), *Picasso: Black and White*, exh. cat., Munich and London 2012

New York and London 1998
K. Varnedoe with P. Karmel, *Jackson Pollock*, exh. cat., New York 1998

Nichols 1992
L.W. Nichols, 'The "Pen Works" of Hendrick Goltzius', *Philadelphia Museum of Art Bulletin*, vol. 88, nos. 373–4 (Winter 1992), pp. 4–56

Norton and Park 2012
C. Norton and D. Park (eds), *Cistercian Art and Architecture in the British Isles*, Cambridge 2012

Ormond 1975
J. Ormond, *Leighton's Frescoes in the Victoria and Albert Museum*, London 1975

Packer 2012
L. Packer, 'Imitation and Innovation in Materials in Early Modern Northern European Art: Pen Prints, Pen Drawings and Pen Paintings, c.1580–1670', unpublished Ph.D. diss., New York University, Institute of Fine Arts, 2012

Packer 2017
L. Packer, 'Prints as Paintings: Willem Van de Velde the Elder (1611–1693) and Dutch Pen Painting c.1650–1665', in S. Karr Schmidt and E.H. Wouk (eds), *Prints in Translation, 1450–1750: Image, Materiality*, Space, London 2017, pp. 42–58

Paik 2015
T.Y. Paik et al., *Ellsworth Kelly*, London and New York 2015

Panofsky 1953
E. Panofsky, *Early Netherlandish Painting, its Origins and Character*, 2 vols., Cambridge, MA 1953

Paris 1989
F. Viatte, *Léonard de Vinci: les études de draperies*, exh. cat., Paris 1989

Paris 2012
R. Blok, *Un Univers Intime*, exh. cat, Paris 2012

Paris 2015
É. de Chassey, *Bridget Riley*, exh. cat., Paris 2015

Paris, Cleveland and Boston 1979
P. Rosenberg, *Chardin*, exh. cat., Cleveland
1979

Paris, Düsseldorf, London and New York
1999–2000
P. Rosenberg, *Chardin*, exh. cat., London and
New York 2000

Paris and London 1985–6
M.K. Talley, '"All Good Pictures Crack": Sir
Joshua Reynolds's Practice and Studio', in
N. Penny (ed.), *Reynolds*, exh. cat., London 1985

Paris, Ottawa and New York 1988–9
J. Sutherland Boggs et al., *Degas*, exh. cat.,
New York and Ottawa 1988

Parkett Series 1995
V. Celmins, A. Gursky, R. Tiravanija, *The Parkett
Series with Contemporary Artists*, no. 44 (1995)

Parry 1987
E. Parry, *The Photography of Gustave Le Gray*,
Chicago 1987

Payne 2013
A. Payne, 'Renaissance *sgraffito* Facades and
the Circulation of Objects in the Mediterranean',
in M. d. Giorgi, A. Hoffmann and N. Suthor
(eds), *Synergies in Visual Culture/Bildkulturen
im Dialog: Festschrift für Gerhard Wolf*, Munich
2013, pp. 229–41

Payne 2016
A. Payne, 'Wrapped in Fabric: Florentine
Facades, Mediterranean Textiles and
A-Tectonic Ornament in the Renaissance', in
G. Necipogli and A. Payne (eds), *Histories of
Ornament: From Global to Local*, Princeton
2016, pp. 274–89

Pike Gordley 1988
B. Pike Gordley, *The Drawings of Beccafumi*,
Ph.D. diss., Princeton University, New Jersey
1988

Pliny, *Naturalis Historia*
Pliny the Elder, *Naturalis Historia*, ed. K.F.T.
Mayhoff, online edition; Pliny the Elder, *Natural
History*, trans. H. Rackham, London 1952

Popham 1945
A.E. Popham, *The Drawings of Leonardo da
Vinci*, New York 1945

Pörschmann and Visser 2012
D. Pörschmann and M. Visser (eds), *4321
ZERO, mit komplettem Nachdruck der
Zeitschrift ZERO*, Düsseldorf 2012

Powell and Briggs 1972
T. Powell and A. Briggs, *'From Today Painting is
Dead': The Beginnings of Photography*, London
1972

Printz and Guidieri 1988
N. Printz and R. Guidieri, *Andy Warhol: Death
and Disaster*, Houston 1988

Quiviger 1987
F. Quiviger, 'Benedetto Varchi and the Visual
Arts,' *Journal of the Warburg and Courtauld
Institutes*, no. 50 (1987), pp. 219–24

Reznicek 1961
E.K.J. Reznicek, *Die Zeichnungen von Hendrick
Goltzius*, 2 vols., Utrecht 1961

Ricart 1956
J.G. Ricart, *Pintura gótica. Ars Hispaniae*, vol. IX,
Madrid 1956

Richter 1995
G. Richter, *The Daily Practice of Painting:
Writings and Interviews, 1962–1993*, ed.
H.U. Obrist, Cambridge, MA 1995

Richter 2009
*Gerhard Richter: Texts, Writings, Interviews and
Letters 1961–2007*, ed. D. Elger and H.U. Obrist,
London 2009

Robertson 1968
G. Robertson, *Giovanni Bellini,* Oxford 1968

The Roman Missal [Third Typical Edition,
Chapel Edition], Collegeville 2011

Rome and Bassano del Grappa 1993–4
G. Pezzini Bernini and F. Fiorani, *Canova e
l'incisione*, exh. cat., Bassano del Grappa 1993

Rosenberg 1952
H. Rosenberg, 'The American Action Painters',
Art News 51/8 (Dec. 1952), pp. 22–3, 48–50

Rosenberg 1959
H. Rosenberg, *The Tradition of the New*,
New York 1959

Rouen 2000
C. Pétry, G. Lacambre and M.-C. Coudert,
.*Gustave Moreau: Diomède dévoré par ses
chevaux*, exh. cat., Paris 2000

Roy 1999
A. Roy, 'The National Gallery Van Dycks:
Technique and Development', *National Gallery
Technical Bulletin*, vol. 20, Paintings in Antwerp
and London: Rubens and Van Dyck, London
1999, pp. 50–83

Rubin and Rosenblum 1986
L. Rubin and R. Rosenblum, *Frank Stella Paintings 1958–1965: A Catalogue Raisonné*, New York 1986

Rudolf 1987
C. Rudolf, 'The "Principal Founders" and the Early Artistic Legislation of Cîteaux', in *Studies in Cistercian Art and Architecture*, vol. 3, Michigan (1987), pp. 1–45

Sanminiatelli 1955
D. Sanminiatelli, 'The Sketches of Domenico Beccafumi', *The Burlington Magazine*, vol. 97, no. 623 (Feb., 1955), pp. 35–41

Sanminiatelli 1967
D. Sanminiatelli, *Domenico Beccafumi*, Milan 1967

Saragossa 1996
A. Ansón Navarro et al., *Francisco Bayeu: 1734–1795*, exh. cat., Saragossa 1996

Schaaf 1979
L. Schaaf, 'Sir John Herschel's 1839 Royal Society Paper on Photography', *History of Photography*, vol. 3, no. 1 (1979), pp. 47–60

Schmitter 2002
M. Schmitter, 'Falling through the Cracks: The Fate of Painted Palace Facades in Sixteenth-century Italy', in C. Anderson (ed.), *The Built Surface: vol. 1, Architecture and the Pictorial Arts from Antiquity to the Enlightenment*, Aldershot 2002, pp. 130–61

Schneider 2008
A. Schneider (ed.), *Alberto Giacometti: Sculpture, Paintings, Drawings*, Munich and London 2008

Schoell-Glass 1999
C. Schoell-Glass, 'En Grisaille – Painting Difference', in M. Heusser, M. Hannoosh, C. Schoell-Glass and D. Scott (eds), *Text and Visuality: Word and Image Interactions III*, Amsterdam and New York 1999

Shatskikh 2012
A.S. Shatskikh, *Black Square: Malevich and the Origin of Suprematism*, trans. M. Schwartz, New Haven and London 2012

Siena 1990
A. Bagnoli, R. Bartalini and M. Maccherini (eds), *Domenico Beccafumi e il suo tempo*, exh. cat., Milan 1990

Snoep 1970
D.P. Snoep, 'Gerard Lairesse als plafond- en kamerschilder', *Bulletin van het Rijksmuseum*, no. 4 (Dec. 1970), pp. 159–220

Spicer 1994
J.A. Spicer, 'Anthony Van Dyck's Iconography: An Overview of Its Preparation', in *Van Dyck 350, Studies in the History of Art*, vol. 46 (1994), pp. 327–56

Stachelhaus 1993
Heiner Stachelhaus, *ZERO: Heinz Mack, Otto Piene, Günther Uecker*, Düsseldorf, Wien, New York and Moskau 1993

Standen 1986
E.A. Standen, 'The Amours des Dieux: A Series of Beauvais Tapestries After Boucher', *The Metropolitan Museum Journal*, 19/20 (1986), pp. 63–84

Stechow 1999
W. Stechow, *Northern Renaissance Art, 1400–1600: Sources and Documents*, Evanston, IL 1999

Steinberg 1962
L. Steinberg, 'Jasper Johns: The First Seven Years of His Art', *Metro* (New York), 4/5 (May 1962)

Steinberg 1972
L. Steinberg, *Other Criteria: Confrontations with Twentieth-Century Art*, Oxford 1972

Steiner 1990
R. Steiner, 'Paradoxien der Nachahmung bei Giotto: die Grisaillen der Arenakapelle zu Padua', in H. Körner (ed.), *Die Trauben des Zeuxis: Formen künstlerischer Wirklichkeitsaneignung*, Hildesheim and New York 1990, pp. 61–86

Stirling 1938
C. Stirling, *La Peinture Française, Les Primitifs*, Paris 1938

Stuttgart 2010
E. Wiemann (ed.), *Hans Holbein d. Ä: die Graue Passion in ihrer Zeit*, exh. cat., Stuttgart 2010

Suida 1929
W. Suida, *Leonardo und sein Kreis*, Munich 1929

Taubert 2015
J. Taubert in M.D. Marincola (ed.), *Polychrome Sculpture: Meaning, Form, Conservation*, Los Angeles 2015

Teasdale Smith 1959
M. Teasdale Smith, 'The Use of Grisaille as a
Lenten Observance', *Marsyas*, vol. 8 (1959),
pp. 43–54

Thurston 1904
H. Thurston, *Lent and Holy Week*, London 1904

Torriti 1998
P. Torriti (ed.), *Beccafumi: l'opera complete*,
Milan 1998

Toulouse 2008
A. Hémery, *Pas la couleur, rien que la nuance!:
trompe-l'oeil et grisailles de Rubens à
Toulouse-Lautrec*, exh. cat., Toulouse 2008

Troutman 1971
Albrecht Dürer, *Skizzenbuch der Reise nach
den Niederlanden, 1520–21/Sketchbook of
his journey to the Netherlands, 1520–21: With
Extracts from his Diary*, commentary by P.
Troutman, London 1971

Upton 1975
J.M. Upton, 'Devotional Imagery and Style in
the Washington Nativity, by Petrus Christus',
Studies in the History of Art, 7 (1975), pp. 49–79

Van Asperen de Boer 1992
J.R.J. van Asperen de Boer, 'Over de techniek
van Jan van Eycks *De Heilige Barbara*', in
*Jaarboek van her Koninklijk Museum voor
Schoone Kunsten Antwerpen*, Antwerp 1992,
pp. 9–18.

Van de Wetering 2000
E. van de Wetering, *Rembrandt: The Painter at
Work*, Berkeley 2000

Van Gelder 1973
J.G. van Gelder, 'Frühe Rembrandt-
Sammlungen', in O. Simson and J. Kelch (eds),
Neue Beiträge zur Rembrandt-Forschung,
Berlin 1973, pp. 189–206

Van Hout 2010
N. van Hout, 'On dead colour', *Jaarboek
Koninklijk Museum voor Schone Kunsten
Antwerpen 2008*, Antwerp 2010

Van Hout 2012
N. van Hout, *The Unfinished Painting*, Antwerp
and London 2012

Van Mander 1994–9
K. van Mander, *The Lives of the illustrious
Netherlandish and German painters, from the
first edition of the Schilder-boeck (1603–1604):
preceded by the lineage, circumstances and
place of birth, life and works of Karel van
Mander, painter and poet and likewise his
death and burial, from the second edition of
the Schilder-boeck (1616–1618)*, 6 vols., ed.
H. Miedema, Doornspijk 1994–9

Varela 1999
F.J. Valera, *Ethical Know-How: Action, Wisdom
and Cognition*, Redwood City, CA 1999

Varela, Thompson and Rosch 1993
F.J. Varela, E. Thompson and E. Rosch, *The
Embodied Mind*, Cambridge, MA 1993

Varnedoe 1996
K. Varnedoe (ed.), *Jasper Johns: Writings,
Sketchbook Notes, Interviews*, compiled by
Christel Hollevoet, Museum of Modern Art,
New York 1996

Vasari 1906
G. Vasari, *Le vite de' piu eccellenti pittori,
scultori ed architettori scritte da Giorgio Vasari
pittore aretino* [1568], vol. IV, ed. Gaetano
Milanesi, Florence 1906

Vasari 1907
G. Vasari, *On Technique*, ed. G.B. Brown, trans.
L.S. Maclehose, London 1907

Vasari 1912–15
G. Vasari, *Lives of the most eminent painters,
sculptors & architects* [1568], 10 vols., trans.
G. du Verre, London 1912–15

Vidier 1910
A. Vidier, 'Le Trésor de la Sainte Chapelle:
inventaires et documents', *Mémoires de la
Société de l'histoire de Paris*, 37 (1910),
pp. 185–369

Da Vinci 1949
L. Da Vinci, *Paragone: A Comparison of the
Arts*, trans. I.A. Richter, London and New York
1949

Washington, London and The Hague 2000–1
R. Baer, *Gerrit Dou, 1612–1675: Master Painter
in the Age of Rembrandt*, exh. cat., Washington
and New Haven 2000

Washington, Munich, London and New York
2013
A. Robison and K.A. Schröder, *Albrecht Dürer:
Master Drawings, Watercolors and Prints from
the Albertina*, exh. cat., Washington, Munich,
London and New York 2013

Washington and New York 1986–7
J.O. Hand et al., *The Age of Bruegel:
Netherlandish Drawings in the Sixteenth
Century*, exh. cat., Washington, Cambridge and
New York 1986

Watson and Rappaport 2013
R. Watson and H. Rappaport, *Capturing the
Light*, London 2013

Wax 1990
C. Wax, *The Mezzotint: The Development of
an Art Form, History and Technique*, New York
1990

Weigert 2003
Laura Weigert, 'Velum Templi: Painted Cloths of
the Passion and the Making of Lenten Ritual in
Reims', *Studies in Iconography*, vol. 24 (2003),
pp. 199–229

Westerbeck 2014
C. Westerbeck, *Chuck Close, Photographer*,
Munich 2014

Westermann 1999
M. Westermann, 'Fray en Leelijck: Adriaen van
de Venne's Invention of the Ironic Grisaille',
Nederlands Kunsthistorisch Jaarboek, vol. 50
(1999), pp. 221–57

Whitehead 1992
J. Whitehead, *The French Interior in the
Eighteenth Century,* London 1992

Wine 2018
H. Wine, *National Gallery Catalogues: The
Eighteenth-Century French Paintings*, London,
forthcoming

Wolfsburg 2017
MKP: Add authors or editors, *Hans op de
Beeck, Out of the Ordinary*, exh. cat., Tielt 2017

Wright and Moisy 1972
B. Wright and P. Moisy, *Gustave Moreau et
Eugène Fromentin: documents inédits*, La
Rochelle 1972

Wuestman 1995
G. Wuestman, 'The Mezzotint in Holland: "Easily
Learned, Neat and Convenient"', *Simiolus*, vol.
23, no. 1 (1995), pp. 63–89

Zierman 2001
H. Zierman, *Matthias Grünewald*, Munich 2001

Zweite 1980
A. Zweite, *Marten de Vos als Maler. Ein Beitrag
zur Geschichte der Antwerpener Malerei in
der zweiten Hälfte des 16. Jahrhunderts*, Berlin
1980

List of Lenders

ANTWERP
Royal Museum of Fine Arts

BARCELONA
Museu Picasso

BERLIN
Staatliche Museen zu Berlin,
  Kupferstichkabinett

CAMBRIDGE
The Syndics of the Fitzwilliam Museum,
  University of Cambridge

CARDIFF
Amgueddfa Cymru – National Museum Wales

CHICAGO
The Art Institute of Chicago

COPENHAGEN
Statens Museum for Kunst

DÜSSELDORF
Kunstsammlung Nordrhein-Westfalen
Museum Kunstpalast
Museum Kunstpalast / Glasmuseum Hentrich
Museum Kunstpalast – Stiftung Sammlung
  Kemp

ESSEN
Museum Folkwang

GENOA
Soprintendenza Archeologia, Belle Arti e
  Paesaggio della citta metropolitana di Genova
  e delle province di Imperia, La Spezia e Savona

HULL
The Ferens Art Gallery: Hull Museums

LEIDEN
Museum De Lakenhal

LILLE
Palais des Beaux-Arts

LONDON
The British Museum
The National Gallery
Pace Gallery
Victoria and Albert Museum

LOS ANGELES
Los Angeles County Museum of Art

MADRID
Museo Nacional del Prado
Museo Thyssen-Bornemisza

MOSCOW
State Tretyakov Gallery

NEW YORK
The Metropolitan Museum of Art

PARIS
Bibliothèque nationale de France
Collection du Mobilier national
Fondation Custodia, Collection Frits Lugt
Musée d'Orsay
Musée du Louvre
Musée des Arts Décoratifs
Musée national Gustave Moreau

ROTTERDAM
Museum Boijmans Van Beuningen

ST PETERSBURG
The State Hermitage Museum

VIENNA
The Albertina Museum

WASHINGTON
National Gallery of Art

OTHER LENDERS
Collection Jasper Johns
Olafur Eliasson; Tanya Bonakdar Gallery,
  New York; neugerriemschneider, Berlin
Private collection, Belgium
Private collection, c/o David Zwirner Gallery
Private collection, Europe
Private collection, Nottingham
Private collections
The Royal Collection/HM Queen Elizabeth II
Studio Hans Op de Beeck

Photographic and Copyright Credits

ANTWERP
© Museum Mayer van den Bergh: fig. 27. © Royal Museum of Fine Arts Antwerp © www.lukasweb. be-Art in Flanders vzw, photo Hugo Maertens: cats 21, 26.

AUBAZINE
Aubazine Abbey, France © Hervé Champollion / akg-images: fig. 2.

BASEL
Art Unlimited, Basel © DACS 2017 / Photo: Studio Hans Op de Beeck: cat. 72.

BARCELONA
Museu Picasso, Barcelona © Succession Picasso / DACS, London 2017 / Photo: akg-images / Album / Ramon Manent: fig. 23; © Succession Picasso / DACS, London 2017 / Photo: Museu Picasso, Barcelona. Gasull Fotografia: cat. 30.

BERLIN
Gemäldegalerie, Staatliche Museen zu Berlin-Preussischer Kulturbesitz © Photo: Wolfgang Gülcker: fig. 11. Kupferstichkabinett – Staatliche Museen zu Berlin © Kupferstichkabinett. Staatliche Museen zu Berlin / Photo: Jörg P. Anders: cat. 11; © Kupferstichkabinett. Staatliche Museen zu Berlin / Photo: Dietmar Katz: p. 53.

BRUSSELS
© Royal Library of Belgium: fig. 10.

CAMBRIDGE
© Fitzwilliam Museum, Cambridge: cats 44, 49; © The Fitzwilliam Museum, Cambridge / Scala, Florence: fig. 17.

CARDIFF
© Amgueddfa Genedlaethol Cymru – National Museum of Wales: cat. 24.

CHICAGO
© The Art Institute of Chicago / Art Resource / Scala, Florence: cats 38, 39.

COLOGNE
Museum Ludwig, Cologne © 2017 The Andy Warhol Foundation for the Visual Arts, Inc. / Artists Rights Society (ARS), New York and DACS, London / Photo: akg-images: fig. 39.

COPENHAGEN
Statens Museum for Kunst, Copenhagen © Gerhard Richter 2017 (12072017). Photo: SMK: cat. 70.

DORTMUND
Institute for Newspaper Research, Dortmund © Institut für Zeitungsforschung der Stadt Dortmund: fig. 42.

DÜSSELDORF
Kunstsammlung Nordrhein-Westfalen, Düsseldorf © The Estate of Alberto Giacometti (Fondation Giacometti, Paris and ADAGP, Paris), licensed in the UK by ACS and DACS, London 2017. Photo: bpk / Kunstsammlung Nordrhein-Westfalen, Düsseldorf / Walter Klein: cat. 25. Museum Kunstpalast Düsseldorf © Gerhard Richter 2017 (0182). Photo: Museum Kunstpalast – ARTOTHEK: cat. 56; © ADAGP, Paris and DACS, London 2017 / Photo: Museum Kunstpalast / ARTOTHEK: cat. 66; © DACS 2017 / Photo: Museum Kunstpalast / ARTOTHEK: cat. 64; © Museum Kunstpalast / Horst Kolberg / ARTOTHEK: cat. 8. Museum Kunstpalast, Düsseldorf – Stiftung Sammlung Kemp © DACS 2017 / Photo: Museum Kunstpalast / ARTOTHEK: cat. 1; © Ellsworth Kelly: cat. 68. Museum Kunstpalast, Düsseldorf / Glasmuseum Hentrich © LVR-Zentrum für Medien und Bildung, Stefan Arendt / ARTOTHEK: cat. 3.

ESSEN
Museum Folkwang Essen © Frank Stella. ARS, NY and DACS, London 2017 / Photo: Museum Folkwang Essen / ARTOTHEK: cat. 67.

ETON
Eton College © Reproduced by permission of the Provost and Fellows of Eton College: fig. 30.

FLORENCE
Galleria degli Uffizi, Florence © Photo Scala, Florence – courtesy of the Ministero Beni e Att. Culturali: fig. 18.

FRANKFURT AM MAIN
Historisches Museum, Frankfurt © akg-images: figs 28, 29.

GENOA
State property on deposit in the Museo Diocesano, Genova © Courtesy of the Ministero dei beni e delle attività culturali e del turismo, Soprintendenza Archeologia, Belle Arti e Paesaggio per la città metropolitana di Genova e le province di Imperia, La Spezia e Savona: cat. 5.

GHENT
Saint Bavo Cathedral, Ghent © Lukas – Art in Flanders VZW / Bridgeman Images: fig. 26.

HAARLEM
© Teylers Museum, Haarlem: fig. 34.

HULL
© Ferens Art Gallery, Hull Museums: cat. 36.

LEIDEN
© Museum De Lakenhal, Leiden : cat. 47.

LILLE
Palais des Beaux-Arts, Lille © RMN-Grand Palais / René-Gabriel Ojéda: cat. 37.

LIVERPOOL
© Walker Art Gallery, National Museums Liverpool / Bridgeman Images: fig. 37.

LONDON
The British Library, London © British Library Board. All Rights Reserved / Bridgeman Images: fig. 6. The British Museum, London © The Trustees of The British Museum: cats 22, 33. © The National Gallery, London: cats 7, 9, 15, 16, 31, 34, 41, 43, 51, 53. Royal Collection Trust / © Her Majesty Queen Elizabeth II 2017: cat. 14. © Samuel Courtauld Trust, The Courtauld Gallery, London, UK / Bridgeman Images: fig. 19. © Victoria and Albert Museum, London: cats 2, 52, 54.

LOS ANGELES
Los Angeles County Museum of Art, California © 2017 The Andy Warhol Foundation for the Visual Arts, Inc. / Artists Rights Society (ARS), New York and DACS, London / Photo: Museum Associates / LACMA: fig. 40; © Museum Associates / LACMA: cat. 50. © The J. Paul Getty Museum, Los Angeles, California: fig. 31.

MADRID
Museo Nacional del Prado, Madrid © MNP / Scala, Florence: fig. 24; © Museo Nacional del Prado, Madrid: cat. 17. © Museo Thyssen-Bornemisza, Madrid: cat. 32.

MOSCOW
© The State Tretyakov Gallery: cat. 60.

NEW YORK
The Metropolitan Museum of Art, New York © The Metropolitan Museum of Art, New York: figs 3, 4, 8, 22; cat. 13; © The Metropolitan Museum of Art / Art Resource / Scala, Florence: cat. 28. The Museum of Modern Art, New York © Succession Picasso / DACS, London 2017 / Photo: Digital image, The Museum of Modern Art, New York / Scala, Florence: fig. 38. © The New-York Historical Society: fig. 35.

OXFORD
© Ashmolean Museum, University of Oxford, UK / Bridgeman Images: fig. 1.

PADUA
Scrovegni Chapel, Padua © A. Dagli Orti/Scala, Florence: fig. 25; © Alinari / Bridgeman Images: fig. 9.

PARIS
© Bibliothèque nationale de France: cat. 4. Centre Georges Pompidou, Paris, Musée national d'art moderne / Centre de création industrielle © The Pollock-Krasner Foundation ARS, NY and DACS, London 2017 / Photo: Centre Pompidou, MNAM-CCI, Dist. RMN-Grand Palais / Adam Rzepka: fig. 43. © Collection du Mobilier national. Photo: Isabelle Bideau: cat. 19. © Fondation Custodia, Collection Frits Lugt, Paris: cat. 27. © Paris, Les Arts Décoratifs / Jean Tholance: cat. 18. Musée de Cluny – musée national du Moyen-Age, Paris © RMN-Grand Palais (musée de Cluny - musée national du Moyen-Age) / Michel Urtado: fig. 7. Musée national Gustave Moreau, Paris © RMN-Grand Palais / René-Gabriel Ojéda: cat. 20. Musée du Louvre, Paris © RMN-Grand Palais (musée du Louvre) / Hervé Lewandowski: cat. 10; © RMN-Grand Palais (musée du Louvre) / Jean-Gilles Berizzi: cat. 40; © RMN-Grand Palais (musée du Louvre) / Michèle Bellot: fig. 5; © RMN-Grand Palais (musée du Louvre) / René-Gabriel Ojéda: cat. 48; © RMN-Grand Palais (musée du Louvre) / Thierry Le Mage: fig. 21. Musée d'Orsay, Paris ©

Musée d'Orsay, Dist. RMN-Grand Palais / Patrice Schmid: cat. 29 ; © RMN-Grand Palais (musée d'Orsay) / Jean Schormans: fig. 20.

PHILADELPHIA
Philadelphia Museum of Art, Pennsylvania © Ellsworth Kelly: fig. 45.

PISA
Pisa Cathedral © Courtesy of the Archivio fotografico dell' Opera della Primaziale Pisana: fig. 14.

POSSAGNO
© Museo Canova / Archivio Fotografico, Possagno: fig. 33.

PRIVATE COLLECTION
Pace Gallery © Chuck Close, courtesy Pace Gallery. Photograph by Bill Jacobson, courtesy Pace Gallery: cat. 57; © Chuck Close, courtesy Pace Gallery. Photograph courtesy the artist and Pace Gallery: cat. 58. Private Collection © Photo courtesy of the owner: cat. 35. © Marlene Dumas. Photo: Peter Cox: cat. 55. © Vija Celmins, Courtesy Matthew Marks Gallery. Photo courtesy of the owner: cat. 59. © The Josef and Anni Albers Foundation / VG Bild-Kunst, Bonn and DACS, London 2017: cat. 61. © Cy Twombly Foundation. Courtesy Archives Nicola Del Roscio: cats 62, 63. © Jasper Johns / VAGA, New York / DACS, London 2017: cat. 65. © Bridget Riley 2017. All rights reserved: cat. 69.

ROME
Galleria Borghese, Rome © Photo Scala, Florence – courtesy of the Ministero Beni e Att. Culturali: fig. 15. Galleria Doria Pamphilj, Rome © 2017 Amministrazione Doria Pamphilj s.r.l.: fig. 32.

ROTTERDAM
Museum Boijmans Van Beuningen, Rotterdam © Museum Boijmans Van Beuningen, Rotterdam. Photographer: Studio Buitenhof, The Hague: cat. 45; © Museum Boijmans Van Beuningen, Rotterdam. Photographer: Studio Tromp, Rotterdam: cats 23, 42.

SAN GIMIGNANO
Santa Fina Chapel, Collegiate Church of San Gimignano © Parrocchia di Santa Maria Assunta in San Gimignano: fig. 13.

ST PETERSBURG
© The State Hermitage Museum, 2017 / Photo: Vladimir Terebenin: cat. 46.

STOCKHOLM
Moderna Museet, Stockholm © Olafur Eliasson. Photo: Anders Sune Berg: cat. 71.

STUTTGART
Staatsgalerie Stuttgart © bpk / Staatsgalerie Stuttgart: fig. 12.

VIENNA
mumok, Museum moderner Kunst Stiftung Ludwig Wien © Jasper Johns / VAGA, New York / DACS, London 2017 / Photo: mumok, Museum moderner Kunst Stiftung Ludwig Wien, On loan from the collection Ludwig, Aachen: fig. 44. © Albertina, Vienna: cat. 12.

WASHINGTON
National Gallery of Art, Washington, Image courtesy of the Board of Trustees, National Gallery of Art, Washington, DC: cat. 6. © The Library of Congress, Washington, DC: fig. 36.

WILLIAMSTOWN
© Sterling and Francine Clark Art Institute, Williamstown, Massachusetts, USA / Bridgeman Images: fig. 16.

ALSO ILLUSTRATED
© Photo 12 / Alamy Stock Photo: fig. 41.

Index

Abderus 72
Aeneas *67*, *68*, 70
Agony in the Garden 38, 39–40
Albers, Josef 17, 186
  'Homage to a Square' series 186, 188
  Study for Homage to the Square 187, 188
Alberti, Leon Battista, *Della Pittura (On Painting)*
  56, 107
Anchises 70
Anthony Abbot, Saint 45
Apollodorus 15–16
Armenini, Giovanni Battista 122
Armida 138, *139*, *140*
Audran, Michel 70

Bacchus 19, 82, *84*, *136*, 147
Balke, Peder, *The Tempest* 165, *167*
Barbara, Saint 79, *80*, 81
Barendsz, Dirck 137
Barocci, Federico 60
  Aeneas and Anchises escaping from Troy 60, *61*
Bartolommeo, Fra 53
Bayeu y Subías, Francisco 65
  The Spanish Monarchy 65, *66*, 68
Beccafumi, Domenico 19, 58
  Saint Matthew 58, *58*, 59
Beeck, Hans Op de, *The Collector's House* 206, *207*
Bellini, Giovanni, *Lamentation over the Dead*
  Christ 81–2, *81*
Benedict, Saint 27
Bernard of Clairvaux, Abbot 28
Bertin, Saint 43
Blanc, Célestin Joseph, *Head of a Girl* 20, 166, *168*,
  169
Boilly, Louis-Léopold 35, 151
  A Girl at a Window 18, 155, *156*, 157, *158–9*
Boucher, François 68
  Venus in the Forge of Vulcan 68, *69*, 70–1
  Vulcan presenting Arms to Venus for Aeneas 68,
  70
  *Vulcan's Forge (Vulcan presenting Venus with
  Arms for Aeneas)* 6, *67*, 70
Bruegel, Jan, the Elder 92
  Visit to the Peasants 10, 92, *92*, 94
Bruegel, Pieter, the Elder 82, 92, 137
  Christ and the Woman taken in Adultery
  82, *83*, 92
Bruegel, Pieter, the Younger 92
Bruzazorzi, Domenico, *The Fall of the Giants*
  124
Buttre, John Chester, *The Lincoln Family* (after
  Francis Bicknell Carpenter) *157*

Campin, Robert 109, 113
Canova, Antonio 129, 131
  Deposition 131, *131*, 133
Carlo 138, *140*, 142
Caroline Murat, Queen of Naples 95
Carpenter, Francis Bicknell, *The Lincoln Family*
  157, *157*
Carracci, Agostino 60
Carrière, Elise 88, *89*, 90
Carrière, Eugène, *Maternity (Suffering)* 22, 23, 88,
  89, 90
Carrière, Sophie 88, 89, 90
Catherine of Alexandria, Saint 34
Celmins, Vija 174, 179, 181
  Night Sky no.3 (1991) 179, *180*, 181
Cennini, Cennino, *Libro dell'arte (The Craftsman's
  Handbook)* 16, 71
Ceres 19, 82, *84*, *136*, 147
Chardin, Jean-Siméon, *Back from the Market
  (La Pourvoyeuse)* 152, 155
Charles III, King of Spain 65
Charles IV, King of France 31
Charles V, King of France 16, 35
Christina, Queen of Sweden 149
Christopher, Saint 45
Christus, Petrus, *The Nativity* 19, *41*, 42, 47
Close, Chuck 174, 175, 177, 181
  Joel (1993) 177, *178*, 179
  Joel (Maquette) (1991) *179*
Cornaro, Francesco 117
Courbet, Gustave 164
Cukor, George, *Camille* 20, *172*, 174
Cupid 82, 149
Cybele 19, 117–19
Cyriacus, Saint 114

Daguerre, Louis 163
  Boulevard du Temple 164
  The Ruins of Holyrood Chapel 163–4, *164*
de Kooning, Willem 94
Degas, Edgar 102
  Ballet Rehearsal 97, *98–9*
  Ballet Rehearsal on Stage 96
Del Pollaiuolo, Antonio 117
Delaroche, Paul 165
Delilah *93*, 94
d'Este, Antonio, *Deposition* (after a model by
  Antonio Canova) 131, *132*, 133
d'Este, Isabella 117
d'Evreux, Jeanne 31–2, *32*, 34–5, 109
di Bondone, Giotto
  fresco decorations in the Scrovegni Chapel 40,
  41, 108–9

Hope 109, *109*
di Credi, Lorenzo 53
Di Giorgio Martini, Francesco 117
Diomedes, King of Thrace 72–3
Donne, Sir John of Kidwelly 45
Doria, Prince Andrea 39
Dou, Gerrit 94
Dumas, Marlene 173
  The Image as Burden 20, *173*, 174
Duquesnoy, François 129
  Bacchanalia of Putti 129, *129*
Dürer, Albrecht
  Christ on the Mount of Olives 39
  Head of a Woman 114–15, *116*, 117, 127
  Heller Altarpiece 114, *115*
  *A Woman in Netherlandish Dress seen from
  Behind (Drapery Study)* 55, 57–8
Dyck, Anthony van 138
  Iconography 138
  Rinaldo and Armida 138, *139*, *140*, 142

Eliasson, Olafur 205, 209–11
  Room for one colour 204, 205–6, 210
  'Some Ideas About Colour' 205
Erhart, Gregor 47
Etienne de Poissy, Bishop 37
Eton College chapel grisaille paintings 119, *122*
Eyck, Hubert van, *The Ghent Altarpiece* 109
Eyck, Jan van 109
  *The Annunciation Diptych (The Archangel
  Gabriel, The Virgin Mary)* 106, 109, 110, *110–11*,
  112–13
  The Ghent Altarpiece 109, *112*
  Saint Barbara 79, *80*, 81

Filarete 56
Flight into Egypt 113, *113*
Francken, Frans II, *The Parable of the Prodigal Son*
  47–8, *49*
Frederik Hendrik, Prince of Orange 138, 142

Gabriel, Archangel 45, *106*, 112, 113
Ganymede *126*, 127
Garbo, Greta 174
Geeraerts, Marten Jozef 127, 129
  Children's Game 128, 129
Geffroy, Gustave 90
Géricault, Théodore, *Race of the Riderless Horses*
  72, 74
Ghirlandaio, Domenico 19, 53
  *Drapery Study (possibly study for Saint
  Matthew and an Angel)* 43, *52*, 53, 56–7, 58
  The Four Evangelists 56, *57*

Giacometti, Alberto 90
   Annette Seated 23, 90, *91*
Giacometti, Annette 90, *91*
Gidal, Peter 172
Giotto 119
Goltzius, Hendrik 19–20, 137, 145
   The Great Hercules 145, *146*
   Right Hand 145, *146*, 147
   Without Ceres and Bacchus, Venus would Freeze
     19, 82–3, *84*, 136, 147, *148*, 149
Gonzaga, Francesco, Duke of Mantua 117
Götz, Karl Otto 193
   Toro 192, 193
grisaille stained glass 28, *29*, 30, 31, *31*
Grünewald, Matthias 114
   Saint Cyriacus 114, *115*
   Saint Lawrence 114, *115*
Gutherz, Rainer 175

Heemskerck, Maarten van 137
Heere, Lucas de 81
Heller, Jakob 114
Henry II, Emperor 124, 125
Hercules 72, 94, 145
Holbein, Hans, the Elder, *The Grey Passion* 45, 47,
   48
Hooch, Pieter de 155

Ingres, Jean-Auguste-Dominique 102
   Le Grand Odalisque 95, *96*
   Odalisque in Grisaille 78, 94, 95–6, *95*, 193
Isaac de Camondo, Count 96

Jean de Berry, Duke 16
Jode, Pieter de, the Younger, *Rinaldo and
   Armida* (after Anthony van Dyck) 138, *141*, 142
Johann Wilhelm II 94
John the Baptist, Saint 109
John of Damascus, *On the Divine Images* 42
John the Evangelist, Saint 109
Johns, Jasper 193
   American Flag paintings 193
   Gray Flag 193
   Two Flags 193, *193*
   Untitled 194, 195
   Jupiter 126, 127

Kandinsky, Wassily 185, 209
Kelly, Ellsworth 196, 199–200
   Black and White Bar I 20, *199*, 200
   Black with a Red Bar 200
   Seine 198, 199

Kline, Franz 196–7
Kruchenykh, Aleksei 185

La Font de Saint-Yenne, Etienne 107
Lawrence, Saint 114
Le Bon, Philippe, Duke of Burgundy 34
Le Gray, Gustave 164–5
   The Great Wave, Sète 164–5, *166*
Le Noir, Jean 34
Leighton, Frederic 68
Lemoyne, Jean-Baptiste 70
Leonardo da Vinci 53, 56, 107
   The Battle of Anghiari (1505) 72, 74
Lépicié, François-Bernard, *Back from the Market
   (La Pourvoyeuse)* (after Jean-Siméon Chardin)
   153, 155
Lincoln, Abraham 157
Livy 117
Louis, Saint 28, 31
Louis IX, King 28, 31
Louis XV, King 70
Lower Rhine Workshop, *Judith with the Head of
   Holofernes* 31, *31*

Mack, Heinz, *White Dynamic Structure on Black 21*
Malevich, Kazimir 209, 210
   Black Square 17, 20, *184*, 185–6
Mallarmé, Stéphane 88
Mander, Karel van 145, 147, 149
   Schilderboek (Painter's Book) 81
Mantegna, Andrea 117, 124
   The Introduction of the Cult of Cybele at Rome 19,
     117–19, *118–19*, *120–1*, 127
manuscript illumination of a veiled crucifix and
   paintings 35, *35*
Marchesini, Giorgio 124
Margaret of York, Duchess of Burgundy 34
Margarita María, Infanta 101–2
Marigny, Marquis de 70
Marmion, Simon, *The Saint Bertin Altarpiece*
   43, *43*
Marshall, Kerry James 94
Mary Magdalene 63
Master of the Moral Treatises and workshop,
   The Celebration of Mass 42–3, *42*
Matthew, Saint *43*, *52*, 53, 56–7, 58, *58*, *59*
Matura, Helga 23, *162*, 175, *176*, 177, *177*
Maturino da Firenze, 122
Memling, Hans
   Saint Anthony Abbot (The Donne Triptych) 46
   *Saint Christopher carrying the Infant Christ
   (The Donne Triptych) 26*, 46

   *The Virgin and Child with Saints and Donors
   (The Donne Triptych)* 45, *46*
Michelangelo 108, 123
Miélot, Jean, *Life of Saint Catherine 33*, 34
Minims 40
Mondrian, Piet 209, 210
Moreau, Gustave
   Diomedes devoured by his Horses 72–3, 74, *74–5*
   Hesiod and the Muses 73
Moulinneuf, Etienne 151
   Back from the Market (La Pourvoyeuse) (after
   Jean-Siméon Chardin) *14*, 151, *154*, 155
Mulbacher, Gustave 96

Niépce, Joseph Nicéphore 163
Nocchi, Bernardino 129
   Deposition (after Antonio Canova) *130*, 131

Opałka, Roman 195–6
   Opałka 1965/1–∞, Detail 612464–638092 195,
   196
Orléans, Jean d'
   The Narbonne Altarcloth 34–5, 35, 37
   *Resurrection of Christ and Saints (The Mourning
   Mitre)* 36, 37
Ovid 117
   Metamorphoses 127

Park Seo-Bo 17
Peiresc, Nicolas-Claude Fabri de 16
Petrarch 107, 108
Pharisees 82
Philip IV, King of Spain 101
Picart, Bernard 63
Picasso, Pablo 20, 96, 102, 170, 181
   The Charnel House 20, *169*, 170
   Guernica 170
   Las Meninas (after Vélazquez) 96, *100*, 101
   Las Meninas (Infanta Margarita María) 101–2, *103*
Pisano, Giovanni, *Madonna and Child* 109
Pliny the Elder 16, 107
Polidoro da Caravaggio, 122
Pollock, Jackson 17, 188–9, 196
   Number 26 A, Black and White 1948 189–90, *189*
Pontius Pilate 142, 145
Porto, Jacopo 124, *125*
Porto, Orazio 123–4
Poseidon 124
Prud'hon, Pierre-Paul 129
Pucelle, Jean, *The Hours of Jeanne d'Evreux* 16,
   31–2, *32*, 34–5, 37, 109

Quinta, Claudia 118

Raphael, *Entombment* altarpiece 40
Rembrandt van Rijn 142
    Ecce Homo 63, 142, *143*, 145
    The Entombment 65
    The Lamentation over the Dead Christ 63, *64*, 65
Reynolds, Joshua, *Lord Rockingham and Edmund
    Burke* 71–2, *72*
Richter, Gerhard 15, 17, 23, 174–5, 181, 202–3
    Grey Mirror – 765 202, 203
    Helga Matura with her Fiancé 23, *162*, 175, *176*,
    177
    Mirror Painting 203
    Table 202
Riley, Bridget 201
    Horizontal Vibration 201, *201*
    Rustle 201–2
    Tremor 201
Rinaldo 138, *139*, *140*
Rodin, Auguste 74
Rosenberg, Harold 189
Rubens, Peter Paul 16, 19, 60, 138, 145
    *The Apotheosis of Germanicus: copy after an
    antique Cameo (The 'Gemma Tiberiana')* 17
    The Birth of Venus 60, 62, *62*
Rudolf II, Holy Roman Emperor 60, 149

Saenredam, Jan 82
Salviati, Francesco 123
Samson *93*, 94
Sauvage, Piat Joseph 129
Schapiro, Joel 177
Scipio, Cornelius 118
Solms, Amalia van 138
Squarcione, Francesco 117
*Stained Glass Panel with Quarries and a Female
    Head 30*
Stella, Frank 196–7
    'Black Paintings' 197–9
    Tomlinson Court Park 1 197, *197*, 198

Talbot, William Henry Fox 163
Tasso, Torquato, *Gerusalemme Liberata* 138
Taylor, Robert 174
Terence 82
    The Eunuch 147
Tiepolo, Giovanni Battista (Giambattista) 123, 124
Tiepolo, Giovanni Domenico (Giandomenico) 123,
    124
    *Jacopo Porto appointed Governor of Vicenza by
    the Holy Roman Emperor Henry II in 1022* 123–4,
    125
Titian, *Portrait of a Lady ('La Schiavona')* 107, *108*
Tofanelli, Stefano 129

Triptych with the Passion of Christ 31, 32
Turner, J.M.W. 164
Twombly, Edwin Parker 'Cy' 190–1
    Untitled [Rome] (1970) *190*, 191–2, *191*

Ubaldo 138, *140*, 142

Valerius Maximus 117
Varchi, Benedetto 108
Varela, Francisco 211
Vasari, Giorgio 107, 117, 122, 123
    Lives of the Artists 16, 53
Veen, Otto van 137
Velázquez, Diego, *Las Meninas* 96, 101, *101*
Velde, Willem van de, the Elder 149
    *The Departure of the Dutch Fleet the 9th of June
    1645 12–13*, 149, *150*, 151, *151*
Venne, Adriaen van de 16, 83
    *Arme Weelde (Poor Luxury), A Procession of
    Revelling Cripples and Beggars* 83, 85, 85, *86–7*
Venus 19, *67*, 68, *68*, *69*, 70, 71, 82, *84*, *136*, 147
Verlaine, Paul 88
Verrocchio, Andrea del 53, 56, 58
Virgil, *Aeneid* 70, 127
Vliet, Johannes (Jan) van, *Christ before Pilate
    (after Rembrandt)* 142, *144*, 145
Vos, Marten de, *The Annunciation* 43, *44*, 45
Vrelant, Willem, *Life of Saint Catherine 33*, 34
Vulcan *67*, 68, *68*, *69*, 70, 71

Warhol, Andy 181
    Black and White Disaster 171, 172, 174
    Death and Disaster series 170, 172, 174, 175
    129 Die in Jet! 170, *170*, 172
Werff, Adriaen van der 94
    Samson and Delilah (?) 93, 94
Whistler, Anna Matilda 88, *88*
Whistler, James McNeill, *Arrangement in Grey and
    Black No. 1* 88, *88*
Widmann, Antonio 131
Wit, Jacob de, *Jupiter and Ganymede 126*, 127
With, Witte de 149
The Wizard of Oz 20
Wool, Christopher 17

Zuccaro, Federico 123
    *Taddeo decorating the Facade of the Palazzo
    Mattei* 123, *123*
Zuccaro, Taddeo 123, *123*